Taxpayers' Ultimate Defense Manual

Nine Devastating Weapons Against IRS Abuse!

by Daniel J. Pilla

WINNING Publications
St. Paul, Minnesota

WINNING Publications
506 Kenny Road, Suite 120
St. Paul, Minnesota 55101

First Edition, October, 1989.

Printed in the United States of America.

Library of Congress Catalog Card Number 89-51321

ISBN: 0-9617124-7-3

Notice from the Author and Publisher

This book is designed to provide the author's findings and opinions based on research, analysis and experience with the subject matter covered. This information is not provided for purposes of rendering legal, accounting or other professional advice. It is intended purely for educational purposes.

The author and publisher disclaim any responsibility for any liability or loss incurred as a consequence of the use and application, either directly or indirectly, of any information presented herein.

Because the United States currently functions under an evolutionary legal system, the reader bears the burden of assuring that the principles of law stated in this work are current and binding at the time of any intended use or application. Caution: The law in this country is subject to change arbitrarily and without prior notice.

Dedication

To the Memory of Esther

"But this *shall* be the covenant that I will make with the house of Israel; After those days, saith the Lord, I will put my law in their inward parts, and write it in their hearts; and I will be their God, and they shall be my people."

Jeremiah 31:33

Writings by Daniel J. Pilla

Taxpayers' Ultimate Defense Manual

How Anyone Can Negotiate With The IRS—And WIN!

Pilla Talks Taxes, A Monthly Newsletter

Special Report on the Taxpayers' Bill of Rights Act

The Naked Truth

Understanding Taxes and Court Procedure

Table of Contents

"Great men, great nations, have not been boasters or buffoons, but perceivers of the terror of life, and have manned themselves to face it."

—Ralph Waldo Emerson

Preface

The Internal Revenue Service is the one government institution we Americans "love to hate." Even those "proud and honored" to be American taxpayers find that the patriotic fervor dies when a letter from the tax collector finds its way into the mailbox. Over the years, the IRS has been verbally bashed and beaten more than any other agency you can name. The IRS has been the subject of grass roots reform movements, organized lobbying efforts and Congressional investigations.

Most recently, the nation seemed to rally behind the latest assault upon "public enemy number one." The assault took the form of the Taxpayers' Bill of Rights Act, signed into law on November 8, 1988.[1] The Taxpayers' Bill of Rights Act is the culmination of decades of hearings, allegations and demands which have been launched at the IRS.

I have been on the forefront of this battle for over a decade. During this period of time, my remarks about the IRS have been less than laudatory. I have openly accused the IRS of dishonesty with respect to its own public documents,[2] fraud in connection with its billing practices[3] and of deliberately and intentionally taking unfair advantage of citizens ignorant of their rights.[4]

Yet, I must confess, throughout all of this time and in the face of my allegations, one thing remains clear, *no abuse would be possible* if people simply took the time to understand their rights. We in this country have become *lazy and arrogant* on the subject of individual rights. We welcome every opportunity to point an accusatory finger at any foreign government which may not respect one's individual rights in the fashion we deem acceptable. Though as citizens, we make almost *no effort* to understand our own constitutional system of law and how it is supposed to protect us from governmental abuse.

Consequently, *the United States Government* is guilty of *abusing the rights and liberties* of its own citizens! Through the vehicle of the IRS and under the cloak of tax collection, *this government* is as guilty as any of oppressing individual liberties.

Each citizen in this country is *expected* to *know* the law. Each citizen in this country is *expected* to *comply* with the law. The presumption that all citizens know the law is, I believe, responsible for the IRS' indifference toward individual rights. After all, if each citizen *knows* his rights, why should the tax collector be concerned about going out of his way to observe them? A person with knowlege of the law and his rights, it is presumed, is in a position to *stand up for them.* He need not be patronized like a child. And it naturally follows that a person with knowledge of his rights may easily call to account any IRS official who would tend to overlook them.

This theory is borne out by an event which occurred recently at the IRS Service Center in Philadelphia. A tax return processing clerk noticed that a number of tax returns filed there contained an error in tax computation. The error was caused by the citizens' failure to give themselves full credit for withheld taxes. As a result, a number of returns showed *more taxes* due than were in fact due.

The conscientious clerk brought the matter to the attention of her supervisor. She suggested that the erroneous returns be returned to the unwitting taxpayer with a cover letter explaining the mistake. This course of conduct naturally would have *saved money* for each taxpayer who made this mistake.

The reply received by the processing clerk was shocking. Her supervisors declared that it was not the responsibility of the IRS to correct the kind of errors which *favor the taxpayer.* The IRS will correct only those errors which *favor the IRS.* As if that were not enough, the clerk was further told that if a taxpayer was "dumb enough to pay more than is owed, we will keep the money!"

It was not until the clerk went public with this outrage, causing the incident to receive newspaper coverage in the eastern United States, that the IRS announced its policy in this respect would be altered. The IRS was, however, careful to point out that its new-found benevolence would apply "only to income and excise tax matters." As far as "estate tax matters were concerned," the policy would remain in "force and effect." In other words, "If you do not know the law and your rights, *tough luck!*"

Unfortunately, it is a well documented fact that

---

1. Public Law 100-647.

2. *Pilla Talks Taxes,* May 1988, issue regarding IRS Publication 908.

3. *The Naked Truth,* WINNING Publications, 1986. See the Introduction therein.

4. *How Anyone Can Negotiate With The IRS—And WIN!,* WINNING Publications, 1988.

almost *nobody* completely understands the tax law, including attorneys, accountants, Congress and the IRS itself. Congress changes the tax law constantly, providing no opportunity for the public or professional community to catch its breath. This affords the IRS a decided advantage when dealing with the public. It provides the IRS with the convenient excuse to take liberties, knowing full well that the public has no clue whether the acts are legal or not. After all, if you are supposed to *know the law*, but do not, whose fault is that?

Continually pointing a finger at the IRS is *not a solution* to the problem. Calling upon Congress to declare this or that type of IRS act illegal is *not the solution* to the problem. Certainly we welcome any legislation which limits the IRS' power over the citizen, but such legislation is effective only if the oppressed citizen *is aware of the proscription*. If the citizen is ignorant of the legal limitation, the legal limitation *does not exist*.

It is for this very reason that I have concentrated not so much on "reforming the IRS," but rather, on educating the taxpayer. Regardless of how the law is written, ignorant citizens remain entirely at the mercy of their government. Under such circumstances, their only hope is that the taskmaster will be humane and compassionate. Sadly, history has proven time and again that governments are not always humane and compassionate toward even their own citizens. Where the IRS is concerned, the United States is no exception.

The solution to the problem, therefore, seems plain. Only educated citizens, willing and able to take action, are capable of preventing government abuse. Where the IRS is concerned, citizens must not only know *what their rights are*, but must also be cognizant of just how those rights may be utilized to protect their own interests. In the absence of such capacity, the willingness of Congress to enact legislation is *worthless*.

The purpose of this manual is to transmit to the individual the concept of a "national defense" and "Ultimate Defense." As a nation, our theory since the end of World War II has been that the superior ability to *defend* one's self will *prevent* an attack by a foreign power. Regardless of your views on the state of our military and related expenditures, you must admit, this theory has merit. I believe that it applies not only at the national level vis-a-vis *foreign* governments, but it applies equally to the *individual* vis-a-vis *his own government*.

A citizen ready, willing and able to vindicate, in the courts, *any violation of the law or his rights by the IRS is the least* likely target of deliberate IRS abuse. We can begin to eliminate IRS abuse *only* when we eliminate the available pool of citizens capable of being abused. In this respect, citizens must not only be aware of their rights, but must have the capacity to *make them stick* in court, if necessary.

Taxpayers' Ultimate Defense Manual is the next installment toward the overall goal of eliminating IRS abuse through citizen education. This book will give you, the average taxpayer, the ultimate *power* not only to say "no" to the IRS, but to *vindicate* any violation of your rights. It is my belief that enough taxpayers with this kind of potent information will finally affect a "balance of power" between the IRS and the taxpayer.

—Daniel J. Pilla
St. Paul, Minnesota

Introduction

As you probably have already surmised from the cover of this manual, the material presented here is *not for spectators!* This manual is for those citizens *determined* to protect themselves from unwarranted intrusion by the tax collector into their financial affairs. I am referring to the abuse of your rights, including the attempted collection of taxes *not legally owed*. IRS abuse can be prevented, and within these pages we find the formula for doing so under nearly every factual scenario.

Like the nuclear capability possessed by the world's superpowers, this manual is not intended to be *an offensive* weapon. Rather, the knowledge derived from these pages is intended to permit you to stand firm against any act of aggression committed against your legal or financial liberties. Just as we assume the United States *will never* wish to *instigate* a nuclear attack against its foes, you *will never* wish to instigate an unprovoked legal attack against the IRS. However, the IRS has declared war and *you* are its intended enemy! It has made plans clear in IRS Docuent Number 6941, entitled, *Internal Revenue Strategic Plan*. This plan was exposed by me in my first book, *The Naked Truth*, and since has been the subject of much debate. In a word, it is a plan to systematically audit *every American taxpayer*, with the goal of collecting more money!

The IRS' own call to ironfisted enforcement policy is justified by its view that there is a "continuing decline in the extent to which taxpayers are willing or able to voluntarily comply with the federal tax laws."[1] The IRS boldly and callously accuses the typical taxpayer—you—of blatantly, intentionally cheating the government. In its own words, the IRS' Declaration of War is justified by, among other things, the following accusations of the conduct and mind-set of middle income Americans:

> "Changes in attitudes toward authority, in some cases manifested as open hostility and organized resistance. Taxpayers are exhibiting a declining respect for and reliance on 'the law' and government in general. A 'decay in the social contract' is detectable; there is a growing feeling, *particularly among middle-income taxpayers,* that they are not getting back, from society and government, their money's worth for taxes paid. The tendency is for taxpayers to try to take more control of their finances, perhaps because they seen an uncertain economic future for themselves; they exhibit a declining willingness to pay the share of governmental expenditures (including expenditures they may strongly disagree with) which government says is theirs to pay." (Emphasis added.) IRS *Strategic Plan,* page 45.

The war is on! Still, with the knowledge that you now have Ultimate Defense capabilities, you may—with confidence—stand toe-to-toe with our nation's tax collection superpower, the IRS. In any legal confrontation with this super-power where your legal rights are threatened by tax collection piracy, you need not be the one to blink. Finally, *you* can make *the other guy blink!*

The Right of Self-Defense

The right to defend one's self from an attack upon his person is one of the most basic rights recognized by our concept of law. Blackstone,[2] in his *Commentaries on the Laws of England,* Book One, speaks thusly of the right:

> "This natural life, as was before observed, the immediate donation of the great creator, cannot legally be disposed of or destroyed by any individual, neither by the person himself nor by any of his fellow creatures, merely upon their own authority."
>
> ★ ★ ★ ★
>
> "Besides those limbs and members that may be necessary to man, in order to defend himself or annoy his enemy, the rest of his person or body is also *entitled to the same natural right to security from the corporal insults of menaces, assaults, beatings, and wounding; though such insults amount not to destruction of life or member.*"[3] (Emphasis added.)

---

1. *Strategic Plan,* page 45.

2. William Blackstone was the 18th Century's most prominent legal scholar. As an English jurist, Blackstone occupied a seat on the bench of the Court of Common Pleas at Michaelmas from 1770-1779. Blackstone was revered for his insight into the rights and liberties of Englishmen. In his *Commentaries on the Laws of England,* Book One, Chapter One, he recorded a ringing diatribe on these rights. Unlike most jurists, Blackstone practiced what he preached, and this was reflected in the decisions which issued from his court. More than any other jurist, Blackstone's influence over the thinking of our forefathers was visibly profound. Blackstone's inexorable posture in support of individual liberties was replete throughout the rulings of our early American judges, and is dangerously absent from the writing of contemporary jurists. Blackstone's four volume series, *Commentaries on the Laws of England,* were first published in 1769. He died in Westminster, England, in February of 1780. His *Commentaries* are still revered as legal classics.

3. See Blackstone's *Commentaries on the Laws of England,* Book the First, pages 128 and 131.

But in the context of this manual, we are not speaking of self-defense in the sense of fending off an attack upon our person at the hands of a common thug. Rather, we speak of an attack by the tax collector upon the liberty of our finances; our right of property. Nevertheless, the right of self-defense exists in this respect and is *at least* as important in this context as is in the former. Blackstone teaches:

> "Of great importance to the public is the preservation of this *personal liberty:* for if once it were left in the power of any, the highest, magistrate to imprison arbitrarily whomever he or his officers thought proper (as in France it is daily practiced by the crown) there would soon be an end of all other rights and immunities. Some have thought, that unjust attacks, even upon life, or property, at the arbitrary will of the magistrate, are less dangerous to the commonwealth, than such as are made upon the personal liberty of the subject. To bereave a man of life, *or by violence to confiscate his estate,* without accusation or trial, *would be so gross and notorious an act of despotism, as must at once convey the alarm of tyranny throughout the whole Kingdom.* "[4] (Emphasis added.)

It follows that if we enjoy a natural property right in our estate, any *unlawful* attack which would threaten the peaceful enjoyment of that estate is subject to *redress.* That is to say, we possess the right to take such steps as are necessary to protect our property. Blackstone again:

> "In all. . .cases it is a general and *indisputable rule,* that where there is a legal right, there is also a legal remedy, by *suit or action at law.*[5] (Emphasis added.)

The concept of a "legal remedy by suit or action at law," *even against the government* for unlawful attacks upon the right of property or liberty, has long been recognized in the Common Law. The right was first expressed in the *Magna Charta, The Great Charter of Liberties,* executed under the Seal of King John at Runnymede, England, on June 15, 1215 A.D.

The *Magna Charta,* signed by King John at the point of a sword as ransom for his Crown, indeed his head, is credited for the establishment of the right of self-determination in government. It is undisputed that *Magna Charta* established the environment of and set in motion the engine of political change which eventually led to our own Constitution and Bill of Rights.

Blackstone himself described the *Magna Charta* thusly:

"There is no transaction in the ancient part of our English History more interesting and important, than the rise and progress, the gradual mutation and final establishment of the Charter of Liberties."[6]

The right of "legal remedy" is referred to in modern vernacular as the "right of redress." Magna Charta speaks pointedly of this right at Chapter 61. Chapter 61 reads:

> "This is the form (all previously declared rights) of the security for the observance of the peace and liberties between the King and the Kingdom. That the Barons may elect twenty-five Barons of the Kingdom, whom they will, who shall take care with all their might to hold and observe, and cause to be observed, the peace and liberties which our Lord the King hath conceded, and by his Charter (the *Magna Charta*) hath confirmed; so that, namely, if the King or the Justiciaries or Bailiffs of the King, or any of his Ministers shall in any case fail in the performance of them towards any person, or shall break through these Articles of peace and security, and the offense be notified to four Barons of the aforesaid five and twenty, they, the four Barons, shall go to our Lord the King, or to his Justiciary, if the King shall be out of the Kingdom, *and laying open the grievance shall petition to have it redressed without delay;* and if the King shall not amend it. . .the four Barons shall refer the case to the remainder of the twenty-five, and they, the twenty-five, with the whole community of the land, shall distain and distress the King *by all means which they can;* that is to say by taking his Castles, Lands, Possessions, and in every other manner which they can, until amendment shall be made according to their decision. . ."

Hence in these words we find the genesis in Anglo-American law of our inalienable right to pursue *even the government* for any violation of a sacred property right. Under *Magna Charta,* not even the King could legally dispossess a subject of his "lands, liberty, or his rights," save the King shall be answerable for the transgression and liable for repayment in order to remedy the violation. Should he fail to correct the infraction, the law afforded *the people* substantial power and might to enforce their rights to liberty and property. The same principles hold true even today.

In fact it was just such a failure which prompted our American forefathers to break their political ties with England, catapulting the Colonies first into War, then

---

4. Ibid, at pages 131-132.

5. Ibid, Book Three, page 23.

6. Blackstone quoted in *An Historical Essay on the Magna Charta of King John,* by Richard Thompson, first published in England in 1829.

into Independence. Our liberties were ensured by the *first* Constitution creating a Republican form of Representative Government. As we all know, the Declaration of Independence, drafted by Thomas Jefferson and unanimously adopted by Congress, July 4th, 1776, set this sequence of events into motion.

The Declaration of Independence was an *indictment* by the Colonies of King George III for his lawless acts. It contained 27 specific charges against the Crown for violations of rights which, according to Jefferson and Congress, manifested in "the establishment of absolute Tyranny over these States."[7] What is lost upon this point, however, is the subtlety that it was not *the acts of despotism themselves* which moved the Colonies to declare their independence from England. Rather, it was the King's failure to *right those wrongs* when presented with the lawful Petitions of the Colonists. In this respect, the Declaration reads:

"In every stage of these Oppressions We have Petitioned for Redress in the most humble terms: Our repeated Petitions have been answered only by repeated injury. A Prince, whose character is thus marked by every act which may define a Tyrant, is unfit to be a ruler of a free people."

This "long train of offenses and usurpations" announced Jefferson in the Declaration, evidenced "a design to reduce (the people) under absolute Despotism." Given such circumstances, Jefferson and the united Colonies declared that it was the people's right, indeed, "their duty, to throw off such Government, and to provide new Guards for their future security." Thus was born the United States of America.

Some 12 years later, on September 13, 1788, eleven States having voted to ratify the new Constitution of the United States, the Continental Congress passed a resolution to put the new Constitution into effect. With it eventually came a series of Amendments known as the Bill of Rights, the one Statement of Law which sets this nation apart from any other in history.

The Courts Belong to the People

At the foundation of the Bill of Rights is the right to hold our Government accountable for its unlawful transgressions; to *redress* the deprivation of personal liberty or property rights as they are expressed in our Constitution. The First Amendment, recognized for its bonding of the right to religious freedom and freedom of the press, is often overlooked as to the equally important guarantee of the "right of redress." The First Amendment reads in applicable part as follows:

"Congress shall make no law. . .abridging the. . .right of the people. . .to petition the Government for a redress of grievances."

Hence, the cornerstone of our system of Government is the *right of the people* to ensure *their own* continued freedom and the integrity of their individual liberties. Naturally, access to the courts is fundamentally necessary to *discharge* this right, as the courts have been established principally for the purpose of settling the disputes which may from time to time arise. Thus, in the truest sense, the courts belong not to the Government, but rather to the people, who when proceeding lawfully, have the full right and duty to quell lawless Governmental actions through the judicial process.

To this end, I maintain that the courts must be *destigmatized*. Americans have come to associate the courts only with "criminals." As such, most have determined that they shall stay clear of their sweep. While it is certainly true that those institutions are rightfully established to consider and determine the verity of *criminal allegations*, we must not renounce those halls as those in which *only criminals* should be found. Rather, honest citizens, aggrieved by the lawless acts of *Government*, must, as is their right and their duty, turn to the courts for reconciliation of those acts. Such is the exercise of one's First Amendment right in its most *pristine* form.

I say that citizens *must* undertake to redress such violations for two reasons. First, as Thomas Paine is credited with saying, "Government, even in its best state is but a necessary evil; in its worst state, an intolerable one." The undisputable history of government among men is that government will become increasingly intolerant of free thought and private property, gradually encroaching the incidental liberties which accompany those rights. So long as *any* unlawful attack by government upon these important rights is permitted to stand unaccosted by the bereaved citizen, government and its institutions will grow *progressively* arrogant in its view of the individual.

Secondly, and equally true, there can be no question that a steady stream of abuses wears heavily upon an otherwise law abiding community. More so than any other of our noble institutions, Government is a teacher. When it acts without regard to the Constitution and its plain and indisputable holdings, it teaches others to do the same. When Government ignores the property rights and individual liberties of its own people, it communicates to the masses that *it will tolerate* lawlessness on a wholesale level.

---

7. The Declaration of Independence.

Pardoxically, Government is then *burdened* with the task of keeping the peace and maintaining order in a society which neither knows of nor cares about such intangibles. In the end, the most violent and obscene attacks upon individual liberties by government are justified to the people in the name of maintaining social order.

We see this phenomenon plainly where the Internal Revenue Service is concerned. The IRS has, over the years, used every manner and means to enforce its edicts, justifying its lawlessness with worn-out platitudes regarding the importance of insuring the integrity of the "public fisc." We know from documented records of court proceedings and Congressional hearings that the IRS has employed such intolerable tactics as illegal wiretaps, outright theft of private records, jury tampering, hiring prostitutes in efforts to spy, using its authority to carry out personal vendettas, fraud in connection with its own publications and fraud in connection with its billing practices. Sadly, this list is not exhaustive.

As the IRS displays total disregard for the law, as it regularly treats citizens unfairly and without respect, a number of those same citizens inevitably conclude that the only appropriate response is to return the lawless conduct *in kind*. As a reactionary measure, certain persons will "cheat" on their income tax returns. Others go "underground," distancing themselves to the fullest extent possible from any records which would trace evidence of "income" to them. Still another response is "tax protesting." While the IRS is loathe to admit it, that organization itself is responsible for the conception, birth and propagation of the "tax protester" movement through the 1970s and into the early 1980s.

The members of that movement attacked the IRS, openly and publicly, through a variety of means, challenging and defying the tax laws and the IRS' tactics at every step. Quashing the tax movement became for the IRS a bureaucratic obsession persisting for over a decade. Throughout the crusade, the end always justified the means, and the IRS was guilty of innumerable lawless acts calculated to convict protest leaders and quell the movement.

Thankfully, the symptoms of lawlessness on the part of citizens have not boiled to a wholesale level. Though the IRS suggests otherwise, the facts are that the incidences of proven criminal tax "cheaters" in this country are an immeasurably small fragment of the overall number of taxpayers.[8] *Yet the very presence of this anathema enables the IRS to justify tightening its grip* on the totality of the American public. The cycle of lawlessness thus feeds upon itself.

Breaking the Cycle of Lawlessness

If the cycle of lawlessness is to be broken, lawless IRS acts *cannot be answered in kind*. Rather, the only legitimate, acceptable manner in which to address such transgressions is to petition for redress under the First Amendment according to the prescribed rules of the legislature and the judiciary. In the absence of such a petition, no other course of conduct will be effective; no other course of conduct can be received by society as viable in light of the Constitution. Having so petitioned, the Government and the Government alone bears the responsibility for the degeneration of society into chaos or revolution should the lawful complaints of beleaguered citizens fall upon deaf ears.

This point is best illustrated by reference to events which occurred in south Texas not many years ago. In Texas, particularly south and west Texas, the spirit of independence soars high. Citizens there tend to be more mindful of their rights, and more willing to exercise them—even in the face of Government intimidation. Jean H., a Texas housewife, is no different.

Jean's husband, V.R., another fiercely independent Texan, posted "No Trespassing" signs at the entrance to the family's 55-acre homestead. The signs were impossible to miss. They measured four feet wide by six feet high. The signs anchored at the property entrance were quite literally the "talk of the town." In addition, V.R. recorded a notice with the office of the County Recorder, declaring that federal agents were not welcome on the premises. A copy of the notice was mailed to the IRS via certified mail and placed into the file which the local tax collectors maintained. By now it should be obvious to you that V.R. and Jean had a long-standing bitter dispute with the IRS.

On November 4, 1981, two special agents of the Internal Revenue Service entered the premises in defiance of the "No Trespassing" signs. They were met at the door by Jean, and they began asking questions. Jean, unflinching, politely inquired as to the agents' authority for their entry upon her posted, private property. In the face of her continued probing, one agent responded, "I'm asking you a question and I'm not going to answer any questions." Later in the conversation, he again stated in response to one of Jean's questions, "We're not going to answer any questions." The agents eventually left Jean's home, having obtained no information.

Jean's reaction to the trespassing is an example of "breaking the cycle of lawlessness" as I have discussed above. Rather than attempt any action herself against

---

8. See my book, *How Anyone Can Negotiate With The IRS—And WIN!*, Chapter 1, pages 48-51. WINNING Publications, 1988.

the agents, Jean exercised her First Amendment right. The next morning, she marched into the County Attorney's office and filed a criminal trespass complaint against the two agents. The result was that the agents were arrested by the local sheriff and eventually tried on the charge of criminal trespass, a misdemeanor violation of Texas State law!

Having been bashed in the teeth by the criminal complaint, the agents and United States Attorney advising them, were faced with a difficult choice. Texas law is clear, *no person* may enter the premises of another if those premises are clearly marked with "No Trespassing" signs. *Not only* was Jean's residence marked with such signs *anybody* could see, but formal *written* notice had been mailed to the IRS stating that V.R. and Jean would take seriously their right to privacy. Consequently, if the agents were to admit that they had seen such signs at the entrance to the property, they would have been guilty of criminal trespass. The solution, then, was to continue their lawless acts.

First of all, *they lied,* claiming that no signs were posted at the entrance to the property. Next, the United States Attorney levied *bad faith,* retaliatory claims against Jean, professing that she unlawfully interfered with the administration of justice by hindering and impeding the agents in the course of their investigation. This theory was grounded upon the false claim that the "No Trespassing" signs were not in fact posted as alleged by Jean in her criminal complaint.

With regard to the false testimony that the signs were not posted at the time agents entered the premises, a court later found that the "evidence overwhelmingly points to a contrary conclusion." The court observed that Jean and V.R. had "adorned their private property with 'No Trespassing' signs, and that 'responsible officials' were well aware of (their) desire to exercise their right to privacy." The false testimony of the agents was rejected by the court.

With regard to the retaliatory claims pointed at Jean by a vindictive United States Attorney, a federal court supported her right under the First Amendment. This was its observation:

"As the Supreme Court has held, the right to petition for redress of grievances is 'among the most precious of the liberties safeguarded by the bill of rights.' (Citation) Inseparable from the guaranteed rights entrenched in the First Amendment, the right to petition for redress of greivances occupies a 'preferred place' in our system of representative government, and enjoys a 'sanctity and a sanction not permitting dubious intrusions.' (Citation) Indeed, 'it was not by accident or coincidence that rights to freedom of speech and press were coupled in a single guarantee with the rights of the people peaceably to assemble and to petition for redress of grievances.' (Citation)★★★
"Having thoroughly reviewed the record. . .we have concluded that (Jean's) actions represent a legitimate and protected exercise of her right to petition for the redress of grievances. The record clearly reveals that (Jean) placed a high value upon her right to personal privacy and genuinely attempted to protect her rights through the orderly pursuit of justice—the filing of citizen complaints with a reasonable basis."[9]

The death knell for the IRS' spitefull retaliation against Jean was the final observation of the court as to the government's act. The court stated, "We cannot condone the imposition of criminal sanction for (Jean's) exercise of her constitutional right."[10]

After the court upheld Jean's First Amendment right of redress, she and her husband have lived peacefully in their small, south Texas community, *unharassed* by the IRS.[11] Though Jean was confronted with the unlawful IRS actions, she did not return those acts in kind. Her *lawful* petition under the First Amendment led to incredible embarrassment on the part of the two offending agents who fabricated stories to justify their actions.

I do not know very many citizens with the mettle of Jean. I do not know many persons willing to challenge an IRS agent on account of his unlawful acts. As an unfortunate consequence, I do know hundreds of people who have been victimized by the IRS. That the IRS leaves Jean alone is testimony to the truthfulness of my longtime hypothesis that the IRS is just like an army in time of war. No commander with any degree of intelligence or experience will attack when his adversary is *prepared for and capable of* doing battle.

This lesson teaches us to be on our guard. If you are to break the cycle of lawlessness, you must prepare for the time when the attack falls upon your doorstep. The IRS itself has announced its intentions; it is now just a question of "When?" This does not mean that you are to scout for trouble. On the contrary, you must continue to make every effort to comply with the law. However, it is equally true that you must not allow yourself to be taken advantage of in the name of the law.

9. See 710 F.2d 1106, 1111-1112 (5th Cir. 1983).

10. Ibid, at page 1112.

11. The full story of Jean, her husband and their battle with the IRS is told by my friend and attorney, Donald W. MacPherson, in his recent book, *Tax Fraud and Evasion, The War Stories* ($17.95), MacPherson and Sons Publishers, Phoenix, AZ, 1989, 602-866-9566. The book is a fascinating "insider's" look at not only some of the over 50 criminal tax trials in which Mac has been involved, but his 18 months experience as a company commander and platoon leader in Vietnam.

The Ultimate Defense Weapon

As we have seen, citizens have a right—indeed a duty—to defend against unlawful government acts. We have also seen when the First Amendment right of petition is used in good faith and in a lawful manner, it will accomplish the intended goal. Jean is no longer the target of improper or illegal IRS actions. She fired her Ultimate Defense Weapon and scored a direct hit, leaving the enemy in tatters.

This manual is all about Ultimate Defense Weapons. With it, you can ensure that any enemy attack upon your stronghold of life, liberty and property can be defended successfully.

PART I
A Blueprint For Victory

CHAPTER
1

Formulating an Effective Defense

To be successful, a decision to carry forth any action, military or otherwise, must always be predicated upon forming strategic assessments or evalutions of the conditions of the campaign. The effectiveness of the operation is measured in direct relation to the accuracy of the assessments. When contemplating battle, a commander must evaluate the enemy's commander, his strengths, weaknesses, experience, and tendencies. He must evaluate the enemy's troop strength and morale. He must evaluate the terrain and likely weather conditions in which the battle will be fought. He must evaluate the conditions in which the battle will be fought. He must evaluate the condition of his own equipment and supplies and the capacity of his own troops to carry the decided strategy into battle successfully. He must evaluate the enemy's political climate and its people's willingness to continue to fund the struggle, both in human and financial terms.

It is no less important, when pondering battle with the IRS, to formulate the necessary strategic assessments in much the same fashion. As I have said, the success of a campaign is measured in direct relation to the accuracy of those assessments. While each element

to be evaluated in the fight against IRS abuse will not involve exactly the same factors as those a general may consider, they are closely parallel, as we shall see.

The Enemy Commander

The armies of the Internal Revenue Service, insofar as the average citizen is concerned, can be identified as these four: the Examination Division, responsible to conduct audits; the Appeals Division, responsible to resolve disputed examination cases; the Collection Division, responsible to collect unpaid taxes; and, the Criminal Investigation Division, responsible to investigate and aid in the prosecution of criminal violations of the tax laws.

The battle plans for each of these armies have already been drawn, approved and placed into effect. These marching orders take the form of the Internal Revenue Manual. The IRS manual contains a portion which addresses itself to each of the functions I have just described. In very large measure, the tendencies, experience, strengths, weaknesses and intelligence of the IRS' commanders and lieutenants along the chain of command, may be accurately assessed through review of the IRS' Manual.

The Internal Revenue Manual, while not openly discussed by the IRS with the general public, is *not classified* material. Any person with the desire to acquire relevant portions, and knowing which bureaucratic buttons to push, can amass this important intelligence information. All or part of the Internal Revenue Manual is available from the IRS Disclosure Officer, located within each IRS district.[1] The Disclosure Officer is responsible to determine whether any particular IRS document may legally be released to the public. If so, he will transmit those documents to the citizen.

In addition, entire copies of the IRS manual may be purchased from the IRS by inquiring to the following address:

> Freedom of Information Reading Room
> Internal Revenue Service
> ATTN: PM:S:DS:P:RR
> 1111 Constitution Avenue NW
> Washington, D.C. 20224

Inquiries to that office should request a copy of the Freedom of Information Price List relative to the IRS. That document lists each of the Internal Revenue Manual parts, the number of pages included in each part and the price.

In the motion picture *Patton,* actor George C. Scott portrayed American General George S. Patton during World War II. In one scene, while fighting German Field Marshal Rommel in North Africa, Patton and his armies are shown lying in wait for Rommel and his armored divisions. Just prior to commencing the attack against Rommel, Patton cries, "Rommel, you b------, I read your book!" While this of course was Hollywood's rendition of the events, it is undisputed that, by using his enemy's own statements of tactics and strategy, Patton was able to defeat Rommel in battle after battle in the deserts of North Africa. His forces eventually drove the Germans out of the continent altogether.

The Internal Revenue Manual is the "book" of strategy and tactics written by the IRS' Generals for use by the men in the fields. In any anticipated confrontation with them, the intelligent commander will acquire the enemy's battle plan, diagnose his strategy and tacts, anticipate his moves based upon those disclosures, and having done so, *defeat him in battle.*

Enemy Troop Strength and Morale

One of the most critical errors a commander can make is to underestimate his enemy's troop strength, morale, and willingness of the enemy soldier to resist. In fact, perhaps the most famous lawsuit of the 1980s, General William Westmoreland's libel suit against CBS, centered upon this very issue. Westmoreland was the Commander-in-Chief of all U.S. Forces in Southeast Asia during the Vietnam fiasco. Years after U.S. witdrawal from the area, CBS alleged, in a *60 Minutes* news broadcast, that Westmoreland was involved with the CIA in supplying false reports of North Vietnamese troop strength and morale to U.S. officials in Washington. The reports, claimed *60 Minutes,* were presented to the President and the Congress through the Pentagon in effort to induce the two to commit further human and financial resources to the war effort.

Whether Westmoreland was or was not involved in any real or imagined CIA coverup, the suit did not ultimately reveal. After several weeks of testimony in a New York City courtroom, and after the expenditure of a mountain of money in legal fees, Westmoreland dropped the suit. We can only assume that the cost of the battle had brought the General to his knees.

What we do know, however, is that the most powerful nation in the world was brought to *its knees* by, as MacPherson writes, "a 12-year old farmer, bare-foot, wearing black pajamas and carrying an out-dated carbine."[2] Somebody somewhere, deliberately or otherwise, seriously—no, *fatally*—underestimated the number of NVA troops which could be thrown into the fight. Perhaps more significantly, the failure was in underestimating the *intensity of purpose* in the hearts of these troops.

When dealing with the IRS, we do not need to covertly plant undercover intelligence operatives to learn or surmise the number of agents we may potentially face in battle. That puzzle can be solved now, once and for all. The typical audit involves *one* auditor. The average appeal involves *one* appeals officer. A garden variety Tax Court case occupies the time of *one* District Counsel attorney. Action within the District Court will involve, in the typical case, *one* attorney from the Justice Department.

One of the most compelling emotions experienced by citizens doing battle wit the IRS is the feeling that they are *overwhelmingly outnumbered.* Concomitantly, one

---

1. See Appendix 1 for map of IRS districts.
2. *Tax Fraud and Evasion,* MacPherson and Sons Publishers, 1989.

must also battle the feelings of hopelessness and desperation. This result is well-planned by the IRS, in keeping with Chinese General Sun Tzu's observation that the most successful army is one which wins *without fighting*.[3] To destroy the enemy's capacity and desire to resist *before* the outbreak of hostilities is, according to Master Sun, the mark of a *superior commander*.

As a matter of fact, however, the IRS *will not send* a battalion of men and equipment to crush a single taxpayer in the routine audit or collection situation. That the IRS has *anyone* convinced to the contrary is a tribute to the cunning and capacity of its generals to wage psychological warfare.

It is important to understand that the IRS will *not* send overwhelming numbers against you. Believing it will is the principal reason citizens usually shy away from a fight with the tax collector. After all, how can anybody withstand the force and might of the United States Government? With all its power and resources, surely it would be futile to resist.

To gain the confidence necessary to engage the enemy in the defense of one's rights, one must understand that the enemy has created the mere appearance of over-whelming numbers to the end that it *will not have to fight*. It is certainly true that the IRS employs over 115,000 persons within its service, but certainly each of these 115,000 persons *will not* be mobilized to attack *you!* As I have already stated, *you* stand to face just one enemy combatant at any one state of hostilities with the IRS. *You are not outnumbered by overwhelming enemy forces!*

Though the IRS does not possess the luxury of endless manpower to throw into the fight, it does have a carefully established, unbroken *chain of command*. This feature contributes to the *illusion* of overwhelming forces. The chain of command begins with the generals in Washington. It filters down to the lieutenants in the local districts, and finally, to the troops in the field. Together with an artfully orchestrated system of centralized communications, it allows the IRS armies to advance in a seemingly smooth, unstoppable fashion.

But in this context, there are *disadvantages* to such a tightly structured chain of command. They are two-fold in my judgment. First, the officers in the field have very little authority to act independently of established procedure. Taken from them is the necessary element of control which every field commander must possess if he is to have the capacity to react to the enemy on the battlefield. The IRS is locked into its manual and can be expected to follow those procedures.

This factor can be exploited by striking quickly, creating confusion within the enemy's camp. To be successful, any attack must be so calculated as to remove from the commander in the field the authority to make such decisions as will affect the outcome of the battle. As Sun Tzu observes, if a field commander is so limited that he must first seek permission to put out a fire, when he returns with the order, all he will find are ashes.

The second problem with the IRS' established chain of command is the manner in which most orders are transmitted. This function is carried out through the vehicle of the IRS manual. This document, as we have already stated, is *written* and can be obtained by any citizen. And since a detailed manual exists by which IRS personnel are instructed to proceed, the IRS can be *expected* to maneuver *within the context of that manual*. Foreknowledge of the provisions of the manual enable you to anticipate the enemy's every move. This of course is of great advantage to you.

In assessing the morale of the IRS troops in the field and their capacity and willingness to carry out the campaigns established for them by their military and political leaders, we must draw some different conclusions than those concerning its troop strength. This assessment is as important as any of the others since an incorrect analysis of the problem will prove disastrous in battle.

For over a decade, leaders of the tax protester movement, believing their cause to be noble and their motivation patriotic, challenged the IRS and our nation's tax laws on various grounds. Chief among them was the proposition that the tax laws were unconstitutional and that no person should be required to pay income taxes. Pointing to the Second Plank of Marx's Communist Manifesto which calls for a heavy, progressive or graduated income tax, protest leaders defied the laws and called upon others to do the same. Its leaders claimed that the tax protester movement was designed to reform serious social, political and economic ills created by what they perceived to be an unconstitutional income tax burden.

The leaders of the movement were very fond of boasting that in the event they were ever confronted by the IRS with respect to their defiance of the law (which they were), the truthfulness of their cause and patriotic motivation would lead the attacking agents to withdraw as a sign of support. It was not uncommon for leaders to publicly declare their *desire* for the IRS to "come after" them. "I'll make tax protesters out of any agent I talk to!" was the battle cry.

This attitude reflected a serious miscalculation of the individual IRS agent's willingness to resist the threat presented by tax protesters. Tax protesters assumed that the "righteousness" of their cause would be

---

3. *The Art of War*, Sun Tzu, 6th Century B.C. Translated by Thomas Cleary, Dragon Publications, 1988.

sufficient to neutralize any enemy resistance. What they failed to consider, however, was the *agent's personal interest* in continuing to resist.

To the vast majorty of persons within the employ of the federal government, their function is "just a job." They perform their task for the sole purpose of earning a living to support their families. They are not motivated by patriotism, they are motivated by money. *They are mercenaries.* Their very existence depends upon their marching to the beat of the drum as sounded out by Congress and their superior officers. In this respect, their tenacity in battle may be pre-determined. They must be expected to carry out their orders or risk losing the very means by which they support themselves. If you think this point is unimportant, consider the observation of Napoleon Bonaparte:

> "In war, morale counts for three-quarters, the balance
> of man-power counts for only one-quarter."

The decision to engage the IRS, therefore, should never be predicated upon the supposition that you will prevail merely because of the righteousness of your case *whatever it may be!* Agents of the IRS are not interested in your cause. They are interested in their own cause, namely, professional advancement and the support of their families.

In reaching your decision to engage the enemy, you must assume and be prepared for utter resistance *at every level of combat.* More clearly stated, do not begin the fight if you do not have the heart or ability to *finish the fight.* You can anticipate no surrender on the part of the enemy.

Field Terrain and Conditions

The military demise of both Napoleon and Hitler began with a common mistake being the failure to perceive, or the miscalculation of, the conditions of battle along the western border of Russia. Mile after endless mile of open field made supply and reinforcement difficult, and the incredibly harsh Russian winter, together with ill-equipped soldiers, rendered sustained battle impossible. Both the French and German armies suffered terrible losses and eventual defeat due to these errors in planning.

In battle with the IRS, it is not rain, snow or mountainous terrain with which we must be familiar. We must be familiar with the structure of the federal court system, and the vehicle of federal administrative procedures, as these are the fields of battle on which we

will engage the enemy. A failure to understand the field of battle will surely spell the demise of your army.

In 1946, Congress passed the Administrative Procedures Act. As I stated in my book, *The Naked Truth,*[4] the Administrative Procedures Act was the beginning of a blatant departure by government from long-established Constitutional standards. It was a major step in an evolutionary process which has transformed our legal system.

Prior the Act, the three powers of government, the legislative, executive and judicial, were vested in three *separate* departments of government. Congress controlled the legislative power, the courts held all judicial power and executive agencies carried out the functions of government expressed in the Constitution. Each department of government held and could exercise at its own discretion a veto power against each of the other two branches. This system of "checks and balances" acted to prevent any one department from acquiring or usurping total power, thus creating a despotism. It is against this type of totalitarian government which our forefathers rebelled.

The transformation brought about by the Administrative Procedures Act has all but destroyed the constitutionally mandated system of checks and balances just described. The Act gives federal administrative agencies, such as the IRS, the authority to create its own laws (referred to as regulations), to judge those laws within its own administrative tribunals, and to enforce those laws through its own administrative police forcce. While the courts insist otherwise, there can be no question that the creation of this hybrid seriously impairs the First Amendment right to petition the government for redress of grievances and the Fifth Amendment right to due process of law.

Theory aside, the courts have time and again upheld the IRS' administrative structure, leaving us with the option of fighting first within that structure, or *not fighting at all.* Within the framework of the IRS' administrative procedures, one has certain rights of appeal in connection with agency decisions. For example, the most common right of appeal is the right to insist upon a review of *any* decision which is made by an IRS auditor. Rather than pursuing the review of any such adverse decision in a court of law, a citizen must first exhaust his administrative remedies within the IRS before the courts will host any debate on the issue. *It is always necessary to exhaust all administrative remedies* before pursuing an issue *in court.* Failure to do so will result in sure and sudden defeat.

The specific administrative procedures peculiar to the various strategies within this manual are discussed

---

4. WINNING Publications, 1986, page 82.

Exhibit 1-1:
Chart of Civil Administrative Procedures Within the IRS

1. Notice of Audit

☐ Return to be Examined

or

☐ Mathematical Recomputation Performed

2. Your Response to Notice of Audit

☐ Explain Nature of Audit, More Time Needed;

or

☐ Demand Abatement

3. Audit Conducted

☐ Return Accepted—Case Resolved;
☐ More Info Needed—Further Meetings

or

☐ Deductions Disallowed

4. Notice of Disallowance Sent

☐ 30-Day Letter Received, You Either:
  ● Accept Disallowance,
  ● Pay Tax,
  ● File Claim For Refund

or

☐ Submit Protest Letter
  to Appeals Division

5. Appeals Conference

☐ Claim For Refund Considered
  ● Hearing on Facts and Law

or

☐ Protest Letter Considered
  ● Hearing on Facts and Law

6. Appeals Action

☐ Grant Claim or Protest—Case Resolved

or

☐ Deny Claim or Protest—In Case of Protest, Deficiency Issued

7. IRS Makes Final Administrative Determination

☐ Denial of Claim For Refund

or

☐ Issuance of Notice of Deficiency—
Either Act Constitutes a Final Determination

on a chapter by chapter basis. However, for a better understanding of the overall structure, refer to Exhibit 1-1, Chart of Civil Administrative Procedures. This road map will enable you to determine where your army is *or should* be headed in your war with the IRS. Observing this chart is much like following a road map. Without it, you will be lost in the jungles and rice paddies of the administrative war zone.

Only after having exhausted all *administrative remedies* is it legally permissable to cross the DMZ into the federal courts. But again, launching an attack into that area requires an understanding of the lay of the land. The chart in Exhibit 1-2 illustrates the structure of the federal courts, vis-a-vis the IRS. Naturally, the chart contains a reference to the administrative process as it is an indispensable step in gaining access to the courts.

In addition to the charts shown above, it is necessary to understand that the Federal courts operate under the rules promulgated by both the Supreme Court and Congress. The rules, known as the Federal Rules of Civil Procedure, contain the guidelines needed to walk a civil case through the federal system. Any hope of success in the federal courts is contingent upon knowing the rules of the game. They, more than anything else, constitute the conditions of battle, and the commander who understands how they may be best put to use will be the commander who prevails in battle.

Exhibit 1-2
Chart of Federal Court Process

1. Final Administrative Determination Received

2. Court Action Commenced

☐ District Court Refund Suit

or

☐ Tax Court Petition

3. Court Decision

☐ Favorable
  ● Refund Issued

  or

  ● Deficiency Set Aside

or

☐ Unfavorable

4. Judicial Appeal — U.S. Court of Appeals

Your Own Troops and Supplies

I stated earlier that unless you have the heart and ability to *finish* a fight with the IRS, you have no business *beginning* one. In this respect, it is a necessary prerequisite to battle to assess your own capacity to carry out the task with which you are faced. More specifically, your supplies annd supply line must remain *intact* at all times. The supplies to which I am referring here are *the law and facts*. All judicial decisions are based upon these two elements. The law is comprised of the legislative rules and judicial decisions governing the subject matter at hand. The facts are the historical occurences which shaped the events surrounding your case.

These elements of war may be considered by you to be *intact* only after you have completely analyzed all of the facts of the case, evaluating their significance, and mustering all of the law which governs the subject matter, *including* the rules and decisions which weigh against you. No reasonably intelligent commander will send troops into battle if it is impossible to supply those troops with the necessary elements of survival once in the field.

By engaging the IRS before these necessary considerations are made, you risk losing the battle before you have an opportunity to come face to face with the enemy. If the position you have taken in your case against the government is *not supported by the law or judicial interpretation,* your case will be lost at the earliest stages of confrontation.

In addition, at any time should your position on the law or the facts come under siege by the enemy, you must be capable, through pre-battle planning, to withstand such a siege. I am referring to a move by the government to have your case *dismissed* before you are given a full opportunity to litigate before a judge or jury. In the vernacular of the law, such a maneuver is referred to as a motion for summary judgment. This maneuver will be discussed later in detail, but for now, suffice it to say that when a motion for summary judgment is presented, the claim is that either or both the law and facts of the case do not justify rendering a judgment in your favor.

You must anticipate such an attack upon your position, and *beforehand,* take the necessary steps to ensure that you will endure such a siege and prevail in battle.

Determining the law is the more difficult aspect of this equation. Yet, through a few simple steps, it is not possible for the average person to accomplish. The law of the United States as passed by Congress is set forth in books known as the United States Code. The Code is organized by subject matter, with each subject given a number, known as a Title. Within Title 26 of the Code, we find all laws relating to the IRS and taxation in the United States.

West Publishing Company, a private publisher, produces a version of the code known as the United States Code Annotated. The term "annotated" refers to a collection of court decisions which have interpreted the code. Thus, all under one roof, one is able to assimilate both the legislative rules (the statutes) and judicial rulings (court decisions) on a given legal matter.

The United States Code Annotated is available at any law library, and many public libraries. The court decisions that are found with the United States Code are organized there in an abbreviated fashion. The full text of any court decision mentioned in the Code is also available in any law library. The court decisions themselves are printed in books called Case Reporters. West Publishing Company is also responsible for producing these books.

In its pamphlet, *West's Law Finder, A Legal Research Manual,* the editors of West describe a simple and concise manner of carrying out legal research. The pamphlet is inexpensive and available from West by writing P.O. Box 64526, St. Paul, MN 55164.

Understanding the law library, something not very difficult to do, is necessary to ensure that your supply line will not be broken in battle.

The Enemy's Political Climate

The last, but certainly not least important strategic assessment is the state of the enemy's political climate. When the civil government is in unity with its military leaders, a nation is at its strongest. When that government is at odds with its military leadership, it is at its weakest. The crafty commander will not attack an enemy when that army will receive all the best support of every kind and description from its government. To do so would ensure a prolonged battle won only at great cost in men and materials.

Rather, the intelligent commander will await evidence of dissension among the civil government vis-a-vis its own army. When the civil government is unwilling or unable to lend unfettered support to its military, an attack will cause confusion, consternation and will inevitably result in the defeat of the torn nation. Sadly, this bitter lesson was taught the United States in southeast Asia.

Where the IRS is concerned, the civil government is beginning to express dissatisfaction with its army. Recently, the hotly debated Taxpayers' Bill of Rights Act passed the Congress with great support. While I have spoken in opposition to the Bill due to its failure to solve many tax abuse problems, it is nevertheless a statement by lawmakers that IRS abuse is indeed a concern which is wreaking havoc on the people of this country.

In addition, I reported in the April, 1989 issue of my newsletter, *Pilla Talks Taxes*,[5] that Congress will begin hearings on revamping the penalty provisions of the tax code. In June of 1989, Congressman J.J. Pickle (D. Tex.), Chairman of the House Ways and Means Oversight Subcommittee, introduced H.R. 2528, the Improved Penalty Administration and Compliance Tax Bill (IMPACT). Congressman Pickle declared on June 1, 1989, when the bill was introduced, that it would streamline and revamp the penalty system "to provide a fairer, less complex, more effective and more rational civil tax penalty system."[6]

Congress and presumably the IRS have finally begun to recognize, as I have argued for years, that the penalties as currently structured do more to *prevent* taxpayers from complying with the law, than they do to *ensure* compliance with the law. Prior to his resignation, former IRS Commissioner Lawrence Gibbs stated, "Penalties have produced tensions that are counter-productive to the goals of tax administration."[7]

Moreover, as I write, hearings before the House Government Operations Subcommittee are being conducted in Washington by Congressman Doug Barnard (D. Geo.). The hearings are probing into alleged *widespread* ethics violations by upper level management personnel within the IRS. The Committee has already uncovered significant evidence of influence peddling, the use of IRS power to carry out personal vendettes and even fraud within the agency.

What this tells me is that the IRS is now vulnerable to attack. Now, more than any other time in my 14 years of dealing with the tax collectors, I see a chain of evidence which suggests that the civil government is not all that happy with the way in which its army of tax collectors conducts itself on the battlefield. Now, more than ever, the IRS is vulnerable to attack by citizens whose rights have been abused by that army.

I cannot and will not guarantee that the courts or Congress will turn their backs on any agent guilty of unlawful conduct. However, I do know that Congress has *handed citizens* some additional weapons with which to *fight back*. They are, of course, discussed in this manual. And I do believe that *the time is right* for fighting back! The IRS' political support seems to be waning! Our supplies are in place! The battle lines are drawn! The enemy has been placed *on notice* that we will tolerate no further intrusions into our rights and liberties! The order has been given—should the enemy cross the line, *commence firing!*

Patton's Principle

As important a consideration as those expressed above is a principle of warfare attributed to General George S. Patton. Patton was fond of saying, "Never fight a battle if nothing is gained by the victory."[8] Relying upon the principle of "economy of forces," Patton realized that no army is capable of winning a war if it engages the enemy at *every possible opportunity*. When *you* choose your fights, fighting only on *your terms*, the chances of prevailing in the war are substantially increased.

No army has an inexhaustible supply of money, weapons, machinery and manpower. Because of this, it is necessary to carefully choose the conditions under which one will fight, making sure that the battle to which one commits his forces will, if successful, contribute in the most significant of ways to the war effort in general.

When we discuss the war against IRS abuse, this principle is *no less true*. It is a fact that the IRS has more money, more weapons, more machinery and more manpower than do you or I. That *does not mean* we cannot win the war against IRS abuse. We can win it. We are winning it. We will win it. What it *does mean* is that as commanders in our army, we must be especially *selective* in terms of the *circumstances and conditions* under which we engage the enemy. Not every fight is *worth winning*, and we must have the wisdom and exercise the patience to know which fights will produce the best long term results.

Believe it or not, the fact that the IRS does possess more in terms of money and equipment than we do, operates, in my opinion, *to our advantage!* The fact that the agency is resource-rich tends to render its commanders judgment-poor. Just as the spoiled "rich kid" has no appreciation for the value of a dollar and will foolishly waste what has been given to him, the IRS tends to engage the citizen in combat *at every turn*. This careless and often reckless command attitude places the IRS in battles which are not only meaningless if victory is achieved, but which are so poorly planned and hastily carried out that *victory is not possible* if any intelligent opposition is put forth.

The reason that the IRS has been so successful in the

---

5. WINNING Publications, St. Paul, MN. One year subscription, $97.

6. Reported in CCH *Taxes on Parade*, June 7, 1989.

7. See April, 1989, *Pilla Talks Taxes*, page 4.

8. *Patton's Principles*, Porter B. Williamson, Simon and Schuster, 1982.

past with its war is not because of its overwhelming resources. The reason is that the advancing army has been met with *almost no opposition.* Like a guerrilla army, we must carefully pick and choose the times, circumstances, and conditions under which we will engage the enemy. Like a guerrilla army, through superior planning and execution, we can bring the army of the IRS, with its formidable manpower and funding, *to its knees!*

Planning The Attack

Another of Patton's Principles is that an army which is on the defensive *cannot* counterattack. This notion of warfare kept Patton's armored divisions on the move through western Europe, gobbling up ground and the German army faster than any other Allied Commander. So long as Patton's forces kept moving and kept the pressure on, the Germans were unable to regroup and mount a counteroffensive.

As with all principles of warfare, this is equally applicable to the fight with the IRS. The sooner one can take the offensive, the sooner he can bring an enemy advance to a standstill and in fact, drive him back. For this reason, it is my considered judgment that *all IRS aggressions* should be met with an immediate counter-attack of the kind authorized by law. In this manner, the IRS can be put on the *defensive,* thus limiting its ability to carry out further aggressive campaigns.

Moreover, it is a settled principle that if you can cause your enemy to *react,* you *control* him. Whenever you have been placed on the receiving end of IRS actions, their ability to destroy you financially will be measured in direct relation to the kind of offense you can muster in the face of the enemy's fire. To be successful, you must strike quickly and with the full force of your garrison.

I mentioned earlier that the richness of the IRS' forces has rendered its commanders, in large part, lacking in strategic judgment. Hence, the first order of business while under attack is to determine the enemy's weakest point as revealed by its attack. We know, given the nature and character of IRS attacks, that they are usually ill-planned and are carried out in haste. This teaches us that in nearly every instance of IRS abuse, there are procedural or legal deficiencies which can be exploited by the aggressive commander.

Once a weakness has been identified, attack it! The moment you go on the offensive, directing your charge at the enemy's exposed flank or rear, his assault *will cease.* He will begin to draw back to protect his exposures. This is when you must *turn up the heat,* for as long as he is completely defensive, there will be no way for him to win the battle. It matters not whether you are outnumbered in terms of men, equipment, money, etc.

If the enemy has "dug in" and remains defensive, he *cannot win.* As long as you stay on the offensive, attacking the enemy's weakest points, victory in battle is virtually assured.

Successful attacks against the IRS and its abusive tactics are assured by following two steps. First, as I have already discussed, it is imperative, *before one commences any action,* to conduct such legal research as is necessary to equip yourself to assert your claims in court. Without the ammunition found in the law library, you will be ill-prepared to win your case.

Legal research of your question must address two aspects of the problem. You must address the *affirmative aspect* of the question, that being the position advanced in court by you. Also, your research must explore the *negative aspect* of the question, or that advanced by the enemy in court. Without equipping yourself to handle *both aspects of the law,* you could very well suffer an ambush on the law which may destroy or seriously impair your offensive.

Do not allow yourself to be intimidated by the idea of "legal research." Anyone who has ventured into a law library no doubt has seen and been awed by the mountain of books contained there. However, you do not have to be an expert on all the issues covered withn those hundreds of volumes. Rather, your question grows out of an isolated set of facts, and is covered, in most instances, by narrow rules of law found within a very few volumes. The pamphlet I mentioned earlier produced by West Publishing Company, will guide you through the process of research, and librarians are generally glad to provide such assistance as is necessary. This is particularly true at public law libraries.

King Henry is reported to have said that a lawyer is not one who *knows* the law, but one who knows *where to find it.* Correct use of the library is the essential first step to taking action and formulating a battle plan.

The second step to establishing a plan of attack against the IRS is to collect intelligence information. Data concerning what the enemy knows and to the extent possible, the nature of its plans, will greatly assist you in carrying out your attack. As a matter of fact, certain intelligence data, such as the date in which a notice of deficiency was allegedly mailed, or whether one was mailed at all, are indispensable to the fight. Without basic intelligence data, you are literally fighting blindfolded and the potential for success is greatly diminished.

Chapter Three of this book is dedicated in its entirety to gathering intelligence from sources within the enemy's camp. The importance of this intelligence, in addition to the IRS Manual which is discussed earlier, cannot be overlooked or overemphaasized. We must know the enemy's stance as to administrative matters, and we must learn what its intended moves and stratagem will be in a given factual scenario. We learn this from our sources of intelligence.

Beyond the Internal Revenue Manual itself, the IRS maintains a computer log of all administrative actions performed in a given case. This computer log is referred to by the IRS as an Individual Master File (IMF). In coded language, the IMF chronologically lists any and all transactions which have taken place in a given taxable year. Because it is a fingerprint of all IRS actions taken in a given case, it is critical to review.

Only after all intelligence sources have been milked for all possible data, and after the library has produced ammunition for the impending battle, may the wheels be set in motion to mobilize your forces in opposition to the IRS' attack.

Conclusion

Success in war is not guaranteed to the army with superior manpower, equipment or resources. Rather, success is guaranteed to the army with superior *resourcefulness*. There are no better examples of this than America herself and her involvement in two wars, her first and her last. In the War for Independence, the decisive battle of Bunker Hill was won by colonists rolling logs down the hill into the British formations. Certainly the logs did not kill any British soldiers, but they did scatter the formations, fatally disturbing the carefully structured British attack, preventing the troops from firing their muskets.

In Vietnam, America was convinced that its mere superiority in equipment, money, training and manpower would eventually overwhelm the enemy. But America lacked purpose in Vietnam. It lacked the commitment from its political leaders, and perhaps even its military leaders, necessary to carry the fight decisively to the enemy. Even the American people were divided as to America's presence in the region. As a result, the mighty United States was defeated in war by a third world nation.

All it has ever required to win in battle is a *total commitment* to win the battle. Dealing with the IRS is no different. We have already examined the reasons why its apparent overwhelming forces, money and equipment are no barrier to success in your fight with them. All you must add to the formula is the commitment to bring IRS abuse to an end in *your* case. It was Thomas Paine who wrote:

> *'Tis the business of little minds to shrink; but he whose heart is firm, and whose conscience approves his conduct, will pursue his principles unto death.*

CHAPTER

2

The Rules of Warfare

As has been previously explained, the battle against assaults upon your liberty takes place in the courts. The vehicle of petition for redress under the First Amendment is the only legitimate manner in which to break the cycle of lawlessness and bring the IRS to account for its unlawful actions. Because of this, if we are to be successful in any measure we must understand how a case is brought to fruition within our federal court process.

Such an undertaking begins with an examination of the Rules of Court. The Federal Rules of Civil Procedure (FRCvP), adopted by the Supreme Court, govern practice before the federal courts in civil cases. The rules are not particularly lengthy, nor are they overly complicated or burdensome. They are, however, binding upon any person entering the court system, and must therefore be the subject of your full attention prior to commencing any court action. West Publishing Company[1] offers a special edition of the *Federal Rules of Civil Procedure* which contains all the rules applicable to federal court practice, including the rules which govern

appeals to the higher courts. The paperback edition also contains the full text of most of the federal statutes which address themselves to procedure within the federal system. That volume is indispensable!

Dropping a Bomb

After the process of gathering intelligence is complete, the weaknesses in the enemy's strike force having been detected, your plan of counterattack may be reduced to writing and given a title. This manual is a compendium of civil actions, proceedings, petitions and even lawsuits directed against the IRS. Each constitutes a counterattack calculated to cure IRS abuse or avoid potential abuse altogether.

A civil case always begins with the filing of a "complaint" or "petition." The complaint constitutes your formal written charge or allegation of wrongdoing against the IRS. For all practical purposes, the complaint is a bomb which is dropped upon the enemy, rudely informing him that he is now involved in hostile action.

Each chapter of this volume contains a complaint or petition, provided for illustrative purposes only. Each will demonstrate the manner in which unlawful acts on the part of the IRS have been successfully prosecuted in the past. In order that the reader will better understand the purpose of certain language contained within each document, we will now examine, in skeletal form, the structure of the complaint.

You will first notice that each complaint or petition, indeed every legal document filed with the court, contains a "heading." The heading identifies the title of the case, the specific court in which the case is found, the parties to the action, and the case number. The case number is assigned by the court clerk at the time the case is filed. See Exhibit 2-1. Just beneath the heading, generally centered on the page, one will find the title of the specific document, in this case, a complaint.

Exhibit 2-2 is the skeleton of a complaint. This format has been used very successfully over the years. You will, of course, note that there is no specific language whatsoever found within this skeleton. This is because the specific language must be modified on a case by case basis. However, the *organizational structure* of that language will remain constant. As we progress from chapter to chapter within this manual, you will find specific language which brings life to the complaint based upon the facts and circumstances we examine. For now, we wish only to understand exactly the purpose of the various sections shown in this skeleton.

Section one of the skeleton is entitled, *Nature of the Action*. The purpose of the two or so paragraphs found there will briefly describe the character of the charge which is embodied within the complaint. It will also summarize briefly the specific relief, or award, which is being sought from the court.

Section two of the skeleton is entitled, *Jurisdiction*. Very few of the sections which we are discussing are *indispensable* to an effective court charge. However, *this section is*. The federal courts of the United States *are not* courts of "general jurisdiction" as are the district or county courts found at the state level. Rather, the "jurisdiction" or authority, of the federal courts (referring to their authority to hear and determine a particular issue) is greatly limited. The jurisdiction or authority of the Federal courts is expressly limited to that which is granted them by Congress. Therefore, in order to ensure that your case will be heard by the federal court, you must state in clear and simple terms

---

Exhibit 2-1: Sample Heading

*   *   *   *   *   *

UNITED STATES DISTRICT COURT
DISTRICT OF MINNESOTA
THIRD DIVISION

```
William E. Citizen,              )

                  Plaintiff,     )      Case No. _____
                                 )
vs.                              )
                                 )
The United States of America,    )
Internal Revenue Service,        )
Willard P. Mean, Internal        )
Revenue Officer,                 )
                                 )
                  Defendants.    )
```

COMPLAINT FOR DAMAGES — JURY TRIAL DEMANDED

*   *   *   *   *   *

the basis of federal court jurisdiction.[2]

Generally speaking, the federal courts have the authority to hear and determine any issue which raises a Constitutional question, grows out of any Act of Congress, or which involves the Internal Revenue laws. The *general* federal jurisdictional provisions of the law are found within Title 28 of the United States Code. They run from about sections 1330-1403. More specific federal jurisdictional provisions relating directly to IRS abuses will be discussed on a chapter by chapter basis in this manual.

At 28 USC §1340, we find the following statement:

"The district courts shall have jurisdiction of any civil action arising under any Act of Congress providing for internal revenue, or revenue from imports or tonnage except matters within the jurisdiction of the Court of International Trade."[3]

Because of §1340's *general* grant of jurisdiction to the federal courts in matters involving tax laws, this section is usually referenced within the complaint's jurisdictional statement. Section 1340 also applies in many taxes cases. One must review it to determine whether it is applicable in a given case. These sections are included in addition to such other specific statutes found within the tax code that speak directly to the subject matter covered in the case.

Because of the rule requiring a "federal question" to be presented by a case brought within the federal courts, it is a good idea to include in the jurisdictional statement, words to the effect that a "federal question" is raised by this action."

Section three of Exhibit 2-2 is entitled, *Venue*. The term venue is defined as the geographic location of the district court in which the case is filed. Title 28 USC §1391(e) provides:

"A civil action in which a defendant is an officer or employee of the United States or any agency thereof acting in his official capacity or under color of legal authority, or an agency of the United States, or the United States, may, except as otherwise provided by law, be brought in any judicial district in which (1) a defendant in the action resides, or (2) the cause of action arose, or (3) any real property involved in the action is situated, or (4) the plaintiff resides if no real property is involved in the action.★ ★ ★"

Section 1402 or Title 28, provides:

"In any civil action in a district court against the United States under subsection (a) of section 1346[4] of this title may be prosecuted only:

"(1). . .in the judicial district where the Plaintiff resides;★★★"

From this we learn that the district court nearest your home is the proper court in which to file the case when your action is directed against the United States, or any officer or agency of the United States. Naturally this is important from the standpoint of your own convenience. However, if property is involved in the law, or if the lawsuit involves questions of legality of any IRS levy or collection action, the suit should be filed where the property is located, or where the unlawful act occurred.[5]

A statement respecting venue and the provisions of 28 USC §§1391 and 1402 is made under the *Venue* heading of Complaint, Section III.

Section four of Exhibit 2-2 is entitled *Parties to the Action*. In this area you will list the persons, including agencies of government, which are named in your complaint. The Plaintiff(s), or persons commencing the case, are listed first, together with their addresses and a brief statement as to why those persons are named as plaintiffs in your case. The Defendant(s), or those against which whom the case is brought, are listed next, with addresses, and with a brief statement as to why they have been named in the case.

Section five of Exhibit 2-2 is entitled, *Background Facts*. This portion of the charge will set forth several paragraphs which provide the factual history of the events which formulate your "cause of action," or reason for proceeding against the defendants. It is important to appreciate that the term "facts" refers only to *historical events* and not to opinion or conjecture. All cases which come before the courts for resolution are decided on the basis of the law *and* the facts. This portion of the complaint or petition is your opportunity to set forth the facts as they occurred in order to justify your claim of legal culpability on the part of the defendant.

A *Background Facts* section which is overly burdensome, or which is replete with irrelevant assertions having no bearing upon your legal claim of the defendant's culpability has no place in your complaint. It is easier to appreciate my observation when you consider that you, as the plaintiff, bear the burden or responsibility, to prove with evidence that your version of the facts is correct. The wider the swatch you paint

---

2. See Rule 8(a), FRCvP.

3. See also 28 USC §1346(a)(1), relating to suits for refund of taxes; §(a)(2) relating generally to constitutional questions, acts of Congress and federal questions; and §(e) relating to other sections of the Internal Revenue Code.

4. See previous footnote.

5. See 28 USC §1402(a) and (c).

Exhibit 2-2: Skeletal Complaint

UNITED STATES DISTRICT COURT
DISTRICT OF MINNESOTA
THIRD DIVISION

William E. Citizen,

    Plaintiff,   Case No. _____

vs.

The United States of America,
Internal Revenue Service,
Willard P. Mean, Internal
Revenue Officer,

    Defendants.

COMPLAINT FOR DAMAGES — JURY TRIAL DEMANDED

NATURE OF THE ACTION

Description of purpose of suit and claim for relief.

(Section Two.)

JURISDICTION

Plain statement as to basis of federal jurisdiction.

(Section Three.)

VENUE

Statement regarding geographic location of court.

(Section Four.)

PARTIES

Describe names and addresses of all parties, with statement as to why such person is a party to the suit.

(Section Five.)

SKELETAL COMPLAINT, Page 1

BACKGROUND FACTS

Describe all facts (historical events) relevent to the claims of wrongdoing and request for relief.

(Section Six.)

COUNT I

State in affirmative fashion the specific facts which establish a violation of law, and make specific statement as to damages incurred as a result of such acts. Each violation should be set forth in a separate count.

(Section Seven.)

DAMAGES

Set forth in specific dollar and other terms, the percise damages which you have suffered.

(Section Eight.)

REQUEST FOR RELIEF

In specific terms, request the relief or judgment you wish the court to enter in your favor, including a request that all damages be paid to you by the Defendant.

The Complaint should then be signed and dated, with your name, address and phone number shown below your signature. Each Plaintiff must also sign in the same fashion.

SKELETAL COMPLAINT, Page 2

within your charge, the more difficult, expensive and time consuming will be the task of proving your case. It takes time and effort to hone the facts to a fine edge, alleging only those facts which are sufficient to make your legal claim viable.

This is not a difficult task if you have done your legal research homework. The statute and case law, upon which you must rely in tandem, will provide the standards to which you must compare the facts of your case. When deciding on the manner in which to frame the factual allegations of your complaint, you must first refer to the law which governs the subject. From the law, you will learn that certain "elements" must exist before any act will constitute a violation or offense justifying action on your part. These "elements" must be set forth as matters of fact in your complaint in order for that document to be legally sufficient to hold the defendants accountable for their lawlessness.

Regardless of the nature of your complaint and its underlying facts, there are two essential allegations which must be made a part of any suit against the IRS. These statements typically follow the historical outline, appearing at the conclusion of the factual statement. The first such contention must truthfully assert, "That all administrative remedies have been exhausted by the Plaintiff without satisfaction." You will recall from our discussion in Chapter One, under the heading, *Field Terrain and Conditions,* that unless all administrative remedies are pursued and exhausted by you before proceeding into the courts, your court action *will not succeed.* That is why it is necessary to include this statement with your complaint or petition. It is also a good practice to set out the specific administrative steps which you did in fact utilize.

The second statement must truthfully claim that your case is, "not a suit to restrain or enjoin the collection of income taxes such as is barred by 26 USC §7421." Code §7421 is the so-called Anti-Injunction Act. Be mindful of the fact that any lawsuit which seeks to restrain or prevent the IRS from collecting taxes pursuant to a *legitimate* assessment is barred, or forbidden by statute. We will study exceptions to this rule in Chapter Eight. When your case is based upon a statutory exception, §7421 *does not apply.*

Section six of Exhibit 2-2 contains the individual "Counts" of the complaint. A "Count" is one specific allegation of wrongdoing on the part of the Defendant. If your charge against the IRS is comprised of several separate allegations of wrongdoing, as many are, each individual act would be set forth as a separate Count. For example, an allegation that the IRS filed an improper lien against your property could be the subject of Count I. Within the same complaint, provided a foundation of Background Facts is supplied, Count II could allege unlawful conduct against the particular agent responsible for the lien. You could then ask for an assessment of damages against him personally.

Care should be taken, when drafting the language of each count, to be sure that your allegations match the provisions of the statute which you believe has been violated. By doing so, you can be sure that your case is sufficient to "state a claim" against the defendant such as will allow the court to grant the award you are seeking. By way of example, the statute governing the failure of the IRS to release a tax lien is Code §7432. It contains the following language:

"If any officr or employee of the Internal Revenue Service knowingly, or by reason of negligence, fails to release a lien under section 6325 on property of the taxpayer, such taxpayer may bring a civil action for damages against the United States in a district court of the United States."

The statute further provides that the citizen is entitled to recover damages, "which, but for the actions of the defendant, would not have been sustained, plus the costs of the action." The statute also contains these conditions:

a. All administrative remedies must be exhausted;

b. The citizen must take steps to minimize, or "mitigate" his damages;

c. The action must be commenced within two years of the IRS' failure to act; and

d. As a part of the administrative remedies, the citizen must serve upon the IRS written notice of that failure and of his intent to sue if not corrected.

As you can see, the statute itself communicates to us the facts which must exist, and which must be set forth in an affirmative nature within a count of the complaint, in order that the complaint may be sufficient to hold the IRS accountable for its unlawful acts. In this example, allegations sufficient to state a claim under §7432 would include the following:

a. That a lien was filed by the IRS on your property;

b. That you served notice on the IRS indicating that the lien was improper and should be removed, that all administrative remedies have been exhausted, and that you intend to file suit if the lien is not removed;

c. That either knowingly or by reason of negligence, the IRS has failed to release the lien;

---

6. For more detailed discussion of this subject, see Chapter Ten.

d. That the presence of the lien has caused damages and financial hardship to you, which, but for the lien, would not have occurred;

e. That you have made every reasonable effort to mitigate those damages; and

f. That the suit was brought within the two year statute of limitations.[6]

It is important to realize that the above explanation is provided by way of *example only*. Obviously, your specific allegations will vary from issue to issue, and naturally, everyone's facts are different. Within the individual chapters of this manual are found firm examples of language applicable to each of the Ultimate Defense Weapons we discuss.

The point to be made here is that regardless of your claim, the specific allegations contained within a single "Count" *must conform* to the language of the governing statute. If you fail in this respect, you cannot hope to meet with success in your case.

Section seven of Exhibit 2-2 is entitled, *Damages*. In this portion of the document you will list all of the adverse effects that have been brought about by the IRS' unlawful conduct. Specific claims for monetary awards, both in terms of out-of-pocket losses and punitive damages should be set forth. Any detrimental fallout other than actual monetary loss should also be declared in this portion of the complaint.

The final section of the complaint is entitled, *Request For Relief*. In it, you will specifically set forth, in the language of an affirmative request, all of the remedial action you expect the court to take based upon the claims made within the complaint. Requests for money or money's worth compensation, as well as any other relief which may be appropriate, should be set out here.

Lastly, the form is dated and signed by all plaintiffs. Their address and phone number should also be shown on the document.

The Right to Trial by Jury

The Seventh Amendment to the United States Constitution provides in part:

> "In suits at common law, where the value in controversy shall exceed twenty dollars, the right of trial by jury shall be preserved, . . ."

To the extent that any issue raised by you in your complaint involves factual questions triable to a jury under the common law, you are entitled to a jury trial as a matter of right. Now frankly, the courts of the United States are *all over the lot* as to which issues are, and which are not, "common law" questions when it comes to tax cases. Most of the time, the courts are undecided themselves, zigging when they should zag, and vice versa. I can state with authority that since the matter is in such a condition of flux, one should always take steps to protect his rights under the Seventh Amendment.

For that reason, I recommend that every complaint be painted at the outset with the same brush. The document should contain a demand for a jury trial on its face. As is the wont of the federal judiciary, it has placed terms and conditions upon Constitutional rights which the framers never dreamed of and certainly never intended. For example, the *absolute* language of the Seventh Amendment is now tranquilized by the provisos found in Rules 38(b) and (d), FRCvP.

Rule 38(b) requires that before any jury trial will take place, the party desiring his right must make a "demand" in writing, "anytime after the commencement of the action," but in any event, "not later than 10 days" after the final pleading is served.[7] Rule 38(d) holds that if a party fails to make the written demand as described, such failure "constitutes a waiver by him of trial by jury."

I do not recall having read any language in the Seventh Amendment to the effect that I must take some type of affirmative action in order to enjoy my right of trial by jury. In fact, the Amendment reads that the right of jury trial shall be "preserved"—period! This tells me that the *court*, not the individual, must take affirmative steps to see that my right to a trial by jury is enforced. Despite this, the rule provides, and is enforced to the effect that, one *ignorant* of his right to a jury trial or the convoluted procedures the courts have created for asserting that right, will in fact, be deprived of the right *regardless* of the Constitution. The moral of the story is, as it always has been, if you do not know your rights, *you do not have any rights.* Worse than that, you cannot always count on the courts to do your thinking for you, even when it comes to matters so basic as the right to trial by jury.

To the fullest extent possible, I will attempt to discuss with authority whether a right of jury trial exists in the instances of the individual sample cases addressed in this manual. But please, if the courts cannot decide the issue, please do not expect me to do it. Of course, I have my own solution to the problem they have created. *Just read the Constitution!* It is quite plain! That, however, seems too simple.

---

7. Rule 7(a), FRCvP, provides, that the "pleadings" in the typical case consist of the complaint and the defendant's answer to the complaint. The court may also order a reply to the defendant's answer if the facts so warrant.

Filing Your Case

Through all of your preparatory steps, you should be confident that your intelligence has revealed a soft spot in the enemy's attack force. You should have completed drafting your complaint or petition focusing upon that soft spot, and you should be ready to launch the attack. A civil court action begins with filing the case with the clerk of court.[8] You must be sure to file the case with the office of the *federal* district court which serves the county in which you live.

Title 28 USC §81-131 describe, on a state by state basis, which divisions of the district court serve the counties within a given state. Proceeding alphabetically, it is a simple matter of finding your state within those sections of law and reading through that one section until you find your county. The statute will specify which division of the court serves your county. The phone book will provide the balance of the information needed to "get your foot in the door."

The clerk is responsible to file the case, but you are responsible to see that copies of the complaint or petition are "served upon" or delivered to each of the Defendants. The process of filing involves paying a fee to the clerk, usually $65, and preparing a form known as the "Civil Cover Sheet." See Exhibit 2-3. The Civil Cover Sheet is nothing more than a questionnaire which seeks very general information about the nature of your case, including the names and addresses of the parties. This document is used only by the clerk for filing purposes.

In addition to providing the Civil Cover Sheet, the clerk will assign a number to your case, known as a docket number or file number. This number identifies your case for filing purposes. It becomes the "address" by which your file and its related matters are tracked by court personnel. You will be asked to provide that number on all future filings related to your case.

The last task performed at the clerk's office at time of filing is the preparation of the Summons.

Service of Process

In order for the case you have just filed to have any effect upon the Defendant, a copy of your complaint or petition must be promptly delivered to each Defendant. This act is known as "service of process." As a means of formally notifying the Defendant that he has been "sued," an official court "Summons" is attached to the complaint when served upon each Defendant. See Exhibit 2-4.

The summons informs the Defendant that a case has been filed against him. It further provides that according to the Rules, the defendant is limited in the amount of time in which he has to respond to the complaint or petition. Ordinarily, a person has 20 days in which to file his "Answer" in response to the complaint. However, when the Defendant is the United States, or an agent or agency thereof, the time in which to respond is increased to 60 days.[9]

Correctly carryng out service of process is essential when proceeding against the government. Rule 4, FRCvP specifies the conditions which must be met to assure efficacious service of process. Service of the summons and complaint cannot, as a general rule, be accomplished by a party to the action. Any person of legal age may effect service of process upon the Defendant. Service is accomplished when a summons, signed by the clerk, with a true copy of the complaint or petition attached, is personally handed to the defendant, or "left at his dwelling house or usual place of abode with some person of suitable age and discretion then residing there or by delivering a copy of the summons and complaint to an agent authorized by appointment or by law to receive service of process.[10]

When a Defendant is the United States, or an officer or agency thereof, service is more technical. Rule 4(d)(4) FRCvP addresses the question in these terms:

"(Service) upon the United States, (is carried out) by delivering a copy of the summons and of the complaint to the United States Attorney for the district in which the action is brought, or to an assistant United States Attorney or clerical employee designated by the United States Attorney in a writing filed with the clerk of the court *and by sending* a copy of the summons and of the complaint by *registered or certified* mail to the Attorney General of the United States at Washington, D.C., and in any action attacking the validity of the order of an officer or agency of the United States not made a party, by also sending a copy of the summons and of the complaint by registered or certified mail to such officer or agency." (Emphasis added.)

It should be obvious that you will need a number of copies of your summons and complaint when the Defendant is the United States, or an officer or agency thereof. With respect to the requirement that a copy of

---

8. See FRCvp 3.
9. See FRCvP 12.
10. See FRCvP(d)(1).

Exhibit 2-4: Summons

SUMMONS IN A CIVIL ACTION   (Formerly D.C. Form No.4da Rev. (6-49))

United States District Court

FOR THE

Your State and District

CIVIL ACTION FILE NO. _____

Name of Plaintiff Here

Plaintiff

v.

Name of Defendant(s) Here

Defendant

SUMMONS

To the above named Defendant

You are hereby summoned and required to serve upon (Plaintiff's name)

plaintiff's attorney , whose address   (Plaintiff's address here)

an answer to the complaint which is herewith served upon you, within 60 days after service of this summons upon you, exclusive of the day of service. If you fail to do so, judgment by default will be taken against you for the relief demanded in the complaint.

Date:

      William Smith, Clerk of Court

         Clerk of Court.

[Seal of Court]

         Deputy Clerk.

NOTE:—This summons is issued pursuant to Rule 4 of the Federal Rules of Civil Procedure.

Exhibit 2-3

JS 44C
(Rev. 7/80)   **CIVIL COVER SHEET**

The JS-44 civil cover sheet and the information contained herein neither replace nor supplement the filing and service of pleadings or other papers as required by law, except as provided by local rules of court. This form, approved by the Judicial Conference of the United States in September 1974, is required for the use of the Clerk of Court for the purpose of initiating the civil docket sheet.

PLAINTIFFS –   DEFENDANTS –

ATTORNEYS (FIRM NAME, ADDRESS, AND TELEPHONE NUMBER)   ATTORNEYS (IF KNOWN)

BASIS OF JURISDICTION (PLACE AN ⊠ IN ONE BOX ONLY)
☐ 1 U.S. PLAINTIFF   ☒ 2 U.S. DEFENDANT   ☐ 3 FEDERAL QUESTION (U.S. NOT A PARTY)   ☐ 4 DIVERSITY

IF DIVERSITY, INDICATE CITIZENSHIP BELOW. (28 USC 1332, 1441)

CAUSE OF ACTION (CITE THE U.S. CIVIL STATUTE UNDER WHICH YOU ARE FILING AND WRITE A BRIEF STATEMENT OF CAUSE)

NATURE OF SUIT (PLACE AN ⊠ IN ONE BOX ONLY)

CONTRACT	TORTS		FORFEITURE/PENALTY	ACTIONS UNDER STATUTES	
☐ 110 INSURANCE	**PERSONAL INJURY**		☐ 610 AGRICULTURE	**PROPERTY RIGHTS**	**OTHER STATUTES**
☐ 120 MARINE	☐ 310 AIRPLANE		☐ 620 FOOD & DRUG	☐ 820 COPYRIGHT	☐ 400 STATE REAPPORTIONMENT
☐ 130 MILLER ACT	☐ 315 AIRPLANE PRODUCT LIABILITY		☐ 630 LIQUOR LAWS	☐ 830 PATENT	☐ 410 ANTI-TRUST
☐ 140 NEGOTIABLE INSTRUMENT	☐ 320 ASSAULT, LIBEL & SLANDER		☐ 640 R.R. & TRUCK	☐ 840 TRADEMARK	**BANKRUPTCY**
☐ 150 RECOVERY OF OVERPAYMENT & ENFORCEMENT OF JUDGMENT	☐ 330 FEDERAL EMPLOYERS' LIABILITY		☐ 650 AIR LINE REGS.		☐ 420 TRUSTEE
☐ 151 MEDICARE ACT	☐ 340 MARINE		☐ 660 OCCUPATIONAL SAFETY/HEALTH		☐ 421 TRANSFER (919b)
☐ 160 STOCKHOLDERS SUITS	☐ 345 MARINE PRODUCT LIABILITY		☐ 690 OTHER		☐ 422 APPEAL (801)
☐ 190 OTHER CONTRACT	☐ 350 MOTOR VEHICLE		**LABOR**		☐ 430 BANKS AND BANKING
☐ 195 CONTRACT PRODUCT LIABILITY	☐ 355 MOTOR VEHICLE PRODUCT LIABILITY		☐ 710 FAIR LABOR STANDARDS		☐ 450 COMMERCE ICC RATES, ETC.
	☐ 360 OTHER PERSONAL INJURY		☐ 720 LABOR/MGMT. RELATIONS		☐ 460 DEPORTATION
REAL PROPERTY	☐ 362 PERSONAL INJURY-MED. MALPRACTICE		☐ 730 LABOR/MGMT. REPORTING & DISCLOSURE ACT		☐ 810 SELECTIVE SERVICE
☐ 210 LAND CONDEMNATION	☐ 365 PERSONAL INJURY PRODUCT LIABILITY		☐ 740 RAILWAY LABOR ACT		☐ 850 SECURITIES COMMODITIES EXCHANGE
☐ 220 FORECLOSURE			☐ 790 OTHER LABOR LITIGATION		**SOCIAL SECURITY**
☐ 230 RENT LEASE & EJECTMENT	**PERSONAL PROPERTY**		☐ 791 EMPL. RET. INC. SECURITY ACT		☐ 861 HIA
☐ 240 TORTS TO LAND	☐ 370 FRAUD OR TRUTH IN LENDING				☐ 862 BLACK LUNG
☐ 245 TORT PRODUCT LIABILITY	☐ 380 OTHER PERSONAL PROPERTY DAMAGE				☐ 863 DIWC
☐ 290 ALL OTHER REAL PROPERTY	☐ 385 PROPERTY DAMAGE PRODUCT LIABILITY				☐ 863 DIWW

CIVIL RIGHTS	PRISONER PETITIONS
☐ 441 VOTING	☐ 510 VACATE SENTENCE (2255)
☐ 442 JOBS	☐ 520 PAROLE COMMISSION REVIEW
☐ 443 ACCOMMODATIONS	☐ 530 HABEAS CORPUS
☐ 444 WELFARE	☐ 540 MANDAMUS & OTHER
☐ 440 OTHER CIVIL RIGHTS	☐ 550 CIVIL RIGHTS

☐ 870 TAX SUITS   ☐ 871 IRS-THIRD PARTY   ☐ 875 CUSTOMER CHALLENGE 12 USC 3410   ☐ 891 AGRICULTURAL ACTS   ☐ 892 ECONOMIC STABILIZATION ACT   ☐ 893 ENVIRONMENTAL MATTERS   ☐ 894 ENERGY ALLOCATION ACT   ☐ 895 FREEDOM OF INFORMATION ACT   ☐ 950 CONSTITUTIONALITY OF STATE STATUTES   ☐ 970 PARA. TITLE III   ☐ 890 OTHER STATUTORY ACTIONS   ☐ 864 SSID Title XVI   ☐ 865 RSI

ORIGIN (PLACE AN ⊠ IN ONE BOX ONLY)
☒ 1 ORIGINAL PROCEEDING   ☐ 2 REMOVED FROM STATE COURT   ☐ 3 REMANDED FROM APPELLATE COURT   ☐ 4 REINSTATED OR REOPENED   ☐ 5 TRANSFERRED FROM (SPECIFY DIST.)   ☐ 6 MULTIDISTRICT LITIGATION   ☐ 7 APPEAL TO DISTRICT JUDGE FROM MAGISTRATE JUDGMENT

Check if THIS IS A CLASS ACTION UNDER F.R.C.P. 23   DEMAND $ Check/Fill in if demanded in complaint: OTHER

RELATED CASE(S) IF ANY   JUDGE   DOCKET NUMBER

CIVIL CASES ARE DEEMED RELATED IF PENDING CASE INVOLVES:
☐ 1. PROPERTY INCLUDED IN AN EARLIER NUMBERED PENDING SUIT
☐ 2. SAME ISSUE OF FACT OR GROWS OUT OF THE SAME TRANSACTION
☐ 3. VALIDITY OR INFRINGEMENT OF THE SAME PATENT COPYRIGHT OR TRADEMARK

CITIZENSHIP OF PRINCIPAL PARTIES (IF DIVERSITY)

	PTF	DEF
CITIZEN OF THIS STATE	☐ 1	☐ 1
INCORPORATED THIS STATE	☐ 2	☐ 2
FOREIGN CORPORATION PRINCIPAL PLACE OF BUSINESS IN ____ (STATE)	☐ 3	☐ 3
OTHER NON-CITIZEN OF THIS STATE	☐ 4	☐ 4

Check YES only if demanded in complaint:
JURY DEMAND: ☒ YES ☐ NO

DATE   SIGNATURE OF ATTORNEY OF RECORD

the summons and complaint be served upon the Attorney General of the United States in Washington, D.C., the requirement is, in fact, that *two* copies be so served. The address at which such service is effected, through the mail as specified in the rule, is:

> United States Attorney General
> US Department of Justice
> Tax Division
> Washington, DC 20044

When the individual Defendants have been served with a copy of the summons and complaint, and after the United States has been properly served, both locally with the United States Attorney's office, and by certified mail to the Attorney General in Washington, D.C., your case against the IRS and any individual agent is a reality. You have begun an attack on the enemy. This attack will put them on the *defensive*, and provided you maintain the intensity of the battle to the fullest extent possible, the IRS will be virtually *unable* to continue its lawless actions against you.

A Word of Caution

If you have carried out each of the procedures I have just described, you have, as a matter of fact, *sued the IRS* for a violation of your statutory or Constitutional rights. If you did not realize it prior to this point in the manual, you had better understand it now—*this is serious*—*this is war!* Legal and technical to be sure; certainly not mortal, but war nevertheless.

Action of this nature cannot be undertaken without careful forethought and without sufficient legal and factual justification. Rule 11, FRCvP, provides that your signature *on any documennt filed with the court*, is your certification that you have read the document, and that:

> ". . .to the best of (your) knowledge, information, and belief, formed after reasonable inquiry it is *well grounded in fact and warranted by existing law* or a good faith argument for the extension, modification, or reversal of existing law, and that it is *not interposed for any improper purpose, such as to harass or to cause unnecessary delay or needless increase in the cost of litigation.**** If a (document) is signed in violation of this rule, the court, upon motion, or upon its own initiative, shall impose upon the person who signed it. . an appropriate sanction, *which may include an order to*

pay to the other party or parties the amount of the reasonable expenses incurred because of the filing of the (document), including a reasonable attorney's fee." (Emphasis added.)

Rule 11, FRCvP, provides authority for the court to order the payment of *reparations* to the party unreasonably attacked through the judicial process. *Make no mistake;* both the party you sue and the court in which the suit is brought will take your actions seriously. You had better as well!

Preventing a Counterattack

I stated earlier, drawing from General Patton's wisdom and experience, that an enemy which is on the defensive cannot counterattack. From this we learn that the simple formula for countering IRS aggression and preventing further attacks in connection with your case is to *stay on the offensive*. The rules of procedure provide a means to stay on the offensive, enabling you to minimize the potential that you will find yourself on the receiving end of such countermeasures as the enemy may conceive.

I speak here of the process of "discovery." Discovery is the means whereby the parties to a suit obtain from one another or from third party sources, information and evidence which can be used to prove or disprove the claims made in the case.[11] The use of the discovery tools provided within the federal rules is an effective means of keeping the pressure on the enemy. Each discovery demand requires the enemy take specific steps to comply with the demand, steps which involve the disclosure of valuable information you may need to prove your case. At the same time, while the enemy is busy responding to the demands you place upon it through discovery, it is hindered in its ability to mount a counterattack against you.

The rules provide four separate methods of obtaining discovery. Discussed one at a time, they are:

Interrogatories. An interrogatory is a question propounded, in writing, by one party to another.[12] Their use is limited to persons named within the suit as "parties to the action." Interrogatories are perhaps the most common form of obtaining discovery due to their simplicity. The task is accomplished by drafting questions, the answers to which will shed light upon the allegations of your complaint. The written questions are delivered via first class mail to the attorney for the Defendants. According to the rule, the question must be

---

11. See generally, Rule 26, FRCvP.
12. See Rule 33, FRCvP.

answered "separately and fully in writing and under oath." The answers to the questions must be served upon the person asking them, "within 30 days after service of the interrogatories."[13]

The answers to the interrogatories are considered evidence which may be used any time during the proceedings, including trial, to prove the matters contained within.

Depositions. Rule 30, FRCvP, permits the taking of "depositions." A deposition is akin to the interrogatory, but rather than propounding the questions in writing, a "deposition" is taken through "oral examination." The questions are asked and the answers are provided by the witness verbally. Unlike the requirement that Interrogatories be used only with parties to the action, one may take the deposition of "any peson" whose testimony is anticipated to shed light upon the allegations of the complaint. This aspect greatly broadens the prospective uses to which depositions may be put.

When seeking the deposition of a party to the action, one need only serve through the mail a "notice of deposition." This simple document informs the deponent of the time, date and location in which his deposition will be taken. Parties are required by the rules to attend the deposition and provide oral testimony pursuant to the notice.

When the deposition of a non-party to the action is sought, one must serve, in addition to the notice, a subpoena under Rule 45, FRCvP,[14] and the appropriate witness fees and travel expenses. The amount of these costs is set by the local district and is available from the clerk of court.

Bear in mind that when a deposition is sought, you must secure that deposition from the witness in the county in which he resides. You cannot require a person to travel great distances to provide testimony in your case.

Request for Production of Documents. The Request for Documents is the process whereby one may obtain specific documents from a party to the action. The items available are, "writings, drawings, graphs, charts, photographs, phono-records, and other data compilations from which information can be obtained."[15]

The individual requets are served on the attorney for the Defendant, and within 30 days, a written response must be forthcoming. The person making the request has an option relative to taking possession of the documents to be transmitted via mail within 30 days, or,

he may establish a "reasonable time, place, and manner of making the inspection" of the documents and photo-copying them himself.[16]

Request for Admissions. A Request for Admission requires that a party specifically admit or deny the truth of an asserted fact. An example of such a request is, "Admit that on (date) you mailed a notice to the Plaintiff demanding that (amount) in taxes, interest and penalties be paid within 30 days."

Having received the specific requests for admission, the Defendant is required to provide written "answers or objections addressed to the matter.[17] If the party does not admit the truth of the statement, he is required to "specifically deny the matter or set forth in detail the reasons why (he) cannot truthfully admit or deny the matter."[18]

This procedure is extremely helpful in narrowing the issues raised in the complaint or petition. It can greatly simplify the litigation process. If you as the Plaintiff are able to obtain admissions from the Defendant as to material facts and allegations contained in your complaint, the task of *proving* those particular allegations has been eliminated. Each and every admission made by the parties under Rule 36, FRCvP, is *binding* for the purposes of the litigation. If, for example, the Defendant in fact admits that, "On (date) a notice was mailed to the Plaintiff demanding (amount) in taxes, interest and penalties," the Defendant is precluded from later claiming that no such notice was sent. The admission binds him to that fact for the duration of the proceeding.

For this reason, it is tactically wise to use the admissions process only after you have gathered all the facts. Admissions should be used as the means to narrow the issues, making your case simpler to prosecute.

The Uncooperative Defendant. It is not uncommon for the government to attempt to stonewall the discovery process. For any number of reasons, not the least of which is the attitude that a non-attorney simply has no means of enforcing his demands, government lawyers will fail or refuse to cooperate in the discovery process. Should this occur, the rules provide a means in which discovery demands may be enforced.

Rule 37, FRCvP, provides that if a person fails to answer interrogatories timely or completely, or fails to appear or answer questions while being deposed, or fails or refuses to produce documents as requested, the aggrieved party may apply to the court for an order

---

13. See Rule 33(a), FRCvP.
14. Available from the clerk's office.
15. See Rule 34(a), FRCvP.
16. See Rule 34(b), FRCvP.
17. See Rule 36(a), FRCvP.
18. Ibid.

compelling his cooperation. If the motion to compel is granted and the uncooperative party is compelled to answer, etc., you would be entitled to recover the fees and costs you expended in bringing the motion.[19] Should the belligerent attitude continue and the party fail to comply with the court's order, again, on application by the aggrieved party, the court may take any of several different steps to punish the party's failure to comply. Those steps include such harsh sanctions as dismissing the disobedient party's case entirely.

It should be noted that, with respect to requests for admissions, a motion for sanctions under Rule 37, FRCvP, is unnecessary should a party fail to properly respond. According to the Rule 36, FRCvP, "the matter is admitted" unless, within 30 days, a specific answer as discussed above is forwarded to the person making the request. This is another reason why admissions are a tactically sound way in which to narrow the issues raised in the case. Without specific details made in a timely manner, the adverse party risks losing his entire case.

The Final Battle

One of the most common complaints made by the average person with respect to civil litigation is that *it takes too long.* The courts are jammed, lawyers engage themselves in complex maneuvers, and the process is dragged out over a period of years. When this occurs, nobody but the lawyers win. All others, plaintiffs and defendants alike, lose much in terms of money, anxiety and time.

This rule of civil litigation does not generally apply to cases against the federal government. While I have certainly seen *selected* cases stretch on over a period of years, the typical case comes to a head without much delay. Naturally, this is to the advantage of the citizen, simply because the government has far more resources, and consequently, far more ability to endure a long battle. Long battles exhaust resources and manpower. You will want to take every possible step to ensure that your victory is swift and decisive.

The Rules provide a means for dong so. Rule 56, FRCvP, allows either party to apply to the court for a "judgment" in his favor if he feels the law and facts support him. The procedure is known as "summary judgment."

Summary judgment is appropriate only when there are no facts remaining in dispute. Under Rule 56, the court is not called upon to make decisions regarding the

facts. If any factual matter material to the resolution of the case remains in dispute at the time summary judgment is applied for, the court should deny the motion and refer the matter for trial. Summary judgment *is not* a substitute for a trial on the merits.

However, when the process of discovery has so *narrowed the issues* that all facts material to the resolution of the case are *no longer* in dispute, summary judgment is appropriate. Under those circumstances, the court is called upon to apply the law, which it will determine, to those settled facts, rendering judgment in favor of the appropriate party.

A common practice for government attorneys is to submit a motion for summary judgment at the earliest possible opportunity. Generally speaking, the government's motion is premature from the standpoint that it is raised at a time when facts material to the resolution of the case remain in dispute. By that I mean only to say that one party views the historical events in one light, while the other party—the government— takes a differing position as to *what has happened.*

One must be on guard to oppose any government motion for summary judgment which is premature. Should you fail to do so, the court is likely to grant the motion, rendering judgment in favor of the government on the issues in the case. This will not only deprive you of a trial on the merits of the case, including a jury verdict, but will deprive you of any of the relief you have demanded in your complaint.

When faced with a motion for summary judgment, it is your burden to demonstrate to the court that material facts remain in dispute. This is done through the filing of affidavits signed by you or other witnesses. You may also present to the court discovery material obtained during the course of the proceedings.[20] The affidavits and discovery material must "set forth specific facts showing that there is a genuine issue for trial. If (you do) not so respond, summary judgment, if appropriate, shall be entered against (you)."[21] The statements of fact contained in the affidavits and discovery material must demonstrate that the government's version of the facts is subject to debate. That is to say, you need not *prove* that its version is *incorrect.* Rather, you need only show, specifically and affirmatively, that its version of the facts *is in dispute.*

Under the appropriate circumstances, summary judgment in your favor can be very helpful. Particularly if your goal is to bring the case to fruition as quickly as possible. Your motion for summary judgment will allege that no material facts remain in dispute and that you are entitled to judgment as a matter of law. In

---

19. See Rule 37(a)(4), FRCvP.

20. Rule 56(e), FRCvP.

21. Ibid.

opposing the motion, the government must show that certain facts remain to be settled and trial is therefore appropriate. Alternatively, the government may argue that *it*, not you, is entitled to judgment as a matter of law.

In most cases involving the IRS, summary judgment is the means by which the case is resolved. Most of the time, such a resolution deprives one of the parties, generally the citizen, to his right of a trial by jury. This is why it is necessary to understand summary judgment and the circumstances under which *it is not appropriate*. You will have to take specific countermeasures in the face of a motion for summary judgment if you wish to preserve your right of trial by jury.

Still, where your case does not involve issues which are properly tried by jury, summary judgment is a quick and effective remedy for bringing to an end what might otherwise develop into lengthy, costly litigation.

Aware that summary judgment, Rule 56, is typically the *final battleground,* you should begin at once to prepare for the fight. This preparation may assume that you will be on the "giving end," or the "receiving end," of the Rule 56 remedy. In either event, you must be prepared with both the law and the facts if you are to carry the day.

Conclusion

Just imagine what would happen to IRS abuse and illegal collection attempts if the government *knew* that every citizen—heck, just ten percent of the citizens— had the *power to fight back and win!* History has proven that it never requires a majority to effect change of any kind, however significant and far-reaching. What is required are a few dedicated citizens with the right tools and information necessary to *make every shot count.*

PART II
Gathering Enemy Intelligence

CHAPTER

"We Have Ways of Making You Talk."

I spoke earlier about the necessity of obtaining as much intelligence data from the enemy as is possible *prior to* undertaking any hostile action. Specifically, I mentioned the importance of the Individual Master File (IMF), a computer log which is maintained by the IRS. The purpose of this chapter is to provide the details of using the enemy's own system of record keeping and disclosure requirements in order to obtain intelligence data. Through these mechanisms, it can be said that, "We have ways of making you talk."

The Freedom of Information Act

On November 21, 1974, Congress passed legislation substantially amending federal information disclosure laws, creating the Freedom of Information Act. Public Law 93-502 completely revamped the federal statutes governing the requirements of administrative agencies, such as the IRS, to maintain records of their activities, procedures and internal operational structure. The law also made it *simpler* in some cases, and *possible* in other cases to obtain information from the various agencies.

Hence, the Freedom of Information Act (FOIA) is the vehicle which, in most cases, provides open access to the IRS' file cabinet of information it maintains concerning you.

The FOIA is now codified in the United States Code as Title 5, USC §552. The law provides, at §552(a)(3), as follows:

"Except with respect to records made available under paragraphs (1) and (2) of this subsection, (each relating to public information, not material peculiar to an individual citizen) each agency, upon any request for records which (A) reasonably describes such records and (B) is made in accordance with published rules stating the time, place, fees (if any), and procedures to be followed, shall make the records promptly available to any person."

This is the basis in the law for access to IRS data.

The FOIA Request in General. We have just learned from the statute itself that when a request for documents is made which conforms to the published standards of the agency in question, that agency must release those documents. The IRS has published regulations which set forth the procedures for making requests under the FOIA. As set out in Rev. Reg. §601.702(c)(3), the IRS' "published rules" regarding disclosure are:

1. The request must be made in writing and signed by the person making the request.

2. It must state that it is made under the Freedom of Information Act, 5 USC §552.

3. It must be addressed to the office or officer within the IRS responsible for control of the requested records. A list of all responsible officers and their addresses is provided in Rev. Reg. §601.702(g). If you do not know who the responsible officer is, "the request should be addressed to and mailed or hand delivered to the office of the director of the Internal Revenue Service district office in the district where the requester resides."[1] I have found that the most efficient manner in which to make the FOIA request is to direct it to the attention of the *Disclosure Officer* within the district in which you reside. If the request is made to a service center, address it to the one which serves your state.

4. You must "reasonably" describe the records you are seeking, but this does not mean that you have to "specifically describe" the documents you are pursuing. To do this would require that you have the document in front of you, in which case the FOIA request would be superfluous. However, any information which you can offer to provide assistance in searching for and identifying the documents you are seeking must be provided. In this respect, some, but not much, guidance is provided by the regulation. It states:

"While no specific formula for a reasonable description of a record can be established, the requirement will generally be satisfied if the requester gives the name, subject matter, location, and years at issue, of the requested records. If the request seeks records pertaining to pending litigation, the request should indicate the title of the case, the court in which the case was filed, and the nature of the case. However, it is suggested that the person making the request furnish any additional information which will more clearly identify the requested records. Where the requester does not reasonably describe the records being sought, the requester shall be afforded an opportunity to refine the request. Such opportunity may, where desirable, involve a conference with knowledgeable Internal Revenue Service personnel. The reasonable description requirement *will not be used* by officers or employees of the IRS as a device for improperly withholding records

from the public." Rev. Reg. §601.702(c)(4); (emphasis added).

The general demand, "Send me my file," will usually produce nothing because of the "reasonable description" requirement.

5. When you are seeking records containing information with respect *to yourself*, rather than general documents of a "public" nature, you must establish your identity and the right to receive information. This is probably the most important portion of the list we are now reviewing. Without meeting this requirement, there is almost no way, due to the tax code's "secrecy provisions," that any such material will be released. The regulation we have been discussing describes three ways in which this requirement can be met. They are:

a. *In the case of a request made in person,* the presentation of a single document bearing a photograph or the presentation of two items of identification which do not bear a photograph but do bear both the name and signature and the person's social security number;

b. *In the case of a request made by mail,* the submission of the requester's signature, address, social security number, and one other identifier bearing the requester's signature;

c. The presentation *in person* or the submission *by mail* of a notarized statement swearing to or affirming such person's identity and his social security number.

6. You must set forth the address where you desire to be notified of the determination as to whether the request will be granted.

7. You must state whether you wish to inspect the records or desire to have them copied and furnished to you without first inspecting them.

8. You must state a *firm agreement* to pay the fees for search and duplication of the records provided pursuant to your request.

From my experience, the IRS does not generally "scalp" a person making an FOIA request. As we all know, they have far more *productive* ways in which to collect money. I have always maintained that the possibility of unexplained costs in connection with a request should not deter one's submitting the request. The necessity and value of the information learned far outweighs the "risk," such as it is, that one may receive a large bill in the mail for the search and reproduction of the records.

This is particularly true in light of the fact that the first two hours of search time, and the first 100 pages of material furnished, are to be provided *without charge*. There—now who ever said the IRS does not *give us*

---

1. See Rev. Reg. §601.702(c)(3)(iii); see also Appendix I for a map of IRS districts.

anything?! In addition, you may state in your letter a *limit* as to the maximum amount of fees you are willing to pay. If the IRS' estimates as to the expenses involved with complying with your request exceeds those limits, it will so notify you, offering you the opportunity to revise the request. If no limit has been stated by you, the IRS' standing maximum is $250. Above that amount, it will always contact you to inform you of the estimated cost of compliance beforehand.[2]

Despite these safeguards, the regulation[3] makes provision for the "waiver or reduction of fees" in connection with FOIA requests. The rule provides that:

"Fees will be waived or reduced...when it is determined that disclosure of the requested information is in the public interest because it is likely to contribute significantly to public understanding of the operations or activities of the IRS and is not primarily in the commercial interest of the requester."

The factors which IRS disclosure officers are to consider in determining whether to waive or reduce fees and costs are:

1. Whether the subject of the records concerns the agency's operations or activities;

2. Whether the records are likely to contribute to an understanding of the agency's operations or activities;

3. Whether the records are likely to contribute to the general public's understanding of the agency's operations or activities;

4. The significance of the contribution to the general public's understanding of the agency's operations or activities;

5. The existence and magnitude of the requester's commercial interest. . .being furthered by the releasable records;

6. Whether the magnitude of the requester's commercial interest is sufficiently large in comparison to the general public's interest.

Persons making the request for a waiver or reduction in fees and costs must "state the reasons why they believe disclosure meets the standards set forth (above)."[4] A request for a reduction or waiver of fees based "solely on indigency" will not be granted. A waiver will be approved only if the requester can demonstrate that one or more of the above criteria are applicable to the disclosure.

I believe that the "waiver or reduction" aspects of the IRS' regulations are important because so many of the requests sought by knowledgeable citizens involve requests for portions of the IRS Manual itself. When records of a particular person are sought, the above criteria do not seem to apply. But surely disclosure of the manual and IRS policies in connection with matters contained in the manual certainly "contribute to the general public's understanding of the agency's operations or activities." Under these circumstances, an argument can be made that the fees and costs should be "waived or reduced" in accordance with the law. The request for waiver and the argument in support should be made within the FOIA request itself.

A written request under the FOIA is not complicated. Though the regulations drone on, describing one requirement after another, the finished product, properly drafted, is short and sweet. Exhibit 3-1 is a sample of a standard FOIA request. It also contains a statement as to the requester's identity, in compliance with the fourth provision of Rev. Reg. §601.702(c)(3). See the previous list of the eight required items. This form of FOIA request has proven very effective in the past.

When to Use the Freedom of Information Act

I have stated many times that the FOIA is your access to government documents. In all but a very few instances, the FOIA will provide the intelligence data you need to determine the IRS' intended action, thus enabling you to counter its acts. We will discuss later in this chapter the steps which can be taken when the IRS refused to provide the material through administrative channels. For now, let us concentrate on what *is learned* from certain records which *are obtained*.

The Individual Master File. The Individual Master File (IMF) is the computerized statement of your account which is created and maintained by the IRS.[5] The IMF contains a complete history of each account transaction according to tax year. It shows the date your return was filed, the date of any tax assessment, the date of all payments, and the amount of interest and penalties, if any, which have been assessed. It also reflects the current status of your account, whether paid in full or in arrears. Because of the all-inclusive nature of the data it provides, the IMF is necessary to obtain *before* any dealings with the IRS are pursued.

---

2. See Rev. Reg. §601.702(f)(3)(ii).

3. See Rev. Reg. §601.702(f)(2)(ii).

4. See Rev. Reg. §601.702(f)(2)(iii).

Exhibit 3-1: Standard FOIA Request Letter

Citizen's Full Name
Address
City, State, Zip
Social Security Number

Date of Request

Disclosure Officer
Internal Revenue Service Center or District Office
Address where records are located
City, State, Zip

FREEDOM OF INFORMATION ACT REQUEST

Dear Sir:

This is a request under the Freedom of Information Act for records relating to the above-mentioned taxpayer. This is a <u>firm agreement</u> to pay the costs of searching for and reproducing all documents requested herein. However, if such costs exceed $50, I wish to be notified before the expense is incurred.

If some of the requested documents are exempt, please furnish me with those portions reasonably segregatable, and provide me with an indexing, itemization and detailed justification concerning information which you are not releasing.

This request pertains to tax years 1983 through 1985.

REQUESTED RECORDS

Please send a complete Statement of Account, i.e., <u>Individual Master File</u> transcript for the tax year 1985.

With respect to the years 1983 and 1984, please send any and all documents which established or in any way relate to the TC 582, lien indicator, shown in requester's IMF for the years 1983 and 1984. Said TC 582 references bear the document locator numbers of 17212-517-57538-2, and 31277-053-77500-3, respectively, and were entered on June 17, 1988.

I may be notified at the above address of the disposition of this request, and this request may be honored by mailing the said documents to that address.

PROOF OF IDENTITY AND RIGHT TO RECEIVE RECORDS

I understand the penalties provided in 5 USC §552a(i)(3) for requesting or obtaining access to records under false pretenses. I certify under penalty of perjury that I am the individual making this request, this is my signature and social security number, and attached is a copy of my driver license.

Citizen's Full Name
Social Security Number

Date of the Request

(Attach copy of Driver License)

Exhibit 3-2 is a sample page from a typical IMF. The names, social security numbers and other identifying features have been removed, but it otherwise is an accurate reproduction of the IMF.

As you can plainly see from reviewing the IMF in Exhibit 3-2, it is *impossible* to decipher its meaning unless one understands the codes it contains. Once the system is understood, the IMF is easy to follow. It begins with the top of the sheet, where we find the tax period, or year, shown within the starred (*) area. Referring to Exhibit 3-2, the tax period shown there is "8112." This reference is to the year 1981, ending with the 12th month. Thus, the tax year covered by Exhibit 3-2 is 1981.

Several lines below the starred box, we find a row of stars covering the width of the entire sheet. Beneath that row begins the codification of the account for the year 1981. The transactions are listed according to the date of the event. The first entry begins with the number "150 080982." Next to that entry, we see the reference, "3,418.00."

The first number in the sequence, number 150, is a "transaction code" or "TC." These codes are numerical abbreviations used to describe the transaction which is recorded. A "TC 150" is used to record the fact that a return was filed, and the tax shown due on the return was officially assessed.

Unless you have access to the list of transaction codes used by the IRS, it is impossible to read and understand the IMF. Therefore I have included here a list of the commonly used transaction codes. (See Exhibit 3-3). Refer to this list while reading your IMF, or better yet, obtain *your own* list of transaction codes from the IRS through the FOIA. Ask for IRS Publication 5576.

Continuing with our analysis of Exhibit 3-2, adjacent to TC 150 is the reference, "080982." This is the date on which TC 150 was recorded. Hence, in this example, the tax return for the year 1981 was filed and the tax assessed, on August 9, 1982. The next number in the sequence is the amount of $3,418. That is the amount of tax shown due on the return which was assessed according to TC 150.

The next series of numbers in the sequence is a document locator number. This number constitutes the "address" within the IRS' information storage system at which the actual return, the subject of TC 150, can be found.

Each entry withn the IMF is patterned in the same fashion. I hope from this you can see the value of obtaining your IMF. Even though you may not be *currently* involved in a dispute with the IRS, the IMF can be enormously valuable. Because it shows the current account balance, the IMF can aid in determining whether any IRS bills or notices have any basis in fact whatsoever.

I invite your attention to the area at the top of Exhibit 3-2, between the starred box and the starred line. Within this area we find information concerning the status of the account *at the time the IMF* is printed out.

The IMF in our example covers the tax year 1981. Yet the printout was made on April 12, 1989. See top center of Exhibit 3-2. By reviewing the account balance data, we find that the "MF Mod Bal," or total amount due on the account, is "0.00." We also find that "Accrued Interest" and "Accrued Penalty" assessments are also "0.00." With this account information in hand, it would be difficult indeed for the IRS to sustain any claim that you owe additional taxes which were allegedly assessed *prior* to April 12, 1989.

In addition, you can determine from the IMF whether the IRS has properly credited any payments you have made against an assessed liability. See Exhibit 3-3, TC's 610 and 670. Regular requests for and review of your IMF can prevent IRS efforts to extract from you more money than you owe.

Another important consideration is, the statute of limitations covering civil assessments of tax liability is three years, compounded from the date the return is filed.[6] Once the liability is officially assessed, the IRS has six years in which to collect that tax.[7] For these reasons, it would also be a good idea to obtain and maintain an up-to-date IMF for each of the past six years. This can be accomplished through the submission of just one FOIA request. See Exhibit 3-1.

I recommend that the IMF be updated at least every year. This is best done *after* your most recent return has been filed and the tax paid, or refund obtained. This will give you substantial information with which to fight should the IRS mail any kind of erroneous notice, or otherwise take any action against you.

Internal IRS Documents. The information gleaned from the IMF is not limited to the material shown on the face of the document. Each transaction code is accompanied by a document locator number. That number, as I have already mentioned, is the address within the IRS' information storage system where the document is located which generated the TC.

---

5. In the case of a business, such as a corporation, the same computer file is referred to as a "Business Master File," or BMF.

6. See Code §6501(a).

7. See Code §6503.

Exhibit 3-2:
Sample IMF Printout

```
0Q0108

PAGE NO-0011   TAX PERIOD 30 8112 (CONTINUED)
                 *IMF MCC TRANSCRIPT-COMPLETE*              EMP NO

ACCOUNT NO                          04-12-89
NAME CONT-                          CYCLE-8914

*************************
* TAX PERIOD 30    8112 *                  REASON CD-            MOD EXT CYC-89
*************************
FS-2         CRINV-  RWMS QUE-  LIEN- 17212-117-57538-2   CAF-   FZ-    -LW
TDA COPYS-          TDA YLD SCR-      TDI COPYS-          TDI YLD SCR-
         INT TOLERANCE-  MATH INCREASE-  HISTORICAL DO-31 BWNC-   BWI-
MF MOD BAL-                  0.00
ACCRUED INTEREST-            0.00   040389
ACCRUED PENALTY-            0.00   040389

***************************************************************************

     150 080982         3,418.00      8230 17212-117-57538-2 D CRD-        SRC-
               RCC-                ERR-                  TAX PER T/P-     3,418.0
                                                      F/C-  AGI-        26,833.0
                                            FOREIGN-         FARM-  MF P-
                                            XRF-                AEIC-      0.0
                                            PIA-     EXFMPT-02 ENRGY-      0.0
                                            LTEX-            TAXABLE INC-  24,833.0
                                            PENALTY SUPP-           SET-      C.0
                                            ACCRTN-       TOTAL WAGES-      0.0
                                            MDP-          TOTAL INC TX-     0.0
                                                         EST TAX BASE-  3,418.0
                                                         PR YR BASE  -       0.0
                                            SHORT YR CD-      ES FORGIVENESS %-0
                                            1ST SE-    0.00       2ND SE-    0.0
                                            ROUTG TRANSIT NUM-         ACCT TYPE-
                                            BANK ACCT NUM-
                                                         CREDIT ELECT-      0.0
                                                         ES TAX PAYMENT-    0.0
     610 041582             0.00      8230
     610 042082         3,418.00-     8218 17212-517-57538-2
                                      PRC-
     425 082582      --------------   8235 31277-236-20000-2
                                      SOURCE-40  ORG-1103  PROJ-     RET REG
     420 090782      --------------   8237 31277-250-00000-2
                                      AIMS #4001103031
     560 022283      --------------   8309 31277-053-77500-3
                                      ASED-041585      CYCLES-
     922 112583             0.00      8324 17277-135-63210-3
                                      PROCESS CD-01-35
     300 070984             0.00      8426 17247-571-10148-4
                                      HC  DC11 870D       ASED       PC  A02
     520 062684      --------------   8427 31277-178-00000-4
                                      COLCLOS-72 PROC-   CLAIM-   PYMT-  AO

MF STAT-10 080982                     0.00   8230
```

Exhibit 3-3
List of Commonly Used Transaction Codes Appearing on IRS Transcripts

Transaction Codes	Title
000	Establish an account
013	Name change
014	Address change
150	Return filed and tax liability assessed
160	Manually computed delinquency penalty
161	Manual abatement of delinquency penalty
166	Generated delinquency penalty
167	Generated abatement of delinquency penalty
170	Estimated tax penalty
171	Abatement of estimated tax penalty
176	Generated estimated tax penalty
177	Generated abatement of estimated tax penalty
180	Deposit penalty
181	Abatement of deposit penalty
186	Generated deposit penalty
187	Generated abatement of deposit penalty
190	Manually assesed interest
191	Abatement of interest
196	Generated assessment of interest
197	Abatement of generated interest
234	Daily delinquency penalty
235	Abatement of daily delinquency penalty
270	Manual assessed failure to pay tax penalty
271	Manual abatement failure to pay tax penalty
276	Computer assessed failure to pay tax penalty
277	Computer abatement of failure to pay tax penalty
290	Additional tax assessed
291	Abatement of prior tax assessment
294	Additional tax assessed-tentative allowance
295	Tentative allowance of tax
298	Additional tax assessed
299	Abatement of prior tax assessment
300	Additional tax by examination division
301	Abatement of prior assessment by examination
308	Additional tax assessment by examination
309	Abatement of prior examination assessment
320	Fraud penalty
321	Abatement of fraud penalty
336	Interest assessed on additional tax
340	Interest assessment
341	Abatement of interest assessment
350	Negligency penalty
351	Negligency penalty abatement
360	Fees and collection costs
370	Account transfer-in
420	Examination indicator
421	Reverse examination indicator
430	Estimated tax payment
459	Prior quarter liability
460	Extension of time for filing
470	Taxpayer claim pending

Transaction Codes	Title
488	Installment and/or manual billing
489	Installment defaulted
500	Military deferment
520	IRS litigation instituted
521	Reversal of TC520
530	Uncollectible account
531	Reversal of uncollectible account
570	Additional liability pending
582	Lien indicator
610	Remittance with return
611	Remittance with return dishonored
612	Correction of TC610 processed in error
640	Advance payment of determined deficiency
642	Reversal of advance payment
650	Depositary receipt-federal tax deposit
660	Estimated tax deposit
662	Reversal of estimated tax deposit
670	Subsequent payment
671	Dishonored subsequent payment
672	Correction of TC670 processed in error
700	Credit applied
701	Reversal of credit applied
706	Generated credit applied from another tax module
710	Overpayment credit applied from prior tax module
712	Correction of TC710
716	Generated credit applied from prior tax module
736	Generated interest overpayment applied
756	Interest on overpayment transferred from IMF
766	Income tax rebate credit
767	Reversal of income tax rebate credit
768	Earned income credit
770	Interest due taxpayer
772	Reversal of interest due taxpayer
776	Generated interest due taxpayer
800	Credit withheld for taxes
806	Credit for withheld taxes and excess FICA
807	Reversed credit from withheld taxes
820	Credit transferred
821	Reversed overpayment credit transfer
826	Generated overpayment credit transfer
830	Overpayment credit elected to be transferred to the next period of tax
832	Reversal of TC830
836	Generated overpayment credit elect transferred to the next period of tax
840	Refund
841	Refund reversed
846	Generated refund
856	Overpayment interest transfer by computer
976	Duplicate return filed
977	Amended return filed

Any TC shown on the IMF will have a supporting document to match. The FOIA will give you direct access to not only the IMF, but the individual documents which comprise the supporting data behind it.

Access to these supporting documents is vitally important for two reasons. First, we know that the IMF will reflect any intended action by the IRS, usually *before* you have been notified. Exhibit 3-2 reflects two such TC's which are most telling. The first is TC 420, entered on September 7, 1982, just weeks after the return was filed. A TC 420 identifies an "examination indicator," telling us that already the return filed has been selected for examination. The document establishing the TC 420 will likely specify the *reasons* why the return was selected for audit. If one were able to obtain the document establishing the TC 420, one would be infinitely *more capable* of preparing for the audit than if he learned of the audit only after receiving a formal notice. Remember, the notice generally *does not provide* adequate time in which to prepare for the audit.[8] The advantage created by this foreknowledge is therefore appreciable.

Another example of this "advance intelligence" is found within Exhibit 3-2. Please notice TC 520. A TC 520 indicates that "IRS litigation has been instituted." Given the channels through which approvals for litigation must flow and the time it takes in which to actually commence the litigation, it may take many months, and in some cases *years* before the citizen will receive official notice of the litigation. Yet the document establishing the TC 520 will tell us what the IRS has up its sleeve long before any notice arrives at your door.

Such advance warning of the gathering storm will enable the citizen to begin intense preparation for the attack, making his baston impenetrable when it finally occurs. In some cases, it may even be possible to thwart the attack through careful planning and appropriate correspondence with the IRS. Naturally, this will depend upon the facts of each case, but it is indisputable that *advanced* knowledge provides a *decided* advantage.

The second reason for acquiring IMF background data involves action *already taken,* but which the IRS has failed to report to the citizen. A common example of this is where a tax lien is filed, but without proper notice to the citizen. The IMF will reveal a TC 582 when the general tax lien is filed. After obtaining a copy of the lien document itself, one can determine the amount of tax allegedly due, as well as the date the lien was filed. This will enable the citizen to file an administrative *protest* to the lien, and if necessary, a proceeding to have the erroneous lien *removed* entirely.[9]

Unless you have knowledge that the lien was filed and take action to remove it, the first you will learn of the encumbrance is when you attempt to sell your home or obtain a loan for any purpose. The lien will appear on your credit report as well as with the county recorder's office. Still, unless you have a copy, you are in the dark. This can and often does cause much hassle, embarrassment, and needless delay and cost in executing your plans.

Worse is the situation where the lien is not removed, even though the tax has been paid. What you have learned from the above discussion will help to correct that inequity as well.

The Internal Revenue Manual. In our discussion of TC 520, we learned that such code indicates the IRS has commenced "litigation." I pointed out that the document establishing the TC 520 will describe the nature of the litigation which the IRS is *anticipating.* Collecting this background data—the supporting documents behind the TC—is necessary to carry out the next step in defense preparations.

Earlier, I observed that the IRS manual is the written battle plan which the enemy will follow, usually inviolate. Now that you have learned the nature of the litigation the enemy is considering, the next step in gathering intelligence is to use the FOIA to obtain that portion of the IRS manual which covers such litigation.

There are a number of reasons why the IRS may be considering litigation. It is probably not productive to attempt to list here every possible action the IRS may contemplate in a given case. What is necessary to understand is, that before the IRS will refer a case to its attorneys for litigation, the agents working the case must make findings and conclusions supporting the referral. This is true of both criminal and civil litigation.

Once we have learned the specific type of litigation under consideration, the portion of the IRS manual which addresses itself to that subject will reveal the aspects of the case which the agents are required to consider. Hence, we see before us a blueprint for the case against you as it appears on the administrative drawing board. What better way in which to approach the matter of defense, counterattack and neutralization of the problem than to have the enemy's plan of attack in front of you?

---

8. See *How Anyone Can Negotiate With The IRS—And WIN!,* at pages 13-16.
9. See Chapter Ten for more details.

Processing the Request

After a valid FOIA request is submitted, the IRS is given just ten days in which to locate and determine whether the records you have requested will or will not be released. If the records cannot be located within that period of time, or due to the volume of records requested, a determination cannot be made whether they will be released, the IRS will seek from you an extension of the 10-day limitation. In granting the request, your right to receive the information or right of administrative appeal if the request is ultimately denied, *are not affected.*[10]

When computing the 10-day period, it is important to note that the time does not begin to run on the day the IRS receives the request "in hand." Rather, after receipt, the disclosure staff reviews the document to determine whether it has met all of the requirements to constitute a *valid* request under the FOIA and IRS regulations. Only when it is determined to be, in fact, a *valid request* will the IRS consider it "received" for purposes of computing the 10-day response period.

I strongly recommend that persons submitting FOIA requests not be "trigger happy" with regard to their appeal rights. The one area in which the IRS seems to be consistent regarding prompt notification and simple explanations of problems, is in the area of FOIA requests. Therefore, patience is the order of business. Keep in mind that the objective of the maneuver is to *obtain the material,* not to engage the enemy. The more "noise" you make while conducting reconnaissance, the less likely your mission will be successful. Be mindful of Patton's Principle: fight only when you stand to gain the victory.

When the Request is Denied

Occasionaly, the IRS does deny requests for records and documents made under the law. The authority for denying certain FOIA requests emanates from §552(b)(1) of the Act. As a matter of fact, the law provides nine specific reasons or circumstances under which the IRS, or any government agency, may withhold documents requested under the FOIA. Because of the cost of paper, my publisher will not permit me to list all nine, as only three of the stated exemptons apply in most IRS cases. They are:

1. The material is specifically exempted from disclosure by statute, provided that such statute (A) requires that the matters be withheld from the public in such a manner as to leave no discretion on the issue, or (B) establishes particular criteria for withholding or refers to particular types of matters to be withheld. IRS Code §6103 is precisely the type of statute to which this exemption refers. It prevents the disclosure of any person's confidential tax return, or return information, to any unauthorized person. That is why, in making an FOIA request for data relative to a "particular person," you must establish your identity and *right* to receive the information.

2. Any inter-agency or intra-agency memoranda or letters which would not be available by law to a party other than an agency in litigation with an agency. This exemption refers to, or is invoked with respect to, legal opinions and the conclusions of personnel within the agency regarding certain legal problems or legal strategy. The opinions and conclusions which attorneys provide to their clients in connection with litigation and related matters are generally not subject to disclosure. Hence, this exemption covers those types of materials.

3. Any investigatory records compiled for law enforcement purposes, but only to the extent that the production of such records would (A) interfere with enforcement proceedings, (B) deprive a person of a right to a fair trial or an impartial adjudication, (C) constitute an unwarranted invasion of personal privacy, (D) disclose the identity of a confidential source and, in the case of a record compiled by a criminal law enforcement authority in the course of a criminal investigation, or by an agency conducting a lawful national security intelligence investigation, confidential information furnished only by the confidential source, (E) disclose investigative techniques and procedures, or (F) endanger the life or physical safety of law enforcement personnel. The IRS will rely upon this, the "law enforcement exemption," usually when a criminal investigation is pending against a citizen. Otherwise, a person is not likely to see this exemption raised in response to his FOIA request.

When the IRS refuses to disclose records pursuant to a lawful request, it is required by law to expressly state its reason or reasons for doing so. It must also cite in its letter of denial the statute under which any exemption is asserted. Further, the letter will state the name and address of the person responsible for making the decision to withhold the documents, and will advise the citizen of his right of administrative appeal.

The appeal must be taken in writing within 35 days after the date of any notification denying your access to

---

10. See Rev. Reg. §601.702(c)(7)(i) and (ii).

documents.[11] The appeal must be addressed to the Commissioner of Internal Revenue at the following address:

> Freedom of Information Appeal
> Commissioner of Internal Revenue
> c/o Ben Franklin Station
> P.O. Box 929
> Washington, D.C. 20224

Additional considerations which must be made part of the letter of appeal, as set out in the regulation,[12] are:

1. You must reasonably describe the records which have been withheld, and which are the subject of the administrative appeal.

2. You must state the address at which you wish to be notified as to the outcome of your appeal.

3. You must give the date of your initial request, the office of the IRS to which it was submitted, and you should provide a copy of both the initial request and the IRS' letter of determination.

4. You must give reasons and arguments to persuade the Commissioner to grant your appeal and release the documents you are seeking. This argument must focus upon the IRS' stated reasons for declining your request for access to the documents, in light of the statutory exemptions under 5 USC §522(b). The most common exemptions asserted by the IRS are set out above. You must demonstrate, through your argument, that the assertions are misplaced and that you are entitled to have the records released.

After receipt by the Commissioner of your appeal, it will be date-stamped and you will be promptly notified that his office has just 20 days, excluding Saturdays, Sundays, and legal holidays, in which to act on the appeal. The letter from the Commissioner will specify the date on which the determination is due. If for some reason, the Commissioner is unable to pass upon your appeal within the 20-day period, he will request your permission to extend the deadline. If you agree, the extension will provide the Commissioner with ten additional days in which to make his decision. However, your appeal rights *will not be affected* if your appeal is later denied.

Ultimate Defense Weapon Number One

The Freedom of Information Act Court Petition

It is important to note that while the IRS does have the power to say "No" to an FOIA request, it's decision is *not final.* The FOIA affords the citizen the right to petition a federal court for an order *requiring* the IRS to release records and documents. Title 5, USC §552(a)(4)(B), reads in part as follows:

> "On complaint, the district court of the United States in which the complainant resides, or has his principal place of business, or in which the agency records are situated, or in the District of Columbia, has jurisdiction to enjoin the agency from withholding records and to order the production of any agency records improperly withheld from the complainant.★★★"

As is always the case when considering court action against the IRS, all administrative remedies must *first* be exhausted prior to filing the petition. We have discussed at length the administrative remedies applicable to FOIA applications, but let us review them now.

First, you must submit a request under the FOIA which meets the conditions of IRS regulation §601.702. These provisions are described earlier under the heading, *The FOIA Request in General.* If the IRS denies the request or fails to release the records within the allotted period of time, you must appeal to the Commissioner of IRS.

The appeal must be accomplished within 35 days of the date of the letter denying your request. The appeal to the Commissioner must also meet the requirements of the regulation. See the above heading, *When Your Request is Denied.* If the Commissioner fails to act within the time allotted or denies your request in whole or in part, you then have the right to file a petition in federal court under Title 5, USC §552(a)(4)(A).

The petition may be filed in any of the court venues described in the statute. See 5 USC §522(a)(b)(B), above. The statute authorizes action only against the Commissioner of IRS, and no *individual agent* may be named as a Defendant. Once the petition is filed, the IRS has just *30 days,* not the traditional 60 days, in which to answer. Also, the matter is expedited on the court's docket to the fullest extent possible to ensure prompt resolution of the dispute.[13]

The one factor which makes the FOIA court petition probably the simplest of all the Ultimate Defense Weapons mentioned in this manual, is the fact that the burden of proof *an all issues* in the case is squarely upon the government.[14] What this means is that the government *must prove* that its actions of withholding records are justified by the law. The citizen *need not* prove that

---

11. See Rev. Reg. §601.702(c)(8).

12. See Rev. Reg. §601.702(c)(8).

13. See 5 USC §552(a)(4)(C) and (D).

14. Ibid, at §(a)(4)(B).

the government's actions were outside the law. The citizen need only prove that he has properly pursued and exhausted all administrative remedies, and that the IRS has refused to release the documents demanded. Of course, when you have a folder of correspondence in hand documenting each step of the process, this becomes a simple task.

Exhibit 3-4 is a sample petition under the FOIA. As you will see upon review, it requests the court to order the IRS to release all of the records which you have demanded. Review it carefully. Notice that in the Background Facts portion of the petition, reference is made to the initial request, the IRS' denial, the administrative appeal, and the Commissioner's denial of that appeal.

It is stated in the petition that these documents are "attached to the petition as Exhibits," but in fact they are not. Since we have already discussed the documents in detail, they have been omitted from the petition. Understand, however, that in the preparation of your *actual* petition, it would be a good idea to include copies of those documents.[15]

Relief Under the Freedom of Information Act

Of course the paramount purpose of the FOIA court petition is to jar loose the records the IRS has refused to provide. To this end, you will have to be prepared to argue *in opposition* to the exemptions which the IRS has asserted as grounds for not releasing them. We have reviewed the most commonly asserted exemptions earlier in this chapter. The IRS is required to state in all its letters to you the precise grounds upon which it relies in refusing to release documents. These communications will put you on notice of the IRS' legal position. This notice will provide you with the time and an opportunity to research the validity of the claims in the law library, both in the context of the statute and the case decisions. This should be done *before* any petition is actually filed.

Prosecuting the FOIA Petition

With the burden on the government to prove that its failure to release records is justified by the law, you will want to take the offensive with discovery at the earliest possible moment. Interrogatories should be directed at the government's attorney, proposing questions which will require the government to state "with specificity" how the records fall within the scope of the exemption it has asserted.

Naturally, when answers to the discovery requests will disclose the very documents which the government is seeking to protect, it may refuse to answer some or all of your discovery demands. Under these circumstances, a Rule 37 motion to compel would be in order. See Chapter Two, under the heading, *Preventing a Counterattack*. Furthermore, in the context of that motion, you could request that the court review the documents *in camera*, or privately, to determine whether the government's claimed exemption is supported by the facts and the law.

Summary Judgment

In an FOIA case, there will be no right of trial by jury. Any question of fact will be determined by the court without a jury. Therefore, summary judgment is sometimes an effective means in which to move the matter quickly to a hearing and resolution. Recalling our discussion of summary judgment, that manner of disposing of a case is appropriate only when all questions of fact have been resolved. Through your discovery, you are able to determine whether the government's claim of exemption relative to the documents has merit or not. Assuming that it does not, summary judgment will place the issue squarely before the court, with the burden on the government to establish facts which justify its refusal.

Beyond the File Cabinet

Relief under the FOIA goes well beyond the act of obtaining the documents you demand. Further relief is available under 5 USC §522(a)(4)(E). That section hands the court the authority to:

> "...assess against the United States reasonable attorney fees and other litigation costs reasonably incurred in any case under this section in which the complainant substantially prevailed."

This section makes it possible to recover from the government all of the costs and fees you have expended in pursuing your rights. The one proviso, however, is

Exhibit 3-4: Sample FOIA Petition

UNITED STATES DISTRICT COURT
DISTRICT OF MINNESOTA
THIRD DIVISION

William E. Citizen,   )
)
             Plaintiff,   )   Case No. _____
)
vs.   )
)
The Commissioner of the   )
Internal Revenue Service.)
)
             Defendant.   )

PETITION FOR RELEASE OF RECORDS UNDER FOIA

NATURE OF THE ACTION

1. This a petition under Title 5, USC §552(a)(4)(B), seeking an order requiring the Defendant to release certain agency records now in its possession or under its control.

2. This petition also seeks a finding by the court that the IRS officer or employee responsible for withholding the documents at issue here acted arbitrarily and capriciously.

JURISDICTION

3. This Petition arises out of the Freedom of Information Act, an Act of Congress, and is authorized by 5 USC §552(a)(4)(B).

4. This Petition raises federal questions.

VENUE

5. Venue is properly grounded within the court above according to 5 USC §552(a)(4)(B), and 28 USC §1402.

PARTIES

6. The Plaintiff, William E. Citizen (address, city, state, zip) is the proper Plaintiff in this case as he is the party aggrieved by the agency's failure to disclose records pursuant to his lawful

request.

7.   The Commissioner of the Internal Revenue Service is properly named as the Defendant in this action under 5 USC §552(a)(4)(B), and Revenue Regulation §601.702(c)(11).

BACKGROUND FACTS

8.   On June 10, 1989, the Plaintiff made a request of the Defendant for the release of records under the Freedom of Information Act, Title 5, USC §552.

9.   The request relates to records within the possession or under the control of the Defendant, and are records which relate to the Plaintiff.

10.   The request for relief substantially complied in all respects with the Defendant's regulations governing application for release of documents under the Freedom of Information Act, as published in Rev. Reg. §601.702.

11.   The Plaintiff's request sought release of the following documents:

    a.   A complete Statement of Account, i.e., <u>Individual Master File</u> transcript for the tax year 1985.

    b.   With respect to the years 1983 and 1984, any and all documents which established or in any way relate to the TC 582, lien indicator, shown in requester's IMF for the years 1983 and 1984. Said TC 582 references bear the document locator numbers of 17212-517-57538-2, and 31277-053-77500-3, respectively, and were entered on June 17, 1988.

12.   A true and accurate copy of the Plaintiff's initial request is attached to this Petition, marked Exhibit A and is

FOIA PETITION - Page 2

incorporated herein by reference.

13. On June 30th, 1989, the Defendant responded to Plaintiff's request, Exhibit A. The response amounted to the release of the documents specified in paragraph 11.a. above, but denied Plaintiff access to the remaining documents as set out in paragraph 11.b. A true and correct copy of the Defendant's reply is attached to this Petition, marked Exhibit B and is incorporated herein by reference.

14. On July 25, 1989, the Plaintiff executed an administrative appeal of the Defendant's letter of denial. Said appeal was carried out in a timely manner, and substantially complied in all respects to the Defendant's regulations governing appeals under the Freedom of Information Act. A true and accurate copy of the Plaintiff's administrative appeal is attached to this Petition, marked Exhibit C and is incorporated herein by reference.

15. On August 15, 1989, the Defendant denied the Plaintiff's administrative appeal. A copy of the said denial is attached to this Petition, marked Exhibit D and is incorported herein by reference.

16. The Plaintiff has pursued and exhausted all administrative remedies in connection with this FOIA request. Nevertheless, the Defendant has failed to and continues to fail and refuse to release the records in question here.

17. The Defendant's agents have acted arbitrarily and capriciously in connection with the failure and refusal to release the records in question here.

COUNT I

18. Plaintiff reasserts all the allegations of paragraphs 1-17, as though fully set out here in Count I.

19. The Defendant is in possession of records relating to the Plaintiff.

20. The Plaintiff has made a lawful request under the FOIA for release of those records, but the Defendant has failed and refused to release the same.

21. The Defendant's failure to release the said records is continuing to this date without justifiable excuse.

22. For this reason, the Plaintiff is entitled to judgment against the Defendant requiring the Defendant to release the said documents forthwith.

DAMAGES

23. The unlawful acts of the Defendant have caused the Plaintiff to be denied access to records and information, which under law, he is entitled to receive.

REQUEST FOR RELIEF

WHEREFORE, based upon all of the foregoing facts, the Plaintiff is entitled to the following relief:

1. An order from the court requiring the Defendant to release all of the documents referred to above without further delay.

2. A finding that the Defendant's agents have acted arbitrarily and capriciously in connection with the refusal to release the records in question here.

3. An order requiring the Defendant to reimburse the Plaintiff for all fees and costs expended in connection with this litigation.

4. For such other relief as the court may deem just.

Dated:

_____

William E. Citizen
Address
City, State, Zip
Area code and phone number

that you "substantially prevail," or *win the case*. You cannot expect to be compensated for filing a case which, after careful scrutiny by the court, was found to be lacking in legal or factual substance. Therefore, as I have been saying throughout, *pick your fights carefully!*

Another provision of the FOIA is indispensible to breaking the IRS' cycle of lawlessness. Section §522(a)(4)(F) of the Act provides that when, (1) the court orders withheld records to be released, (2) orders an assessment of fees and costs against the government, and, (3) draws the conclusion that:

> "the circumstances surrounding the withholding (of the documents) raise questions whether agency personnel acted arbitrarily or capriciously with respect to the withholding, *the Civil Service Commission shall promptly initiate a proceeding to determine whether disciplinary action is warranted against the officer or employee who was primarily responsible for the withholding.*" §522(a)(4)(F); (emphasis added).

This provision of law, when properly enforced by the citizen, is an important weapon in assuring that IRS personnel *will not* unlawfully withhold documents from a citizen. If, in fact, it is found through the Civil Service Commission inquiry that an IRS employee did act "arbitrarily or capriciously," the Commission is require to recommend "corrective action." At that point, the IRS is required to "take the corrective action that the Commission recommends."[16]

Conclusion

We have seen that the FOIA is a useful and simple tool in which to obtain needed intelligence data from the internal files of the IRS. Beyond that, we have learned an important technique for ensuring that the disclosure requirements of the FOIA are not abused or misused by IRS personnel. These two aspects of Ultimate Defense Weapon Number One are vitally important to you in the war against IRS abuse. When you know what the enemy is planning and how the enemy is thinking, you are in the best possible position to defeat the pending attack.

---

16. See Rule 10(c), FRCvP.

PART III
Defending The Money In Your Pocket

CHAPTER

Heading Off an Attack

The single most common attack the IRS will instigate against the American Taxpayer is the dreaded *tax audit*. Millions of Americans are terrified at the prospect of a tax audit, and the IRS milks the fear and apprehension to its fullest potential. Capitalizing on the typical citizen's ignorance of tax audit procedures, his rights during and after an audit, and most importantly, his obligations in connection with the audit, the IRS extracts millions in additional taxes, penalties and interest which are, at best, of *doubtful* legality. So successful is the IRS at this game, that its records show that on the average, over $4,100 in additional taxes were assessed per face-to-face audit in 1988.[1]

My book *How Anyone Can Negotiate With The IRS—And WIN!* had, as its paramount purpose, blowing the lid off the secrets behind the tax audit. My primary goal was to disclose the fact that the IRS tax auditor *has absolutely no power whatsoever* to lien, levy or sieze the assets of *any person under any circumstances!* Tearing down this facade will eventually do more toward

evening the odds with the IRS than any other single achievement, but there is more to the equation.

In declaring these facts on nationwide radio, I have been repeatedly asked, "But can't the IRS simply take the money from you, whether or not you agree with the tax auditor?" In the context of the audit, the answer is, "No, it cannot." The reason is that you *must always* be afforded the opportunity to *contest* the auditor's findings and reasoning before you are thrust into enforced collection action. This is true *regardless of the amount in question.*

Tentative citizens hesitant to say "no" to unreasonable or unlawful demands must realize that they, not the auditor, possess the power to make their words stick. This power lies, not only in the right of appeal, fully discussed in *How Anyone Can Negotiate With The IRS—And WIN!*, but in the ability to avoid *all* enforced collection action prior to obtaining a court decision on the legitimacy of the IRS' demands. In this manner, we can "Head off the attack!"

---

1. See *Internal Revenue Highlights,* 1988, Statistical Tables 7 and 8.

The United States Tax Court

The United States Tax Court was designed and created solely for the purpose of resolving disputes between citizens and the IRS concerning the question of the lawful amount of tax due in a given year. The Court, in its present form, was created in 1969 by an Act of Congress.[2] With its legislative "magic wand," Congress created a court which was to function within the Executive branch of Government, rather than through the constitutionally mandated Judicial branch. The seemingly insignificant divergence from constitutional stipulation allows the government the luxury of a court in which traditional constitutional rights *need not* be afforded to citizens.[3]

Does this subtlety thereby render the Tax Court an unconstitutional tribunal? Constitutional purists would respond affirmatively, arguing that Article III of the Constitution mandates that the "judicial power of the United States, shall be vested in one supreme Court, and in such inferior Courts as the Congress may from time to time ordain and establish.[4]

general powers of the Congress to "legislate." In so doing, Congress created a hybrid, which in turn, purportedly eliminated the need to afford citizens their constitutional rights. Among those rights now ignored in the Tax Court is the right of trial by jury.[5]

Despite the clear, unarguable departure from the constitutional formula, the courts have regularly held that the Tax Court is a "constitutional court."[6] This attitude has left us staring squarely in the face of the reality that the Tax Court is the only remedy available to defuse an unjust ruling unless one is willing and able to first pay the tax.[7]

From a purely *practical standpoint*, discounting for now the constitutional implications of the court's structure and authority, the process for litigating an unjust audit determination is most convenient, not to mention simple. Once a basic understanding of the Tax Court process is appreciated, it becomes *impossible* for the IRS to collect *one dime* which is not lawfully due and owing. Constitutional or not, the Tax Court is the *only recognized* "judicial-type" forum available for contesting an audit determination *prior to payment of the*

United States Tax Court—Opinions

Prevailing party (by decision line)		Summary & small tax case bench opinions		Published, memorandum & regular bench opinions		Total	
		1987	1988	1987	1988	1987	1988
Decided in favor of the government	Number	240	182	285	324	525	506
	Percent	50.3	45.8	31.6	36.7	38.1	39.5
Decided in favor of the taxpayer	Number	22	20	50	40	72	60
	Percent	4.6	5.0	5.5	4.5	5.2	4.7
Decided Rule 155*	Number	204	186	461	384	665	570
	Percent	42.8	46.9	51.1	43.4	48.2	44.5
Miscellaneous	Number	11	9	106	136	117	145
	Percent	2.3	2.3	11.8	15.4	8.5	11.3
Total opinions		477	397	902	884	1,379	1,281

*Rule 155, TC Rules, is invoked when the decision is partially in favor of the IRS, and partially in favor of the citizen.

While it is certainly true that Congress "ordained and established" the Tax Court, it is equally true that they did so *outside the paramaters of Article III*. Instead, the court was created under Article I, which addresses the

tax.

Furthermore, in most cases, the Tax Court will serve the interests of the citizen in determining the correct amount of taxes which are lawfully due. For example, in

---

2. The Tax Reform Act of 1969, P.L. 91-172 §951, creating Internal Revenue Code §7441.

3. *Philips v. Commissioner*, 382 U.S. 589 (1931), speaking of the Board of Tax Appeals, the forerunner to the present United States Tax Court.

4. Constitution, Art. III, §1.

5. *Sonel Research and Development v. Commissioner*, 34 TCM 1021 (1975).

6. *Stix Friedman & Co. v. Commissioner*, 467 F.2d 474 (8th Cir. 1972); *Euzent v. Commissioner*, 78-2 USTC para. 9788 (DC MD 1978).

7. Chapter Five discusses one's alternatives when payment is made.

1988, of the 1,281 decisions rendered by the court, 49.2 percent of all citizens were successful, in whole or in part, with their cases in the Tax Court. Please see the chart entitled *United States Tax Court Opinions.* It is taken from *IRS Highlights 1988,* page 22. It reflects the statistics I have just mentioned.

For some time, I have maintained that the tax audit process is comprised of "90% bluff." I have also maintained that in order to keep your money in your pocket, where it belongs, you must be equipped to say, "No," and to *make it stick.* This is where the Tax Court enters the picture.

When to Use the Tax Court

It can never be said that the tax law is clear and well-settled in very many respects. However, this is not true when it comes to the disallowance of itemized deductions and the addition of unreported income to your tax return. When the IRS has designs to accomplish either or both of these goals, it must mail a notice of deficiency before the proposed tax may lawfully be assessed and collected.

These tax-procedure "basics" are referred to as "the Deficiency procedures."[8] Without first pursuing them in proper fashion, the courts are settled that the attempted collection of taxes by the IRS is simply unlawful.[9] The notice of deficiency, commonly referred to as the "90-day letter" is the IRS' final administrative action indicating its intent to alter your tax liability as reported on your return. Before the proposals are made final, you have the right to a hearing before a judge of the Tax Court.

This fact is what affords you so much power when dealing with the revenue agent in the typical tax audit situation. When the agent proposes adjustments to your tax return, you must be provided with a notice of deficiency *prior* to the IRS making its proposals final. The beauty and irony of the situation is that the individual agent, acting alone, has *neither* the power to issue the notice himself, nor to insist that one be issued.

Each decision he makes in connection with the allowance or disallowance of items on a return is reviewed and must be authorized by a supervisor. Only after the supervisor has "signed off" on the examination will the notice of delinquency be mailed. Consequently, my observation that the agent *has no power over you* to collect one dime is entirely true. It is certainly possible that his cold eyes and the apparent ice water in his veins

has led you to the conclusion that his word is law, but the contrary is true. In fact, I am convinced that if every citizen realized exactly how *little* power IRS tax examiners possess, the tax audit would take on an entirely different perspective. I am not suggesting that it would become a carnival worthy of an admission fee and popcorn, but certainly it would be considerably less intimidating and with that, the IRS would collect only those dollars which are lawfully due.

The Deficiency Determination. The United States Tax Court *is not* a court of general jurisdiction. What this means is that its power and authority, and the circumstances under which a citizen may invoke that power and authority, are extremely limited. The general rule, applicable to the vast majority of citizens, is that *unless* the IRS has made the determination that a "deficiency" in your income tax liability exists for a given year, a case in the Tax Court may not be commenced.

The term "deficiency" is defined by law. Code §6211(a) stipulates that a deficiency is:

> "(1) the sum of:
>   "(A) the amount shown as the tax by the taxpayer upon his return, if a return was made by the taxpayer and an amount was shown as the tax by the taxpayer thereon, plus
>   "(B) the amounts previously assessed (or collected without assessment) as a deficiency, over—
> "(2) the amount of rebates, as defined in subsection (b)(2), made."

A simple explanation of the statutory language is best illustrated by example. Suppose you file a tax return covering tax year 1989. The return shows a tax liability, after all exemptions, deductions and credits are computed, of $2,500. In time, the IRS audits the return, later disallowing several of your deductions. Based upon the disallowance, your "correct tax liability" is determined to be $3,500, rather than the $2,500 you reported on the return. The difference between the $3,500 liability "determined" to be due, and the $2,500 liability you reported, is a "deficiency" under the law.

The Tax Court once described the term "deficiency" using the following mathematical equation:

> "Deficiency = correct tax - (tax on return + prior assessments - rebates) or Deficiency = correct tax - tax on return - prior assessments + rebates."[10]

---

8. See 26 USC §6211, 6212 and 6213.

9. *Bothke v. Fluor Engineers,* 713 F.2d 1405 (9th Cir. 1983). The only exception to this rule is the unusual case of the jeopardy assessment, but even then, the IRS is required to mail a deficiency notice after the assessment, providing an opportunity to contest the assessment in the Tax Court. See 26 USC §7429. Jeopardy assessments are rare and are not discussed in this manual. See *The Naked Truth,* WINNING Publications, pages 115-120 for more information.

10. See *Kurtzon v. Commissioner,* 17 TCM 1542.

You will note that §6211(a) makes reference to "a return made by the taxpayer." You may be asking yourself whether, if *no return is filed*, the IRS is therefore *incapable* of asserting the existence of a deficiency. The answer, vehemently disputed by certain "tax protester" elements, is, "Yes, it certainly may." In support of my conclusion I not only point to the *thousands* of citizens who have fallen victim to this faulty reasoning, but to Code §6020(b). It reads as follows:

"(b)(1) Authority of Secretary to Execute Return.—If any person fails to make any return required by an internal revenue law or regulation made thereunder at the time prescribed therefor, or makes, willfully or otherwise, a false or fraudulent return, the Secretary shall make such return from his own knowledge and from such information as he can obtain through testimony or otherwise.

"(2) Status of Returns.—Any return so made and subscribed by the Secretary shall be prima facie good and sufficient for all legal purposes."

Hence, we see that even in the event no return is filed *by the citizen,* when the IRS prepares the so-called "substitute for a return" under §6020(b), *that* return is considered equally valid for all legal purposes, including §6211(a).

As you have observed, §6020(b) requires the Secretary to make the return "from his own knowledge and from such information as he can obtain through testimony or otherewise." This is where the "information return system" enters the scheme. Forms W-2 and 1099 are submitted by employers and others paying non-employee compensation, or when dividends, interest, and royalties, etc., are paid. Those information returns are cross-checked with the master file of tax returns.

When the verification process discloses the presence of an *information return,* but does not reflect the presence of a *tax return,* the IRS will, if necessary, rely upon §6020(b) to prepare a return for the delinquent citizen. Having done so, the legal effet is much the same as though one had prepared the return *himself.* This enables the IRS to *in fact* determine a deficiency under §6211(a).

Make no mistake about it; failing to file a tax return does not handicap the IRS when it comes to eventually collecting a tax, if indeed there is a deficiency.[11]

The Notice of Deficiency. Having made the administrative determination that a deficiency exists for a given year, the IRS is required to mail a "notice of deficiency." The notice is required *before* the liability may lawfully be assessed. Exhibit 4-1 is an example of the cover pages of a notice of deficiency. Included with the cover pages is the IRS' explanation as to how it arrived at the deficiency amount. Those pages will be discussed later.

The notice of deficiency is your ticket into the Tax Court. Without a notice such as Exhibit 4-1 in your hand, you will be forbidden access to the Tax Court. The sole premise of the court's jurisdiction or authority, which we know to be extremely limited, is to "redetermine" any tax deficiency established by the IRS. If we think of the notice of deficiency as an allegation that additional taxes are due, the function of the Tax Court is to determine whether that allegation is correct under all of the facts and circumstances of the case.

Please take note of the language within the second paragraph of Exhibit 4-1. It provides that if you wish to contest the deficiency determination, you must file a petition with the United States Tax Court within 90 days of the date stamped on the front of the notice. In our example, the date shown is November 8, 1988. (See top of Exhibit 4-1.) The 90-day period is computed by *counting* 90 calendar days, *including* Saturdays, Sundays and holidays. The date shown on the notice is not included in this computation.

It is critical that one determine the last day for filing a Tax Court petition as soon as he receives his notice of deficiency. Any petition which is not filed timely with the Tax Court *will not be considered.* The time for filing the petition is fixed by Code §6213(a). It cannot be extended! Therefore, extreme care should be taken to determine the filing deadline and to have your petition filed with the Court before that period expires.

Failure to do so will not only prevent any Tax Court litigation, but will lead to further difficulty. For example, Code §6213(c) provides:

"If the taxpayer does not file a petition with the Tax Court within the time prescribed in subsection (a), the deficiency, notice of which has been mailed to the taxpayer, shall be assessed, and shall be paid upon notice and demand from the Secretary."

Thus we see that it is not the notice of deficiency itself which creates the assessment, nor is it the auditor's threats which create the assessment. Rather, it is your *failure* to timely file a petition in the Tax Court which creates the assessment. I cannot count the number of persons I have encountered with collection problems,

---

11. See *Hartman v. Commissioner,* 65 TC 542 (1971); *Callow v. Commissioner,* 43 TCM 1060 (1982); *Roat v. Commissioner,* 847 F.2d 1379 (9th Cir. 1988).

Exhibit 4-1

Internal Revenue Service
District Director

Department of the Treasury

Date:

NOV 0 8 1988

Social Security or
Employer Identification Number:

Tax Year Ended and Deficiency:
See Details, Page Two

Person to Contact:
ESP:STP

Contact Telephone Number:

CERTIFIED MAIL

Dear Mr.

We have determined that there is a deficiency (increase) in your income tax as shown above. This letter is a NOTICE OF DEFICIENCY sent to you as required by law. The enclosed statement shows how we figured the deficiency.

If you want to contest this deficiency in court before making any payment, you have 90 days from the above mailing date of this letter (150 days if addressed to you outside of the United States) to file a petition with the United States Tax Court for a redetermination of the deficiency. To secure the petition form, write to United States Tax Court, 400 Second Street, NW., Washington, D.C. 20217. The completed petition form, together with a copy of this letter must be returned to the same address and received within 90 days from the above mailing date (150 days if addressed to you outside of the United States).

The time in which you must file a petition with the Court (90 or 150 days as the case may be) is fixed by law and the Court cannot consider your case if your petition is filed late. If this letter is addressed to both a husband and wife, and both want to petition the Tax Court, both must sign the petition or each must file a separate, signed petition.

If you dispute not more than $10,000 for any one tax year, a simplified procedure is provided by the Tax Court for small tax cases. You can get information about this procedure, as well as a petition form you can use, by writing to the Clerk of the United States Tax Court at 400 Second Street, NW., Washington, D.C. 20217. You should do this promptly if you intend to file a petition with the Tax Court.

You may represent yourself before the Tax Court, or you may be represented by anyone admitted to practice before the Court. If you decide not to file a petition with the Tax Court, we would appreciate it if you would sign and return the enclosed waiver form. This will permit us to assess the deficiency quickly and will limit the accumulation of interest. The enclosed envelope is for your convenience. If you decide not to sign and return the statement and you do not timely petition the Tax Court, the law requires us to assess and bill you for the deficiency after 90 days from the above mailing date of this letter (150 days if this letter is addressed to you outside the United States).

(over)

316 N. Robert St., St. Paul, Minn. 55101

Letter 531(DO) (Rev. 1-87)

If you have questions about this letter, please write to the person whose name and address are shown on this letter. If you write, please attach this letter to help identify your account. Keep the copy for your records. Also, please include your telephone number and the most convenient time for us to call, so we can contact you if we need additional information.

If you prefer, you may call the IRS contact person at the telephone number shown above. If this number is outside your local calling area, there will be a long distance charge to you.

You may call the IRS telephone number listed in your local directory. An IRS employee there may be able to help you, but the contact person at the address shown on this letter is most familiar with your case.

Thank you for your cooperation.

Sincerely yours,

Laurence B. Gibbs

Commissioner

By

Enclosures:
Copy of this letter
Statement
Envelope

CONTINUATION OF FORM 531(DO)

PAGE - 2

Taxable Year Ended		Deficiency
December 31, 1985	Income Tax	$7,855.00
	Addition to the tax-Section 6653(a)(1)	393.00
	Addition to the tax-Section 6653(a)(2)	*
	Addition to the tax-Section 6661	1,964.00
Total deficiencies, taxes and penalties		$10,212.00

* 50% of the interest due on $7,855.00 (See Statutory Notice Statement.)

Letter 531(DO) (Rev. 1-87)

which problems were created by failing to file a petition in the Tax Court in a timely manner. Very often, the lack of understanding of the nature of the notice and the proper manner in which to proceed upon receiving it, causes the citizen to *ignore* it. This, of course, is the worst possible response to the problem.

Proof of the Bluff. One tax examiner after another will lead citizens to believe that they have the power of *assessment and collection* of a tax liability. In *How Anyone Can Negotiate With The IRS—And WIN!*, I related the story of a man who was told by an examiner that if he did not agree to the proposed assessment, the agent would, "write it up," despite his objections. This demand, as well as other threats and innuendos, led the citizen to the conclusion that he had no choice in the matter. Whether he agreed with the figures or not, the IRS, apparently under the direction of the self-declared authority of the agent, would collect the money *regardless.*

The deficiency procedures clearly illustrate that this idea is patently false. Unquestionably, it is a contrived measure calculated to eliminate any potential resistance to assessment that the average citizen may be inclined to offer, *before* it is presented. An understanding of these deficiency procedures will *terminate* the abuse of citizens by tax examiners.

One of the most important aspects of the deficiency procedures is found at Code §6213(a). That law provides:

> ". . .no assessment of a deficiency in respect of any tax, and no levy or proceeding in court for its collection shall be made, begun, or prosecuted until such notice (of deficiency) has been mailed to the taxpayer, not until the expiration of such 90-day or 150-day[12] period, as the case may be, nor *if a petition has been filed with the Tax Court,* until the decision of the Tax Court has become final.***" (Emphasis added.)

The law is quite plain. *No tax* may be assessed without the IRS first mailing a notice of deficiency. Having been mailed, no assessment may be made if the citizen has filed a timely petition in the Tax Court. Without a valid assessment made in accordance with these rules, *any effort* to collect those taxes is *unlawful.* The moral of the story is that the notice of deficiency is the touchstone from which all assessment authority flows. Without the notice, there can be no valid assessment.

The Tax Court's Authority. We have already stated that the notice of deficiency is your ticket to the Tax Court, but what is the purpose of the trip? By now you must appreciate the significance of being able to turn to the court for a determination of whether the demands placed upon you by a lowly tax auditor are indeed legitimate. Given the fact that you have the ability to demand a notice of deficiency if negotiations break down, the IRS will always be required to exercise extreme caution when disallowing any deduction, or adding unreported income to your return.

The power wielded by the Court then, is to *correct* any erroneous actions taken by the IRS in connection with your return, whether it be the disallowance of a deduction or the addition of unreported income. In determining whether to petition the Court for a redetermination of the deficiency, one must first ascertain whether an error has been committed by the IRS. This is done by carefully reviewing the supporting documents which accompany the notice of deficiency.

The first document which one must examine is IRS Form 4549A, Income Tax Examination Changes. This document, prepared by the tax examiner, provides a line-by-line analysis of the agent's proposed changes to your return. The sum of those changes accounts for the income tax deficiency alleged in the notice. Exhibit 4-2 is an example of Form 4549A. Let us review it together.

Beginning with the top of the sheet, we find the name and address of the citizen and generally, the name and office address of the auditor. Beneath those entries we find the explanation of the changes made to the return. Line 1 is entitled, "Adjustments to Income." To the right of that we find the year or years in question. Beginning with line 1.A., a brief statement is made describing what specific adjustment to the return has been made.

In the example shown in Exhibit 4-2, at line 1.A., we see that the first entry states, "Schedule C Expenses." To the right of that entry we find the amount of, "$20,226." This tells us that the examiner *disallowed* $20,226 in Schedule C expenses which were claimed on the return. The next entry at line 1.B. reads, "Cost of Goods Sold." The amount reflected there is, "$11,469." From this we learn that $11,469 worth of Cost of Goods Sold claimed on the return were also *disallowed.*

Each of the proposed changes, whether a *disallowance* of a deduction, or the allowance of a deduction not claimed on the original return,[13] will be reflected in

---

12. Applicable to persons living outside the United States.

13. Additional deductions not claimed on the return are reflected as minus items. See Line 1. C., Exhibit 4-2.

Exhibit 4-2:
Form 4549A

Department of the Treasury - Internal Revenue Service
Income Tax Examination Changes

Name and Address of Taxpayer	S S or E I Number	Filing Status	Return Form No
		JOINT	1040
	Person with whom examination changes were discussed	Name and Title	

1. Adjustments to Income	Year: 1985	Year:	Year:
A. Schedule C Expenses	$ 20,226	$	$
B. Cost of Goods Sold	11,469		
C. Earned Income	-12,000		
D. MARRIED COUPLE DEDUCTION	317		
E. ITEMIZED DEDUCTIONS	1,000		
F.			
G.			
H.			
I.			
J.			
K.			
2. Total Adjustments	21,012		
3. Taxable income shown on return or as previously adjusted	9,489		
4. Corrected taxable income	30,501		
5. Tax 85-Table	4,837		
6.			
7. Corrected tax liability	4,837		
8. Less A.			
Credits B.			
C.			
D.			
9. Balance (line 7 less total of lines 8A thru 8D)	4,837		
10. Plus A. SELF-EMPLOYMENT TAX	4,113		
Additional B.			
Taxes C.			
D.			
11. Total corrected income tax liability (line 9 + 10A,B,C,D)	8,950		$
12. Total tax shown on return or as previously adjusted	1,095		
13. Deficiency or Overassessment (line 11 adjusted by line 12)	7,855		
14. Adjustments to prepayment credits	0		
15. Balance due or Overpayment (line 13 adjusted by line 14)	7,855		$
16. Penalties, if any	2,357		

Other Information

Bernard Dignat

Examiner's Signature	District	Date
	St. Paul (DO-41)	09/27/88

Form 4549A (SF-DES)

Exhibit 4-3:
Form 886-A

Form 886-A	EXPLANATION OF ITEMS	Schedule No. or Exhibit
Name of Taxpayer		Year/Period Ended 8512

SCHEDULE C EXPENSES

Expenses and income have been allowed as verified and provided for by law. Attached is a schedule of specific adjustments to Schedule C. Many of the items have been adjusted because you failed to establish that the expense was incurred in 1985 and that the expense was ordinary and necessary business expense.

WIFE'S WAGES

The adjustments are in accordance with our previous discussion.

TWO-EARNER DEDUCTION

The qualified earned income is figured separately for each spouse, without regard to community property laws. We have refigured your qualified earned income and adjusted your deduction accordingly.

MEDICAL AND DENTAL

Only the amount of medical expenses that exceeds a certain percentage of your adjusted gross income is deductible. Since your adjusted gross income has been changed, we have adjusted your medical expense deduction.

SELF-EMPLOYMENT TAX - TAXPAYER

We have adjusted your self-employment tax due to a change in your net profit from this self-employment.

This report supersedes all prior reports.

Department of the Treasury - Internal Revenue Service   Form 886-A
                                                                Page ____

Lines 1.A.-1.K. In addition, any alleged unreported income will be revealed in that area. Line 2, entitled, "Total Adjustments," is the grand total of all disallowed items, minus any allowed items not originally claimed on the return. Line 2 reflects the taxable income which the agent reasons should be *added to your return,* based upon the adjustments proposed.

Please note the entry on Line 3. This amount is the taxable income originally disclosed on the return. Line 3 is added to Line 2 (total adjustments) to arrive at the taxable income the IRS believes you had during the year in question. See Line 4. Of course, this amount is typically *higher* than that shown on your return. Without an increase in taxable income, there can be no increase in your tax liability.

Line 5 shows the amount of tax which is due on the taxable income shown on Line 4. This amount is also greater than that shown on the original return. The same amount is shown again in Line 7, and Line 8 will compute any credits to which you may be entitled. Lines 9 and 10 combined constitute the total corrected tax liability, taking into consideration all credits to which you may be entitled. See Line 11.

Having computed the "correct" tax "liability," we may now determine the "deficiency." On Line 12, the amount of tax paid per the original return is displayed. Line 13 reflects the "deficiency" after the amount shown as the tax on your return is subtracted from the "correct" liability as shown on Line 11.

Line 16 reflects the addition of any penalties which the IRS believes are appropriate under the circumstances.

In this manner, we have determined just exactly how the IRS has arrived at the deficiency it claims is due from you. What we do now know as yet, is whether the figures themselves and the claims *behind* the figures are correct or incorrect. In order to determine this, we must turn to IRS Form 886-A, Explanation of Items, also a part of the supporting documents provided to you with the notice of deficiency. See Exhibit 4-3, Explanation of Items.

The Explanation of Items, as its title suggests, provides explanation behind the numbers shown on Form 4549A (Exhibit 4-2). One need simply read down the items shown on that page or pages to determine the IRS' reasoning behind the disallowance of any given item as shown on Form 4549A. As an example, Exhibit 4-3, under the heading, "Schedule C Expenses," referring to Form 4549A, Line 1.A., (see Exhibit 4-2) states that:

"* * *Many of the items (shown on Schedule C) have been adjusted because you failed to establish that the expense was incurred in 1985 and that the expense was (an) ordinary and necessary business expense."

Now that we have discovered the reasoning behind the disallowance, we may answer the critical question, "Is the disallowance proper under the circumstances?" If the answer is "yes" *as to each and every item,* then no justification exists for pursuing the matter into Tax Court. *However,* if the answer is "no" as to *even one item,* then justification does exist for pursuing the matter further.

The Tax Court has the authority to correct any mistakes the IRS has made in determining the deficiency it claims you owe. Your job is to demonstrate that a mistake has in fact been made, and the extent of the error. Provided you can accomplish this goal, you will prevail in your Tax Court proceeding. Most importantly, you have stripped the tax examiner *of all power* which he claims to exercise over you in connection with this issue. The court, now the auditor, will resolve the issues, once and for all.

Exhausing Administrative Procedures

If you are not as yet weary of hearing about administrative procedures, you will be by the time you have completed studying this manual. So be it! Given the importance of the subject and far-reaching implications involved, I would be remiss if I were to slight the matter in the least particular.

When dealing with a notice of deficiency, it is not difficult to overlook administrative procedures altogether. Since the onus is on the IRS to mail the notice lest it waive its right to assess a tax, one may lose sight of not only the *need* to exhaust his remedies, but he may fail to *recognize* what his remedies are. After all, if the notice is issued, the remedy is to petition the Tax Court, is it not?

While this is certainly true and cannot be diminished, *in most cases* there is an intermediate stop along the way. This brief but important detour leads one directly to the office of the Appeals Division. As I have discussed at length in prior publications, the Appeals Division is established solely for the purpose of affording the citizen the opportunity and forum in which to correct an improper audit determination.

The Appeals Division is a separate and distinct division of the IRS. It is not a part of the District Office and not under the authority of the district director. The Appeals Division is under the authority of the Director of Appeals, and hence, Appeals Officers are not directly answerable to the same "boss" as are tax auditors. This degree of independence has led me to describe the two functions of Examination and Appeals thusly: The purpose of Examination is to *cause problems,* while the purpose of Appeals is to *solve problems.*

In my experience of nearly 14 years of dealing with the IRS, the office of Appeals has proven largely to be staffed with competent, reasonable persons eager to arrive at a conclusion which is *correct*, and not necessarily one which lines the coffers of the federal government. Sound impossible? Give it a try! *IRS Highlights 1988* reveals that 86 percent of all cases before the Appeals Division in 1988 were settled *by agreement*. See Table 15, *Appeals Workload*.[14]

Regardless of the prospects for success, without

Without a doubt, the penalty under this law is very potent. It was intended to act as a deterrent to persons raising frivolous arguments in the Tax Court, but the Tax Reform Act of 1986 *added* the provision permitting assessment of the penalty if one "unreasonably fails to pursue available administrative remedies." This expansion of the statute increases the need for one to avail himself of the remedy of administrative appeal. Without doing so, the court may enforce the $5,000 penalty against you.

Table 15. — Appeals workload not before the tax court (nondocketed)

	Number of cases[1]	
	1987	**1988**
Received	60,199	57,364
Regular work	39,738	36,942
Tax shelters	20,461	20,422
Disposed of by agreement	45,441	49,129
Regular work	29,201	34,649
Tax shelters	16,240	14,480
Disposed of as unagreed[2]	2,808	3,037
Regular work	2,765	2,897
Tax shelters	43	140

[1] A case represents taxpayers grouped together by tax periods with common or related issues that may be considered and disposed of together.
[2] Cases docketed in the Tax Court in response to a notice of deficiency issued by Appeals are not included because they remain in inventory, merely shifting from nondocketed to docketed status. However, such cases are considered unagreed for purposes of computing a nondocketed agreement rate of 88.9 percent.
NOTE: Workload shown for FY 1987 has been adjusted to include receipts (10,756) and disposals (6,475) of penalty appeal and employee plan/exempt organization cases so as to create comparability with FY 1988 data.

exercising the "right of appeal" as an administrative remedy, one faces significant risks later in Tax Court. With the passage of the Tax Equity and Fiscal Responsibility Act of 1982, Congress increased the penalty provison of Code §6673. Previous to the 1982 Act, the maximum penalty allowable under the law was $500. Now, the maximum allowable penalty is $5,000! But, "penalty for what?" you may ask. Let us read the statute:

"Whenever it appears to the Tax Court that proceedings before it have been instituted or maintained by the taxpayer primarily for delay, that the taxpayer's position in such proceeding is frivolous or groundless, *or that the taxpayer unreasonably failed to pursue available administrative remedies,* damages in an amount not in excess of $5,000 shall be awarded to the United States by the Tax Court in its decision. Damages so awarded shall be assessed at the same time as the deficiency and shall be paid upon notice and demand from the Secretary and shall be collected as a part of the tax." (Emphasis added.)

The careful language of the statute has persuaded me that the penalty is not "automatic" should one fail to exercise the right of appeal. The statute states that one must *"unreasonably"* fail to pursue his administrative remedies before the penalty applies. If one has solid grounds for not having exercised the right of appeal, or if for some reason, the right of appeal was not made available, it seems plain that the penalty is not applicable.

One example comes to mind. The "knowledgeable citizen" is cognizant of the fact that the appeal is affected *after* the examining agent has issued the so-called 30-day letter. The 30-day letter, or examination report, indicates that additional taxes are due and invites citizens to either pay the tax or submit a written protest letter requesting an appeal. The protest letter must be submitted within 30 days, accounting for the common reference to the letter. Exhibit 4-4 is an example of a 30-day letter. The attachments to the letter will be much the same as those already described earlier under the heading, *The Tax Court's Authority*.

However, 30-day letters are *not always sent*. Almost as

---

14. This table is reproduced from page 39 of the 1988 *Highlights*.

Exhibit 4-4: 30 Day Letter

Internal Revenue Service   Department of the Treasury
District Director

Date: APR 27 1988   **Tax Year Ended:**
                                                     December 31, 1985
                                                     Person to Contact:

                                                     Contact Telephone Number:

—   Dear Taxpayers:

Thank you for the information you gave us about your Federal income tax liability
for the above year. We considered it carefully. The item checked below applies to you.

☐ We did not change our previous determination because you did not establish that
   you furnished more than half the total support of the dependents in question.

☐ We did not change our previous determination for the reasons given on the enclosed
   form(s).

☒ We adjusted your tax liability as shown in the enclosed revised examination
   report.

☐

If you agree with our findings, please sign and return either the consent on the
examination report, or the agreement form if one is enclosed. If a waiver form is
enclosed, we would appreciate your signing and returning it. If additional tax is due,
you may pay it now and limit the interest charge; otherwise we will bill you.

If you do not agree, you may do one of the following:

1. Ask for a meeting with an examiner at one of our local offices, if the examination
   was conducted entirely by mail. During this informal discussion, you may furnish
   any additional information you would like considered. Please write or phone us,
   and if necessary we will transfer your case. You will be contacted so that a
   convenient time and place can be arranged.

2. Request a hearing with a member of our Office of Regional Director of Appeals.
   The Appeals Officer will be someone who has not examined your return. Please
   write or phone us and we will transfer your case to the Appeals Office nearest

   you and they will contact you. However, if the examination was conducted entirely
   by mail, we would appreciate your first discussing our findings with an examiner,
   as explained in item 1.

The publications previously given you explain your appeal rights.

Please reply within 30 days from the date of this letter. We have enclosed an
envelope for your convenience.

If you have any questions, please contact the person whose name and telephone
number are shown in the heading of this letter.

Thank you for your cooperation.

                                                     Sincerely yours,

                                                     C. Schnitzer

                                                     District Director

Enclosures:
☒ Examination report
☒ Agreement form
☐ Waiver of notice of claim disallowance
Envelope

cc: **Letter 692(DO) (Rev. 2–82)**

often, the Examination Division or the Service Center will simply issue the notice of deficiency, apparently bypassing the right of appeal. Once the notice of deficiency is in hand, the only remedy is to file the Tax Court petition within 90 days or face an assessment of the amount demanded. Under these circumstances, no direct appeal is available, though plainly the step was not avoided by any conscious act of the citizen. Certainly the IRS' failure to issue the 30-day letter would constitute one ground for not having taken a direct appeal of the matter.

However, a new statute, a part of the Tax Reform Act of 1986, may, if followed, virtually guarantee that one otherwise deprived of a 30-day letter will have the opportunity to pursue and exhaust his administrative remedies within the Appeals Division before being forced to petition the Tax Court. In so doing, the risk of incurring §6673 sanctions is *de minimus*. The law, Code §6612(d) states in part:

> "The Secretary may, with the consent of the taxpayer, rescind any notice of deficiency mailed to the taxpayer.* * *"

In the event the notice is rescinded, the citizen may not file a petition in the Tax Court, but neither can the IRS assess the tax. According to the Congressional Committee which reviewed the law before it was passed in 1986, "Once the notice has been properly rescinded, it is treated as if it never existed."[15] In 1988, the IRS issued a Revenue Procedure designed to implement the conditions under which a notice of deficiency would be rescinded.[16]

Under the terms of the new procedure, the IRS will rescind a notice of deficiency under any of the following grounds:

1. The notice was issued as a result of administrative error, such as when a notice is sent at a time when the IRS has not considered a properly executed Form 872, consent to extend the assessment time period. This is also applicable if the notice is sent to the wrong person or covers the wrong year;

2. The citizen provides information establishing that the actual tax due is less than the amount stated within the notice; or

3. The citizen *specifically* requests a conference with the Appeals Division for the stated purpose of entering into settlement negotiations.

I believe that this new section of law is very important. Provided it is employed at the appropriate juncture, it could very well eliminate the need to petition the Tax Court, particularly when one has not been given the opportunity to pursue the matter with the Appeals Division. More importantly, even if one's effort to rescind the notice of deficiency is unsuccessful, the Tax Court would be *hard-pressed* indeed to render a finding that the citizen "unreasonably failed to pursue available administrative remedies."

The recision is accomplished with Form 8626, Agreement to Rescind Notice of Deficiency. See Exhibit 4-5. The notice is prepared under the direction of the Review Staff and should be filed with that office. To execute the recision agreement, one should notify the "person to contact" identified on the face of the notice of deficiency. That person is usually a part of the Review Staff. See Exhibit 4-1, top right portion. That person will inform you of the manner in which to proceed so that arrangements can be made to complete Form 8626. Be careful to take these steps *well before* the 90-day period for petitioning the Tax Court expires.

The new Revenue Procedure also speaks to the conditions under which the IRS *will not* rescind a notice of deficiency. They are very important. First of all, the IRS will not rescind the notice if the statute of limitations on the assessment of the tax[17] is due to expire within 90 days or less, *unless* the citizen agrees to execute Form 872.[18]

Secondly, the IRS will not rescind the notice if the 90-day period for filing a petition with the Tax Court has expired, with no petition having been filed. Under those circumstances, assessment of the tax is permitted under §6213, and the matter will become an issue for the Collection Division. Third, the notice will not be rescinded if the citizen has filed a petition with the Tax Court. When that occurs, the office of District Counsel becomes involved as the legal representative of the IRS. Resolution of the matter will then be handled through that office. Lastly, the notice will not be rescinded if a Form 872-A has been executed.

Even if one is not successful with his efforts to rescind the notice of deficiency, all is not lost. Administrative remedies are nevertheless available though one has been forced into the Tax Court. This is *especially* true when the IRS has failed or refused to issue the 30-day letter prior to mailing the notice of deficiency.

The Appeals Division does not lose its settlement

---

15. Committee Report on P.L. 99-514.

16. See Rev. Proc. 88-17, 1898-11 IRB 23.

17. See Code §6501.

18. Form 872 is an agreement to extend the statutory period in which assessment may be made. See *How Anyone Can Negotiate With The IRS—And WIN!*, pages 150-153.

Exhibit 4-5

Form **8626** (Rev. September 1987)	Department of the Treasury — Internal Revenue Service **Agreement to Rescind Notice of Deficiency** *(See instructions on reverse)*	In reply refer to: SSN or EIN:

Pursuant to section 6212(d) of the Internal Revenue Code, the parties, _____ ,

                                                                            Name(s)

taxpayers of _____ , and the District Director of

                                (Number, Street, City or Town, State, Zip Code)

Internal Revenue, Regional Director of Appeals or Service Center Director consent and agree to the following:

   1. The parties mutually agree to rescind the notice of deficiency issued on _____

to the above taxpayer(s) stating a deficiency in Federal _____ tax due and, where applicable,

                                                Kind of tax

additions to the tax for the year(s) as follows:

		Additions to Tax:	Additions to Tax:
Tax Year Ended	**Deficiency**	_____	_____

   2. The parties agree that the statute of limitations has not expired as to the above tax year(s) and can be further extended at the time of this agreement or at a later date under applicable provisions of the Internal Revenue Code.

   3. The parties agree that good reasons have been shown to exist for the action being taken in this agreement. The parties agree that the effect of this rescission is as if the notice of deficiency had never been issued. The parties are returned to the rights and obligations existing on the day immediately prior to the date on which the rescinded notice of deficiency was issued. Included among those rights and obligations is the right of the Commissioner or his delegate to issue a later notice of deficiency in an amount that exceeds, or is the same as, or is less than the amount previously determined, from which amount the taxpayer(s) may exercise all administrative and statutory appeal rights.

   4. The taxpayers affirmatively state that at the time of signing this agreement they have not petitioned the United States Tax Court contesting the deficiencies in the notice of deficiency.

Your Signature	Date
Spouse's Signature	Date
Taxpayers' Representative	Date
Corporate Name	
Corporate Officer Title	Date
Commissioner of Internal Revenue or Delegate	Date

authority merely because the citizen has filed a timely petition with the Tax Court. It is true that the Office of District Counsel will represent the IRS in all Tax Court proceedings, but the Appeals Division will retain jurisdiction for a time.[19] Under IRS procedures, the Appeals Division will assume responsibility for settling the case at the time the matter is received from District Counsel.

An Appeals Officer assigned to the case will, within 45 days of receiving the file from District Counsel, attempt to conduct a conference with the citizen. The goal is to settle the case without the need of a trial. Appeals Division jurisdiction is limited to a period of four months, but can be extended if there is a substantial likelihood of settlement within a reasonable period of time. The extension will provide an additional 60 days in which to negotiate with the Appeals Officer on the case.

In all, one has at least six months after filing a petition in Tax Court in which to pursue settlement at the administrative level. Naturally, this opportunity should be exploited to the fullest. Failure to do so could result in an assessment of the $5,000 penalty we have been discussing. Not only will a good faith settlement effort avoid the $5,000 penalty, it could very well eliminate the need for a trial altogether. As we have already seen, most cases at the Appeals level are settled in a fair and amicable manner. One would do well to take full advantage of the opportunity.

Ultimate Defense Weapon Number Two

The Tax Court Petition

The timely filing of a petition with the United States Tax Court will guarantee several important concerns. First, the tax cannot lawfully be assessed until the Tax Court rules on the merits of your claim. Second, you will have an opportunity to present evidence to support your contentions that the IRS has committed errors in computing your tax liability. Third, you will be given at least two opportunities to settle your case prior to trial. The first of these we have already reviewed when we discussed the administrative processes available before and after the petition is filed. The second opportunity will be described later, under the heading, *The Stipulation Process*.

Drafting the Petition. The procedures which govern cases within the Tax Court are set forth in the Rules of Practice and Procedure, United States Tax Court. This pamphlet is available from the clerk of the Tax Court. The address is 400 Second Street NW, Washington, DC 20217. Before any effort is made to submit a Petition to the Tax Court, one should review the rules.

Rule 34(b), Tax Court Rules, describes the requirements for an adequate Tax Court petition. The seven specific mandates which must be included are:

1. Your name and legal residence, including your social security number, and the office of the IRS in which the tax return for the period in question was filed.

2. The date the notice was mailed, including the city and state of the IRS office which issued the notice of deficiency. That information is shown on the cover page of the notice itself. (See Exhibit 4-1.) The cover page of the notice of deficiency should also be attached to the petition as an exhibit.

3. The amount of the deficiency, the period in question, the nature of the tax in question and the amount of the deficiency which is disputed.

4. A clear and concise statement of each of the errors which you believe the Commissioner has made in computing the liability. It is vitally important to set out each of the alleged "errors" in a separate paragraph, and to be sure that your statement covers all the discrepancies you have identified in the notice of deficiency. The reason is that, according to Rule 34(b)(4), "Any issue not raised in the assignment of errors shall be deemed to be conceded."

5. A clear and concise statement of the facts on which you rely as the basis of your claims that the Commissioner erred in computing your liability. The Statement of Facts should also be separately lettered to correspond with the Statement of Errors described in paragraph 4.

6. A statement setting forth the relief you are seeking from the Court.

7. Your name and address must be shown at the conclusion of the petition, together with your signature.

Of the seven stipulations just described, three are especially important to observe. First, you *must* be careful to include the date of the notice of deficiency. You will recall that if your petition is filed late the Court will not accept it. Thus, declaring the date within the petition will demonstrate that your petition is timely filed.

Next, it is *critical* to include a statement of errors in your petition. The law applicable to the notice of deficiency is that unless it is shown to contain errors, the Court will not disturb the IRS' ruling. Therefore, you

---

19. See Rev. Proc. 78-9, 1978-1 CB 563 and Rev. Proc. 79-59, 1979-2 CB 573.

Exhibit 4-6: Tax Court Petition

UNITED STATES TAX COURT

```
William E. Citizen                  )
                                    )
                Petitioner,         )     Docket No. _____
                                    )
vs.                                 )
                                    )
Commissioner of Internal Revenue,   )
                                    )
                Respondent.         )
```

PETITION FOR REDETERMINATION

William E. Citizen hereby makes this Petition for Redetermination. The basis for his case is as follows:

1. The Petitioner is William E. Citizen with his legal residence now at (Address, City, State, Zip).

2. The Notice of Deficiency was mailed to the Petitioner on (date of notice), and was issued by the Office of (city and state of IRS office). Attached hereto is a copy of the cover page of said notice evidencing the Court's jurisdiction in this case.
(Note: Please see Exhibit 4-2 for source of numbers used here.)

3. The alleged deficiency as determined by the Commissioner is for income taxes for the calendar year 1985, in the total amount of $10,212, all of which is in dispute.

4. The alleged deficiency herein is based upon the following errors:

a) The Commissioner has erroneously and wrongfully disallowed $20,226 in Schedule C expenses claimed by Petitioner.

b) The Commissioner has erroneously and wrongfully disallowed $11,469 in Costs of Goods Sold as claimed on Schedule C during the year in question.

c) The Commissioner has erroneously and wrongfully redetermined Petitioner's Married Couple Deduction, increasing Petitioner's income by $317 during the year in question.

d) The Commissioner has erroneously and wrongfully disallowed $1,000 in Schedule A deductions claimed by the Petitioner during the year in question.

e)   The Commissioner has erroneously and wrongfully made adjustments to Petitioner's self-employment tax liability based upon the adjustments made to the Schedule C.

f)   The Commissioner has erroneously and wrongfully included an assessment of the penalties provided for under §§6653(a)(1) and (2) and 6661 of the Code.

5.   A statement of the facts upon which the Petitioner relies as the basis of his case is as follows:

a)   Petitioner accurately reported all expenses on his Schedule C. The disallowance of expenses was improper as all were incurred in the ordinary course of business and were necessary to the operation of Petitioner's business.

b)   Petitioner accurately reported on Schedule C all Costs of Goods Sold in connection with his business. All items reported as cost of goods were sold during the year in question.

c)   Petitioner correctly computed and reported his Married Couple Deduction during the year in question.

d)   The Petitioner correctly and accurately reported all itemized deductions on Schedule A. All deductions claimed there were expended in the manner shown and during the year in question.

e)   The Petitioner's self-employment income tax liability was correctly reported on the Schedule SE for the year in question in that it was based upon a correct Schedule C.

f)   Petitioner has at all times acted in good faith in connection with his tax affairs. Therefore the claim for penalties under the code sections referenced above is misplaced.

g)   On oath and affirmation, and under penalty of perjury, the Petitioner states that he does not owe the additional tax alleged to be due by the Commissioner.

WHEREFORE, Petitioner respectfully request that the Notice of Deficiency herein be dismissed.

Dated:

_____

William E. Citizen
Petitioner
Address
City, State, Zip

Exhibit 4-7:

Places of Trial

APPENDIX IV
PLACES OF TRIAL
(See Rules 140 and 177)

A partial list of cities in which regular sessions of the Court are held appears below.* This list is published to assist parties in making requests under Rules 140 and 177. If sufficient cases are not ready for trial in a city requested by a taxpayer, or if suitable courtroom facilities are not available in that city, the Court may find it necessary to calendar cases for trial in some other city within reasonable proximity of the designated place.

LIST

ALABAMA:
Birmingham
Mobile

ALASKA
Anchorage

ARIZONA
Phoenix

ARKANSAS
Little Rock

CALIFORNIA
Los Angeles
San Diego
San Francisco

COLORADO
Denver

CONNECTICUT
New Haven

DISTRICT OF COLUMBIA
Washington

FLORIDA
Jacksonville
Miami
Tampa

GEORGIA:
Atlanta

HAWAII
Honolulu

IDAHO
Boise

ILLINOIS
Chicago

INDIANA
Indianapolis

IOWA
Des Moines

KANSAS
Kansas City

KENTUCKY
Louisville/Frankfort

LOUISIANA
New Orleans

MARYLAND
Baltimore

MASSACHUSETTS
Boston

MICHIGAN
Detroit

MINNESOTA
St. Paul

MISSISSIPPI
Biloxi
Jackson

MISSOURI
Kansas City
St. Louis

MONTANA
Helena

NEBRASKA
Omaha

NEVADA
Las Vegas/Reno

NEW JERSEY
Newark

NEW MEXICO
Albuquerque

NEW YORK
Buffalo
New York City
Westbury

NORTH CAROLINA
Winston-Salem

OHIO
Cleveland
Cincinnati
Columbus

OKLAHOMA
Oklahoma City
Tulsa

OREGON
Portland

PENNSYLVANIA
Philadelphia
Pittsburgh

SOUTH CAROLINA
Columbia

TENNESSEE
Knoxville
Memphis
Nashville

TEXAS
Dallas
El Paso
Lubbock
San Antonio

UTAH
Salt Lake City

VIRGINIA
Richmond

WASHINGTON
Seattle
Spokane

WEST VIRGINIA
Charleston/Huntington

WISCONSIN
Milwaukee

*The Court sits in about 35 other cities to hear Small Tax Cases. A list of such cities is contained in a pamphlet entitled "Election of Small Tax Case Procedure and Preparation of Petitions," a copy of which may be obtained from the Clerk of the Court.

must set out in "clear and concise terms" just what the errors are that you feel have been committed.

The third item of priority is the statement of facts in support of the claimed errors. This statement does not have to be lengthy. However, it must describe sufficient facts to support the claim that errors have been made in the computation of your liability.

The manner in which these allegations are most effectively included in the petition document is shown in Exhibit 4-6. Exhibit 4-6 is an example of the typical Tax Court Petition. The document is not intended to constitute a "fill-in-the-blank" answer to *your* notice of deficiency. Still, it does provide the formula you will need to properly structure your Tax Court Petition. Be aware of the three most critical aspects of the petition, taking care to include them in your draft.

Filing the Petition. The petition is filed with the clerk of Tax Court by mailing one original document, and "four conformed copies" to the clerk's address.[21] The original document must be signed and a filing fee of $60 must be paid to the clerk.[22]

If one is unable to pay the filing fee, Rule 20(b) permits the court to waive the fees if the petitioner "establishes to the satisfaction of the Court by an affidavit containing specific financial information that he is unable to make such payment."

The Location of Your Tax Court Trial. The United States Tax Court has its principal office in Washington, DC, and that is where all documents are to be filed. However, your Tax Court trial will not occur in Washington unless you are willing to travel there for that purpose. Normal procedure calls for the judges of the Tax Court to ride a circuit throughout the United States, hearing cases in selected cities as they go. In order to insure that you will not be required to travel to Washington to present your case, you would be wise to designate any one of many pre-selected cities in which to have your trial.

Appendix IV to the Tax Court Rules is a list of the cities in which regular Tax Court cases may be tried. See Exhibit 4-7. One should make his request for trial in a particular city by filing with the Tax Court a document entitled, *Request for Place of Trial.* See Exhibit 4-8.

Exhibit 4-8: Request for Place of Trial

UNITED STATES TAX COURT

William E. Citizen)
)
     Petitioner,) Docket No. _____
)
vs.)
)
Commissioner of Internal Revenue,)
)
     Respondent.)

REQUEST FOR PLACE OF TRIAL

The Petitioner hereby requests that the trial of the herein

matter be held in (City, State -- See Exhibit 4-7).

   Dated:

   _____

   William E. Citizen

---

21. See Tax Court Rule 23(b).
22. See Tax Court Rule 20(b).

The *Request for Place of Trial* is attached to the petition as the final page, and will be acknowledged by the Clerk when received. Should you fail to make your request for place of trial at the time of filing your petition, the IRS has the option to do so.[23] In addition, any time before the case has been set for trial, you may file a motion with the court seeking permission to have the place of trial changed to a location more convenient to you.[24]

Prosecuting Your Tax Court Case

The nature of a Tax Court case has been the subject of much debate over the years, and has been the source of a great deal of misunderstanding. Citizens are easily confused as to their obligations in the context of a Tax Court proceeding due to the vast procedural departure from settled principles of American jurisprudence.

We Americans are akin to the proposition that we are "innocent until proven guilty." This attitude carries into our confrontations with the IRS, causing many to assume that, "unless they prove it, it ain't so." Unfortunately, this rule of law does not apply to the IRS when we are discussing a Tax Court matter.[25] Tax Court Rule 142(a) provides that the Petitioner (citizen) carries the "burden of proof" with respect to the errors alleged in his petition.

Thus, to put this into clearer perspective, we can say that the notice of deficiency—the IRS' determination that you owe taxes—is presumptively correct. What that means is, unless you come forth with specific evidence to prove that the IRS has made some type of error in rendering its determination, either with regard to the law or the facts, the notice of deficiency will stand. Whether or not you believe this twist to be constitutional, it is a procedural reality and the courts will adhere to it. Count on it!

Therefore, in order to prevail in the Tax Court proceeding, you must become the "prosecutor." You must take the offensive and you must keep the pressure on the IRS in an effort to settle the case to your liking. One way in which to accomplish this is to use your opportunities to negotiate with the Appeals Division to their fullest potential. But more than that, the Rules of Tax Court will enable you to do the same thing if followed properly. Two particular angles come to mind in this regard. The first is to use the discovery provisions

of the rules, and the second involves the requirement to "stipulate." We shall discuss them in turn.

Tax Court Discovery. In Chapter Two, I discussed the discovery provisions of the Federal Rules of Civil Procedure. See Chapter Two, under the heading, *Preventing a Counterattack.* We learned that there were four principal methods of obtaining discovery, or evidence, for use in your civil case. The Federal Rules of Civil Procedure *do not* apply carte blanche to the Tax Court, but discovery is provided for in the Tax Court's own rules. The methods are the same as those I have already described. Using discovery can be a very helpful way in which to keep the pressure on the IRS.

Before embarking upon the discovery discussion, however, it is important to understand that in most cases, you—not the IRS—will be called upon to present evidence regarding the claims raised in your petition. Do not make the mistake of believing that discovery can be used as a means of somehow shifting the burden of proof to the IRS. Always be aware of the fact that you must prove that the IRS' deficiency notice is erroneous, based upon the facts and circumstances of the case. You must bring forth the evidence to prove this truth.

On the other hand, many notices of deficiency are *unclear* at best, as to the IRS' reasoning for disallowing a given deduction, or for adding phantom income to your tax return. Without a doubt, you are entitled to learn why the IRS has disallowed a deduction. Knowing this will enable you to be better prepared for whatever argument district counsel may present in opposition to your claim.

The rules require that before any formal discovery procedures may be invoked, the parties are expected to "attain the objectives of discovery through informal consultations or communication."[26] Through letters and conferences, you are entitled to obtain whatever information the IRS possesses concerning the actions it took regarding your return. Again I must emphasize that this technique will not permit you to argue to the court that the IRS failed to adequately justify its actions. But it certainly can, and will, enable you to correctly structure your presentation to the court in *light of the IRS' actions.*

In the event that informal "consultations or communications" have failed to provide the information you are seeking, you are free to invoke the formal discovery provisions of the Tax Court's rules.[27]

The Stipulation Process. At some point during the

---

23. See Tax Court Rule 140(a).

24. Ibid, at subsection (d).

25. This does hold true, however, when the subject is criminal wrongdoing or issues which *are not* originally raised in the notice of deficiency. See *The Naked Truth*, pages 147-152. See also *Denman v. Commissioner*, 42 TCM 249 (1981) and Tax Court Rule 142(b).

26. See Tax Court Rule 70(a)(1).

27. See Tax Court Rules 70-90.

course of the proceeding, the district counsel attorney will call upon you to meet for the purpose of developing "stipulations" under Rule 91.[28] This is a critical aspect of the Tax Court proceeding, and if you fail to properly pursue this function, you risk having your case dismissed by the Court.[29]

A "stipulation" is nothing more than an agreement between the parties. Rule 91 holds that:

> "The parties are required to stipulate, to the fullest extent to which complete or qualified agreement can or fairly should be reached, all matters not privileged which are relevant to the pending case, regardless of whether such matters involve fact or opinion or the application of law to fact. Included in matters required to be stipulated are all facts, all documents and papers or contents or aspects thereof, and all evidence which fairly should not be in dispute.* * *"

The rule is interpreted to mean that the parties are required to meet, thoroughly examine all of the issues, and to agree to the fullest extent possible on the facts of the case and the manner in which the law applies. The purpose of the rule is to narrow the issues to be decided by the court. At the very least, the process will reduce the time necessary to try the case. Believe me when I tell you that the judges of the Tax Court are *very serious* about enforcing this rule!

Because the rule requires that stipulations be executed, and because the court *will enforce the rule,* it is best to go on the offensive with regard to stipulation. The more facts to which you can persuade the IRS lawyer to agree, the easier it will be for you to eventually prevail on the issue. Even if you cannot obtain agreement on the ultimate issue, press for agreement on as many of the underlying facts as possible. This process of "chipping away" will only make your task at trial that much simpler.

Going on the offense with regard to stipulations involves either making contact yourself with district counsel, or capitalizing on any opportunity offered you by district counsel. You should attend stipulations conferences fully prepared to prove your case. All of your documents should be in hand, as should your summaries of the testimony of any witnesses you intend to call at the trial. This information will form the basis of the facts to which you will ask district counsel to stipulate.

Properly orchestrated, and provided you have done your homework, you can expect that forceful stipulations conferences will ultimately lead to a settlement of the case without the need of a trial. If you are able to prove to the satisfaction of district counsel that you are entitled to the claims you have made in your petition, (or an agreed upon variation thereof) the need to take the matter before a judge will be eliminated.

The Tax Court Trial

If you have not fully settled your case, either through the appeals process or through your discussions with district counsel, you will be entitled to a trial before a judge. The time of your trial will be announced to you via official notice from the clerk of the court. You must be prepared to go forward with your case at that time. If you have filed a *Request for Place of Trial,* your case will be heard in the Tax court city which you have designated.

The Tax Court trial is not the kind of trial you are accustomed to viewing on *L.A. Law.* In the first place, there will be no jury to decide your case. The law is settled that a citizen is not entitled to a jury trial in Tax Court. You will recall our earlier discussion regarding the Tax Court as an Article I court, not an Article III court. This fact is chiefly responsible for your being denied a trial by jury in this context. Whether or not this comports with your view of the Seventh Amendment is of no moment. The court will not provide a jury trial—period.

In the second place, the trial is a bifurcated, or two-part process. The first segment of the trial focuses upon the facts. This is the only portion of the trial in which you will actually be in a courtroom. With a judge presiding, you will have the opportunity to present to the court any and all evidence supporting your claims, including the stipulations you have reached with district counsel. You may testify on your own behalf and you may call witnesses to testify on your behalf.

The second segment of the trial is known as the "argument" portion. Because there is no jury to decide the facts, the court will not entertain a "closing argument." Hence, there is no need to stand before the court exhibiting emotional pleas for understanding, lenience or justice *ala* Perry Mason. It is just as well, because the rules provide that all arguments are submitted to the court *in writing.* This is accomplished well after the trial on the facts has been completed.[30]

---

28. See Tax Court Rule 91.

29. See *Levy v. Commissioner,* 86 TC 794, and Tax Court Rule 123(b).

30. See Tax Court Rule 151.

Because your argument is written, referred to as a "Brief," you have plenty of time to carefully structure it to ensure full and adequate treatment of your subject.

After both parties have submitted their briefs, the court will render its decision in the case. This decision is the final resolution by the court of the issues, though either party may appeal that decision to the United States Court of Appeals.

Exhibit 4-9 is a flowchart depicting the progress of a case through the Tax Court, beginning with the issuance of a notice of deficiency.

Conclusion

The Tax Court Petition is a powerful weapon available when dealing with the IRS. Its potency is derived from the fact that when you realize the option exists and communicate to the auditor or Appeals Officer that you realize the option exists, fair and reasonable settlements of disputes at those levels have a way of materializing from thin air.

On the other hand, if IRS personnel, particularly auditors, suspect that you have no understanding of your right of appeal and the availability of a Tax Court trial, you will inevitably pay more taxes than are lawfully owed.

The key to success is, as always, *understanding your rights.*

Exhibit 4-9
Flowchart of Tax Court Case

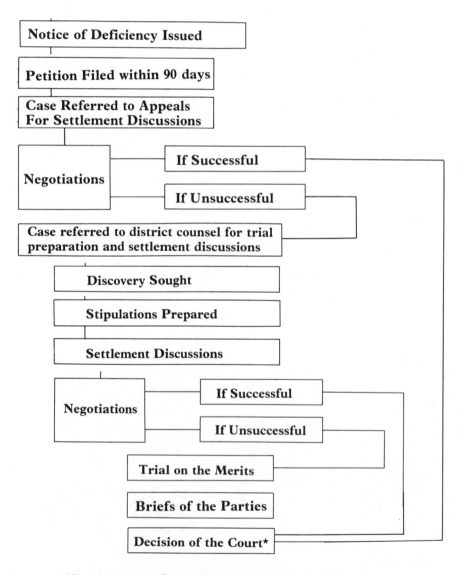

*All settled cases are finalized by "decision documents" which reflect the agreements the parties have reached. The decision documents are signed by the court. Even if there has been no trial, the parties and the court will execute decision documents since a petition has been filed invoking the court's jurisdiction.

CHAPTER

Recapturing Your Losses

The Internal Revenue Service is masterful in the art of psychological warfare. It has convinced the masses that resistance to its demands is futile. This has led to the unprecedented ability of the IRS to collect additional dollars from the public without the need to as much as justify its demands with a reasonable explanation. For years, the IRS has used an obscure tool provided it by Congress to collect additional dollars. The tool enables the IRS to administratively alter a tax return, but only if that return contains *mathematical* errors. It may then, in turn, bill the citizen for any deficiency which might exist after the error is corrected.

However, the IRS has strayed far beyond the limits of the law, employing the mechanism to alter returns *which are not incorrect.* The IRS' annual reports reveal that it used this technique to collect millions in taxes, most of which are probably not due. My exposure to the country via radio has granted me the luxury of speaking directly with thousands of disgruntled citizens who faced this frustrating experience. The reports I receive are painfully similar, revealing that almost no one is able to obtain intelligent answers to reasonable questions about

the bill when the IRS' "help lines" are phoned. IRS operators simply inform the confused citizen that the computer reflects a balance due, and that the amount "must be paid—now."

It is even common for tax practitioners such as accountants and enrolled agents to throw their hands up in utter frustration when attempting to get to the heart of these bills. As a result, it is commonplace for citizens to be told by their tax guardians to just "pay it." Fortunately (I think) for most people faced with these demands, is the fact that the amount tends to be relatively small. As a matter of fact, on more than one occasion I have marveled at the IRS' capacity to match the amount of the bill to the individual citizen's threshold of resistance, demanding an amount which is just *slightly* below the line. This ensures that as the citizen's frustrating in addressing the problem rises, his willingness to resist diminishes *in direct relation.* All the while one tells himself, "It's not that much money. I'm not going to drive myself crazy over a few hundred dollars."[1]

Finally, when an IRS operator points out, in a cold,

1. Chapter One of my book, *How Anyone Can Negotiate With The IRS—And WIN!*, pages, 45-48, demonstrates how one may successfully object to such a bill, placing the burden on the IRS to prove its correctness before it must be paid.

calculated manner, that if the bill is not paid, "enforcement action will be taken," the will to resist evaporates like a puddle in the Mojave. A check is written, a stamp is affixed to an envelope, and with quiet resolve, the two are deposited in the mail. All the while, the confounded citizen wonders how the system could be so *messed up*. Shaking his head, he asks himself, "Why can't the left hand *ever* figure out what the right hand is doing?"

The saddest part of this tale is *not the fact* that the IRS has mailed millions of bogus bills to citizens all across the United States; nor the fact that the vast majority of these bills were paid, some of them without even an *effort* to determine their validity. No, the saddest part of the tale is the fact that when the check is deposited into the mail, the issue *is forgotten!* Most victims of this mail order robbery chalk the event up to experience and pray that it never happens again. Rare is the effort to hunt for the money once it has been paid, in an endeavor to obtain a refund.

In this chapter we demonstrate that even when you *believe* the fight is lost, it probably is not. Even after the IRS has unjustly extracted money from you, with or without your participation, there are procedures available which will enable you to *recapture your losses*.

Recovering What Was Taken

In the previous chapter we discussed all of the measures with which one must comply to ensure that one will not be forced to pay taxes which are not lawfully due. The ability to call the IRS' bluff in an audit hinges upon your eventual right to file a petition in the United States Tax Court. But we also learned that the right to gain access to the Tax Court is contingent upon the IRS' issuing a notice of deficiency, or 90-day letter. In the absence of a 90-day letter, or if for some reason, the citizen permits the 90-day time period to lapse, there is no right to a Tax Court determination of your liability.

Does this fact mean that there is no right to pursue money that is paid under these circumstances? Certainly not, but it does mean that one must be cognizant of his right to pursue his money. He must carefully plan his strategy so that the time-sensitive right is not lost through inaction.

Internal Revenue Code §6402 authorizes the IRS to record credits or issue refunds of taxes which are "overpaid." The law states:

"(a) General Rule.—In the case of any overpayment, the Secretary, within the applicable period of limitations, may credit the amount of such overpayment, including any interest allowed thereon, against any liability in respect of an internal revenue tax on the part of the person who made the overpayment and shall, subject to subsections (c) and (d), refund any balance due such person."

The term "overpayment" is not specifically defined by the Code. As incredible as that may seem, it is nevertheless true. Generally, however, the term "overpayment" is taken to mean any amount which is paid in excess of the amount lawfully due. Section 6401 of the Code discusses the term "overpayment," but does so only in the context of examples.

Some examples of an overpayment are given there. One is where a tax is assessed or collected *after* the period of limitations has expired.[2] Another is where withholding taxes paid during the year exceed the amount of the tax shown due on the return at the end of the year.[3]

The statute itself does not pretend to be exhaustive on the matter, providing just a few, rather limited examples. I am reluctant to leave the question at this point for one reason. When a word is defined only by way of example, some people tend to allow themselves to be limited *only* to the examples. They do not allow themselves the privilege of straying into areas which might not be encompassed within a given example, but nevertheless may fairly be included in the definition of the term at issue. For this reason, I have looked to the Supreme Court for a more worthy definition of the term. We find just the ticket in *Jones v. Liberty Glass Company*.[4]

The high Court has expressed this opinion regarding the word "overpayment" as it is used in the tax code:

"We read the word 'overpayment' in its usual sense, as meaning any payment in excess of that which is properly due. Such an excess payment may be traced to an error in mathematics or in judgment or in interpretation of facts or law. And the error may be committed by the taxpayer or by the revenue agents. Whatever the reason, *the payment of more than is rightfully due* is what characterizes an overpayment." (Emphasis added.)

From this more lucid language we learn that an overpayment exists anytime you have paid more taxes

---

2. See Code §6401(a).

3. See Code §6401(b).

4. 332 U.S. 524, 531 (1947).

than you owe—period. The existence of an over-payment creates the rights expressed under §6402 of the Code. That section is quoted above. The right affords you the option of either having the overpayment credited against future liabilities, or to have it refunded to you.[5] The option is exercised by filing a timely *Claim for Refund.*

The Claim For Refund

There are many critical aspects of the claim for refund, all of which we shall examine. However, none is more important than the element of *timeliness.*

The Claim Must Be Timely. The right to obtain a refund of any amount of overpayment is inextricably linked to time. Whenever a claim is made outside the statutory period for doing so, the right is lost. This is so regardless of the fact that it may otherwise be perfectly valid in every other particular.[6] Code §6511(a) sets out the time periods in which a claim must be filed before it will be considered by the IRS. The statute reads, in part:

"(a) Period of Limitation of Filing Claim.—Claim for credit or refund of an overpayment of any tax imposed by this title in respect of which tax the taxpayer is required to file a return shall be filed by the taxpayer within 3 years from the time the return was filed or 2 years from the time the tax was paid, whichever of such periods expires the latter, or if no return was filed by the taxpayer, within 2 years from the time the tax was paid.★★★"

Generally speaking, a claim for refund is made by most citizens each year on the face of a Form 1040. When a return is filed showing an excess amount of withheld taxes or an overpayment of estimated taxes, that return constitutes a claim for return. Even if the return is filed after April 15th, one's right to a credit or refund is protected if the return is submitted.[7]

For purposes of determining when the three-year period (beginning with the date of filing the return) begins to run, let us consider statutory provisions.

Under the law,[8] a tax return filed *in advance* of the filing deadline is considered filed on the last day prescribed for doing so. For example, in the case of your personal income tax return, its filing is required on or before April 15th of the year following the close of the tax year in question. A return for the year 1989 is due to be submitted on or before April 15th, 1990. But if your return for 1989 is filed on January 30th, 1990, the return is deemed to have been filed on April 15th. The three-year period in which the claim for refund may be made will begin to run on that later date.

However, if the return is filed late, either by extension or otherwise, the date of the *actual filing* is the day on which the statute of limitations for claiming a refund will begin to run.[9]

The claim for refund is considered timely so long as it is made within three years of the time the original return was filed, or within two years from the time the tax was paid, whichever of these two periods has the later expiration.

The Tax Must Be Paid In Full. Another vitally important aspect of the claim for refund is that the tax must be paid in full before any rights to a refund exist.[10] There is no requirement that the tax be paid "under protest" in order to enjoy the right to claim a refund. On the contrary, whether or not the liability is satisfied with reservation, the right to claim a refund is protected.[11]

If your desire is to withhold payment until the matter is resolved by the courts, or you cannot afford to pay the tax, the claim for refund process is not a viable option. Under those circumstances, the Tax Court (see Chapter Four) is the manner in which you must proceed to settle the dispute. Unless the tax is paid in full prior to making the claim, the IRS will not consider the claim to be valid. Moreover, the eventual right to pursue the matter in the district court (not the Tax Court) is linked directly to full payment of the liability.[12]

The importance of paying the tax prior to submitting the claim for refund requires us to examine the rules the IRS has established on this subject. As with the filing of a return, the matter is determined by statute. The very first consideration regarding payment is that a remittance to the IRS will not be considered a "payment" unless a tax has been assessed against you.[13]

---

5. However, if there are outstanding assessments for other periods, the overpayment will be applied to those delinquencies first, with any excess then being refunded. See §6402(c) and (d).

6. See Code §6511(b).

7. It is important to note, however, that if the return is filed more than *three years late,* the right to a credit or refund is lost! *Haun v. Commissioner,* 29 TCM 527 (1970).

8. Code §6513(a).

9. See *Habig v. United States,* 390 U.S. 222 (1968); *Foster v. United States,* 221 F. Supp. (NY 1963).

10. *Flora v. United States,* 362 U.S. 145 (1960).

11. See Code §7422(b).

12. See Code §7422(a).

13. *Rosenman v. United States,* 323 U.S. 658 (1945).

This can be significant when pre-assessment deposits are made for the purpose of terminating the accumulation of interest. Not until the tax has been assessed and the deposit posted to the account is the tax considered "paid."[14]

The manner in which tax withholdings and quarterly estimated payments are treated is also regulated by statute. The law provides[15] that:

"(1). . .any tax actually deducted and withheld at the source during any calendar year. . .shall, in respect of the recipient of the income, be deemed to have been paid by him on the 15th day of the fourth month following the close of his taxable year. . .

"(2). . .any amount paid as estimated income tax for any taxable year shall be deemed to have been paid on the last day prescribed for filing the return under section 6012 for such taxable year. . ."

The statute teaches than when we are discussing tax payments withheld from your wages during the course of a year, the amount deducted is considered paid on April 15th, the last day prescribed for filing the return. The statute of limitations on filing the claim would begin to run on that date. Similarly, estimated payments made during the course of the year are considered paid on the 15th day of the fourth month (usually April 15th) following the close of the taxable year.

Another consideration when determining the date of payment arises when the tax has been paid in installments. It is not uncommon for this circumstance to materialize when a tax was paid through enforced collection. Taxes collected either through a wage levy or through monthly payments made pursuant to an agreement are considered "installment payments." Extensions of time in which to pay the tax, "or an election to pay the tax in installments, shall not be given any effect" when considering the statute of limitations under Code §6511.[16]

The import of this provision is best illustrated by example. Darryl filed his return for 1980 on April 15th, 1981. The return claimed an overpayment of withheld income taxes. The IRS promptly refunded the money shown due on the return. A short while later, the IRS audited the return and determined that a deficiency existed in the amount of about $35,000. Darryl did not exercise his Tax Court option when the notice of deficiency was issued. Consequently, his only alternative was to pay the tax, then later submit a claim for refund.

The excessive amount of the tax, with accumulated interest and penalties, meant that a lump sum payment was impossible. Hence, Darryl fell under the effects of a wage levy, though he later negotiated a payment arrangement with the revenue officer. Under the agreement, Darryl paid $2,000 per month until the liability, with interest and penalties, was paid in full.

The wage levy began in November of 1984. For six months, the IRS confiscated nearly all of Darryl's paycheck of just over $5,000 per month. Payments of $4,700 per month were credited to his account for six months during this period, for a total of $28,200. The levy was terminated when a payment agreement was reached. Under the terms of the agreement, Darryl paid an additional $2,000 per month to the IRS over the ensuing 20-month period. In all, full payment of the tax was spread over a period of two and one half years. A total of nearly $70,000 was paid, considering the interest and penalties which mount on a continuing basis.

After the tax was paid in full, Darryl filed a claim for refund. As we shall examine later, the claim delineated the grounds upon which it was based, and specified an amount of money to which Darryl asserted entitlement. The critical aspect of Darryl's claim, and that which is common to all those submitted at the conclusion of an installment arrangement, is that Darryl was entitled to a refund of only those funds paid within two years of the date of filing the claim. Bear in mind the rules earlier quoted: the claim must be filed within two years of *paying* the tax.[17]

This rule seems rather unfair given the fact that unless the tax is paid in full, no claim for refund may be submitted. If, as in Darryl's case, the installment arrangement extends beyond the two-year period, some portion of the total amount paid will be unrecoverable. This of course assumes that *no part* of the additional assessment was legally justified. If the additional tax was justified in part, only the payments which *exceed* the lawful amount will be recoverable. Under that scenario, the entire amount of such overpayment may well be recoverable. Naturally, determining that will require careful scrutiny of the facts, including a determination of the date each installment was made to the IRS and the amount which the IRS is legally entitled to collect, if any at all. Care must always be taken to determine these facts prior to submitting the claim in order to ensure compliance with the rules and to maximize your refund.

Establishing the Date of Payment. Because the timeliness of the claim is so important, it is imperative that the exact date on which full payment occurred must

---

14. *How Anyone Can Negotiate With The IRS—And Win!,* Chapter Five, explores all the details of transmitting funds to the IRS in a fashion which will assure the intended result.

15. Code §6513(b).

16. See Rev. Reg. §301.6513-1(a).

17. Code §6511(a); Rev. Reg. §301.6513-1(a).

be firmly established. This is even more important when the tax was paid in installments, because each separate payment is linked to the two-year period of limitations. Any payment made outside of the two-year claim for refund window will be lost.

For this reason, it is necessary to obtain the IMF for the year in which the claim for refund will be filed. The IMF, as explained, is the fingerprint of administrative action taken in regard to a particular case. The IMF for the year in question will show the precise date any payments were posted to your account, and the amount of the payment. For example, a TC 610 indicates a remittance with the return, while TC 670 indicates a subsequent payment made after an additional liability has been assessed.

Because the IMF reflects the date on which the payment was posted to the account, and not the date on which it was mailed to the IRS by you (or seized from you), the IMF provides a more reliable record for use in determining the date of payment. No effort to discover the deadline for filing a claim for refund should be made without carefully reviewing your IMF for the year in question.

When Should You File a Claim For Refund

This question could be answered with the simple direction to file the claim anytime the IRS has taken more money than the law allows. Such a general answer, however, ignores the importance of setting forth *examples* of the conditions under whic the claim for refund may produce beneficial results in a given case. Therefore, specific examples are in order.

The Arbitrary Notice. I am fond of discussing the subject of the arbitrary notice. I believe that it, more than any other single attribute of the IRS' bureaucratic personality, reveals its true character. Under the cloak of its statutory authority,[18] the IRS often mails "mathematical recomputations" to citizens after their returns are filed. The IRS is authorized under the law to correct any math error discovered in a return. Under ordinary circumstances, the subsequent assessment of additional tax consistent with the math error is not subject to the deficiency procedures established by the Code.

However, the assessment must be cancelled when the citizen, within 60 days of receiving the notice of tax due responds, in proper fashion.[19] The proper response is to mail a letter within the time allotted which points out

that you do not owe the tax demanded. The letter must also demand an abatement of the assessed liability, and request that a notice of deficiency be mailed to afford you the right to contest the matter in Tax Court.

When these components are structured in a written demand, the IRS is mandated by law to abate, or cancel, the assessment in full. If it is persuaded that an error was in fact made on the return, its burden is to promptly mail a notice of deficiency. Naturally, the notice of a deficiency provides you with all of the computations necessary to determine whether the tax is indeed correct or is, as I suspect in most cases, *bogus*. In fact, if the tax were bogus in the first place, history has shown that no notice of deficiency will follow. Rather, the abatement is made and the matter forgotton. When a notice of deficiency is mailed, you can then make an intelligent decision whether to pay the tax or invoke your rights as described in Chapter Four.

Unfortunately for countless numbers, the IRS is not in the habit of explaining these procedures to the public. Moreover, I doubt seriously whether it will soon begin the practice on the face of the assessment letter. True, IRS Publication 1, *Your Rights as a Taxpayer,* created as a result of the *Taxpayers' Bill of Rights Act,*[20] passed in November of 1988, *does describe* the procedure. Still, the assessment letter itself *does not.* I find it difficult to believe that the uninformed taxpayer will, after reading the vague language of Publication 1, arrive at the conclusion that the *specific* language of a tax due notice and demand for payment may be negated by merely drafting a letter which includes the magic words, "I demand that you abate the tax."

Thus, the tragic pattern is for persons to struggle through phone calls with the IRS and meetings with their tax accountants or preparers, striving to find an answer to the question, "Where did this bill come from?" All too often the answer is that there is no answer. For those with enough moxie to refuse to pay, or who write letters replete with demanding tones but short of the statutory mark, will eventually find—much to their chagrin—that the IRS will simply *take the money.*

While a guest on a popular Atlanta radio talk program, I spoke with a lady who had run into the wall of frustration presented by the arbitrary notice. The IRS demanded just a bit in excess of $300, which to her was king's ransom. She was recently divorced, was raising three small children on a paultry stipend, and public support was her only source of funds. It was difficult to conceive how the bill could have been valid given the brief factual picture she painted while on the

---

18. Code §6213(b).

19. Code §6213(b)(2)(A).

20. See my *Special Report on the Taxpayers' Bill of Rights Act,* WINNING Publications, 1989.

air with me.

She told of her several frustrating encounters with IRS "assisters" at its 1-800 "help" lines. She explained how she had pleaded with certain "assisters" to work with her to look further into the matter as she was certain there was an error. She could not possibly have owed the additional amounts and her suspicion was verified by a well-known tax preparation firm to whom she brought her return for review. Since the return was a *short form,* there simply was not much that *could* have been incorrect.

She went on, relating how her frustration turned to agony when the IRS moved in and seized the money from her bank account. It happened that the funds represented the sum of the resources available for the support of her three small children. Three hundred dollars may not seem like a lot of money to you, but to her, it was *all she had.* Laid next to the responsibility of supporting three children, no reasonable person could suggest that she did not have a problem.

As the months following the levy dragged on, she gradually recovered from the financial hurricane which swept over her family, but then her desperation turned to rage. "How dare they take *my last dime,* and without so much as justifying the bill?! Something is wrong here! What can I do?"

My answer was simple, and for all those who have experienced the same injustice, the suggestion is thus, "File a claim for refund!"

We have already examined the law which gives one this right. Under the circumstances of the arbitrary notice, one has two years from the date the tax is paid in which to submit the claim. The claim need only be filed within that period of time to permit the matter to be reopened and the file examined. Provided the caller was correct and there was no error in her return as she insisted, she would be entitled to a refund of all the money taken, *plus interest.*

The Audit Bluff. I have written many times in the past of a common IRS bluff used at the termination of a routine audit. The bluff revolves around IRS Form 870, *Tax Assessment Waiver.*[21] The Form 870 is presented to the citizen by the revenue agent at the conclusion of the audit. It accompanies the bill for additional taxes, penalties and interest.

After all is said and done, the revenue agent will inform you that the audit is complete, that additional dollars are due, and that the next step of the procedure is to sign the Form 870. In some cases, I have seen revenue agents candidly explain the upshot of signing the form, but most tend to minimize its significance, hoping to obtain a signature without hesitation.

For those who may not be aware of Form 870 and its implications, they can be summarized quite simply. As its title implies, a signed Form 870 acts as a valid *waiver* of the restrictions placed against the IRS on the assessment of the tax claimed due by the auditor. In signing the form, you agree that the IRS may assess *and collect* the tax in question *without* the necessity of first issuing a notice of deficiency.

A common ruse used by the revenue agents to obtain a signature on Form 870 is the claim that if the tax is assessed and paid "now," one will avoid the accumulation of further interest. He may also suggest that despite the fact that you signed the form, you may still contest the assessment "later." This representation tends to indicate that the IRS will somehow notify you concerning this "future right." Let me tell you, its the stuff that farce is made of!

In one case, a North Dakota farmer and his wife had gone through a most difficult audit. The auditor forced the poor woman to rifle through hundreds of cancelled checks in an effort to match each check with both an invoice and receipt for each and every dime of expense deducted. After spending weeks and weeks digging, searching, phoning and cross-checking, the agent's demands were met. Taking the evidence, and without so much as a second look, he hastily thumbed through the stack much as one would page through a telephone book in search of a particular letter of the alphabet.

After completing this "analysis" of the documents, he began ritualistically marking those items which he intended to disallow. In an exhibition I am convinced was designed to flaunt his "power" as an auditor, most of the evidence was arbitrarily rejected and discarded with lightning dispatch and without so much as a question regarding the purpose of the expense. By the time he had completed the charade, tens of thousands of dollars worth of feed, fuel and veterinary expenses incurred in the farming operation had been disallowed. The result was a tax bill which exceeded $25,000. Naturally, the auditor included penalties in the demand for payment.

To add insult to injury, the agent then slid a Form 870 across the table and demanded a signature from both citizens. They offered a mild protest, suggesting that the disallowance of their deductions was carried out with little if any consideration of the evidence.

Unimpressed, the agent rebuffed the objection with the same determined resolve he had used to brush off the evidence. Humorlessly, he again demanded a signature, which he promptly obtained. Upon leaving the IRS office, the couple were under the impression that they would be notified by the IRS concerning their

---

21. See *How Anyone Can Negotiate With The IRS—And WIN!,* pages 147-149.

protests. After all, they made it clear that they did not agree with the agent's decision and wished to pursue the matter.

To their dismay, they never did receive any instructions regarding alternatives available to them in the face of the agent's decision. What they did receive were threatening bills which included interest on the assessed liability. The bills demanded immediate payment, as do all IRS notices. Also, they instructed that if such payment were not forthcoming, "enforced collection action would be taken." Fearing the worst, the couple headed to the bank, obtained a loan and paid the tax, interest and penalty—lock, stock and barrel.

The reason the couple did not receive any instructions regarding their protest is that the signature on Form 870 operated as a *waiver,* or surrender, of their right to protest the agent's decision. Had they refused to sign the form, the only "power" the agent would have had over them is the power to issue a 30-day letter and Examination Report detailing the changes to the return he *proposed.* As we know by now, the agent has no power to actually change the return or to disallow *anything.* He can only propose those changes, but short of citizen acceptance of the proposal, his decision is not final. This of course leads to the right of Tax Court review, which we spoke of in detail in Chapter Four.

The 1988 IRS statistics show that 89 percent of all audits result in a signed Form 870, indicating acceptance by the citizen of the IRS' findings. That does not mean those findings were *correct,* only that the citizen signed the 870 and waived his right to appeal. This of course means that just 11 percent of all audit cases were appealed by the citizen.[22] During the same period, the IRS prevailed outright in Tax Court in just 39.5 percent of the cases.[23] What this extrapolates to is that, of the persons who signed Form 870 in 1988 but *did not* pursue any further action to obtain a refund, about 60.5 percent have some or *all* of their money coming back to them *with interest.* Considering that in 1988, the average tax audit netted the IRS an *additional* $4,123.98 in increased taxes and penalties, the fact that over half of those audited have money coming back to them is most significant.[24]

Looking back on our couple from North Dakota, these figures were much more than just cold numbers on a sheet of paper. They did file a claim for refund after paying the arbitrary assessment created by an over-zealous tax auditor. The claim for refund was considered in a far more reasonable and intelligent light and when the matter was closed, a refund of nearly *every* *dime* was received by them from the United States Government.

What we learn from this is that if you have signed a Form 870 in haste, without considering the possibility of appeal, you retain the right to file a claim for refund within two years of the date the tax is paid.

The Questionable Notice of Deficiency. The notice of deficiency is truly a double-edged sword. The IRS views it as the final administrative decision that you owe additional taxes. Outwardly it indicates that you lost the struggle and must pay. However, it has been made plain throughout this disclosure that the notice of deficiency operates at least as much to the advantage of the citizen as it does the government in disputed tax confrontations.

On the side of the citizen is the important fact that unless the notice is mailed to his last known address, the IRS—in all but a few limited circumstances—is precluded from making an assessment or collecting additional taxes. Also on the side of the citizen is the fact that the notice of deficiency, in all but a few rare cases, will fully explain the IRS' rationale, or lack thereof, for disallowing deductions or adding phantom income to your return. Unless you are *blind,* you can easily determine whether the IRS' perception of your tax liability is correct or not.

Equally advantageous to the citizen is the fact that the law provides a period of 90 days in which one may evaluate his options upon receipt of the Notice of Deficiency. Within that time period, he may either petition the Tax Court without the necessity of pre-paying the liability, or he may pay the tax. If the election to pay is made, this gives rise to another procedural evaluation to consider. The citizen may either accept responsibility for the liability, thus allowing the matter to die, or he may file a claim for refund within two years of paying the tax.

The advantage of time—the 90-day grace period—is of paramount importance to the citizen. It comes into play in cases where the IRS' determination of tax liability is just *partially* correct. Rare indeed is the single-issue notice of deficiency. The overwhelming majority of cases involves multiple issues, such as the disallowance of several categories of deductions, in whole or in part. A respectable number of notices of deficiency also include a claim of unreported income, thus broadening further the scope of issues joined by the notice.

Though I would never admit this in public, the IRS is not wrong *every time.* (Please, let's keep this between

22. See *IRS Highlights 1988,* page 38, table 11.

23. Ibid, page 22, Chart Three. That chart is shown in Chapter Four, page 56.

24. Ibid, pages 32-33, table 7.

you and me, okay?) Now then, realizing that *your* notice of deficiency may be *partially* correct, it is decision time. If you petition the Tax Court, you can reasonably expect to prevail only on those issues in which the IRS is clearly mistaken. (You cannot expect to prevail on the issues in which the IRS is clearly correct.) The best you will hope to achieve from the Tax Court is a split in its decision. But in light of the length of *time* required to litigate in the Tax Court, this may not translate to any measurable gain. The reason is that *interest* charged on unpaid liabilities accrues even while your case is in court!

Section 6601 of the Code provides:

"(a) General Rule.—If any amount of tax imposed by this title. . .is not paid on or before the last date presribed for payment, interest on such amount at the underpayment rate established under section 6621 shall be paid for the period *from such last date to the date paid.*" (Emphasis added.)

Section 6621 of the Code establishes the rate of interest at three points *above* the average short-term "Federal rate."[25] The current interest rate is announced by the IRS on a monthly basis. For example, the applicable federal rate for July of 1989 is 8.86 percent.[26] This translates to an interest rate of 11.8 percent (Federal rate plus three points) which is assessed by the IRS on unpaid liabilities during the month of July, 1989. Moreover, interest is compounded on a *daily* basis.

Given these facts, it is not uncommon for interest to substantially increase a tax bill over a relatively short period of time. Consequently, the notice of deficiency would have to be at *least* 50 percent incorrect in order for you to hope to break *even* in your litigation with the IRS. And by breaking even, I am speaking in terms of the notice of deficiency, *not* in terms of the tax return! The notice of deficiency demands *more money* than was paid with the return.

We *are not* leading to the conclusion that litigation with the IRS is futile and should always be avoided. On the contrary, the IRS has used the interest factor well to its advantage, persuading countless thousands to abandon their legitimate claims on threat of accumulated interest. The point to be made is that the claim for refund provides a perfectly viable solution to the dilemma created by the accumulation of interest over long periods of time. Given the factual scenario I painted earlier, where the notice of deficiency is

partially incorrect, one employing this weapon could stand to save not only thousands in taxes and penalties, but *all of the interest* as well.

The 90-day grace period provides ample time for one to review the notice and make an analysis of its "ratio of correctness," ie., that portion which is correct versus that portion which is incorrect. Using a correctness ratio of 50 percent, one may not stand to gain greatly even if successful in the Tax Court. Alternatively, one could stand to benefit substantially if he were to pay the entire tax and then claim a refund of the 50 percent (or 100 percent for that matter) of the amount deemed to be erroneously paid. Bear in mind that not only will further interest cease the day the tax is paid, but interest in your favor will accrue at the rate of *two* points above the applicable Federal rate. Interest is computed beginning with the date the tax is paid by you, until it is refunded to you.[27]

This aspect of tax litigation transforms otherwise risky procedures into a *no risk* proposition. After paying the tax, nothing further can be lost by pursuing the matter through the remedy of the claim for refund. You have only to gain, provided your claim is made in good faith and is based upon reasonable grounds.

General Ignorance. There is another aspect that makes awareness of the right to claim a refund of taxes paid an overriding concern. It is the fact that *ignorance* of the right to petition the Tax Court or procedures for doing so is rampant among the public. Most are under the impression that the IRS can do whatever it pleases, making resistance worthless. Many of those who may receive a notice of deficiency inviting a Tax Court petition are simply at a loss as to where to begin, short of calling a *very expensive* tax attorney. At that point, the sentiment tends to be, "If I must pay the attorney, win or lose, I might as well just pay the tax and be rid of the hassle."

One or more of these factors leads the public to pay millions in taxes, interest and penalties which are not owed. Yet these persons have a remedy available to correct the injustice. Since the tax has been paid, the right to claim a refund within two years of the date of doing so exists under the law. Properly prosecuted and upon success, you are entitled to a return of your money with interest in your favor.

Recovering or Cancelling Penalties. Section 6404(a) of the Code provides the authority to the IRS to abate, or cancel:

". . .the unpaid portion of the assessment of any tax or

---

25. That rate is based upon the average market yield of outstanding marketable obligations of the United States with remaining periods of maturity of three years or less. See Code §1274(d) and 6621(a)(2).

26. Internal Revenue News Release IR-89-75, June 20, 1989.

27. See Code §§6321(a) and 6511(d).

any liability in respect thereof, which

"(1) is excessive in amount, or

"(2) is assessed after the expiration of the period of limitations properly applicable thereto, or

"(3) is erroneously or illegally assessed."

The same statute also provides authority to abate interest and penalties attributable to IRS delays in connection with the case, and erroneous written advice provided by an IRS "assister."[28] It should be noted, however, that the abatement referred to above *does not apply* to income tax assessments, nor does it apply to estate and gift tax assessments.[29] Clearly, however, penalties and interest are covered by the statute.

Penalties are *big* business for the IRS. As shown by the table in Exhibit 5-1,[30] in 1988 the Internal Revenue Service assessed 26,589,303 separate penalties—more than half—were assessed against individuals, like yourself. After abatements, the IRS was successful in collecting just over $2 billion in penalties from individuals.

The claim for refund is a viable tool for recovering penalties which you believe were improperly assessed, but nevertheless paid. In addition, under the circumstances discussed by Code §6404(a) (see above), penalty assessments may be abated even though they have not been paid in full. The IRS is indeed trigger-happy when it comes to penalties. The claim for refund is your opportunity to disarm this weapon.

Exhibit 5-1
Table 14.—Civil penalties assessed and abated (dollars in thousands)

	Assessments		Abatements		Net penalties	
	Number	Amount	Number	Amount	Number	Amount
Individual						
Delinquency	1,870,495	700,734	185,096	131,045	1,685,399	569,689
Estimated tax	3,114,574	440,028	120,585	57,810	2,993,989	382,218
Failure to pay	7,564,587	521,439	668,594	53,513	6,895,993	467,926
Bad check	242,518	3,360	10,812	571	231,706	2,789
Fraud	9,304	141,407	871	44,413	8,433	96,994
Negligence	1,127,882	353,476	45,239	52,336	1,082,643	301,140
Other¹	161,448	228,933	14,608	32,027	146,840	196,906
Total	14,090,808	2,389,377	1,045,805	371,715	13,045,003	2,017,662
Corporation²						
Delinquency	152,190	498,350	45,803	490,809	106,387	7,541
Estimated tax	293,027	377,143	46,936	263,030	246,091	114,113
Failure to pay	390,790	277,008	126,442	249,943	264,348	27,065
Bad check	3,089	161	367	40	2,722	121
Fraud	535	82,171	57	8,342	478	73,829
Negligence	3,304	45,920	167	1,886	3,137	44,034
Other	913	41,080	74	4,070	839	37,010
Total	843,848	1,321,833	219,846	1,018,120	624,002	303,713
Employment³						
Delinquency	2,267,293	764,678	375,181	272,002	1,892,112	492,676
Failure to pay	4,680,681	368,485	835,546	136,258	3,845,135	232,227
Federal tax deposits	3,545,691	2,612,727	726,335	1,206,943	2,819,356	1,405,784
Bad check	113,285	2,684	4,457	216	108,828	2,468
Fraud	704	2,316	8	19	696	2,297
Other	3,377	3,392	1,320	1,577	2,057	1,815
Total	10,611,031	3,754,282	1,942,847	1,617,015	8,668,184	2,137,267
Excise⁴						
Delinquency	149,131	40,430	22,251	13,993	126,880	26,437
Daily delinquency	40,713	57,703	30,244	52,363	10,469	5,340
Failure to pay	235,042	20,799	50,131	12,735	184,911	8,064
Federal tax deposits	50,020	75,432	9,422	40,677	40,598	34,755
Bad check	4,186	121	349	79	3,837	42
Fraud	887	10,114	206	241	681	9,873
Other	205	3,107	44	1,384	161	1,723
Total	480,184	207,706	112,647	121,472	367,537	86,234
Estate and Gift						
Delinquency	6,354	47,221	2,409	39,835	3,945	7,386
Failure to pay	8,800	25,330	4,910	20,571	3,890	4,759
Bad check	203	112	34	47	169	65
Fraud	10	273	3	29	7	244
Negligence	34	337	5	62	29	275
Other	264	1,403	72	380	192	1,023
Total	15,665	74,676	7,433	60,924	8,232	13,752
All Other⁵						
Delinquency	208,676	509,405	112,635	475,935	96,041	33,470
Failure to pay	144,857	13,541	47,582	8,802	97,275	4,739
Bad check	2,882	161	188	20	2,694	141
Negligence	79	479	24	232	55	247
Missing information	10,807	35,702	5,701	19,483	5,106	16,219
Other	140	525	14	154	126	371
Total	367,441	559,813	166,144	504,626	201,297	55,187
Non-return⁶	180,326	2,603,812	68,275	1,174,652	112,051	1,429,160
Total, all civil penalties	26,589,303	10,911,499	3,562,997	4,868,524	23,026,306	6,042,975

Note. With the exception of estimated tax, assessments and abatements can apply to any tax year.
1 Includes taxpayer identification number, failure to report tips, miscellaneous and false withholding.
2 Includes Forms 1120, 990C and 990T.
3 Includes Forms 940, 941, 942, 943 and CT-1.
4 Includes Forms 1041A, 5227, 990PF, 990, 4720, 4638, 2290, 11, 11C, 720 and 730.
5 Includes Forms 1041, 1065 and individual retirement account file.
6 Includes penalties assessable under the Tax Equity and Fiscal Responsibility Act of 1982, the Tax Reform Act of 1984 and the Tax Reform Act of 1986.

28. Code §6404(e) and (f).

29. The exception to this rule is the right to demand abatement of a mathematical recomputation. See Chapter Nine.

30. This table is from the *IRS Highlights* of 1988, page 39.

Exhibit 5-2: Form 1040X

Page 1

Form **1040X**
(Rev. October 1988)

(X)

Department of the Treasury—Internal Revenue Service
Amended U.S. Individual Income Tax Return

OMB No. 1545-0091
Expires 9-30-90

This return is for calendar year ▶ 19_____ , OR fiscal year ended ▶ _____ , 19_____

| Your first name and initial (if joint return, also give spouse's name and initial) | Last name | | Your social security number |

Present home address (number, street, and apt. no. or rural route). (If you have a P.O. Box, see Instructions.) | Spouse's social security number

City, town or post office, state, and ZIP code | Telephone number (optional) ( )

Enter below name and address as shown on original return (if same as above, write "Same"). If changing from separate to joint return, enter names and addresses used on original returns. (Note: You cannot change from joint to separate returns after the due date has passed.)

A Service center where original return was filed

B Has original return been changed or audited by IRS? ☐ Yes ☐ No
If "No," have you been notified that it will be? ☐ Yes ☐ No
If "Yes," identify IRS office ▶

C Are you amending your return to include any item (loss, credit, deduction, other tax benefit, or income) relating to a tax shelter required to be registered? ☐ Yes ☐ No
If "Yes," you MUST attach Form 8271, Investor Reporting of Tax Shelter Registration Number.

D Filing status claimed. (Note: You cannot change from joint to separate returns after the due date has passed.)
On original return ▶ ☐ Single ☐ Married filing joint return ☐ Married filing separate return ☐ Head of household ☐ Qualifying widow(er)
On this return ▶ ☐ Single ☐ Married filing joint return ☐ Married filing separate return ☐ Head of household ☐ Qualifying widow(er)

Income and Deductions (see Instructions)

		A. As originally reported or as adjusted (see Instructions)	B. Net change—increase or (Decrease)—explain on page 2	C. Correct amount
1	Total income			
2	Adjustments to income			
3	Adjusted gross income (subtract line 2 from line 1)			
4	Deductions			
5	Subtract line 4 from line 3			
6	Exemptions			
7	Taxable income (subtract line 6 from line 5)			

Tax Liability
8	Tax (see Instructions). (Method used in col. C _____)			
9	Credits (see Instructions)			
10	Subtract line 9 from line 8. Enter the result, but not less than zero			
11	Other taxes (such as self-employment tax, alternative minimum tax)			
12	Total tax liability (add lines 10 and 11)			

Payments
13	Federal income tax withheld and excess FICA and RRTA tax withheld			
14	Estimated tax payments			
15	Earned income credit			
16	Credits for Federal tax on fuels, regulated investment company, etc.			
17	Amount paid with Form 4868, Form 2688, or Form 2350 (application for extension of time to file)			17
18	Amount paid with original return, plus additional tax paid after it was filed			18
19	Add lines 13 through 18 in column C			19

Refund or Amount You Owe
20	Overpayment, if any, as shown on original return (or as previously adjusted by IRS)			20
21	Subtract line 20 from line 19 (see Instructions)			21
22	**AMOUNT YOU OWE.** If line 12, col. C, is more than line 21, enter difference. Please pay in full with this return			22
23	**REFUND** to be received. If line 12, column C, is less than line 21, enter difference			23

Please Sign Here
Under penalties of perjury, I declare that I have filed an original return and that I have examined this amended return, including accompanying schedules and statements, and to the best of my knowledge and belief, this amended return is true, correct, and complete. Declaration of preparer (other than taxpayer) is based on all information of which the preparer has any knowledge.

Your signature ▶ _____ Date _____
Spouse's signature (if joint return, BOTH must sign) ▶ _____ Date _____

Paid Preparer's Use Only
Preparer's signature ▶ _____ Date _____ Check if self-employed ☐ Preparer's social security no. _____
Firm's name (or yours if self-employed) and address ▶ _____ E.I. No. _____ ZIP code _____

For Paperwork Reduction Act Notice, see page 1 of separate Instructions.
BE SURE TO COMPLETE PAGE 2

Page 2

Form 1040X (Rev. 10-88) Page 2

Part I — Exemptions (see Form 1040 or Form 1040A Instructions)

If you are not changing your exemptions, do not complete Part I.
If claiming more exemptions, complete lines 1–8 and, if applicable, line 9.
If claiming fewer exemptions, complete lines 1–7.

		A. Number originally reported	B. Net change	C. Correct number
1	For tax years beginning after 1986—yourself and spouse. **Caution:** For tax years beginning after 1986, if someone (such as your parent) can claim you as a dependent, you cannot claim an exemption for yourself.	1		
2	For tax years beginning before 1987—yourself and spouse, 65 or older, blind	2		
3	Your dependent children who lived with you	3		
4	Your dependent children who did not live with you due to divorce or separation	4		
5	Other dependents	5		
6	Total exemptions (add lines 1 through 5)	6		
7	Multiply $1,950 ($1,900 for tax year 1987, $1,080 for tax year 1986, $1,040 for tax year 1985) by the number of exemptions claimed on line 6. Enter the result here and on page 1, line 6.	7		

8 Dependents (children and other) not claimed on original return:
Note: Complete column (b) or (c), whichever applies, only if amending your 1987 or 1988 return.

(a) Full name (first, initial, and last name)	(b) Check if under age 5	(c) If age 5 or older, dependent's social security number	(d) Relationship	(e) No. of months lived in your home

No. of your children on 8 who lived with you ▲
No. of your children on 8 who didn't live with you due to divorce or separation (see Instructions) ▲
No. of other dependents listed on 8 ▲

9 If your child listed on line 8 didn't live with you but is claimed as your dependent under a pre-1985 agreement, check here ▲ ☐

Part II — Explanation of Changes to Income, Deductions, and Credits
Enter the line number from page 1 for each item you are changing and give the reason for each change. Attach all supporting forms and schedules for items changed. Be sure to include your name and social security number on any attachments.

If the change pertains to a net operating loss carryback, a general business credit carryback, or, for tax year 1985, a research credit carryback, attach the schedule or form that shows the year in which the loss or credit occurred. See the Instructions. Also, check here ▲ ☐

Part III — Presidential Election Campaign Fund
Checking below will not increase your tax or reduce your refund.
If you did not previously want to have $1 go to the fund, but now want to _____ check here ▲ ☐ ☐
If joint return and your spouse did not previously want to have $1 go to the fund, but now wants to _____ check here ▲ ☐ ☐

Exhibit 5-3: Form 843

Form 843 (Rev. December 1987)
Department of the Treasury
Internal Revenue Service

Claim

▶ See Instructions on back.

OMB No. 1545-0024
Expires 9/30/90

If your claim is for an overpayment of income taxes, do NOT use this form. (See Instructions.)
(Use this form ONLY if your claim involves one of the taxes shown on line 8 or a refund or abatement of interest or penalties.)

Please type or print

Name of taxpayer or purchaser of stamps

Telephone number (optional)
( )

Number and street

City, town, or post office, state, and ZIP code

Fill in applicable items—Use attachments if necessary

1 Your social security number
2 Spouse's social security number
3 Employer identification number

4 Name and address shown on return if different from above

5 Period—prepare separate form for each tax period
From ___, 19___, to ___, 19___
6 Amount to be refunded or abated $

7 Dates of payment

8 Type of tax or penalty
☐ Employment ☐ Estate ☐ Excise ☐ Gift ☐ Stamp ☐ Penalty IRC section ▶

9 Kind of return filed
☐ 706 ☐ 709 ☐ 720 IRS No. (s) ▶
☐ Other (specify) ▶
☐ 940 ☐ 941 ☐ 990-PF ☐ 2290 ☐ 4720

10 If this claim involves refund of excise taxes on gasoline or special fuels, please indicate your tax year for income tax purposes.

11 Explain why you believe this claim should be allowed and show computation of tax refund or abatement of interest or penalty.

Under penalties of perjury, I declare that I have examined this claim, including accompanying schedules and statements, and to the best of my knowledge and belief it is true, correct, and complete.

Signature (Title, if applicable) _____ Date _____
Signature _____ Date _____

For Internal Revenue Service Use Only
☐ Refund of taxes illegally, erroneously, or excessively collected
☐ Refund of amount paid for stamps unused, or used in error or excess
☐ Abatement of tax assessed (not applicable to estate or gift taxes)

For Paperwork Reduction Act Notice, see instructions on back.

Director's Stamp
(Date received)

Form **843** (Rev. 12-87)

Form 843 (Rev. 12-87) **Page 2**

Instructions

(Section references are to the Internal Revenue Code.)

Paperwork Reduction Act Notice. We ask for this information to carry out the Internal Revenue laws of the United States. We need it to ensure that you are complying with these laws and to allow us to figure and collect the right amount of tax. You are required to give us this information.

Purpose of Form. This form can be used to claim certain refunds and abatements. Use Form 843 to file a claim for refund of overpaid taxes (except in the case of income tax), interest, penalties, and additions to tax. For example, if on your employment tax return you reported and paid more Federal income tax than was actually withheld from an employee, use this form to claim a refund.

Form 843 is also used to file a claim for abatement of an overassessment, or the unpaid portion of an overassessment, if more than the correct amount of tax (except in the case of income, estate, and gift taxes), interest, additional amount, addition to tax, or assessable penalty has been assessed.

New section 6404(e) gives IRS the authority to abate interest in cases where the additional interest was caused by IRS errors and delays. Section 6404(e) applies only if there was an error or delay in performing a ministerial act (defined below) and only relates to a tax of the type for which a notice of deficiency is required by section 6212(a), which includes the taxes relating to income, generation-skipping, estate, gift, and certain excise taxes imposed by chapter 41, 42, 43, 44, or 45. Section 6404(e) does not authorize the abatement of interest for employment taxes or other excise taxes.

Ministerial Act. The term "ministerial act" means a procedural or mechanical act that does not involve the exercise of judgment or discretion and that occurs during the processing of your case after all prerequisites of the act, such as conferences and review by supervisors, have taken place. Get **Publication 556,** Examination of Returns, Appeal Rights, and Claims for Refund, for more information.

Special Instructions for Requesting Abatement of Interest Under Section 6404(e). Across the top of Form 843, write "Request for Abatement of Interest under Rev. Proc. 87-42," fill in your name and address, and complete lines 1 through 4, whichever are applicable.

Line 5 should show the tax period involved.

Skip lines 6, 8, and 9.

Line 7 should show dates of any payment of interest or tax liability with respect to the tax period and type of tax to which the claim relates.

Line 11 should state the type of tax involved, writing with respect to the deficiency or payment, when you were first contacted by the Service in writing with respect to the deficiency or payment, the specific period for which you are requesting abatement of interest, the circumstances of your case, and the reason or reasons why you believe that failure to abate the interest would result in grossly unfair treatment.

A separate Form 843 should be filed for each tax period for each type of tax. However, if the interest assessment resulted from the Service's error or delay in performing a single ministerial act that affected a tax assessment for multiple tax years or types of tax (for example, where 2 or more tax years were under examination), only one Form 843 is required.

Special instructions for requesting refund, credit, or abatement of interest treated as erroneously paid or assessed as a result of the amendment of section 6601(c). Taxpayers may recover or have abated, interest imposed with respect to the suspension period on interest that accrued before January 1, 1988. A claim for refund or credit must be filed within 3 years from the time the return of tax to which the interest relates was filed or within 2 years from the time the interest was paid, whichever is later.

If you are filing for a refund of suspension period interest, write across the top of Form 843 "Request filed under Rev. Proc. 87-43" and leave lines 5, 6, and 10 blank. Line 7 should show the date the interest was paid if known and state whether the claim is for a credit or refund. Leave line 7 blank if the interest has been assessed but not paid.

The following statement should be included on line 11: "Interest on a deficiency or .... (enter the type of tax; e.g., income, estate, or gift tax) for the tax period ending .... was suspended pursuant to section 6601(c) of the Internal Revenue Code. This is a claim for credit, refund, or abatement of the interest collected or assessed for the period the suspension was in effect."

General Instructions. Do not use this form to make a claim for overpayment of income tax. Individuals who filed Form 1040, 1040A, or 1040EZ must use **Form 1040X,** Amended U.S. Individual Income Tax Return, to claim an overpayment. Corporations who filed Form 1120 or Form 1120-A, must use **Form 1120X,** Amended U.S. Corporation Income Tax Return, to claim an overpayment. Other income tax filers

should file a claim on the appropriate amended tax return. (Follow the instructions on the appropriate form for filing an amended return.)

Your agent may make a claim for you. In this case, the original or a copy of the power of attorney must be attached to the claim.

If you are filing the claim as a legal representative for whose return you filed, attach to the claim a statement that you filed the return and are still acting as the representative. If you did not file the decedent's return, attach to the claim certified copies of letters testamentary, letters of administration, or similar evidence to show your authority.

If a corporation is making the claim, the person authorized to act in its behalf must sign the claim and show his/her title.

Specific Instructions. Lines that are not explained below are self-explanatory.

Lines 1 and 2. If you are claiming a refund based on an overpayment on a joint return, such each spouse's social security number must be entered.

Line 8. Check the appropriate box to show the type of tax or penalty. If you are filing a claim for refund or abatement of an assessed penalty, check the box and enter the applicable Internal Revenue Code (IRC) section. For example, if the penalty was assessed under section 6700, check the penalty box and enter 6700 in the space provided. Generally, the IRC section can be found on the Notice of Assessment you receive from the Service Center.

Line 9. Check the appropriate box to show the kind of return, if any, that was filed. If the box for Form 720 is checked, enter the IRS No.(s) in the space provided. The IRS No. can be found on Form 720 to the right of the entry space for the tax.

Line 11. Specify in detail your reasons for filing this claim and show your computation of the tax credit, refund, or abatement. Also attach appropriate supporting evidence.

Signature. If you are claiming a refund based on an overpayment made on a joint return, such as a refund for overpaid windfall profits tax, each spouse must sign the refund claim.

Where To File. File your claim with the Internal Revenue Service Center where you filed your return.

If your claim is for alcohol and tobacco taxes, see the regulations for that particular tax to determine whether you should file with the Regional Director, Bureau of Alcohol, Tobacco and Firearms.

For Internal Revenue Service Use Only

Transcript of Claimant's Account

(Complete only for miscellaneous excise taxes and alcohol, tobacco, and certain other excise taxes imposed under subtitles D and E, Internal Revenue Code.)

The following is a transcript of the record of this office covering the liability that is the subject of this claim.

A—Assessed Taxes

Tax Period and Class of Tax (a)	Document Locator No. (b)	Reference and Date (c)	Amount Assessed (d)	Date or Sched. No. (e)	Paid, Abated, or Credited Amount (f)	AB. (g) PD. CR.	Remarks (h)

B—Purchase of Stamps

To Whom Sold or Issued (i)	Kind (j)	Number (k)	Denomination (l)	Date of Sale (m)	If Special Tax Stamp: State: Amount (n)	Document Locator No. (o)	Period Commencing (p)

Prepared by (initials) _____ Date _____ Office _____

☆ U.S. Government Printing Office: 1987—201-993/60166

Form **843** (Rev. 12-87)

Drafting the Claim For Refund

If you determined that you made an overpayment of taxes to the IRS, voluntarily or otherwise, and have determined that a claim for refund with respect to that overpayment would be timely, the next step is to prepare and submit the claim. The single most important factor to consider in drafting the claim for refund is the injunction in a supervisory regulation. It reads:

"The claim must set forth in detail each ground upon which a credit or refund is claimed and facts sufficient to apprise the Commissioner of the exact basis thereof. The statement of the grounds and facts must be verified by a written declaration that it is made under the penalties of perjury. A claim which does not comply with this paragraph will not be considered for any purpose as a claim for refund or credit." Rev. Reg. §301.6402-2(b)(1).

The IRS has developed forms for use in making a claim for refund, but the instructions for each do not address themselves sufficiently to this aspect of the claim. IRS Form 1040X *Amended Individual Income Tax Return,* is the common form used to claim a refund of personal income taxes. See Exhibit 5-2. IRS Form 843, *Claim,* is used for a host of tax refund claims, such as employment tax overpayments, penalties, excise taxes, etc. See Exhibit 5-3.

Both the 1040X and the 843 provide spaces in which to explain the grounds upon which the refund is based, but neither is particularly explicit as to the importance of the full and complete factual disclosure that is demanded under the regulation discussed above. See Exhibit 5-2, Part II, and Exhibit 5-3, line 11. In particular, the instructions for Form 1040X *are silent* as to this important facet of the claim. The instructions for Form 843, while they do at least address the issue, do not rise to the level of completeness demanded by the circumstances. Regarding the necessity to "apprise the Commissioner of the exact basis" of the claim, the instructions tell us:

"Specify in detail your reasons for filing this claim and show computation of credit, refund or abatement. Also attach appropriate supporting evidence."

The "reasons for filing the claim" may be that "you need the money," but of course that does not come close to meeting the requirements of the regulation. The regulation specifically states that the explanation supporting the claim for refund must set forth the "grounds and facts" upon which the refund is based. Neither the Form 1040X or the 843 adequately communicates this admonition.

Necessity being the mother of invention, I have devised a claim for refund which does meet all of the required provisions of the regulations. There are eight key elements to a claim for refund. They are:

1. The year involved;
2. The citizen's name and address;
3. The place of filing the original return and its status, i.e., whether it was examined, etc.;
4. A statement of the revised income and deductions, and a statement of the over-payment credits;
5. The computation of the overpayment;
6. An explanation of the tax computations;
7. Supporting schedules or documentation;
8. The signature of the citizen, with a declaration that the claim is made under the penalties of perjury.

Exhibit 5-4 is a sample of the Claim for Refund form we just discussed. Please examine it carefully to appreciate the manner in which each of the above elements is set forth.

In reviewing the claim form, you will note that there are no legal arguments contained in the document. That is because there is no requirement that any legal arguments be set out there, only that the "grounds and the facts" be stated in a manner which fairly advises the IRS of the nature of the claim. A "ground" should include an item of income, a deduction or an exemption or credit that gives rise to an "overpayment." In any event, one must realize that non-specific grounds within the claim will not meet the requirement of apprising the IRS of the nature of the claim.[31]

The general rule with regard to claims for refund is that *specific grounds* which are not asserted within the claim itself when filed with the IRS, are waived. That issue may not later form the basis of a suit for refund if the IRS denies the claim.[32] For example, if one ground entitling you to a refund is that the IRS wrongfully disallowed $5,000 paid as a charitable contribution, you must specifically state that as a ground in your claim. Great care should be taken to cover every possible ground for refund within the claim, making sure that a full and complete statement of facts supporting the

---

31. *Belt Ry. of Chicago v. United States,* 567 F.2d 717 (7th Cir. 1977).

32. Code §7422(a); *United States v. Felt & Tarrant Mfg. Co.,* 283 U.S. 296 (1931).

ground is included. Each ground upon which your claim for refund is sought should be set out as a separate paragraph.

Another important drafting consideration is that each individual year for which a refund is sought must be the subject of a *separate* claim. You are not permitted to file one claim form encompassing multiple tax years.

Filing the Claim for Refund

The claim for refund must be filed with the service center[33] in which the return in question was filed. It may also be hand-delivered to the District Director for the district in which you reside. In any event, those which are mailed should be mailed via certified mail, return receipt requested. When hand-delivered to the District Director, one should have a copy of the claim date-stamped by the IRS employee accepting the claim. This will adequately demonstrate receipt of the claim by the IRS and establish the date of filing. Certified mail receipts will also establish the date of mailing if the question of timeliness ever becomes an issue.

Demanding Abatement Of Penalties

As we already explained, Code §6404(a) provides authority for the citizen to demand that penalties be abated without the necessity of paying them in full. When making a demand for abatement, it is recommended that one use Form 843. In the top margin of the form, above the word "Claim" one should type the phrase, "Demand for Abatement of Penalties Under Code §6404(a)." See Exhibit 5-3.

In line 11, where one is asked to provide the grounds upon which the claim is based, you should set forth in as much detail as possible the reasons why the IRS should abate the penalties in question. When seeking an abatement of penalties, you are required to demonstrate that you acted in good faith and not out of a deliberate intent to violate the IRS' rules and regulations. Care should be taken to communicate facts to the reader who will evaluate your claim such as will allow that person to come to the conclusion that you made every reasonable effort to comply with the law, but through no fault of your own, were unable to do so. One example is where you hire a professional tax preparer to compute your liability, but it is later shown that an error was made.

Your good faith in hiring the professional will bear upon the question of whether the penalty assessed on account of the error is appropriate.[34]

An Important Limitation

There is an important limitation on the right to claim a refund of taxes paid which we must discuss now. That limitation arises in cases where one has petitioned the Tax Court regarding a notice of deficiency and in connection with that petition, has received a judgment from the Tax Court on the merits of the petition. If the Tax Court has rendered judgment on the merits adverse to your interests, you may not pay the resulting tax and then file a claim for refund.[35]

The IRS' Reaction

When the claim is filed with the service center, IRS personnel will review the document to determine whether it meets the requirements of a valid claim for refund. In particular, they will attempt to establish whether the tax has been paid in full and whether the claim is submitted in a timely manner. They will then determine whether the case should be handled within the service center itself or must be referred to the district for an examination before the claim is acted on.

Claims involving mathematical errors which gave rise to an overpayment will generally be handled by the service center. Upon determination that the claim is valid, a refund check will be issued. However, when the claim involves much more than a mathematical error, the case will generally be referred to the district for an examination before any refund check will be issued. The examination conducted pursuant to the claim for refund is no different than the audit of a tax return. The examination is conducted to determine whether the grounds set forth in the claim for refund are correct and whether you have sufficient evidence to support your statement of facts.

Because of the likelihood that the claim will be audited, one must be prepared at the time it is drafted to present evidence to support it. Any ground or fact which cannot be buttressed with firm evidence to support it should not be included in the claim.

When the claim is allowed, the IRS will issue a check. But if the claim is disallowed, the IRS will issue either Form letter 916 or 917. Each letter explains that the

---

33. See Appendix I for map of IRS districts.

34. See Chapter One of *How Anyone Can Negotiate With The IRS—And WIN!* for further discussion on abating penalties.

35. *Hammond v. United States,* 77-1 U.S.T.C. Paragraph 9442 (DC Cal. 1977).

Exhibit 5-4: Claim for Refund

IN THE INTERNAL REVENUE SERVICE
FOR THE INTERNAL REVENUE DISTRICT OF MINNESOTA

In re the matter of:)
)
William E. & Jane M. Citizen,   )
SSN: 000-00-0000   )
)
          Petitioners.   )
)
_____

ADMINISTRATIVE CLAIM FOR REFUND AND DEMAND FOR HEARING

TAX YEAR 1986

This is an Administrative Claim for Refund of Taxes, Interest
and Penalties erroneously paid, and for a District or Appeals
Conference, pursuant to 26 USC §§6401 and 6511(b).

This claim is made upon the following facts, arguments, and
disclosures:

1. <u>The year involved</u> -- The year involved with this claim is
tax year 1986.

2. <u>Taxpayer's identity</u> -- The claimants are William E. and
Jane M. Citizen, SSN: 000-00-0000, whose address is, (address, city,
state, zip).

Note: These facts are hypothetical. You must use your own facts.

3. <u>Original return</u> -- The original return was timely filed
with the Internal Revenue Service Center in (city, state). A
subsequent examination of the return led to the assessment of
additional taxes on (date). All of the additional taxes, with
interest and penalties, have been paid.

4. <u>Revised income and deductions, and payment credits</u> -- The
claim for refund herein is based upon the following revision of
claimant's income and deductions for the year in question:

    a. The examination assessment was based upon the
allegation that taxpayers had taxable income in the amount of

CLAIM FOR REFUND, PAGE 1

$81,069.13. The correct amount of taxable income which the claimants had is $75,009.32.

b. The examination assessment allowed no deductions or exemptions of any kind against the alleged income. The correct amount of deductions and exemptions are:

1) Schedule A deductions of $10,662.84;

2) Schedule D loss of $261.44; and

3) A total of four exemptions, two for taxpayers and one each for two dependent children.

4) Taxpayers are also entitled to the married filing jointly tax rates.

c. The full amount of the assessed liability, interest and penalties was satisfied on September 24, 1988. Claimants paid a total of $54,832.77 against the assessment.

5. Computation of overpayment -- The amount to be refunded to taxpayers is:

a. Amount paid - erroneous assessment = $54,832.77

b. Correct tax liability   = $ 0.00

c. Amount to be refunded
   Together with interest   = $54,832.77

The figure of $54,832.77, or such greater amount as is allowed by law, claimed as the refund amount includes interest and penalties paid by the taxpayers as of the date mentioned in ¶4c.

6. Explanation in tax computation -- The following is an explanation of the changes accounting for the overpayment herein demanded.

a. Income. The erroneous tax assessment was computed on the basis of a misunderstanding of the taxpayers' correct income and deductions. The taxpayers' correct gross income is $89,672.16. This is determined by reference to the taxpayers' form W-2, showing $87,306.88 in wages, $206 in Schedule C income, $2,290 in Schedule E income, and a $130.72 Schedule F loss.

      b. <u>Exemptions</u>. Taxpayers have four exemptions to which they are entitled, having paid at least 51% of the support of such number of persons.

      c. <u>Filing Status</u>. They are entitled to the married filing jointly tax rates, having been married and living together during the year in question.

      d. <u>Deductions</u>. They have excess Schedule A deductions of $10,662.84 as shown in the attached Schedule A.

Upon computation of these factors, taxpayers' correct tax liability for the year in question is $27,783.03, all of which was paid with the return when it was filed. They are therefore entitled to a refund of all additional amounts paid, such amounts being $54,832.77, or such greater amount as is lawfully refundable.

7. <u>Schedules</u> -- Attached hereto and made a part hereof for the purposes of fully apprising the Commissioner of the nature of this claim, and the grounds upon which it is based, find Form 1040, for the year 1986, together with accompanying schedules. Such form and attachments demonstrate, in addition to the above explanation, how the herein demanded refund is computed. (Return not attached for purposes of this illustration.)

8. <u>Attestation</u> -- Under penalty of perjury, the undersigned, William E. and Jane M. Citizen, hereby declare that the facts contained in this claim for refund, together with the accompanying forms and schedules, are true and correct to the best of their knowledge and belief.

      Dated:

_____

William E. Citizen

_____

      Jane M. Citizen

claim has been denied for one or more of the reasons shown. Exhibit 5-5 is an example of Letter 916.

The receipt of a letter denying your claim for refund creates the right to file a lawsuit for refund in the United States District Court.

Ultimate Defense Weapon Number Three

The Lawsuit For Refund

Thankfully, the IRS does not have the last word on whether your claim for refund should be granted. The letter of denial, Exhibit 5-5, constitutes a final administrative determination on the issue, and is a necessary prerequisite to the proceeding. However, the district court may override the IRS when the law and facts so justify.

Section 7442 of the Code establishes district court jurisdiction to determine suits for refund when all administrative procedures have been properly pursued and exhausted. The law states in part:

"No suit or proceeding shall be maintained in any court for the recovery of any internal revenue tax alleged to have been erroneously or illegally assessed or collected, or of any penalty claimed to have been excessive or in any manner wrongfully collected, *until* a claim for refund or credit has been duly filed with the Secretary, according to the provision of law in that regard, and the regulations of the Secretary established in pursuance thereof." (Emphasis added.)

After one has properly pursued the remedy of claim for refund, it is well-settled that §7422 does not permit the lawsuit for refund. However, as suggested by the next-to-the-last paragraph in the letter of denial (Exhibit 5-5) your right to file a lawsuit in the district court is, like all rights with the IRS, time-sensitive. The statute of limitations[36] provides that one *may not* commence a suit for refund *before the expiration of six months from the date the claim for refund is filed, or later* than two years after the date the claim for refund is denied. The six-month waiting period is required in order to provide the IRS with the opportunity to act upon the claim before the suit in court is initiated. If the IRS fails to act within the six-month period, or if the claim is denied, whichever occurs first, the two-year limitation period begins to run

from that date. Failure to adhere to these strict limitations will spell the end of your suit for refund.

Drafting the Complaint. The lawsuit for refund is commenced when a "complaint" is filed with the clerk of the district court.[37] The suit is filed with the clerk of the court serving the district in which you reside.[38] The statute creating the right to sue for refund[39] expressly provides that the sole defendant that may be named in the suit is the United States of America. Any other person or entity named in the suit will be dismissed.[40] From this we learn that the suit for refund under §7422 *is not* a viable means in which to proceed against a particular agent of the IRS. Other means must be used to accomplish that goal. These are discussed later in this manual.

The most important aspect of the complaint alleging entitlement to a refund is the fact that all grounds for refund alleged in the complaint must first be stated in the *claim for refund.* Any ground for refund presented in the complaint which was not first raised in the claim will usually be set aside by the court. In this respect, the complaint is merely a restatement of the claim, but structured in a manner which conforms to the Federal Rules of Civil Procedure.

The Rules of Civil Procedure present a requirement that three general elements must be set forth in the complaint.[41] They are:

1. A short, plain statement of the court's jurisdiction;

2. A short, plain statement of the claim showing that you are entitled to the relief you are seeking from the court; and,

3. A demand for the specific judgment you seek from the court.

In Chapter Two, under the heading, *Dropping a Bomb*, we discussed the mechanics of drafting a complaint, including an illustration of many points of importance. Let me state further, however, regarding this specific complaint, that your factual statement must establish that the jurisdictional prerequisites for the suit for refund are met. In this regard, you must state:

1. That you paid the tax in full pursuant to an assessment;

2. That a timely and proper claim for refund was submitted; and,

3. That the claim was either denied in whole or in part, or that six months have lapsed from the time the claim was filed and the IRS has failed to act.

One should always attach to his complaint as exhibits

---

36. Code §6532.
37. Rule 3, Federal Rules of Civil Procedure (FRCvP).
38. 28 USC §1402(a)(1).
39. Code §7422(f)(1).
40. Code §7422(f)(2).
41. Rule 8(a), FRCvP.

Exhibit 5-5: Letter of Denial

Internal Revenue Service
District Director

Department of the Treasury

Date: DEC 3 1 1987

Refund Claimed: 1978 – $64,947.88
                   1979 – $24,607.97
Kind of Tax: 1980 – $43,650.74
Income
Tax Period Ended: December 31, 1978
                      December 31, 1979
Person to Contact: December 31, 1980

Contact Telephone Number:

We have reviewed your claim for refund, but we cannot allow it for the reason checked below.

☐ It was received after the deadline for filing.

☐ It is based on your view that certain tax laws are unconstitutional; only the courts have authority to pass on such matters.

☐ As consideration in a previous settlement, you waived your right to claim the refund.

☐ This matter has already been settled under the terms of a Closing agreement we made for the tax period in question. (See section 7121 of the Internal Revenue Code.)

☐ This matter was disposed of by a final order of the United States Tax Court or other court.

☐ This matter was settled in your favor in an earlier determination of your liability.

This letter is your legal notice that we will not consider your claim.

If you want to bring suit or proceedings for the recovery of any tax, penalties, or other moneys for which this disallowance notice is issued, you may do so by filing such a suit with the United States District Court having jurisdiction, or the United States Court of Claims. The law permits you to do this within 2 years from the mailing date of this letter.

If you have any questions, please contact the person whose name and address are shown in the heading of this letter.

Thank you for your cooperation.

Sincerely yours,
District Director

316 N. Robert St., St. Paul, Minn 55101

Letter 916(DO) (Rev. 8-79)

copies of all relevant correspondence, including the claim for refund itself.[42] It is also worthy of notation that each of the grounds for relief set forth in the claim for refund should be restated in the complaint, each in a separate paragraph. In this manner, one can be sure that he will not *overlook* a ground which may be appropriate to plead, nor will he *include* an issue which has not previously been raised in the claim. Care must be taken to fully set out the grounds upon which the refund is sought.

Exhibit 5-6 is a sample Complaint for Refund. It contains the elements which we have been discussing and, as you will see, follows the general format for a complaint that we set out in Chapter Two.

Filing the Complaint. The complaint must be filed with the clerk of the court serving the district in which you reside. At the time of filing, the clerk will assign a number to your case, known as the case or file number. This number must be affixed to your complaint and included on all future filings. You must also pay a filing fee of approximately $75 and complete a Civil Cover Sheet. See Exhibit 2-3.

You are responsible to see that the complaint is served upon the United States. This requires that you obtain from the clerk and complete a Summons form if that task is not carried out by the clerk. See Exhibit 2-4. Service is accomplished by delivering the complaint to the defendant United States in accordance with the Rules of Procedure.[43] For more details, see Chapter Two, under the heading, *Service of Process.*

Prosecuting the Complaint for Refund

The most important consideration in submitting a complaint for refund is to realize that *you* have the burden to prove with evidence that you are entitled to a refund of the money paid. You must be prepared to present evidence to demonstrate that your factual allegations are correct and that your view of the law governing the subject matter is binding under the circumstances.

In this regard, you should consider using the discovery tools of the Federal rules to elicit from the government any financial information within its possession which may assist you in preparing your case for trial. In addition, you should give thought to issuing Requests for Admissions upon government counsel. As you will recall from our discussion in Chapter Two, this mechanism is a handy method of achieving admissions from the government concerning important factual assertions made within your complaint. Every fact to which the government concedes is one less matter which you must prove later.

On the other hand, because of the nature of your case, you cannot expect to carry the day solely with material obtained from the government's file cabinet. You are, or should be, the one in possession of evidence regarding your financial affairs and must be prepared to present this evidence. However, if the complaint revolves around, for example, an "arbitrary notice," your discovery requests for facts supporting the IRS' demand for payment will prove quite interesting—to say the least! Without a doubt, discovery is very helpful. If for no other reason, one can employ it to pin down the government's attorney as to *his* position regarding the facts of the case.

At the same time, be mindful of the fact that discovery is available to the government as well. No doubt, the Justice Department attorney handling the case will make every effort to discover your evidence, hoping to have your case dismissed before you are able to obtain a favorable judgment.

Right to a Trial by Jury

The Seventh Amendment ensures the right of a jury trial in cases where the amount in controversy exceeds $20. This right, while seriously erroded by the federal courts, is intact where refund suits in the district court are concerned.[44] The right of jury, in order to be protected and enjoyed, must be claimed under the terms of Rule 38, FRCvP. See Chapter Two, under the heading, *The Right to Trial by Jury.*

Motion for Summary Judgment

A motion for summary judgment is governed in accordance with Rule 56 FRCvP. One must always assume in tax litigation that the government *will,* at some point, submit a motion for summary judgment. As we have alredy discussed, a motion for summary judgment is only appropriate after all the facts material to a just resolution of the case are resolved. If facts material to the case are unresolved at the time the

---

42. Rule 10(c), FRCvP.

43. See Rule 4(d)(4), FRCvP.

44. *Calhoun v. United States,* 591 F.2d 1243 (9th Cir. 1978).

Exhibit 5-6: Complaint for Refund

UNITED STATE DISTRICT COURT
DISTRICT OF MINNESOTA
THIRD DIVISION

William E. and Jane M. Citizen,	)	
	)	
Plaintiffs,	)	Civil Case No. _____
	)	
vs.	)	JURY TRIAL DEMANDED
	)	
The United States of America,	)	
	)	
Defendant.	)	

COMPLAINT FOR REFUND OF TAXES ERRONEOUSLY PAID

NATURE OF THE ACTION

1. This is a civil action for refund of taxes erroneously paid to the Internal Revenue Service.

JURISDICTION

2. The Jurisdiction of the court is invoked under the authority of 26 USC §§7422, and 6532, establishing jurisdiction in refund suits.

3. This case involves the internal revenue laws of the United States and hence, raises a federal question.

VENUE

4. Venue within the above-named court is proper according to 28 USC §1402, in that the United States is a defendant in this case.

PARTIES

5. The Plaintiffs, William E. and Jane M. Citizen, (address, city, state, zip, SSN) are properly named as the Plaintiffs to this action as the unjust assessment was made against them and they paid

COMPLAINT FOR REFUND, PAGE 1

the tax.

6. The Defendant, United States of America, through its agency the Internal Revenue Service, caused the unjust tax to be assessed and collected against the Plaintiffs.

BACKGROUND FACTS

7. The Plaintiffs filed a timely US Individual Income Tax Return, Form 1040 for the year 1986, with the Internal Revenue Service. The return was filed with the IRS Service Center at (city, state).

8. The return was later examined by agents of the IRS, after which all of Plaintiffs' deductions and exemptions were disallowed. In addition, agents of the IRS arbitrarily increased the gross income of the Plaintiffs for the year 1986.

9. On August 30, 1988, the IRS assessed an additional tax, with penalties and interest against the Plaintiffs. That assessment was based upon the afore-mentioned examination.

10. The full amount of the assessed liability, interest and penalties was satisfied on September 24, 1988. Plaintiffs paid a total of $54,832.77 against the assessment to the IRS at (city, state).

11. On January 10th, 1989, subsequent to paying the tax in full, the Plaintiffs filed a timely Claim for Refund of all taxes, penalties and interest paid. A true and correct copy of such Claim, with its exhibits, is attached to this Complaint and marked Exhibit A.

12. On June 15th, 1989, the Internal Revenue Service issued a letter denying the claim for refund in full. A copy of said letter is

COMPLAINT FOR REFUND, PAGE 2

attached hereto and marked Exhibit B.

13.   Said denial constitutes a final administrative determination adverse to the Plaintiffs. This complaint for refund is filed in a timely manner according to 26 USC §6532.

14.   Plaintiffs properly pursued and exhausted all available administrative remedies in connection with the overpayment, yet the IRS has failed and refused to refund the money lawfully due.

15.   The Claim for Refund, and hence this suit for refund, is based upon the following grounds:

a.   The original erroneous tax liability was computed on the basis of a misunderstanding of the taxpayers' correct income and deductions. The taxpayers' correct gross income is $89,672.16. This is determined by reference to the taxpayers' form W-2, showing $87,306.88 in wages, $206 in Schedule C income, $2,290 in Schedule E income, and a $130.72 Schedule F loss;

b.   Taxpayers are entitled to claim four exemptions from income, having paid at least 51% of the support of such number of persons;

c.   They are entitled to the married filing jointly tax rates, having been married and living together during the year in question;

d.   They have excess Schedule A deductions of $10,662.84 as shown on the Form 1040, Schedule A, attached hereto and made a part hereof.

16.   Upon computation of these factors, taxpayers' correct tax liability for the year in question is $27,783.03, all of which was

COMPLAINT FOR REFUND, PAGE 3

paid with the return when it was filed.

17.   They are therefore entitled to a refund of all additional amounts paid, including penalties, such amounts being $54,832.77, or such greater amount as is lawfully refundable.

COUNT I

18.   Plaintiffs restate all of the allegations contained in paragraphs 1-17 as though fully set forth here in Count I.

19.   Plaintiffs made erroneous payments of taxes, interest and penalties to the Internal Revenue Service for tax year 1986.

20.   Said payments were made in satisfaction of an erroneous tax assessment made against Plaintiffs by the Internal Revenue Service.

21.   Said assessment of taxes, including all interest and penalties, has been paid in full.

22.   Plaintiffs filed a timely and accurate Claim for Refund of all taxes, penalties and interest, but said claim was denied by the IRS.

23.   Plaintiffs have in all things pursued and exhausted their administrative remedies in connection with such overpayment, but the IRS continues to fail and refuse to refund such overpayment.

24.   Plaintiffs are entitled to a refund of the overpayment, such amount being $54,832.77, or such greater amount as is allowed by the law, including interest on the overpayment according to law.

DAMAGES

25.   The Plaintiffs have been deprived of the use and enjoyment of their lawful money in the amount of $54,832.77, since

COMPLAINT FOR REFUND, PAGE 4

that money was paid to the IRS.

26. The Plaintiffs have suffered the loss of interest on said amount since the time it was paid to the IRS.

<u>REQUEST FOR RELIEF</u>

WHEREFORE, based upon all of the foregoing, Plaintiffs request judgment against the Defendant as follows:

1. That the Defendant be ordered to refund to the Plaintiffs the amount of $54,832.77, plus statutory interest, or such greater amount as is allowed by law.

2. That the Defendant be ordered to pay all of the Plaintiffs' costs and disbursements incurred in connection with prosecuting this refund claim.

3. For such other relief as the court may deem just.

Dated:

_____   _____
William E. Citizen   Jane M. Citizen

Address
City, State, Zip
Area Code and Phone Number

motion is submitted, summary judgment is not appropriate.[45]

I am not suggesting that it is always undesirable to dispose of a case through the vehicle of summary judgment. Under the appropriate circumstances, it may well be the most effective way in which to resolve the dispute. However, *you* should choose the battleground, *not* the enemy. When the government raises the motion, it is suggested that *it* is entitled to judgment as a matter of law, and that *your* claim should be denied. If the motion is granted, you would of course lose the case. Thus, in order to prevent the government from obtaining relief on its motion, you must demonstrate to the court that facts material to the issues in the case have yet to be resolved.

This is done through the submission of affidavits and any relevant discovery material obtained during the course of the proceedings. Failure to respond to the motion in that manner will usually mean that the motion will be granted. Rule 56, FRCvP, is explicit in this regard. The party *opposing* the motion must demonstrate the existence of facts which have yet to be resolved. Let me provide an example. Suppose your complaint alleges that the IRS acted improperly in disallowing a deduction of $5,000 which you claim was made to charity. Whether or not you made the contribution of $5,000 to the charity claimed is a question of fact. That question of fact is material to the issue of whether you are entitled to the refund you claim. The question of fact must be resolved, one way or the other, before the court can correctly apply the law and arrive at a just decision. Therefore, to demonstrate that this material issue of facts remain in dispute, you must submit an affidavit containing affirmative statements to the effect that such funds were donated as claimed on the return.

In opposition to a motion for summary judgment, you may not rest upon the mere allegations of your complaint. Affidavits which are direct and pointed in their statements of fact must be submitted. If you prevail on the government's motion for summary judgment, your right to trial on the merits are assured.

Negotiating a Settlement

Most civil cases are settled without the need of a trial. Suits for refund are frequently settled on this basis as well. However, it should be noted that the Justice Department will usually *not* initiate settlement negotiations. That is left to the citizen. Therefore, if you are serious about pursuing settlement negotiations, you should be the one to open the door.

At the same time, there are no rigid government standards which must be met before a settlement will be considered. The only existing standard is quite simple, "Can a mutually satisfactory agreement be reached?" If so, the case will be disposed of through the "stipulation," or agreement, process.

While the manner in which one arrives at his proposed settlement is as varied as the circumstances, the most common starting point in refund litigation is the "percentage basis." Under this procedure, one proposes a cash settlement amounting to a percentage of that claimed in the complaint. If a $15,000 refund is demanded in the complaint, a 50 percent cash settlement would mean that $7,500 is paid to the citizen in settlement of all issues.

In transmitting the terms of the settlement to the government's attorney, you should be careful to include all conditions under which you will settle the case, including:

1. Dismissal of your case;

2. An agreement that the case is resolved as to all issues;

3. The specific amount you expect in return for dismissal;

4. The extent to which you will expect interest to be included as part of the settlement.

In some cases, settlement with the Justice Department is effectuated through the offer in compromise.[46] If the Justice Department seeks settlement through this vehicle, you should be prepared to submit the appropriate documents on the IRS' forms. Care must be taken to be sure that the final version of the documents comports with the terms of the settlement as they were agreed upon.

The Trial

If settlement cannot be reached, the case will be submitted for trial. As I have already stated, you are legally saddled with the burden of proof on the issues in the complaint. Therefore, you must be prepared to go forward with evidence to prove your claims to the satisfaction of the court or jury. In this regard, all evidence you possess and have obtained through the discovery process should, if relevant to the issues, be presented to the court.

---

45. *Belt Railway of Chicago v. United States,* 76-1 USTC Paragraph 168 (DC Il. 1976), aff'd 567 F.2d 717 (7th Cir. 1978).

46. See *How Anyone Can Negotiate With The IRS—And WIN!,* Chpter Five.

In any trial, all evidence is submitted through the testimonoy of witnesses. You may testify on your own behalf or call such witnesses whose testimony will be helpful to resolve the facts. After the evidence is submitted, the court or jury will determine the facts of the case and render judgment accordingly. A written instrument will be issued to the parties at the conclusion of the trial. This instrument will reflect the judgment of the court and constitutes the final order in the case.

Exhibit 5-7 is a flow chart depicting the progression of a refund case through the district court.

Conclusion

The cliche "better late than never" was never more appropriate than where a citizen failed initially to exercise all his rights under the law to prevent paying taxes that were not due and owing. It is never too late to learn your rights. Fortunately in many cases, it is also not too late to recover what you once thought was lost. If this information gives you hope of recovering what was already paid, it is now your obligation to yourself, as well as to other citizens, to make this claim. Thus, you do your part to end IRS abuse and to break the cycle of lawlessness.

Exhibit 5-7
Flowchart of Suit for Refund Procedure

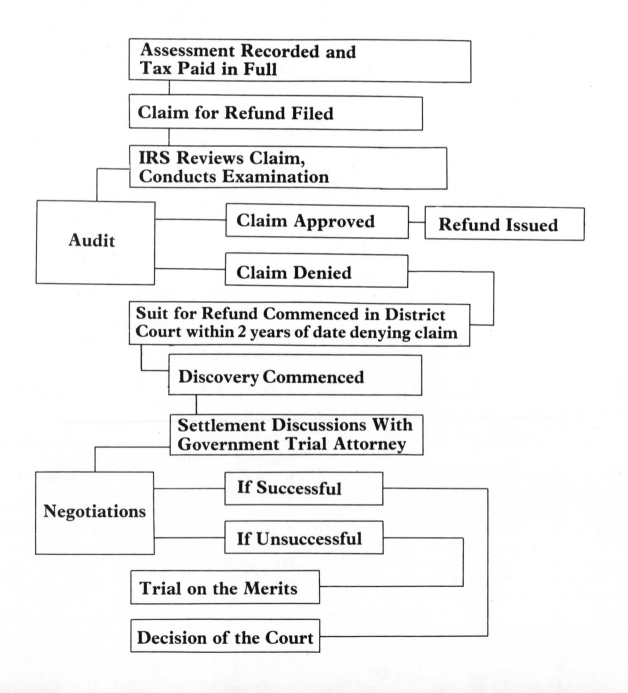

CHAPTER

Barricade Your Business

For many citizens, their business is their life. Small businesses comprise the majority of the employers in the United States, providing needed income and resultant security to tens of millions of people. At the same time, the government has heaped incredible demands upon businesses of all sizes. Costs ranging everywhere from minimum wage requirements to mandatory social security "contributions" for all employees translate to billions of dollars each and every year. For large corporations, these costs are merely passed on to the consumer. However, to the small business proprietor unable to effectively shift the burden of the expense, these millstones often spell the difference between success and failure in the business world.

All too often, failure materializes in the person of the IRS. Precipitated by an inability to pay federal employment tax obligations, the IRS closes the doors on innumerable small business operations. Over the years, my experience with small businesses has led me to the conclusion that the employment tax nemesis must be understood at the outset if the destruction it can cause is ever to be avoided. With an understanding of just how the federal employment tax scheme operates, we may then examine methods of avoiding problems entirely, and of solving those that presently exist.

Understanding Employment Taxes

When one agrees to hire a worker, pay him a salary and provide him with steady income, several obligations, in addition to the payment of the wage, attach to the relationship. First of all, the employer must withhold from the employee's pay a certain amount of money to cover the *employee's* federal income tax liability. The amount is determined by reference to a Form W-4 which is filed by the employee with his employer. The W-4 contains a declaration as to the number of withholding allowances to which the employee is entitled. Based upon that number, the correct amount of federal income tax is computed and withheld from the employee's pay. That amount must then be paid by the employer to the IRS.[1]

---

1. Code §§3401, 3402 and 3403.

In addition to income taxes withheld directly from the employee, the employer is required to withhold and pay in the same manner, the *employee's* social security tax (FICA) liability.[2] In 1989, every employee is required to pay social security taxes in the amount of 7.51 percent of wages paid to him. The tax is assessed against the first $48,000 of income earned.[3]

The combination of the *employee's* withheld federal *income* and *social security taxes* are referred to by the IRS and the Courts as "trust taxes." The reason for this designation is simply that the money *belongs* to the employee, since it is withheld directly from his pay. When the money is withheld by the employer, he becomes a "fiduciary" acting on behalf of the employee. A "trust" relationship is thereby created. In that relationship, the employer is legally responsible to accurately withhold, account for and pay over these "trust" amounts to the IRS on the employee's behalf.[4]

In addition to "trust taxes" the employer is responsible for other taxes imposed upon the payment of wages. First of all, the employer is required to *match* the employee's social security tax payments. The employee pays 7.51 percent on his wages, and the *employer* must also pay 7.51 percent on those same wages.[5] Thus, if an employer pays an employee $10 per hour, the employer will be liable to the IRS in the amount of 75 cents for each hour the employee performs services. This constitutes the *employer's* share of the social security tax obligation.

Employment tax liabilities do not end there. The Federal Unemployment Tax Act (FUTA) imposes on employers an *additional* tax based upon the total amount of wages paid during the year.[6] In 1989, each employer is required to pay to the IRS the amount of 6.2 percent of the total wages paid to his employees.[7]

As a result of FICA and FUTA tax obligations, employers are required to pay total taxes to the government equal to 13.71 percent of wages paid to employees. This is *not* money withheld from the employees and paid over by the employer. This is money which comes out of the *employer's pocket.* Consequently, these *are not* considered "trust taxes."

Both the employee's share and the employer's share of FICA taxes are reported on Form 941, Employer's Quarterly Federal Tax Return. That return is required to be filed no later than one month after the close of the calendar quarter. For example, a Form 941 for the first

quarter of 1989 is due to be filed no later than April 30th, 1989. The FUTA tax is reported on Form 940, Employer's Annual Federal Unemployment Tax Return. That return is filed at the close of the calendar year. It must be submitted within 30 days of that time. Thus, Form 940 for the year 1989 is due on or before January 31, 1990.

All taxes just described represent *federal* employment tax liabilities only. Virtually each state in the nation also imposes employment tax liabilities akin to those we have just examined. For example, most states assess an unemployment tax against the wages paid to employees[8] and also extract workmen's compensation insurance from the employer.

At this juncture, I wish to caution the reader that I have no designs to debate here the relative merits of any of the employment taxes just identified. My purpose is merely to examine the nature of the taxes imposed against an employer by reason of his engaging workers on his behalf. For the moment, the reader will draw such inferences and conclusions regarding the propriety of such assessments independent of my personal observations.

How The Problems Begin

Having discovered the various taxes for which the average business is responsible, we will now examine the principle reasons for the demise of small businesses in light of these tax obligations.

The Cash Flow Crisis. Businesses under market or other economic pressures often experience a cash flow crisis. While the business may remain profitable in the long-term, it is difficult, for a variety of reasons, to meet its short-term obligations. When this occurs, some business owners begin to work from what is referred to as a "net payroll" arrangement.

A "net payroll" arrangement functions in this manner: the employer determines the amount of the "gross pay" owed to his employees, based upon their hourly rate and the number of hours worked. Then, the employer determines the amount of money which is to be withheld from the employee's pay according to all federal and state employment tax laws.

Solely for purposes of example, we shall assume that such amount is 30 percent of the employee's gross pay.

---

2. Code §3102(a).

3. Code §3101.

4. Code §3403.

5. Code §3111(a).

6. Code §3301.

7. This amount is determined *without* reference to any credits to which one may be entitled by virtue of paying into any state unemployment fund.

8. The federal law allows a credit against federal unemployment tax obligations when similar payments are made to a state. See Code §3302.

Further assuming that the employee's gross pay is $1,000 per pay period, his "take home" share, after all deductions are computed, is $700. A check is written to the employee for this "net amount" of $700. At the same time, the employer is responsible to retain possession of the remaining $300 (plus the employer's share), which represents all taxes due on the gross payroll. The money is required to be paid to the IRS via Form 941 on a quarterly basis.

However, in light of the cash flow crisis constricting the operations of the business, one of two events occurs. Either the $300 *never existed,* in which case the employer is prevented from paying the money to the IRS for that reason, or the $300 is used in some measure to pay the operating expenses of the business. Persons in the midst of this crisis commonly look ahead to a time in the "near future" when a "big score" or a "certain loan" will produce sufficient funds to satisfy all accumulating tax obligations.

In any event, the delinquency creates a problem of great magnitude. The difficulty is intensified when, as is typical, the employer files his quarterly payroll tax returns, Forms 941, but *does not* transmit the funds to the IRS as required. As we now know, whenever a return is filed, an assessment is born. The presence of an assessment, we also know, enables the IRS to begin immediate collection action. When the subject is employment taxes, the IRS is particularly aggressive due to the fact that the unpaid liabilities represent "trust taxes." The IRS takes a most stern view of the employer who, in its judgment, has taken money which does not belong to him and expended that money in his business.

More commonly, however, the money never existed, as opposed to having been used to fund the operating expenses of the business. Nevertheless, the IRS' attitude is to pursue collection action to its fullest potential. Often this results in the business making enormous monthly installment payments against the debt, during which time revenue officers closely monitor the business to be sure that it remains in compliance as to all later quarters. In the event the business is unable to fund sufficient installment payments or defaults on such payments, the IRS will proceed to close the business without much delay.

The Reclassification of Workers. The second most common source of employment tax difficulty arises when the IRS, after conducting an "employment tax audit," redesignates the company's workers, branding them "employees" rather than independent contractors. After doing so, it will assess employment taxes against the business, with interest and penalties included, on a retroactive basis.

Allow me to explain what is meant by "reclassifying workers." It is not uncommon for many industries to function through the use of "independent contractors" or "sub contractors" rather than employees. An independent contractor is nothing more than a self-employed person who, under the terms of a contract agreement, consents to perform services for another. When one has contracted with an independent, self-employed person to perform services on his behalf, the "contractor" is not required under federal law to withhold and pay to the IRS any of the employment taxes we discussed. Since the independent worker is "self-employed" in his own right, his social security taxes are paid by him on the basis of the extent to which his business is profitable during the year.[9]

The "contractor" is, however, required to transmit to the IRS a Form 1099, Information Return, at the end of the year.[10] The Form 1099 is used to inform the IRS that non-employee compensation has been paid to a given person during the course of the year. The form is required when payments in excess of $600 are paid to any one person during a particular calendar year.[11]

Employment tax audits are conducted by the IRS on a regular basis. They are conducted to ensure that employers are in compliance with all withholding regulations. They are also conducted vis-a-vis contractors for the purpose of verifying that the independent contractors with whom they do business are in fact independent contractors under the law, not merely employees masquerading as independent contractors. The most common problem associated with the independent contractor relationship is the risk that the IRS will "reclassify" the independent contractors, ruling that such workers are in fact *employees.* In this event, all the employment taxes which should have been paid on those employees are assessed against the contractor. When this occurs, immediate efforts to collect the employment taxes, with interest and penalties, are undertaken.

These types of audits are conducted under a new program created by the IRS for the sole purpose of detecting improper "independent contractors." The program is the Employment Tax Examination Program (ETEP). Audits under the program are conducted by Revenue Officers, not Revenue Agents. You may recall that the principal function of the Revenue Officer is to *collect* tax assessments, while the primary function of the Examination Division is to conduct audits.

---

9. See Schedule C and Schedule SE, used with Form 1040.

10. Code §§6041 and 6041A.

11. Ibid.

However, under the ETEP, a hybrid has been created. Designated Revenue Officers working with the ETEP are referred to as Revenue Officer Examiners. These Revenue Officer Examiners, acting on leads usually from within the Collection Division, conduct employment tax examinations. The purpose is to determine whether a given business is improperly classifying its workers as independent contractors, rather than as employees, solely for the purpose of avoiding employment tax obligations.

The 100 Percent Penalty. Another area of difficulty with employment tax obligations arises when the business is a corporation. While it is true that the two situations discussed above could very easily apply to small corporations as well as sole-proprietorships, the problem of the 100 percent penalty will materialize only when the business in question is a corporation.

Section 6672 of the Internal Revenue Code creates the so-called "100 percent penalty." It is referred to as the 100 percent penalty because it represents 100 percent of the "trust fund" taxes which were required to be paid over to the IRS by the corporation, but which *were not* paid over. The statute authorizes the IRS to assess against "any person required to collect, truthfully account for, and pay over" 100 percent of the trust taxes which were required to be withheld, accounted for and paid over to the IRS, but which, for whatever reason, were not.

Whenever a corporation has unpaid employment tax debts, the IRS will seek to satisfy those debts from the *corporate assets.* However, where the corporation either has no tangible assets or is bankrupt or otherwise defunct, the IRS will undertake to locate an *individual* against whom the assessment of the 100 percent penalty may be made.

The coordination of 100 percent penalty cases is handled by the Collection Division. A Revenue Officer will generally lead the charge for the collection of the tax, first from any available corporate assets, and next from one or more individuals alleged to be the "responsible person." After conducting interviews and investigating any possible evidence as to who may have been responsible for the corporation's failure to pay its employment tax debts, the Revenue Officer will propose the assessment against one or more persons.

The proposal comes in the form of IRS Form 2751. That document, discussed at length in *How Anyone Can Negotiate With The IRS—And WIN!,* sets forth the amount of tax, referred to as the 100 percent penalty, which is to be assessed. It also states the name of the individual against whom the tax is to be assessed. Moreover, the form contains a "waiver" provision which is most significant. If signed by the individual as requested by the Revenue Officer, that person *agrees* that the penalty may be assessed against him. By signing it, he waives his right to request an abatement of the penalty. Together with Form 2751, a notice is generally mailed stating that the penalty is proposed and that you have either 10 days or 30 days (depending upon the particular notice) in which to make an appeal to the Appeals Division.

If no appeal is taken, or if the appeal is unsuccessful, the tax is assessed and collection is undertaken. In this manner, the employment tax obligations of a financially unsound corporation become the problem of the corporate officers or employees who are alleged to be responsible for failing to pay the taxes in the first place.

How the Problem is Compounded

We examined three major reasons why businesses, and sometimes individuals, encounter employment tax difficulty. Now we shall answer the question, "Why do employment tax difficulties so often escalate into the worst possible scenario, where the IRS seizes the assets of the business or individual in question?"

The answer to the question is simple. Employment tax assessments, unlike income tax assessments, *are not* subject to the deficiency procedures we reviewed at length in the prior chapters of this manual. Previously, we discussed the need for the IRS to mail a notice of deficiency to the citizen prior to making an assessment of additional income tax obligations. In the absence of a proper notice of deficiency, we demonstrated that any subsequent assessment was patently invalid.

However, this binding rule of law has no application to the discussion of employment tax liabilities. Employment tax obligations are "assessable taxes,"[12] meaning simply that the deficiency procedures applicable to income tax debts are of no moment when it comes to employment tax debts. Furthermore, the United States Tax Court has no jurisdiction to entertain questions relating to employment tax assessments or proposed assessments.[13]

Because of this extreme limitation on the rights of the citizen in this area, the IRS appears to maneuver within the realm of the employment tax battlefield *unfettered* by any statutory restrictions. Despite the illusion of invincibility in this particular, the citizen does enjoy

---

12. Code §§6205 and 6672.
13. Code §§6213(a) and 6672.

rights which, if exercised properly and in a timely manner, can greatly reduce, and in some cases eliminate the hardships created by assessed employment tax liabilities.

The Right to Review Employment Tax Assessments

Notwithstanding the fact that employment taxes are assessable without regard to the deficiency procedures applicable to income tax assessments, such assessments are nevertheless reviewable. In a word, the process of review is accomplished through the vehicle of the Claim for Refund, which we addressed in much detail in Chapter Five.

In this chapter, we will not "re-invent the wheel" already forged in Chapter Five. However, we will set forth the specific circumstances under which claim for refund procedures may be used in the employment tax context, and the manner in which one will set out to employ that remedy.

When to Seek Review of Employment Tax Assessments

Proposed employment tax assessments are transmitted to the citizen in much the same manner as are income tax assessments. While one will *not* receive a notice of deficiency, he will be informed that assessments are proposed and will be given an opportunity to appeal the proposed assessment.

Analyzing the Examination Report. In Exhibit 6-1, I have presented the standard 30-day form letter the IRS utilizes to transmit the examination report concerning employment tax assessments. You will probably note that the form very closely resembles the one used by the Examination Division to transmit the news of a proposed income tax deficiency. However, substantial differences are revealed in the examination report.

The letter (Exhibit 6-1) explains that there is a right of appeal with regard to the proposed assessment. The right of appeal is in reference to the administrative appeal taken to the Appeals Division of the IRS. This is carried out by submitting a written protest letter within 30 days, explaining why the proposed assessment is improper in light of the facts and circumstances of the

case.[14] If no written protest is filed within that time, the tax will be assessed. A notice of deficiency will not be mailed.

At the time the tax is proposed, the IRS will ask you to sign a Form 2504. That Form is a consent to an immediate assessment of the proposed tax. If signed, that form will permit the IRS to begin collection action immediately. If left unsigned, the assessment will generally not be made until the Appeals Division is given an opportunity to review the matter more thoroughly.

Business owners should be aware of the fact that the letter displayed in Exhibit 6-1, and the accompanying examination report is used only if no employment tax returns were filed by the business during the periods under consideration. If, for example, the business functioned through independent contractors rather than employees and the IRS reclassifies those workers, the findings of the audit will be transmitted via Exhibit 6-1. However, if employment tax returns were filed but the tax was not paid, the return itself creates the assessment.

Under the latter circumstance, no further administrative action by the IRS is necessary to enable it to lawfully collect the tax. In addition to demanding payment of the taxes shown due on the return, the IRS will include a host of penalties. Penalties are *always* subject to review and abatement provided the citizen is able to present sufficient facts justifying an abatement. I have adopted the position that one should request an abatement of penalties as a matter of course when presented with any collection problem.[15]

As part of the examination report, the IRS will transmit Form 4666, *Summary of Employment Tax Examination.* That form relates in summary fashion the liability for employment taxes which the IRS believes is appropriate. See Exhibit 6-2. One will also receive IRS Form 4667, *Audit Changes-Federal Unemployment Tax.* That form communicates specifically the manner in which the tax under the FUTA, required to be paid via Form 940, was computed. (See Exhibit 6-3.) The next form which will be mailed as part of the examination report is Form 4668, *Employment Tax Examination Changes Report.* (See Exhibit 6-4.) That form relates to the FICA and withheld income taxes required to be reported on Form 941. Together, these forms paint the picture of the precise *amount* of employment taxes the IRS believes to be due for the periods in question.

Not shown here, but also a part of the employment tax examination report will be Form 886-A, *Explanation*

---

14. See IRS Publication 5 which discusses the right of appeal and the preparation of written protests. For more information, see *The Naked Truth,* WINNING Publications, 1986, pages 70 and 71.

15. See Chapter Five, under the subheading, *Recovering or Cancelling Penalties.*

Exhibit 6-2: IRS Form 4666

Department of the Treasury - Internal Revenue Service

Form 4666 (Rev. 8-76)

Summary of Employment Tax Examination

Name and Address of Employer

Employer Identification Number:

Date of Report: 1-4-85

Type of Report

[X] Delinquent tax (Return not filed)

[ ] Increase (Decrease) in tax (Return filed)

[ ] Agreed (This report is subject to review and you will be notified by the District Director when it is accepted)

[X] Unagreed

Following is a summary of the results of my examination of your returns as shown on the attached pages of this report.

a Calendar Year	b Return Form Number	c Delinquent Tax Increase (Decrease) in Tax	d Penalty Code Section	d Penalty Amount	e Total	Page Number of Report
1980	940	938|20	6653(b)	469|35	1,454|91	
			6656	46|94		
1980	941	8906|63	6656(b)	4453|33	13,444|58	
			6656	84|72		
1981	940	845|52	6653(b)	422|72	1,310|52	
			6656	42|28		
1981	941	12,409|72	6653(b)	6204|87	18,738|51	
			6656	123|72		
1982	940	989|07	6653(b)	494|59	1,533|06	
			6656	49|45		
1982	941	12,116|94	6653(b)	6,058|49	18,296|94	
			6656	121|53		
1983	940	665|48	6656	323|74	1,031|49	
			6656	33|27		
1983	941	6,350|62	6653(b)	3,175|31	9589|62	
			6656	63|69		
Total		43,222|68		22,177|07	65,399|75	

Other Information

Examining Officer's Signature

District

Form **4666** (Rev. 8-76)

☆ U.S. GOVERNMENT PRINTING OFFICE: 1977—720.104/3308 2-1

Exhibit 6-1: 30-day Letter

Internal Revenue Service
District Director

Department of the Treasury

Date: **JUL 08 1987**

In Reply Refer to:

Person to Contact:

Contact Telephone Number:
(313)   (not toll free)
Tax Year Ended and Deficiency/
Overassessments:

See Report

Ladies/Gentlemen:

We have enclosed a copy of our examination report explaining why we believe an adjustment of your tax liability is necessary.

If you accept our findings, please sign and return the enclosed agreement or waiver form. If additional tax is due, you may want to pay it now. If so, please follow the instructions in the enclosed Publication 5.

If you do not accept our findings, you may request a conference with our Office of Regional Director of Appeals. Most cases considered at that level are settled satisfactorily. If the proposed increase or decrease in tax is $2,500 or less, a written protest is unnecessary. You may want to send us, with your conference request, a written statement outlining your position. If the proposed increase or decrease in tax is more than $2,500, please submit a written protest, in accordance with the enclosed Publication 5, so that a conference can be arranged. Publication 5 also explains your appeal rights. If you request an Appeals conference, please send your written statement or protest to the District Director, who will forward it to the appropriate Appeals Office. An envelope is enclosed for your convenience. You will be contacted so that an appointment can be scheduled with Appeals.

If we don't hear from you within 30 days, we will have to process your case on the basis of the adjustments shown in the examination report.

If you have any questions, please contact the person whose name and telephone number are shown above.

Thank you for your cooperation.

Sincerely yours,

District Director

Enclosures:
Examination Report
Agreement or Waiver Form
Publication 5
Notice 609
Envelope

P.O. Box 32500, Stop 16, Detroit, MI 48232

Letter 950(DO) (Rev. 1-32)

Exhibit 6-4: IRS Form 4668

Form 4668 (Rev. January 1986)	Department of the Treasury — Internal Revenue Service Employment Tax Examination Changes Report					Page 1 of 1 Page

		Return Form No. 941
Employer Identification No.		Calendar Year 198?
		Last quarter of this examination 3-93

Name and Address of Employer

Total tax plus penalty, or (decrease) in tax $ 18,738.51

( ) Agreed (It is understood that this report is subject to acceptance by the District Director)
(X) Unagreed

Examination discussed with (Name and title)

	(a) Applicable Rate	(b) 1st Quarter	(c) 2nd Quarter	(d) 3rd Quarter	(e) 4th Quarter
1. Social security wage adjustment subject to tax under IRC 3101 & 3111 (IRS Ref. .004)	13.3	10,946.20	12,057.30	8,931.00	5,299.95
2. Social security wage adjustment subject to tax under IRC 3509 (IRS Ref. .004)	N/A				N/A
3. Social security tip adjustment subject to tax under IRC 3101 (IRS Ref. .005)	N/A				N/A
4. Income tax withholding wage adjustment subject to tax under IRC 3402	20.0	10,972.20	12,057.20	8,934.00	5299.95
5. Income tax withholding wage adjustment subject to tax under IRC 3509	N/A				N/A
6.					
7. Adjustment to social security tax	N/A				N/A
8. Adjustment to income tax withholding	N/A				N/A
9. Total social security tax (IRS Ref. .007) (Line 1 x rate) + (Line 2 x rate) + (Line 3 x rate) plus/minus Line 6		1,459.93	1,603.84	1,187.22	704.89
10. Total income tax withholding (IRS Ref. .003) (Line 4 x rate) + (Line 5 x rate) plus/minus Line 7		2,195.24	2,411.96	1,786.20	1,059.99
11. Delinquent tax or increase (decrease) in tax (Line 8+9)		3,655.07	4,015.75	2,974.02	1,764.88
12. Penalty Code Section 6651	N/A				N/A
13. Penalty Code Section 6656 5% [Line 1 × Employer Share]		36.50	40.10	29.70	17.62
14. Penalty Code Section 6653(b) 50% Line 10		1,827.54	2,007.88	1,487.01	882.44
15. Maximum wages subject to tax abatement IRC 3402(d)					

Under IRC sections 6051 and 6071 and the regulations under those sections, you are required to furnish Form W-2 (Wage and Tax Statement) or Form W-2c (Statement of Corrected Income and Tax Amounts) to each of the __ employees whose wages were adjusted by this report. In addition, you are required to file the original of these statements by the last day of February __ employees whose wages provide penalties for failure to file and failure to furnish these statements by the required dates. Please file these statements with:

Internal Revenue Service
Chief, Examination Division
Attn: Examination Support and Processing

Examiner's signature		Group No.	District No.	Date

Form 4668 (Rev. 1-86)

Exhibit 6-3: IRS Form 4667

Form 4667 (SEPT. 1970)	DEPARTMENT OF THE TREASURY - INTERNAL REVENUE SERVICE AUDIT CHANGES – FEDERAL UNEMPLOYMENT TAX	PAGE __ OF __ PAGES

	CALENDAR YEAR 1981
NAME AND ADDRESS OF EMPLOYER	DATE OF REPORT 1-4-85

EMPLOYER IDENTIFICATION NUMBER	TYPE OF REPORT

TYPE OF REPORT
(X) DELINQUENT TAX (RETURN NOT FILED)
( ) ADDITIONAL TAX OR (OVERASSESSMENT) (RETURN FILED)
( ) AGREED (This report is subject to review and you will be notified by the District Director when it is accepted)
(X) UNAGREED

1. TOTAL TAXABLE WAGES AS REPORTED OR AS PREVIOUSLY CORRECTED	$	0
2. INCREASE (DECREASE) IN TAXABLE WAGES		24,868.20
3. CORRECTED TOTAL TAXABLE WAGES		24,868.20
4. GROSS FEDERAL UNEMPLOYMENT TAX AS CORRECTED (3.4 % OF LINE 3 ABOVE)	$	845.52
5. Less: CREDIT FOR CONTRIBUTIONS PAID TO STATE UNEMPLOYMENT FUND (Line 22 below)		0
6. CORRECTED TAX	$	845.52
7. Less: UNEMPLOYMENT TAX AS REPORTED OR PREVIOUSLY ADJUSTED		0
8. DELINQUENT TAX, ADDITIONAL TAX OR (OVERASSESSMENT)		845.52
9. PENALTIES IRC 6651 $ ___, IRC 6653(b) $ 422.76		465.24

Your allowable credit for contributions paid State unemployment fund has been computed as indicated below:

	STATE	
10.		
11. EXPERIENCE RATE PERIOD		
12. EXPERIENCE RATE (Enter 2.7% if no experience rate or if actual exceeds 2.7%)	%	%	%
13. TAXABLE PAYROLL (As defined in State Act but limited to FUTA wages)	$	$	$
14. 2.7% OF LINE 13		
15. Less: CONTRIBUTIONS PAYABLE AT EXPERIENCE RATE (Line 13 × Line 12)	%	%	%
16. ADDITIONAL CREDIT (Line 14 less Line 15)		
17. CONTRIBUTIONS TIMELY PAID		
18. LESSER OF: (a) 90% OF CONTRIBUTIONS PAID LATE (b) 90% OF CREDIT ALLOWABLE IF SUCH CONTRIBUTIONS HAD BEEN TIMELY		
19. TENTATIVE CREDITS (Sum of lines 16, 17, 18)		
20. TOTAL TENTATIVE CREDITS (Sum of amounts on line 19)	$
21. 2.7% OF LINE 3 ABOVE	$
22. ALLOWABLE CREDIT (Lesser of line 20 or 21)	$

OTHER INFORMATION

EXAMINING OFFICER'S SIGNATURE	DISTRICT

FORM 4667 (9-70)

*U.S. GOVERNMENT PRINTING OFFICE:1974 620-423/3663 1-3

of Items. That form is shown in Chapter Four. (See Exhibit 4-3.) You will recall that Form 886-A communicates the IRS' reasoning behind the particular changes which are recommended as a result of an examination. The information learned from Form 886-A will enable you to determine exactly what, if any, errors were made by the IRS, either in its analysis of the facts or its application of the law in your case. By carefully reviewing all of the above documents, in particular the 886-A, you will be able to develop your arguments in opposition to the tax proposed. Your arguments will be presented to the Appeals Officer later.

If no appeal is taken from the 30-day letter (Exhibit 6-1) the tax will be assessed and will be subject to collection. When an appeal is taken by submitting a timely written protest, collection will generally be stayed until such time as the Appeals Division has had an opportunity to review the matter and rule on the case.

Reviewing Penalty Assessments. I stated earlier that the 30-day letter and examination report will be issued when no employment tax returns are filed. When returns are filed but the tax is not paid, the tax is assessed without the necessity of an examination report. At that point the matter will immediately become the responsibility of the Collection Division and collection action will be pursued.

However, the Collection Division may also assess substantial penalties as part of the bill. These penalties include the failure to pay penalty[16] the failure to deposit penalty,[17] and the negligence penalty.[18] Each of these penalties is subject to be abated by the IRS upon application by the citizen. We have discussed the specific procedures for requesting a penalty abatement in Chapter Five. Use of the Form 843, *Claim,* structured under the authority of Code §6404(a), will aid in the abatement of penalties.[19] Also, one may write a letter addressed to the Revenue Officer setting forth the abatement. Bear in mind that when seeking the abatement, you must show "reasonable cause" for the action or inaction which is the subject of the penalty.[20]

In the event the Revenue Officer refuses to abate the penalties pursuant to your demand, you should take immediate action. You have 15 days from the date the Revenue Officer refuses to abate penalties, even if that refusal is oral, in which to submit a written protest. The written protest (see IRS Publication 5) should request a conference before the Appeals Division and should set out the facts you feel justify abatement of the penalty. This action should be taken without delay.

Reviewing the Reclassification of Workers. If any one area of the employment tax audit arena may be termed "hot," this is it. The IRS is "on a mission" to prevent the use of independent contractors to the fullest extent humanly possible. The reason is simple. In an independent contractor relationship, the contractor (the person for whom services are performed) is not required to withhold and transmit to the IRS any money from the pay of the worker. Not only is the IRS' "safety net" of withholding bypassed, but it also loses revenue in terms of social security and unemployment tax assessments. Whether or not the independent contractor arrangement is legal and proper is often *another matter.* The compelling issue in the eyes of the IRS is, "We need the money."[21]

Another problem identified by the IRS is that persons who perform services under contract relationsips, but who are not formally self-employed, are often transient-type workers. Traveling from town to town, or area to area, they are difficult to trace. With no funds withheld from their pay, there is little incentive for some to file tax returns, leaving the IRS in the lurch in that respect. Even though none of this is the fault of the contractor, the brunt of the problem is dropped in his lap. Often it is the contractor who is forced to pay additional income, social security and unemployment taxes by reason of the fact that one or more of his workers has filed regarding his own tax obligations.

There are many businesses which are dependent upon contract workers for the profitability of their operations and for the latitude it provides in bidding on work. Independent contractors are just that; they are, in their own right, self-employed persons who offer their services to the public for a fee. Their presence enables the contractor to avoid the difficulties which accompany an in-house work force, such as labor disputes, coordination of the hours of work, and workmen's compensation costs. The self-employed independent person will determine each of these matters for himself, with the contractor receiving completed work at a specified fee.

While there are literally a hundred reasons why a particular business may become more efficient through

---

16. Code §6654-6655.

17. Code §6656(a).

18. Code §6653(a).

19. See footnote 15.

20. See *How Anyone Can Negotiate With The IRS—And WIN!,* pages 39-44.

21. The Supreme Court case of *United States v. Lee,* 102 S.Ct. 1051 (1982), offers an interesting, if not disheartening discussion of the government's attitude when it comes to "getting the money." The case is discussed at length in *The Naked Truth,* Chapter Six.

the use of independents, the IRS takes a singular view of the matter; the move is made to avoid taxes—period. Such bureaucratic tunnel vision makes it necessary to review the law regarding independent contractors with an eye toward enabling one to establish that his independents are legitimate, self-employed workers, not employees disguised as independents for the sole purpose of avoiding taxes.

The difficulty in this area begins with the fact that the Internal Revenue Code contains *no clear and concise definition* of the term, "employee." For purposes of employment taxes and the withholding of income taxes, an employee is described by the Code in somewhat vague terms. Section 3121(d)(2) of the Code, applicable to employment tax matters, addresses the term "employee" thusly:

> "(A)ny individual who, under the usual common law rules applicable in determining the employer-employee relationship, has the status of an employee;. . ."

The definition, though devoid of specific elements which may be applied to determine whether one performing services is in fact an "employee," does provide some direction in which to turn to solve the problem. The "common law" test of determining the employer-employee relationship is age-old. The development of the law in the area has left us with 20 specific considerations to which one may look in determining the relationship of himself to his workers. These 20 factors, loosely referred to as "the 20 common law tests,"[22] are:

1. Whether the worker is required to comply with specific *instructions* given by the contractor;

2. Whether the worker is required to undergo specific *training* offered by the contractor;

3. Whether the services of the worker have been *integrated* into the day-to-day operations of the contractor's business;

4. Whether the contractor requires the worker to perform the services *personally;*

5. Whether the contractor may *hire, supervise and pay* assistants to the worker;

6. Whether a *continuing relationship* exists between the contractor and the worker;

7. Whether the contractor has the right to *establish the hours of work;*

8. Whether the worker must devote *full time* or substantially full time to the contractor's business;

9. Whether the work is required to be performed on the contractor's *premises;*

10. Whether the work must be performed in an *order or sequence* specified by the contractor;

11. Whether *oral or written reports* are required by the contractor;

12. Whether payment of the worker is by *hour, week, month;*

13. Whether the contractor will reimburse the worker for his *traveling or business expenses;*

14. Whether the worker is required to furnish his own *tools and materials;*

Whether the worker has a *significant investment* in his own facilities which are used for his business;

16. Whether the worker has the potential to realize a *profit or a loss* on a particular venture undertaken for the contractor;

17. Whether the worker performs services for *more than one firm;*

18. Whether the worker makes his services available *to the general public;*

19. Whether the contractor retains a *right to discharge* the worker for any reason; and

20. Whether the worker has the *right to terminate* his relationship with the contractor without incurring any liability.

Exhibit 6-5 is the portion of Revenue Ruling 87-41 which sets forth the "20 common law" tests we have listed above. In addition to the test itself, Rev. Rul. 87-41 offers a brief explanation as to the manner in which each test is applied. Thus further guidance is provided to us.

It should be noted that the "20 common law" tests have been developed as guidelines only. More importantly, *no one factor* is to be considered dispositive in determining the existence of an employer-employee relationship. In fact, Rev. Rul. 87-41 itself states:

> "As an aid to determining whether an individual is an employee under the common law rules, twenty factors or elements have been identified as indicating whether sufficient control is present to establish an employer-employee relationship. The twenty factors have been developed based on an examination of cases and rulings considering whether an individual is an employee. The degree of importance of each factor varies depending on the occupation and the factual context in which the services are performed. The twenty factors are designed only as guides for determining whether an individual is an employee;* * *"

While the "20 common law tests" provide guidelines on the question of whether a worker is an employee, the employment tax examination will attempt to answer the one question which all are agreed is dispositive on the issue; namely, whether the contractor has the right to

---

22. Rev. Rul. 87-41, 1987-1 CB 296.

(whether or not he actually does) exercise any control over the worker as to anything other than performing the services to a specified standard. If, for example, the contractor may determine the times at which the work is to be performed, or the specified manner in which the work is to be performed, these elements will weigh in favor of determining that the worker is in fact an employee, not an independent contractor.

Furthermore, one must be aware of the fact that in examining the relationship of the parties to one another, the IRS will consider the *substance of the relationship*, overlooking the form thereof, if there are differences. For example, it is common for persons attempting to establish an independent contractor relationship to draft a *pro forma* written contract agreement. The contract may state that an "independent contract relationship" exists and that the contractor "may exercise no control over the worker" in connection with the service performed. However, if it is revealed through examination that the element of control is indeed present in the relationship, the contract will be set aside, considered non-dispositive as to the question.

In this respect, Rev. Rul. 87-41 provides:

"* * *(S)pecial scrutiny is required in applying the twenty factors to assure that formalistic aspects of an arrangement designed to achieve a particular status to not obscure the substance of the arrangement (that is, whether the person or persons for whom the services are performed exercise sufficient control over the individual for the individual to be classified as an employee).* * *"

To aid in the examination, the IRS regularly uses a questonnaire designed to test the "form over substance" aspect of the arrangement. The question-naire is Form SS-8, *Information for Use in Determining Whether a Worker is an Employee for Purposes of Federal Employment Taxes and Income Tax Withholding.* See Exhibit 6-6. A copy of Form SS-8 is provided to both the worker and the contractor. Each is asked to complete the form and return it to the examiner. The answers are compared with one another and wit the language of any written contract. Through this process, as well as from discussions with the worker and the contractor, the examiner will determine whether an employer-employee relationships exists, despite a written agreement to the contrary.

Any person suffering the reclassification of workers is likely faced with substantial proposed tax assessments. Because employment taxes are assessable without the need of a notice of deficiency, it is mandatory that one's appeal rights are exercised. It is also mandatory that one be aware of the so-called "safe-haven" rules. Under the Revenue Act of 1978,[23] Congress stepped in to provide relief to persons who, despite making every effort to comply with the law, suffered the reclassification of workers as employees. Noting that the ensuing tax liabilities could be crushing to any business, Congress passed §530 as part of the 1978 Act.

The law provides that if such workers were treated as independents during the tax period in question, then such person will "be deemed *not to be* an employee" for the same period, if the contractor had a "reasonable basis for not treating such individual as an employee."[24] The law goes on to define exactly what constitutes "a reasonable basis for not treating an individual as an employee." Section 530(a)(2) provides as follows:

"(2) For purposes of paragraph (1), a taxpayer shall in any case be treated as having a reasonable basis for not treating an individual as an employee for a period if the

Exhibit 6-5: 20 Common Law Tests

1. *Instructions.* A worker who is required to comply with other persons' instructions about when, where, and how he or she is to work is ordinarily an employee. This control factor is present if the person or persons for whom the services are performed have the *right* to require compliance with instructions. See, for example, Rev. Rul. 68-598, 1968-2 C.B. 464, and Rev. Rul. 66-381, 1966-2 C.B. 449.

2. *Training.* Training a worker by requiring an experienced employee to work with the worker, by corresponding with the worker, by requiring the worker to attend meetings, or by using other methods, indicates that the person or persons for whom the services are performed want the services performed in a particular method or manner. See Rev. Rul. 70-630, 1970-2 C.B. 229.

3. *Integration.* Integration of the worker's services into the business operations generally shows that the worker is subject to direction and control. When the success or continuation of a business depends to an appreciable degree upon the performance of certain services, the workers who perform those services must necessarily be subject to a certain amount of control by the owner of the business. See *United States v. Silk*, 331 U.S. 704 (1947), 1947-2 C.B. 167.

23. Public Law 95-600.

24. See Act §530(a)(1). Note: §530 has not been codified into the Internal Revenue Code. Therefore, Act §530 *is not* Code §530.

4. *Services Rendered Personally.* If the services must be rendered personally, presumably the person or persons for whom the services are performed are interested in the methods used to accomplish the work as well as in the results. See Rev. Rul. 55–695, 1955–2 C.B. 410.

5. *Hiring, Supervising, and Paying Assistants.* If the person or persons for whom the services are performed hire, supervise, and pay assistants, that factor generally shows control over the workers on the job. However, if one worker hires, supervises, and pays the other assistants pursuant to a contract under which the worker agrees to provide materials and labor and under which the worker is responsible only for the attainment of a result, this factor indicates an independent contractor status. Compare Rev. Rul. 63–115, 1963–1 C.B. 178, with Rev. Rul. 55–593, 1955–2 C.B. 610.

6. *Continuing Relationship.* A continuing relationship between the worker and the person or persons for whom the services are performed indicates that an employer-employee relationship exists. A continuing relationship may exist where work is performed at frequently recurring although irregular intervals. See *United States v. Silk.*

7. *Set Hours of Work.* The establishment of set hours of work by the person or persons for whom the services are performed is a factor indicating control. See Rev. Rul. 73–591, 1973–2 C.B. 337.

8. *Full Time Required.* If the worker must devote substantially full time to the business of the person or persons for whom the services are performed, such person or persons have control over the amount of time the worker spends working and impliedly restrict the worker from doing other gainful work. An independent contractor, on the other hand, is free to work when and for whom he or she chooses. See Rev. Rul. 56–694, 1956–2 C.B. 694.

9. *Doing Work on Employer's Premises.* If the work is performed on the premises of the person or persons for whom the services are performed, that factor suggests control over the worker, especially if the work could be done elsewhere. Rev. Rul. 56–660, 1956–2 C.B. 693. Work done off the premises of the person or persons receiving the services, such as at the office of the worker, indicates some freedom from control. However, this fact by itself does not mean that the worker is not an employee. The importance of this factor depends on the nature of the service involved and the extent to which an employer generally would require that employees perform such services on the employer's premises. Control over the place of work is indicated when the person or persons for whom the ser-

vices are performed have the right to compel the worker to travel a designated route, to canvass a territory within a certain time, or to work at specific places as required. See Rev. Rul. 56–694.

10. *Order or Sequence Set.* If a worker must perform services in the order or sequence set by the person or persons for whom the services are performed, that factor shows that the worker is not free to follow the worker's own pattern of work but must follow the established routines and schedules of the person or persons for whom the services are performed. Often, because of the nature of an occupation, the person or persons for whom the services are performed do not set the order of the services or set the order infrequently. It is sufficient to show control, however, if such person or persons retain the right to do so. See Rev. Rul. 56–694.

11. *Oral or Written Reports.* A requirement that the worker submit regular or written reports to the person or persons for whom the services are performed indicates a degree of control. See Rev. Rul. 70–309, 1970–1 C.B. 199, and Rev. Rul. 68–248, 1968–1 C.B. 431.

12. *Payment by Hour, Week, Month.* Payment by the hour, week, or month generally points to an employer-employee relationship, provided that this method of payment is not just a convenient way of paying a lump sum agreed upon as the cost of a job. Payment made by the job or on a straight commission generally indicates that the worker is an independent contractor. See Rev. Rul. 74–389, 1974–2 C.B. 330.

13. *Payment of Business and/or Traveling Expenses.* If the person or persons for whom the services are performed ordinarily pay the worker's business and/or traveling expenses, the worker is ordinarily an employee. An employer, to be able to control expenses, generally retains the right to regulate and direct the worker's business activities. See Rev. Rul. 55–144, 1955–1 C.B. 483.

14. *Furnishing of Tools and Materials.* The fact that the person or persons for whom the services are performed furnish significant tools, materials, and other equipment tends to show the existence of an employer-employee relationship. See Rev. Rul. 71–524, 1971–2 C.B. 346.

15. *Significant Investment.* If the worker invests in facilities that are used by the worker in performing services and are not typically maintained by employees (such as the maintenance of an office rented at fair value from an unrelated party), that factor tends to indicate that the worker is an independent contractor. On the other hand, lack of investment in facilities indicates dependence on the person or per-

sons for whom the services are performed for such facilities and, accordingly, the existence of an employer-employee relationship. See Rev. Rul. 71–524. Special scrutiny is required with respect to certain types of facilities, such as home offices.

16. *Realization of Profit or Loss.* A worker who can realize a profit or suffer a loss as a result of the worker's services (in addition to the profit or loss ordinarily realized by employees) is generally an independent contractor, but the worker who cannot is an employee. See Rev. Rul. 70–309. For example, if the worker is subject to a real risk of economic loss due to significant investments or a bona fide liability for expenses, such as salary payments to unrelated employees, that factor indicates that the worker is an independent contractor. The risk that a worker will not receive payment for his or her services, however, is common to both independent contractors and employees and thus does not constitute a sufficient economic risk to support treatment as an independent contractor.

17. *Working for More Than One Firm at a Time.* If a worker performs more than de minimis services for a multiple of unrelated persons or firms at the same time, that factor generally indicates that the worker is an independent contractor. See Rev. Rul. 70–572, 1970–2 C.B. 221. However, a worker who performs services for more than one person may be an employee of each of the persons, especially where such persons are part of the same service arrangement.

18. *Making Service Available to General Public.* The fact that a worker makes his or her services available to the general public on a regular and consistent basis indicates an independent contractor relationship. See Rev. Rul. 56–660.

19. *Right to Discharge.* The right to discharge a worker is a factor indicating that the worker is an employee and the person possessing the right is an employer. An employer exercises control through the threat of dismissal, which causes the worker to obey the employer's instructions. An independent contractor, on the other hand, cannot be fired so long as the independent contractor produces a result that meets the contract specifications. Rev. Rul. 75–41, 1975–1 C.B. 323.

20. *Right to Terminate.* If the worker has the right to end his or her relationship with the person for whom the services are performed at any time he or she wishes without incurring liability, that factor indicates an employer-employee relationship. See Rev. Rul. 70–309.

taxpayer's treatment of such individual for such period was in reasonable reliance on any of the following:

"(A) judicial precedent, published rulings, technical advice with respect to the taxpayer, or a letter ruling to the taxpayer;

"(B) a past Internal Revenue Service audit of the taxpayer in which there was no assessment attributable to the treatment (for employment tax purposes) of the individuals holding positions substantially similar to the position held by the individual; or

"(C) long-standing recognized practice of a significant segment of the industry in which such individual was engaged."

Provided one has formulated his position regarding his workers on a "reasonable basis" as defined above, he will avoid an assessment of employment taxes for the period under audit. However, that will not alter the fact that his workers have been reclassified, requiring them to be treated as employees, *in the future*. He will, however, avoid back taxes, penalties and interest.

There are two further conditions which must exist before the "safe haven" rule will apply, however. First of all, the contractor must have filed "all Federal tax returns (including information returns) required to be filed by the taxpayer (contractor) with respect to such individual for such period. . ."[25] Second, the contractor's treatent of the worker must have been "consistent" with both the tax returns filed regarding such person, and with the manner in which the worker was treated, *prior* to enactment of the "safe-haven" rule.

Thus, a failure to file Forms 1099 relative to the worker may well vitiate the protection offered by Act §530. Or, if Forms W-2, rather than 1099s were filed regarding the workers, this will weigh against the contractor when considering "safe-haven" protection. Also, if one has *altered* the manner in which he treats the worker, this factor will weigh against the contractor.[26] Consistency in the treatment of the worker is very important to whether the protection of Act §530 will apply. One is not free to alter the status of his employees to independent contractors merely because he is aware that the "safe-haven" rule is in effect. To enjoy "safe-haven" protection, the workers must have been treated as independent contractors from the beginning.

In addition to arguing the *merits* of your independent contractor treatment of workers (relying upon the "20 common law tests" for your ammunition) you should also assert your right to "safe-haven" protection under Act §530. Thus, even in the event you are unable to prevail on the merits of the case, you will nevertheless avoid an assessment of back taxes, penalties and interest which could strangle your business.

Reviewing the 100 percent Penalty Assessment. We already stated that the 100 percent penalty under Code §6672 is assessed against one or more "responsible persons" when a corporation has outstanding employment tax debts. The statute provides for assessment of the penalty against the "person responsible" to withhold, truthfully account for and remit the employment taxes, but who fails to do so.

Before going any further, let us understand *what is not* to be included within an assessment of the 100 percent penalty. The penalty is to include *only* the *employee's share* of income and social security tax debts—the "trust fund" taxes. The 100 percent penalty *does not apply* to the *employer's share* of FICA AND FUTA taxes, and *does not apply* to any delinquency penalties or interest due on those taxes prior to the assessment of the penalty.[27] Thus, the first consideration is to determine that no inappropriate corporate taxes have been included in the proposed 100 percent penalty assessment.

The proposed 100 percent penalty is communicated via form letter by the IRS to the citizen. The letter points out that the IRS has been unsuccessful in collecting the taxes from the corporation's assets, and that it intends to assess the 100 percent penalty against the individual as an alternative. Exhibit 6-7 is a sample of the letter just referred to. Please review it.

To avoid an immediate assessment of the penalty, one must execute an appeal within 30 days of the date shown on the letter. The appeal is critical and as with all employment tax matters, could prevent the assessment entirely.

There are two primary considerations when contesting an assessment of the 100 percent penalty. We have already identified what they are, and will now address them in turn. First, the penalty must only be assessed against the "person responsible" to withhold, truthfully account for and pay to the IRS the taxes in question. In determining whether a person was "responsible" to carry out those duties, the Supreme Court has established three primary elements.[28] Under its ruling, a person will be termed "responsible" if:

1. He possessed the *power* to see that the taxes were paid;

2. He possessed the *power* to determine which

25. Act §530(a)(1)(B).

26. Act §530(a)(3).

27. See Rev. Reg. §301.6672-1.

28. *Slodov v. United States*, 436 U.S. 238 (1978).

Exhibit 6-6: Form SS-8

Form **SS-8**	Information for Use in Determining Whether a Worker Is an Employee for Purposes of Federal Employment Taxes and Income Tax Withholding	OMB No. 1545-0004
(Rev. Nov. 1981) Department of the Treasury Internal Revenue Service		Expires 11-30-84

Paperwork Reduction Act Notice.—The Paperwork Reduction Act of 1980 says we must tell you why we are collecting this information, how we will use it, and whether you have to give it to us. We ask for the information to carry out the Internal Revenue laws of the United States. We need it to ensure that you are complying with these laws and to allow us to figure and collect the right amount of tax. If you want a determination of employment status, you are required to give us this information.

Instructions

A. This form should be completed for **ONE** individual who is representative of the class of workers whose status is in question. When a written determination is desired for more than one class of workers, a separate Form SS-8 should be completed for one worker from each class whose status is typical of that class. A written determination for any worker will be applicable to other workers of the same class, provided the facts are not materially different from those of the worker whose status was ruled upon.

B. Please complete section 1 of the form in all cases. In sections II, III, IV, and V, complete only the information relating to the worker's occupational group.

C. You will need to answer items that do not have "Yes" or "No" check boxes in a letter with paragraphs numbered to correspond with the related items. If any item does not apply to the services performed, enter "N/A," "not applicable," in the margin beside the item. Responses should contain sufficient detail to explain the circumstances under which the worker performs services.

D. The word "firm," as used in this form, includes an individual, corporation, partnership, association, or any other business organization.

E. The term "written determination," as used in this form, means a ruling, determination letter, or technical advice memorandum.

F. All copies of contracts and other documents submitted with this form become a part of the records of the Internal Revenue Service and will not be returned.

G. Please return Form SS-8 to the Internal Revenue Service office that provided the form. If the Internal Revenue Service did not ask you to complete this form but you wish a determination on whether a worker is an employee, file Form SS-8 with your District Director.

Name and identification number of firm

Address of firm

Nature of firm's business

Form of organization (check one):
☐ Sole proprietorship
☐ Partnership
☐ Corporation
☐ Other (specify) ▶

IRS District Office for the locality where you file your tax returns, if known ▶

Name of worker

Home address of worker

Social security number

Occupation (check one):
☐ Agent-driver or commission-driver
☐ Life insurance salesperson ☐ Home worker
☐ Traveling or city salesperson
☐ Other (specify) ▶

Under section 6110 of the Internal Revenue Code, the text and related background file documents of any ruling, determination letter, or technical advice memorandum will be open to public inspection. This section provides that, before the text and background file documents are made public, identifying and certain other information must be deleted. See "Section 6110(c) of the Internal Revenue Code" on page 4 for details.

If the only items you want deleted are names, addresses, and taxpayer identifying numbers, please check this box . . ▶ ☐

If you believe additional deletions should be made, please submit a copy of this form and copies of all supporting documents indicating, in brackets, those parts you believe should be deleted in accordance with section 6110(c) of the Code (see page 4). Attach a separate statement indicating which specific exemption provided by section 6110(c) applies to each bracketed part.

Complete Section 1 in All Cases

Section I. General

1 Total number of workers in this class (if more than one, please answer item 33) ▶

2 This information is about services performed by the worker from ▶ .... (Month, day, year) to .... (Month, day, year)

3 What was the first date on which the worker performed services of any kind for the firm? ▶ .... (Month, day, year)

Is the worker still performing services for the firm? . . . . ☐ Yes ☐ No

If "No," what was the date of termination? ▶ .... (Month, day, year)

4 Please attach copies of any written agreements, leases, sales contracts, etc., between the firm and the worker. If the Social Security Administration has considered the status of the worker, or of any other individual who performed services for the firm under similar circumstances, what decision was made by the Social Security Administration? If the decision related to a worker other than the individual named above, state the name, address, and social security number of the worker.

Please answer items that do not have "Yes" or "No" check boxes in a letter and attach it to this form.

Form SS-8 (Rev. 11-81)

Page 2

	Yes	No			Yes	No
5 If the agreement for the worker's services is not in writing (item 4), state the complete terms and conditions of the firm's oral agreement with the worker, including a statement whether the services were to be performed full-time, part-time, for a particular job, or for an indefinite period, etc.				If "Yes":		
				(a) List the items furnished by the firm and state whether any charge is made to the worker for their use.		
6 Does the actual working arrangement differ from that contemplated by the original agreement?				(b) List the items furnished by the worker and the approximate value of each item.		
If "Yes," please explain such differences and the circumstances that gave rise to the changes. Specify the date such changes took place.				(c) If any item furnished by the worker was obtained from the firm (by purchase, lease, or otherwise), please attach a copy of the written agreement, if the agreement is oral, state and detail the financial arrangement giving purchase price, terms of payment, etc.		
7 Describe in detail the specific types of services performed by the worker.				18 Does the worker wear a uniform or special clothing while performing the services?		
8 Where does the worker perform the services?				If "Yes":		
9 Does the firm require the worker to perform services during regular working hours?				(a) Is this a requirement of the firm?		
If "No," state the firm's requirements.				(b) Who pays for the uniform or special clothing?		
10 Does the worker follow a daily, weekly, etc., routine established by the firm?				(c) Who pays for the cleaning?		
If "Yes," what is the routine?				19 Does the firm's arrangement with the worker contemplate that all of the services are to be performed by the worker personally?		
11 Is the worker restricted to a specific territory?				If "No," under what circumstances are the worker's services performed by others?		
If "Yes," is the worker required to cover such territory within a specified time or with specified frequency?				20 Does the worker engage helpers to assist in the work?		
12 Does the worker sell goods or services for the firm?				If "Yes":		
If "Yes":				(a) What services do the helpers perform?		
(a) Are leads to prospective customers furnished?				(b) Are the helpers engaged with the express or implied consent of the firm?		
(b) Is the worker required to follow up or report on such leads?				If "No," explain.		
(c) Is the worker required to adhere to prices, terms, and conditions of sale established by the firm?				(c) Who supervises and pays the helpers?		
(d) Are orders submitted to and subject to approval by the firm?				(d) May the firm discharge the helpers?		
(e) Is the worker expected to attend sales meetings?				If "No," can the firm require the worker to discharge them?		
If "Yes," what is the result if the worker fails to attend?				(e) Are Federal Insurance Contributions Act employee tax and income tax withheld from the helpers' wages?		
13 Are the worker's services supervised or reviewed by the firm?				If "Yes," who withholds, reports, and pays such taxes?		
If "Yes," describe in detail the methods used.				21 How is the worker paid for the services (that is, salary, commissions, percentages of fares or fees, hourly wage, piecework rate, percentage of profits, lump-sum payment, difference between purchase price paid by worker and amount received by the worker from resale, etc.)?		
14 Does the worker report in person, by telephone, in writing, or otherwise to the firm or its representative?				22 Does the firm guarantee a minimum amount of compensation to the worker?		
If "Yes," how often, for what purpose and in what manner is the reporting made? Please furnish copies of any report forms, route sheets, etc.				23 Does the firm allow the worker a drawing account or advance against anticipated earnings?		
15 Is the worker given instructions or training by the firm?				If "Yes":		
If "Yes," give specific examples of instances in which the firm instructed the worker how to perform the work and state the circumstances under which such instructions were given. Please attach representative copies of any written instructions, procedures, or operating manuals.				(a) Is the worker paid such advances at regular and stated intervals?		
				(b) If the worker is required to repay the excess of advances over actual earnings, how is the repayment accomplished?		
16 Is the worker required to meet a minimum quota?				24 (a) What expenses are incurred by the worker in the performance of services for the firm?		
17 Are facilities or equipment (such as office, store, showroom, warehouse, office equipment, tools, machinery, business forms and stationery, stenographic service, telephone, automobile, delivery truck, etc.) used by the worker in performing services for the firm?				(b) Does the firm pay the worker any amount that is specifically designated as an allowance or reimbursement for such expenses, or does the worker pay such expenses from gross remuneration?		
				(c) Does the worker account for his or her expenses to the firm?		
				25 Is the worker eligible for bonuses, pensions, sick pay, etc.?		

Form SS-8 (Rev. 11-81) Page 3

Yes No

26 Does the firm make contributions toward hospital or medical insurance for the worker? . . . . . .

27 (a) Under what circumstances and for what reasons are the worker's services subject to termination by the firm?

(b) May the worker terminate the services at any time? . . . .

28 (a) Under whose name does the worker operate when performing services for the firm?

(b) Does the worker hold himself or herself out to the public as available to do work of a similar or related nature to that performed for the firm? . . . .

(c) Does the worker advertise in newspapers, etc., or maintain a business listing in the telephone directory? . . . .

(d) Does the worker maintain an office or shop? .

If "Yes," where are such quarters located?

29 Is a license necessary for the work? . . . . . .

If "Yes":

(a) What kind of license is required?
(b) By whom is it issued?
(c) In whose name is it issued?
(d) By whom is the license fee paid?

30 Does the worker perform similar services for others? . . . .

If "Yes":

(a) List the names and addresses of such other persons and briefly describe the services.

(b) Are the worker's services for such other persons performed regularly during the course of the same working day in which services are performed for the firm? . . . .

(c) What percentage of the worker's total working time is spent in performing services for such other persons?

(d) Does the firm have top priority on the worker's time and efforts? . . . .

If "No," explain.

31 (a) Do you believe the worker is an employee for purposes of Federal employment taxes and income tax withholding? . . . . .

Please state the reasons for your belief.

(b) Has the firm withheld the Federal Insurance Contributions Act employee tax and income tax from the worker's remuneration? . . . .

32 To your knowledge, is the same issue being considered by any office of the Internal Revenue Service in connection with the examination of the worker's or firm's tax return? . . . .

If "Yes," please give the office and location.

33 List the names and addresses of all of the workers referred to in item 1, or the names and addresses of 10 such workers if there are more than 10.

34 If you are the worker, do you object to the disclosure to the firm of your identity or a copy of the information you furnish? . . . .

35 Please furnish any additional information you consider important.

If the Worker Comes Within One of the Occupational Groups Covered by the Following Sections, Complete the Appropriate Section

Section II. Agent-driver or Commission-driver

Yes No

36 List the products and/or services distributed by the worker, such as meat, vegetable, fruit, bakery products, beverages (other than milk), or laundry or dry cleaning services. If more than one type of product and/or service is distributed, specify the principal one.

37 (a) Were the route or territory and a list of customers assigned to the worker by the firm or another person? . . . .

If "Yes," please identify the person who made the assignment.

(b) Did the worker pay the firm or person for the privilege of serving customers on the route or in the territory? . . . .

If "Yes," how much did the worker pay (not including any amount paid for a truck or racks, etc.)? What factors were considered in determining the value of the route or territory?

(c) How are new customers obtained by the worker? Explain fully, showing whether the new customers are those who call the firm for service, those solicited by the worker, or both.

Section III. Life Insurance Salesperson

Yes No

38 Is the worker's entire business activity the selling of life insurance or annuity contracts for the firm? .

If "No," state the extent of his or her other business activities.

39 Does the worker sell other types of insurance for the firm? . . . .

If "Yes," state the percentage of the worker's total working time spent in such other selling.

40 State if, at the time the contract was entered into between the firm and the worker, it was their intention that the worker would be considered as selling life insurance for the firm (a) on a full-time basis, or (b) on a part-time basis. State the manner in which such intention was expressed.

Section IV. Home Worker

Yes No

41 Does the worker perform work on materials or goods furnished by the firm? . . . .

If "No," where and how does the worker obtain such materials or goods?

42 Is the worker furnished with specifications, samples, or instructions to follow in performing the services? . . . .

If "Yes," explain.

43 Does the firm require that the finished product be returned to it or to a person designated by it? . . . .

Section V. Traveling or City Salesperson

44 Specify from whom the worker principally solicits orders on behalf of the firm. If the worker solicits orders from wholesalers, retailers, contractors, or operators of hotels, restaurants, or other similar establishments, specify the percentage of the worker's time spent in such solicitation.

45 Is the merchandise purchased by the customers for resale by them, or is it purchased for use by them in their business operations? If used by the customers in their business operations, describe the merchandise and state whether it is equipment which is installed on their premises or is a consumable supply.

Form SS-8 (Rev. 11-81) Page 4

General Rules for Determination of Employer-Employee Relationship

The determination of whether a worker is an employee, for purposes of the Federal Insurance Contributions Act, the Federal Unemployment Tax Act, and the income tax withholding provisions of the Internal Revenue Code, is based on the usual common law rules applicable in determining the employer-employee relationship.

Under the usual common law rules, the relationship of employer and employee generally exists when the person for whom services are performed has the right to control and direct the individual who performs the services, not only as to the result to be accomplished by the work but also as to the details and means by which that result is accomplished. That is, an employee is subject to the will and control of the employer not only as to what shall be done but how it shall be done. It is not necessary that the employer actually direct or control the manner in which the services are performed; it is sufficient if he or she has the right to do so. The right to discharge is also an important factor indicating that the person possessing that right is an employer. Other factors characteristic of an employer, but not necessarily present in every case, are the furnishing of tools and a place to work.

In general, if an individual is subject to the control or direction of another person merely as to the result to be accomplished by the work and not as to the means and methods for accomplishing the result, the individual is an independent contractor. Also, if it is possible for the individual to sustain a loss, the individual is usually an independent contractor. An individual performing services as an independent contractor is not, as to such services, an employee under the usual common law rules. Individuals such as physicians, lawyers, dentists, veterinarians, construction contractors, public stenographers, auctioneers, etc., engaged in the pursuit of an independent trade, business, or profession, in which they offer their services to the public, are independent contractors and not employees.

Whether the relationship of employer and employee exists under the usual common law rules will be determined after the examination of the particular facts of each case.

If the relationship of employer and employee exists, the designation or description of the relationship by the parties as anything other than that of employer and employee is immaterial. If such relationship exists, it is of no consequence that the employee is designated as a partner, coadventurer, agent, independent contractor, or the like.

All classes or grades of employees are included within the relationship of employer and employee. Thus, superintendents, managers, and other supervisory personnel are employees.

Additional Rules Applying to Status of Workers in Certain Occupations for Purposes of the Federal Insurance Contributions Act and the Federal Unemployment Tax Act

If a worker in certain occupational groups, namely, an agent-driver or commission-driver, a full-time life insurance salesperson, a homeworker, or a traveling or city salesperson, is not an employee under the usual common law rules, then the worker's status, for purposes of the Federal Insurance Contributions Act, is determined under the statutory definition of "employee" contained in Section 3121(d)(3) of such Act. The worker's status, for purposes of the Federal Unemployment Tax Act, is also determined under the statutory definition of "employee" contained in section 3121(d)(3) of the Federal Insurance Contributions Act except that subparagraphs (B) and (C) do not apply.

Section 3121(d)(3) of the Federal Insurance Contributions Act reads, in part, as follows:

"EMPLOYEE.—The term 'employee' means—

* * * * *

"(3) any individual * * * who performs services for remuneration for any person—

"(A) as an agent-driver or commission-driver engaged in distributing meat products, vegetable products, fruit products, bakery products, beverages (other than milk), or laundry or dry-cleaning services, for his principal;

"(B) as a full-time life insurance salesman;

"(C) as a homeworker performing work, according to specifications furnished by the person for whom the services are performed, on materials or goods furnished by such person which are required to be returned to such person or a person designated by him; or

"(D) as a traveling or city salesman, other than as an agent-driver or commission-driver, engaged upon a full-time basis in the solicitation on behalf of, and the transmission to, his principal (except for side-line sales activities on behalf of some other person) of orders from wholesalers, retailers, contractors, or operators of hotels, restaurants, or other similar establishments for merchandise for resale or supplies for use in their business operations;

if the contract of service contemplates that substantially all of such services are to be performed personally by such individual; except that an individual shall not be included in the term 'employee' under the provisions of this paragraph if such individual has a substantial investment in facilities used in connection with the performance of such services (other than in facilities for transportation), or if the services are in the nature of a single transaction not part of a continuing relationship with the person for whom the services are performed."

Section 6110(c) of the Internal Revenue Code

"(C) Exemptions From Disclosure.—Before making any written determination or background file document open or available to public inspection under subsection (a), the Secretary shall delete—

"(1) the names, addresses, and other identifying details of the person to whom the written determination pertains and of any other person, other than a person with respect to whom a notation is made under subsection (d)(1), identified in the written determination or any background file document;

"(2) information specifically authorized under criteria established by an Executive order to be kept secret in the interest of national defense or foreign policy and which is in fact properly classified pursuant to such Executive order;

"(3) information specifically exempted from disclosure by any statute (other than this title) which is applicable to the Internal Revenue Service;

"(4) trade secrets and commercial or financial information obtained from a person and privileged or confidential;

"(5) information the disclosure of which would constitute a clearly unwarranted invasion of personal privacy;

"(6) information contained in or related to examination, operating, or condition reports prepared by, or on behalf of, or for use of an agency responsible for the regulation or supervision of financial institutions; and

"(7) geological and geophysical information and data, including maps, concerning wells.

The Secretary shall determine the appropriate extent of such deletions and, except in the case of intentional or willful disregard of this subsection, shall not be required to make such deletions (nor be liable for failure to make deletions) unless the Secretary has agreed to such deletions or has been ordered by a court (in a proceeding under subsection (f)(3)) to make such deletions."

For further information, see section 6110 of the Internal Revenue Code.

Note: Section 530 of the Revenue Act of 1978 provides relief from employment taxes on payments to certain workers, and Public Law 96–541 extends this relief until July 1, 1982. If you have a reasonable basis for treating a worker other than as an employee for periods before July 1, 1982, there is no liability for employment taxes on the payments to that worker. To get this relief, you must have filed all required Federal tax returns, including information returns, on a basis consistent with your treatment of the worker. Also, you (or your predecessor) must not have treated any worker holding a substantially similar position as an employee for any period after 1977.

Under penalties of perjury, I declare that I have examined this request, including accompanying documents, and to the best of my knowledge and belief, the facts presented are true, correct, and complete.

Signature ▶ Title ▶ Date ▶

If this form is used by the firm in requesting a written determination, the form should be signed by an officer or member of the firm.

If this form is used by the worker in requesting a written determination, the form should be signed by the worker. If the worker wants a written determination with respect to services performed for two or more firms, a separate statement should be furnished for each firm.

Additional copies of this form may be obtained from any Internal Revenue Service office.

☆U.S. GOVERNMENT PRINTING OFFICE 1981 343-549

creditors were paid; or

3. He possessed the *power* to make final decisions regarding the manner in which the funds of the business would be disposed.

In determining whether a particular person possessed such powers, the IRS will consider who signed the employment tax returns during the periods in question (or prior periods), who had signature power over the corporation's checking accounts, who was considered responsible for employment tax matters within the corporation's bylaws or minutes, and who the particular corporate officers and directors were at the time the withholding crisis developed. The revenue officer responsible to assess the tax will generally take a very shortsighted view of the problem, tending at the outset to assess the penalty against the corporate officers jointly, regardless of which individual fits the descriptions shown above.

Therefore, your defense must revolve around the question of financial control over the funds of the corporation during the periods in question. It is settled that the issue of control in this regard is the major, overriding consideration in determining who is responsible for the corporation's failure to pay its employment tax obligations. If you had no control, or possessed no *final authority* on the matter of disposing of the corporation's funds, you cannot be held responsible for the tax.

Exhibit 6-7: Sample 100 Percent Penalty Letter

Internal Revenue Service
District Director

Department of the Treasury

Date: May 10, 1988

Person to Contact:

IRS Contact Address:

IRS Contact Telephone Number:
(313) 334-3255

Employer Identification Number:

Name and Address of Corporation:

Our effort to collect the Federal taxes described in the enclosed Form 2751 have not resulted in full payment of the corporate tax liability.

We therefore propose to assess a penalty against you, as a person required to collect, account for, and pay over withheld taxes for the above corporation. This penalty, provided by law, equals the total not paid to the Government of the employment tax withheld from the corporation's employees or the excise tax collected from its patrons. The penalty is to be assessed and collected like tax.

If you agree to the proposed assessment, please sign Part 1 of Form 2751 and return it to me in the enclosed envelope. Part 2 is your copy of the assessment agreement. It includes a report of the corporation's unpaid tax liability.

If you do not agree and have additional information to support your case, please contact the person whose name appears above within 10 days from the date of this letter.

You also have the right to appeal. You may do so within 30 days from the date of this letter (60 days if the letter is addressed to you outside the United States). The instructions on the back tell you where and how. They also explain how to prepare a protest. If you ask for one, a hearing will be arranged.

If we do not hear from you within 30 days (or 60 days as the case may be), we will have to assess the penalty and bill you.

Sincerely yours,

Enclosures:
Form 2751
Envelope

Letter 1153(DO) (Rev. 12-84)

Another important consideration is the *time periods* in which the employment tax obligatons arose, *relative* to the time in which you became responsible for the operations of the corporation. It is not uncommon for a corporation to be delinquent in its withholdings *before* you became associated with it, or *before* you acquired sufficient power to direct the disbursement of its funds. Under these circumstances, you cannot rightfully be held responsible for the corporation's employment tax failures.

The second aspect of the test under Code §6672 is the issue of "willfulness." It is not enough that the tax was not paid in order that it be assessable against the "responsible person." The responsible person must also be guilty of "willfulness" in connection with his failure to pay the tax.

The term "willfulness," as you might imagine, has been the subject of much litigation and controversy. However, the courts have settled on the definition, declaring that the failure to pay must be a voluntary, conscious, and intentional act. It must be shown that the "responsible party" was aware of the outstanding tax debts and knowingly and intentionally used the funds to pay operating expenses or other debts of the business. It is not necessary that any "evil or bad intent" be present, just that the "responsible person" voluntarily, knowingly or willingly failed to pay the money to the IRS.[29]

The question of whether one acted in a willful fashion may only be determined by examination of all the facts and circumstances of the particular case. However, the case law seems clear on the notion that mere "reasonable cause" for not paying the tax does not extinguish the element of "willfulness" needed to assess the penalty.[30] The critical issue in this regard is whether *other creditors* were preferred over the United States at a time when knowledge exists that employment taxes were unpaid. When this factor is present, most other "reasonable cause" grounds will not override the preferential treatment given others.[31]

On the other hand, where it can be shown that the corporation *had no funds* at the time payment of employment tax obligations was due, this has been held to vitiate "willfulness" under the statute.[32] In addition, failure to pay was held not to be willful when, through no fault of its own, the debts due a corporation by its customer went unpaid, leaving the corporation unable to meet its obligations. Under the circumstances, it was determined that since the corporation exercised ordinary and necessary business care and prudence and was nevertheless unable to meet its obligations, willfulness did not exist.[33] Where the IRS was paid sufficient funds to satisfy a corporation's withholding obligations, but the IRS, without the knowledge or consent of the corporation's officers, applied those funds to *other* tax obligations, the failure to pay was held not to be willful.[34]

Because the IRS will apply payments in the manner which best suits the Treasury, it is imperative that all payments to the IRS be properly "designated" by the citizen. When making payments of employment tax obligations, such payments should be designated with notations on the face of the check that they are to be applied to "Form 941 taxes for ____ quarter, (year)." In the absence of such a designation, the IRS may apply the payments elsewhere. It is common for undesignated payments to be applied to the *non-trust* portion of the employment taxes, since that portion *may not be assessed* against any individual.

This practice allows the IRS to *maximize* its collection efforts. Since Code §6672 allows the assessment of the *trust portion* of employment taxes to be made against "responsible persons," the IRS will often forego the application of payments by the corporation to those liabilities. Thus, without the knowledge or consent of the individuals, payments they believe are being applied to the trust taxes are in fact being applied to non-trust tax liabilities. Care must be taken to see that this problem is avoided.

The key issues in determining willfulness, then are: (1) control over the disposition of the corporation's funds, (2) preference of other creditors at a time when employment tax debts were outstanding, and (3) knowledge that employment tax debts were outstanding and that other creditors were nevertheless being preferred over the government. In absence of such knowledge, a person cannot have acted willfully.[35] If the citizen can demonstrate the presence of one or more of these factors, he can be successful in preventing an assessment of the 100 percent penalty.

---

29. See IRS Manual §5632.2(1) (3-18-87).

30. *Barnett v. United States*, 594 F.2d 219 (9th Cir. 1979).

31. *Barnett v. United States*, supra; *Garsky v. United States*, 600 F.2d 86 (7th Cir. 1979); *Thibodeau v. United States*, 828 F.2d 1499 (11th Cir. 1987).

32. *Campbell v. Nixon*, 207 F.Supp. 826 (DC Mich. 1962).

33. *Glenwal-Schmidt, Joint Venture v. United States*, 78-2 USTC Paragraph 9610 (DC Dis. Col. 1978).

34. *Watson v. United States*, 86-1 USTC Paragraph 9122 (DC Ky. 1986).

35. *Teel v. United States*, 529 F.2d 903 (9th Cir. 1976); *Moody v. United States*, 275 F.Supp. (DC Mich. 1967); *Matter of Brahmn*, 52 BR 606 (Bky. Ct. Fla. 1985).

When the Appeal Fails

Not every appeal on the matter of employment tax assessments will be successful. One must be prepared to avail himself of the next right which the law affords. We already declared that the right of petitioning the Tax Court is inoperative in the case of employment taxes. Therefore, the only remaining alternative is a refund suit in the United States District Court. The nature of the district court remedy necessitates *payment of the tax,* followed by the timely filing of a claim for refund. See Chapter Five, under the heading *The Claim for Refund.*

You may now be thinking that the requirement to pay the employment tax assessment *prior* to submitting a claim for refund could, by itself, destroy your business. While this may be true, there is an important exception to the rule requiring *full payment* of the tax prior to instigating refund litigation. The rule applies *only to employment taxes.* It grows out of an early Supreme Court decision[36] in which the court held that employment taxes, including the 100 percent penalty, are in the nature of "excise taxes and are therefore divisible."

The rule suggests that the excise tax applicable to wages paid an employee attaches to each *individual payment* of wages. This enables the citizen to divide the total tax into its smallest components, which would be the tax due on the wages paid to *one employee for one quarter.* This rule makes it possible to pay just a portion of the total assessed tax, provided the portion paid represents full payment of the tax due on the wages paid to one employee for the quarter. That amount, naturally, would be substantially less than the total assessment, amounting in most cases to just a fraction of the total assessed liability.

After paying that small amount, the citizen then enjoys his right to claim a refund of those taxes and request an abatement of the balance.[37] Under the conditions we described in detail in Chapter Five, the claim is submitted to the Service Center and will be acted upon by the IRS. If the assessment was preceded by an Appeals conference, it is unlikely that the citizen will be given a second opportunity to present his case within the administrative arena. The IRS is likely to simply deny the claim without further hearing. However, if no Appeals consideration was made on the case prior to assessment of the penalty, the citizen should ask for, and will probably be afforded an Appeals conference by the IRS prior to acting on the claim.

The citizen must afford the IRS a period of six months in which to act on the claim. Prior to the expiration of that period, no suit in court may be commenced. However, if the claim is denied, or if six months lapse with no action taken by the IRS, the right to file an action in the district court is born.[38] See Chapter Five, under the heading *Filing the Complaint.*

Chapter Five also contains a sample claim for refund. See Exhibit 5-4. However, when adapting that claim form to employment taxes, one must be careful to set out the facts and circumstances applicable to the employment tax issue.

Ultimate Defense Weapon Number Four

The District Court Action For Refund and Abatement

The quick trigger finger often displayed by Revenue Officers while holding the employment tax assessment weapon necessitates that one be prepared to exercise his Ultimate Defense relative to this attack. Within two years of the time the IRS has denied a claim for refund, but not before six months have lapsed from the time the claim was filed, one may submit an action in the district court demanding a refund of the employment taxes paid, and request an abatement of the balance due.

All of the rules applicable to the suit for refund which we have discussed in Chapter Five apply to the action for refund in the context of employment tax assessments.

Care must be taken, when the claim for refund is drafted, to include *all of the issues* which one believes apply to the facts of the case. Any ground for refund which is not contained in the administrative claim may not later be raised in your action in the district court. Exhibit 5-6 is an example of a complaint for refund. That complaint demands a refund of *income* taxes which were erroneously assessed and collected by the IRS. When that form is adapted for use in the *employment* tax controversy, care must be taken to specifically set out the nature of the tax in question, the periods involved, and the grounds upon which the refund is sought, including a request that the unpaid balance of the assessment *be abated.*

---

36. *United States v. Flora,* 362 U.S. 145 (1960).

37. Code §3503.

38. Code §6532(a).

Prosecuting the Action for Refund and Abatement

The process by which one will prosecute his action for refund and abatement within the district court is not much different than that which we discussed in Chapter Five. One major difference is worthy of some attention. When a divisible tax is just partially paid prior to the commencement of the action, the government can be expected to file a "counterclaim" seeking a judgment for the balance of the amount due.

A counterclaim is nothing more than the government's claim that, rather than your being entitled to a *refund* of the amount paid, you are in fact liable for the *balance* due. As we have already stated, you bear the burden to prove that the tax in question was assessed improperly. Carefully review the facts of the case and applicable rules of law to determine where the IRS went wrong in its reasoning. These are areas which must be identified in your claim for refund, and re-alleged in the complaint commencing the action for refund and abatement.

The Right of Trial by Jury

Without a doubt, the issue of willfulness and whether the facts of a given case do or do not justify the imposition of the 100 percent penalty, is a question for a jury to resolve.[39] In order to preserve one's right to a jury trial, a demand under Rule 38, Federal Rules of Civil Procedure, should be made at the outset on the face of your complaint.

As is common for government attorneys, an effort to settle the case through the vehicle of summary judgment (Rule 56 FRCvP) is often made. When this occurs, one must be prepared to demonstrate that facts material to the issues involved in the case have yet to be resolved. When questions of fact remain unresolved, particularly those revolving around the question of willfulness and the time periods associated with the failure to pay employment taxes, summary judgment is not an appropriate means by which to dispose of the case.[40] Care should be taken to preserve the case for jury trial by submitting affidavits and other material authorized by Rule 56 in opposition to the government's motion for summary judgment. See Chapter Five, under the heading, *The Motion for Summary Judgment.*

Negotiating a Settlement

We discussed settlement negotiations in Chapter Five. I believe that it is important, in the context of this type of proceeding, to be mindful of the possibility of settling the case without a trial. One should never lose sight of the fact that in all litigation, especially federal tax litigation, the hazards associated with a trial are substantial. Regardless of what may be considered an "open and shut case," there is always the risk that you may lose your case.

By this, I am not suggesting that *every case* be settled without trial, regardless of the facts. However, I am saying that too often, stubborn persons unwilling to enter into a reasonable settlement end up "holding the bag" at the conclusion of a trial. One must always *objectively* consider the risks of trial, including the costs in terms of fees, expenses and time, against the cost of a reasonable settlement. It is important to keep an open mind.

The Trial

If settlement cannot be reached, the case will be submitted for trial. As I already stated, you are legally saddled with the burden of proof on the issues in the complaint. Therefore, you must be prepared to go forward with evidence to prove your claims to the satisfaction of the court or jury. In this regard, all evidence you possess and have obtained through the discovery process should, if relevant to the issues, be presented to the court.

In the trial, all evidence is submitted through the testimony of witnesses. You may testify on your own behalf or call such witnesses whose testimony will be helpful to resolve the facts. After the evidence is submitted, the court or jury will determine the facts of the case and render judgment accordingly. A written instrument will be issued to the parties at the conclusion of the trial. The instrument will reflect the judgment and constitutes the final order in the case.

Exhibit 6-8 is a flow chart depecting the progression of a refund case through the district court.

---

39. *Dudley v. United States,* 428 F.2d 1196 (9th Cir. 1970); *Fitzgibbons v. United States,* 522 F.2d 1353 (5th Cir. 1975).
40. *Louisville Credit Men's Asso. v. United States,* 73-2 USTC Paragraph 9740 (ED Ky 1970).

Conclusion

Employment tax assessments, in particular the 100 percent penalty, are sources of much grief in this country. Countless individuals are assessed employment taxes and made liable for their payment merely because they are ill-equipped to suggest effective reasons why such an assessment should not be made. In addition, recent developments in the IRS' Employment Tax Examination Program make it mandatory that one understand his rights when it comes to employment tax assessments.

These tax assessments are dangerous and highly destructive simply because the deficiency procedures available in income taxes cases do not apply to employment tax assessments. This feature of the law increases the risk for the unwary citizen. Regardless of the apparent advantage the IRS has in this area, it can accomplish nothing in the way of unlawful collection if you are faithful in the exercise of your rights as illustrated above. As long as you are prepared to meet the enemy at every turn, you hold the advantage. Remember, the IRS' goal is to collect taxes, not litigate with each citizen it encounters in the process.

Exhibit 6-8:
Flowchart of Action for
Refund and Abatement

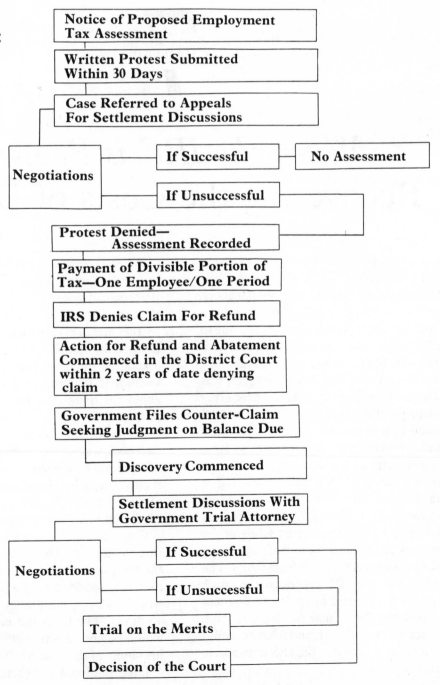

When the IRS is Beaten Recovering the Costs of Battle

Some time ago, I became aware of a problem a young couple was having with the IRS. It involved tax year 1986 and was caused by the IRS misapplying a check mailed in payment of those taxes. The amount in question was comparatively small, about $650, but to Greg and his wife, it represented all the money they had. It all started when Greg mailed a check in payment of the liability with the return. The check, however, was written to the IRS by Greg's sister-in-law, Chris. Greg obtained a loan to pay the taxes due. When the IRS received the mailing, it noted that Greg and his wife filed their return, but credited the payment to Chris, rather than to the return with which it was sent.

Several months later, the IRS began demanding of Greg that the tax be paid. This, of course, caused much confusion, because as far as Greg understood, the tax was paid with money he borrowed from Chris at the time the return was filed. As a matter of fact, Greg obtained a copy of the cancelled check from Chris. The document revealed that the IRS processed the check which was subsequently honored by the bank. This was proof positive, assumed Greg, that the tax was paid. What Greg did not know, however, and what he would not learn until much later, was that the IRS improperly applied the funds he mailed.

When threatening letters began to arrive, Greg went to see the family tax advisor and return preparer. The professional wrote a letter and included in it a copy of the cancelled check (which itself revealed no evidence as to the manner in which it was applied). The letter pointed out that Greg paid the tax with the return. He asked that the matter be straightened out immediately. Confident that the problem was solved, Greg went about his daily activities, nearly forgetting about the problem.

Then, without further warning, the bomb hit. Greg's paycheck was seized by the IRS, leaving him with just $75 per week on which to support himself, his wife and their young son. Greg charged back to the tax preparer's office in a huff. "What's going on here?" he demanded. "I thought this was straightened out!"

Greg learned, much to his chagrin, that it was not straightened out. He learned that, rather than informing the tax preparer that it corrected the mistake, the IRS merely responded with a form letter explaining that it would look into the matter and would respond "within 45 days." The letter did not explain that the response would be hostile action which would deprive Greg and his family of the means by which to support themselves.

Greg implored the preparer to write another letter.

"Explain what's going on here," Greg begged. "We can't live on $75 per week!"

Another letter was written, but it generated only a computer notice stating that taxes were due and declaring the amount which must be paid. By that time, interest and penalties were added to the original amount. Greg had a low paying, factory job. His wife did not work outside the home. Circumstances did not look good if the levy were to remain in effect for any length of time.

After the bad news was received from the IRS a second time, Greg pleaded with the preparer, "You've got to do something!"

"I think you should just pay the tax," the preparer responded. "It will cost too much to fight."

"Pay it with what," Greg quipped desperately. "I had to borrow money to pay it the first time!"

Despite his protestations, Greg was persuaded that the only sensible approach to the problem was to borrow again, and pay the IRS. When it was shown that Greg would have to pay the preparer several hundred dollars to correct the situation, it became a matter of choosing between the lesser of two evils. After all, Greg rationalized to himself, he could work a few hours a week overtime, and maybe a weekend here and there. In six or eight months, he could have the money paid back—again. At least this way, the IRS was off his back. By the time Greg raised the money to pay the IRS, the bill ticked up to $1,100.

The False Hypothesis

The scenario I have just related is repeated throughout the United States on a daily basis. The sad part is not so much that the IRS collects money not lawfully due. Rather, the unfortunate part of the scenario is the false hypothesis which seems to permeate the attitude of the tax paying community. The false hypothesis is present among, and directs the conduct of taxpayers and tax professionals alike. The false hypothesis that it costs more to *win* than it does to *lose!*

Nothing could be further from the truth! The IRS has been wildly successful over the years in collecting unjust taxes from ignorant citizens because those citizens are programmed to *shortsightedness* with regard to the problem. Those responsible for the false hypothesis *refuse* to consider the long-term effects of their failure or refusal to *fight* battles which can be won. The most glaring long-term hazard of clinging to the hypothesis is, that with each unlawful act successfully committed, the IRS *becomes stronger and bolder.* Power is not content with the status quo Power feeds upon itself! Power is like a cancer! It may start small and appear controllable, but the longer it is allowed to

dominate the host, the greater the likelihood that it will destroy the host.

This is even more true of *unlawful* power. Unlawful power can only exist in an environment of fear. When the element of fear is removed, unjust power can exercise no control over its host. The very existence of unjust power is dependent upon the proliferation of its unjust manifestations. Thus is created the cycle of lawlessness which I described in the Introduction to this manual. When one succumbs to unjust demands of illegitimate power without a struggle, he contributes to the cycle of lawlessness!

Hence, the price of appeasement is *far greater* than that of victory, since with victory comes a return to the rule of law and the destruction of the cycle of lawlessness. Therefore, it is not only desirable that society resist unlawful demands, but *such resistance is mandatory* if society is to retain any measure of liberty whatsoever! Freedom, like all of life's treasures, is *not free.* It comes at a price. Samuel Adams, the great American revolutionary leader, stated in 1771:

"The liberties of our country, the freedom of our civil constitution, are worth defending at all hazards; and it is our duty to defend them against all attacks. We have received them as a fair inheritance from our worthy ancestors: they purchased them for us with toil and danger and expense of treasure and blood, and transmitted them to us with care and diligence. It will bring an everlasting mark of infamy on the present generation, enlightened as it is, if we should suffer them to be wrested from us by violence without a struggle, or be cheated out of them by the artifices of false and designing men."

I must at this point raise a caution: I am not inciting the reader to *rebellion* against the *lawfully* constituted authority of this or any other government. No indeed! The first responsibility of a citizen under a Republican form of constitutional government is to *respect and obey* the law. At the same time, however, these very same demands are placed upon the heads of government as well. *They are not above the law.* They are without license to abuse the rights and liberties of the people just as we are without license to abuse the rights and liberties of one another. When such heads of government manifest designs to erode or dissolve those liberties, Jefferson observed in the Declaration of Independence that we the people, retain the lawful authority to prevent such an eventuality. In this regard, Adams, in 1776, defending his call to arms of the American colonies, declared:

"What has commonly been called rebellion has more often been nothing but a manly and glorious struggle in opposition to the *lawless power of rebellious* kings and princes." (Emphasis in original.)

Adams, in that now famous call to arms delivered in Philadelphis before Congress assembled, concluded with a ringing denouncement of those unwilling to take up arms in defense of liberty. He cried:

"If ye love wealth better than liberty, the tranquility of servitude better than the animating contest of freedom, go home from us in peace. We ask not your counsels or arms. Crouch down and lick the hands which feed you. May your chains set lightly upon you, and may posterity forget that ye were our countrymen."

Awake America! Arise and cast off the yoke of fear which has gripped you about the throat for a generation! It is unnatural for you to live in fear of *your own government!* Moreover, it is unnatural for *your own government* to threaten the liberty and tranquility of your peaceful existence under the law. You cannot continue to endure lawless conduct lest you feed the cycle of lawlessness. You have no responsibility under the law to tolerate the abuses of the liberties which you have inherited at great cost to your forefathers. However, you do have a great responsibility to see that those liberties are passed on to posterity. I declare to you America, just as Captain John Parker declared to his men at Lexington Green in April of 1775, while facing a contingent of British troops:

"Stand your ground! Don't fire unless fired upon, but if they mean to have a war let it begin here!"

The Payment of Reparations

There is another, more worldly reason for marching to the sound of the guns where IRS abuse is concerned. It is based upon the proposition that any nation guilty of unlawful aggression is liable for *reparations* to the nation it has attacked. Congress has agreed to hold the IRS liable to you for *reparations* when it is guilty of an unlawful attack upon the liberty of your property or finances. The combination of having destroyed the false hypothesis that there is any "security" in appeasement, and the reality that the IRS may be held accountable to you for any unlawful attack, justifies *standing firm* against its onslaught. In a very real sense, you have

nothing to lose, but *everything to gain,* when lawlessness is opposed at every turn!

In November of 1988, former President Ronald Reagan signed the Taxpayers' Bill of Rights Act into law.[1] With it came an amendment to §7430 of the Code. The amendment removed much of the risk associated with opposing unlawful IRS actions. The law provides:

"In any administrative or court proceeding which is brought by or against the United States in connection with the determination, collection, or refund of any tax, interest, or penalty under this title, the prevailing party may be awarded a judgment or a settlement for—

"(1) reasonable administrative costs incurred in connection with such administrative proceeding within the IRS, and

"(2) reasonable litigation costs incurred in connection with such court proceeding."

The language we have just examined reflects a substantially broader position than that which existed under the prior law. Prior to the amendment,[2] the law authorized recovery of fees and costs only in "civil proceedings." The courts took the narrow view that a "civil proceeding" was one occuring only in the courts of the United States. Thus, in order to recover costs, one was required to in fact sue the IRS, something very few are willing to attempt.

Under the *new* law, however, it is clear that one need not actually sue the IRS to recover the costs of rectifying unjust collection action. The addition to the statute of the term "administrative" clearly reveals that one need not exercise the ultimate remedy for correcting tax collection ills. When successful in negotiations with the IRS at the administrative level, the law provides the authority for you to recover costs and fees when appropriate under the circumstances.[3]

The statute defines the terms "reasonable litigation costs" and "reasonable administrative costs." Under §7430(c), "reasonable litigation costs" are said to include: (1) reasonable court costs, (2) the reasonable expenses of expert witnesses in connection with a court proceeding (but such fees may not exceed those paid to expert witnesses hired by the government), (3) the reasonable costs of any study, analysis, engineering report or project which is necesary for the preparation of your case, and (4) reasonable fees paid to an attorney

---

1. Technical and Miscellaneous Revenue Act of 1988, P.L. 100-647.

2. The new law applies to proceedings commenced after November 10, 1988.

3. Code §§7430(c)(2), (c)(4)(B), and (f)(2).

hired for the purpose of the litigation.

The term "reasonable administrative costs" are said to include: (1) any administrative fees or similar charges imposed by the IRS, and (2) all of those expenses which we have just listed in the preceding paragraph.

There are some limitations which we must examine before reviewing the specific procedures involved in obtaining a judgment or settlement permitting an award of fees and costs. First, the statute states that before fees and costs will be awarded, you must "prevail" in your case against the IRS. A prevailing party is one who establishes that the position of the United States in the proceeding was "not substantially justified," and one who "has substantially prevailed with respect to the amount in controversy" or, "with respect to the most significant issue or set of issues presented" in the case.[4]

Another limitation is that the party "prevailing" *may not recover* his fees and costs if his net worth exceeds $2 million. Businesses and local organizations will not be permitted to recover such costs if their net worth exceeds $7 million or they have more than 500 employees.[5]

Still another limitation is that the "prevailing" party must have exhausted all administrative proceedings applicable to his case. We have gone to great lengths in this manual to describe, accurately and in detail, all of the administrative procedures available to a person engaged in a dispute with the IRS. If for no other reason than to ensure that one will be able to recover his fees and costs, extra care should be taken to correctly pursue all adminstrative remedies with the IRS. If at any point you are in doubt as to what those procedures are, you must request specific, *accurate* information relative to those procedures from the IRS representative with whom you are working. Failure of the IRS to provide such information has been used as grounds for awarding fees and costs.[6]

The final limitation to an award of fees under §7430, is found at subsection (b)(4) of the statute. It stipulates that:

> "No award for reasonable litigation and administrative fees may be made under subsection (a) with respect to any portion of the administrative or court proceeding during which the prevailing partry has unreasonably protracted such proceeding."

I stated earlier in this manual that lengthy delays in tax litigation were of no benefit to the citizen. Considering the potential for the accrual of interest alone, any gain which one may achieve in litigation could well be cancelled by interest. Here we find further impetus for exercising every possible remedy in the swiftest fashion. Deliberate delays in battle generate nothing but expense. In this case, the expense translates to the loss of the ability to recover your fees and costs from the government.

When to Request an Award of Fees and Costs

A request for the payment of fees and costs should be made anytime you are successful in your civil or administrative litigation with the IRS. It should be known, however, that the payment of fees and costs is not available when the case is before the Examination Division of the IRS. The Congressonal Committee Reports which describe the legislative intent of the law state that relief is available after an "unjustified position" is advanced by the IRS when the case is before "IRS district counsel administratively." Therefore, as a general principle, fees and costs are unavailable when the case is "in the audit or appeals process."[7]

There is some confusion between the language of the statute and the comments of Congress reflected in the Committee Reports. The Committee Reports seem to reflect an intent that one be permitted to recover fees and costs *any time* the IRS has issued a 30-day letter, or after the date on which the relevant evidence under your control, as well as all relevant legal arguments, were presented by you to the IRS.[8] This would mean that fees are recoverable even when the case is within the Appeals Division.

On the other hand, the statute itself states that the "substantially unjustified position" of the United States must be asserted as of "the date of the receipt by the taxpayer of the notice of the decision of the IRS Appeals Office, or, the date of the notice of deficiency."[9]

In either event, such notice appears after the appeals process is complete. It seems that, if the intent of Congress was to permit recovery of fees and costs in

---

4. Code §7430(c)(4).

5. This proviso is lifted from the *Equal Access to Justice Act,* 28 USC §2412. See IRS Code §7430(c)(4)(A)(iii).

6. *Golden v. United States,* 86-2 USTC Paragraph 9626 (DC Mo. 1986).

7. Congressional Committee Report on P.L. 100-647.

8. Ibid.

9. See Code §7430(c)(7).

connection with an *appeal,* the language of the statute is overly restrictive. However, if Congress did not intend one to be entitled to fees and costs, then its remarks in the Committee Report are entirely superfluous; something I believe to be unlikely.

Through all of this, one point immerges clear: I believe that one should take steps to preserve his rights under §7430 at the earliest possible opportunity. That, according to the Congressional Committee Report, is after an *appeal* is successful, in which you provided all relevant data and legal arguments on the subject matter to the IRS. Thus, if one is successful in his case before the Appeals Division where the IRS advanced a position substantially unjustified by the law and the facts, he would do well to demand that his fees and costs be reimbursed by the IRS.

Regardless of the possible ambiguity on the matter at the *administrative* level, there is *no confusion,* either in the statute or the Committee Reports, with regard to one's rights when in *litigation* with the IRS. If, in the Tax Court or the district court, the attorneys of the United States have advanced a position which is not substantially justified by the law or the facts of the case, you *are entitled* to recover your fees and costs.

Ultimate Defense Weapon Number Five

The Proceeding to Recover Fees and Costs

The proceeding to recover fees and costs is quite simple compared to the other defense weapons discussed in this manual. The reason is that this procedure is an adjunct to those we have already discussed. It is not, in the strictest sense of the word, a proceeding independently pursued. Before one is entitled to recover his fees and costs, he must have successfully utilized one of the procedures we already explained. At the very least, he must have exercised his right of appeal after his tax audit.

Making the Request For Fees and Costs

A request for fees and costs should always be made in writing. When drafting the demand for fees and costs

one must be careful to set out each of the elements of the statute.

The Elements of the Statute. We discussed many of the provisions of §7430, both in terms of its limitations and in terms of what in fact, it permits. A summary of those requirements is:

1. That you were involved in litigation or an administrative proceeding with the IRS in which you prevailed;

2. That the position of the United States advanced by its representatives in that litigatoin or administrative proceeding was substantially unjustified based upon the law and facts of the case;

3. That you substantially prevailed with respect to the amount in controversy, or with respect to the most significant issue or set of issues presented;

4. That you exhausted all administrative remedies available under the Internal Revenue Code and regulations:

5. That you did not unreasonably protract the proceedings in any particular;

6. That you incurred fees and costs in connection with the litigation or proceeding in the following amounts, for the following purposes, at the following times: (list all expenses, including the date incurred and the purpose of the expense); and

7. That your net worth does not exceed $2 million (for an individual).

In Exhibit 7-1, I have set forth an example of a written demand for reimbursement of fees and costs. The example substantially meets all of the elements of the statute, providing a guideline which may be followed in structuring your demand for fees and costs. Be careful to substitute your facts and circumstances, and to include a listing of all expenses incurred, and the dates and purposes of the costs, including attorney's fees.

Filing the Demand For Fees and Costs. The written demand for recovery of fees and costs should be submitted no later than 30 days from the date the IRS or the court makes a determination in your favor. The demand should be submitted to the authority who ruled in your favor on the merits. However, if one is seeking the *dismissal* of a court action commenced against him by the government, the request for fees and costs should accompany the motion for dismissal of the case. It has been held in at least one case that after the court in fact dismisses the case against the citizen, it loses jurisdiction to rule upon the demand for fees and costs. Therefore, it should be submitted prior to the court's dismissing the case.[10]

---

10. *Sanders v. Commissioner,* 813 F.2d 859 (7th Cir. 1987); but see *Weiss v. Commissioner,* 850 F2d 111 (2nd Cir. 1988), to the contrary.

Exhibit 7-1: Demand for Fees and Costs

UNITED STATES TAX COURT

William E. and Jane M. Citizen,	)	
Petitioners,	)	Docket No. _____
vs.	)	
Commissioner of Internal Revenue,	)	
Respondent.	)	

DEMAND FOR FEES AND COSTS

PLEASE TAKE NOTICE, that the Petitioners in the above-entitled proceeding, hereby move this Court for an order granting them an award of the fees and costs which they have expended in connection with the prosecution of this case, pursuant to 26 USC §7430.

This demand is based upon all of the files, records and proceedings in this case, upon the Rules of Practice for the Tax Court, and upon the following:

GROUNDS

1. Petitioners assert that they have substantially prevailed on the merits of this case. Attached to this demand and made a part hereof, the court will find a copy of the Findings of Fact and Opinion of the Court which was entered on (date). The text of the Opinion describes the issues on which it was held that the Petitioners prevailed.

2. The opinion of the court reflects that the Petitioners substantially prevailed with respect to the amount in controversy. (Alternatively) The opinion of the court reflects that the

DEMAND FOR FEES AND COSTS, PAGE 1

Petitioners prevailed with respect to the most significant issue or issues presented.

3. The position of the Commissioner as advanced by his legal representatives in this case was not substantially justified. In support of this contention, the Petitioners show the court: (list all facts and circumstances, including legal references, which support your allegation that the government's position was not substantially justified.)

4. That the Petitioners exhausted all administrative procedures available to them within the IRS, including the following: (list all steps and procedures taken which were in satisfaction of administrative procedure requirements, or which were calculated by you to settle the case without the need of a trial, including efforts to negotiate with Appeals or district counsel personnel.)

5. The Petitioners at no time took any steps, or failed to take any steps, the effect of which was to unreasonably protract these proceedings. At all times, Petitioners proceeded in good faith with an eye toward settling this dispute.

6. The Petitioners incurred fees and costs in connection with the prosecution of this case. Those fees and costs are itemized as follows:

Date   Amount of Expense   Purpose of Expense

(Enter all amounts paid, with an explanation and date of payment.)

Receipts for all such fees and costs are attached hereto and made a part hereof.

DEMAND FOR FEES AND COSTS, PAGE 2

Total Fees and Costs Demanded = $ (amount)

7.   The Petitioners' net worth is well below $2 million.

8.   Petitioners hereby declare under penalty of perjury that all of the statements of fact contained in this Demand for Fees and Costs are true and correct in all respects.

WHEREFORE, based upon the above showing, the Petitioners hereby request that the Court award them the fees and costs they have expended in connection with the prosecution of this case, as shown in paragraph 6, in accordance with 26 USC §7430.

Dated:

_____   _____
William E. Citizen   Jane M. Citizen

Address
City, State, Zip
Area Code and Phone Number

NOTE: This form should be adapted when used in connection with a district court proceeding, or in administrative proceedings before the IRS.

Proving the Government's Position Was Unjustified

The Senate amendment proposed that the burden of proof on the issue be *shifted* to the government. Under that procedure, all the citizen would be required to do would be to *allege* that the government's position was substantially unjustified, and the government would bear the burden to disprove the assertion. However, that proposal did not find favor with Congress. The conference committee chose to retain the requirements of law which existed prior to November of 1988.

Therefore, the citizen is required to demonstrate that the IRS' position in the litigation or administrative proceeding was substantially unjustified. Whether the government's position was unjustified is determined by examining its action *or inaction* in connection with the case. If the government's factual position or legal arguments can find no support in the context of the issues of the case, this will bear upon the question whether its position was substantially unjustified.

To a great extent, in passing §7430 of the tax Code, Congress intended to incorporate many of the provisions of the Equal Access to Justice Act, codified at 28 USC §2412. In particular, under the EAJA, the question of whether the government's position in a litigated matter is substantially unjustified is answered by examining both the government's in-court litigation conduct and any "action or failure to act taken by the agency upon which the civil action is based."[11]

Thus, any conduct which tends to reflect upon the question of whether the government's position was justified, should be advanced as grounds for granting the demand for fees and costs. Any actions or failures to act which have placed you in the position of being *forced* to litigate also bear upon this question.[12] Because it is your burden to prove that the government's position was not substantially justified, you should include any factual references to the events of the case, as well as references to the law which tend to support your claims.

Most importantly, you must prove that you have actually expended the funds you are seeking to recover. If you have represented yourself in connection with the case, you will be entitled to recover all the costs you have expended, but you will not be entitled to any attorney's fees.[13]

Any demand made to the IRS in an administrative vein which is denied by them may be appealed to the Tax Court.[14] The Tax Court is then empowered to overrule the IRS and grant you an award of fees when conditions so warrant.

Conclusion

In many cases, resisting the unjust claims of the IRS and its efforts to collect additional taxes can be defeated with the expenditure of just one postage stamp. When it comes to the arbitrary notice or demands for additional penalties, the time it takes to write a letter is the only burden one faces in the war for tax justice. However, when the matter extends beyond mere letter writing, the cost of battling the IRS can, without a doubt, become great.

This factor is chiefly responsible for deterring resistance to unjust demands. The thought that it is simpler to "just pay" than it is to fight leads most people to reach into their pockets for the checkbook. "After all," they reason, "my peace-of-mind is worth something too. At least this way, they are off my back." Regardless of the manner in which it is rationalized, the IRS may well have committed a lawless act, and the unwary citizen, through his inaction, has contributed to the cycle of lawlessness.

We have the affirmative duty to break this cycle of lawlessness. Our liberties are worthy of defense—at all costs. Despite this truth, one need not risk his fortune to defend his lawful position. Because one is able, under §7430, to recover fees and costs he has expended in the war against unjustified government action, he may effectively wage the war *at no expense.*

Given this fact, there is no longer any further excuse in my mind; when the IRS makes unlawful demands, *say no!* And when you are successful, make them pay the bill for fighting back!

---

11. See 28 USC §2412(d)(2)(D); *Trichilo v. Secretary of H&HS*, 823 F.2d 702 (2nd Cir. 1987).

12. See *Weiss v. Commissioner,* supra.

13. *Frisch v. Commissioner*, 87 TC 838; *Moran v. Commissioner*, 87 TC 738.

14. Code §7430(f)(2); Code §7463.

PART IV
Eliminating IRS Abuse

CHAPTER

Specialized Training

The rallying cry to which proponents of the recently enacted Taxpayers' Bill of Rights Act responded was the need to provide increased protection to citizens from the dreaded IRS tools of lien, levy and seizure. As a matter of fact, the proponents of the Bill of Rights Act used evidence of the IRS' almost indiscriminate use of these tax collection weapons as proof of the need for a Bill of Rights Act.

In its early stages, there were two versions of the Taxpayers' Bill of Rights Act introduced before Congress. The first, S.579, was introduced on February 23, 1987, by Senator Harry Reid of Nevada. The second, S.604, was introduced three days later by Senator David Pryor of Arkansas.[1] Senator Pryor's bill, S.604, was ultimately passed into law, after some revision, as part of the Technical and Miscellaneous Revenue Act of 1988.[2]

Senator Pryor's Bill of Rights Act is not the first Taxpayers' Bill of Rights ever proposed. The idea of a Taxpayers' Bill of Rights bounced around Congress for

many years. Several congressmen and senators proposed such amendments and additions to the Internal Revenue Code as they believed would increase the level of protection afforded the average taxpayer. All such moves however, failed in the past. David Pryor is the Chairman of the Subcommittee on Private Retirement Plans and Oversight of the Internal Revenue Service. That Subcommittee is part of the Senate Committee on Finance, of which Lloyd Bentsen of Texas, was Chairman.

Among those in Congress supporting Pryor were Senators Charles Grassley of Iowa and Carl Levin of Michigan. In 1980, Senator Levin as Chairman of the Senate Subcommittee on Oversight and Government Operations, held hearings on the "impact of IRS collection practices upon small businesses."[3] In his prepared statement, made part of the record of the hearings on June 22, 1987, Senator Levin claims that the Tax Equity and Fiscal Responsibility Act (TEFRA) of 1982, represents "some progress" in the area of

---

1. A companion bill to S.604 was also introduced into the House of Representatives by Congressman Robin Tallon of South Carolina. The House version was H.R.1313.

2. The full text of the Act as passed by Congress is reproduced in the Appendix to the *Special Report* on the Taxpayers' Bill of Rights Act, WINNING Publications, 1989.

3. Transcript of S.604 Hearings held June 22, 1987, pages 15-16, and prepared statement of Senator Levin, page 1.

improving "taxpayers' rights."[4]

With my knowledge of TEFRA and the effects that it had not only on "revenue enhancement," but upon IRS collection practices, I find it nothing short of astonishng that Senator Levin would refer to TEFRA as manifesting "some progress" in the area of "taxpayer rights." Not only did TEFRA represent the largest single tax increase in the history of the United States,[5] but the law added countless new information reporting and penalty provisions to the Code. Ironically, many of the penalty provisons were so structured as to legally bypass the deficiency procedures of the Code,[6] thereby rendering the penalties immediately collectible without any right of taxpayer appeal prior to assessment. These very penalty provisions are now being reexamined by Congress after harsh criticism from former IRS Commissioner Lawrence Gibbs.[7]

Besides adding many new so-called "assessable penalties," to the Code,[8] TEFRA added a total of 5,223 IRS employees for the *express purpose* of achieving "better compliance with the internal revenue laws."[9] Of the 5,000-plus new employees, 3,000 were Revenue Officers whose sole function is to collect assesed taxes. Revenue Officers are the IRS employees who are empowered to execute seizures, liens and levies, the collection tools that received the most criticism by Senator Pryor and others in his Bill of Rights hearings.

For example, Senator Levin pointed out some startling statistics. He claims that, "In fiscal year 1981, there were 8,848 seizures by the IRS nationwide. In fiscal year 1986, there were 22,450, over two and a half times as many (154 percent increase). The number of levies has also more than doubled, going from 740,103 in fiscal year 1981 to 1,617,982 in fiscal year 1986 (119 percent increase.)"

"During this same period," Levin continued, "the number of tax delinquent accounts rose by only about a third, going from 1,436,000 in fiscal year 1981 to 1,938,000 in fiscal year 1986 (35 percent increase.)"[10]

Levin's apparent dismay over these dramatic increases defies understanding. *It was Congress,* in 1982, that gave the IRS the tools and initiative to "collect additional tax revenues of at least $1 billion in fiscal year 1984 and $2 billion in fiscal year 1985."[11] It was Congress who handed the IRS more laws designed specifically to utilize the seizure, lien and levy power which only IRS collection officers command. Along with this power, Congress handed the IRS over 5,000 additional employees—60% of which were hired solely to wield these formidable collection weapons. Finally, it was Congress which handed the IRS additional funding to carry these directives to the people.[12]

Should Levin, or any other Senator for that matter,[13] be *confused* as to why the IRS so dramatically increased its enforced collection action where there is no corresponding increase in delinquent tax accounts? I think not, since the Senate Report discloses that these enforcement personnel were *projected to collect* a total of $10.1 billion in the five years beginning 1982-1987.[14] The facts seem to indicate that these 5,000 plus tax collectors are doing their jobs quite efficiently.

The only issue now is whether the very same Senators who gave the IRS their awesome and arbitrary power and the means to exercise it have, through the Taxpayers' Bill of Rights, earnestly and sincerely moved to emasculate the Frankenstein monster they have created. History alone will be the judge. In the meantime, we must ask ourselves whether we stand safe from the potential for IRS abuse of these most destructive tax collection weapons in light of the Taxpayers' Bill of Rights Act. The answer to that question is, that while the Bill of Rights Act has lent some *degree* of assistance to the beleaguered taxpayer, it is *far from being the ultimate* solution to the problem.

The ultimate solution to the problem, as declared throughout this manual and elsewhere in my writings, is citizen awareness of his rights and the manner in which they may most effectively be put to use. IRS abuse is not, and will not be a "thing of the past" until each and every citizen of the United States is ready, willing and able to stand firm against an impending unlawful IRS onslaught. Only then will the IRS end its reign of terror over the American citizen. Until then, citizens must be aware of the manner in which they can defeat the abuse by the IRS of its weapons of lien, levy and seizure. Part IV of this manual is dedicated to that very goal.

---

4. Statement of Levin, page 3.

5. The July 12, 1982, Senate Finance Committee Report announced that the "budget effects" of the law would raise a total of $288.3 billion over the six year period from 1982-1987.

6. See Chapter Four.

7. See Chapter One, under the heading, *The Enemy's Political Climate.*

8. Defined as those which may be collected without any taxpayer right of appeal before assessment.

9. Finance Committee Report on TEFRA, page 310.

10. See Levin's prepared statement, page 2.

11. Finance Committee Report on TEFRA, page 310.

12. Ibid, page 311.

13. It should be noted that Senator Grassley was a member of the Senate Finance Committee in 1982, and had a hand in the TEFRA legislation.

14. TEFRA Report, page 414.

To be successful in this regard, however, there are certain principles of law which we must examine and be prepared to put into use prior to taking the offensive. We shall discuss them in turn.

The Anti-Injunction Act

Two terms with which the reader will become familiar during this disclosure are "injunction" and "Anti-Injunction Act." The former speaks of a "court order" directed againt a party to a legal proceeding. The order prevents a party from executing certain threatened acts against another. In the context of this discussion, any "injunction" directed toward the IRS would be calculated to prevent it from carrying out any threatened action, such as the seizure or sale of property. "Injunctive relief" speaks to the order of a court which actually *precludes* the act.

Any lawsuit which seeks an injunction against the IRS faces a serious legal obstacle from the outset. That obstacle is the "Anti-Injunction Act." Regardless of the facts of the case and the seriousness of the IRS' conduct, this law creates a roadblock to injunctive relief in many cases. The Anti-Injunction Act is found at Code §7421. That statute is relied upon heavily by government tax attorneys. It reads as follows:

> ". . .no suit for the purpose of restraining the assessment or collection of any tax shall be maintained in any court by any person, whether or not such person is the person against whom such tax was assessed."[15]

This statute has probably caused more IRS abuse than any other single factor that I can imagine. The reason is that the statute, on its face, takes the authority away from *all courts* to even *consider* a case against the IRS involving the "assessment or collection of taxes." Stated more clearly, the IRS enjoys, according to the statute, *unfettered power and authority* to take any steps it deems necessary to assess or collect taxes, and nobody, *including the courts,* has the power to stop it. If you are looking for something to write your Congressman about, this would be a good subject. How can it be said that we live in a Constitutional Republic when this type of law is on the books?

Exceptions to the Anti-Injunction Act

As one would truly hope, however, there are exceptions to the apparently unbending language of the law. The exceptions are few, but are necessary to understand if we are to successfully engage the enemy in battle. The first type of exceptions are those which are, like the Anti-Injunction Act itself, created by statute.

The Premature Assessment. The *first exception* arises when a Petition in the United States Tax Court has been timely filed.[16] As we learned, the Tax Court is an administrative tribunal established solely for the purpose of resolving disputes as to tax liability *before the tax is assessed.* One's ticket to the Tax Court is obtained when he receives a notice of deficiency from the IRS.

The notice of deficiency is the final administrative determination that the citizen owes additional taxes. When received, the citizen may either pay the tax, or if he disagrees with the tax computations set out within the notice, he may fiie a petition with the Tax Court within 90 days of the date stamped on the face of the letter. Provided a petition is filed within the 90-day grace period, the IRS is forbidden from pursuing *any* action whatsoever "until the decision of the Tax Court has become final." The express language of the proscription reads:

> "* * *Except as otherwise provided. . .no assessment of a deficiency in respect of any tax imposed by subtitle A or B,. . .and *no levy or proceeding in court for its collection* shall be made, begun, or prosecuted until such notice (of deficiency) has been mailed to the taxpayer, not until the expiration of such 90-day. . .period, nor, if a petition has been filed with the Tax Court, until the decision of the Tax Court has become final. *Nothwithstanding the provisions of section 7421(a) (the Anti-Injunction Act), the making of such assessment or the beginning of such proceeding or levy during the time such prohibition is in force may be enjoined by a proceeding in the proper court,* including the Tax Court.* * *" Code §6213(a); emphasis added.

A timely petition filed with the Tax Court acts in much the same manner as an injunction against the IRS. The statute expressly forbids the assessment of the tax before the expiration of the 90-day period. When a Tax Court Petition is timely filed, the statute expressly forbids the IRS not only from assessing the tax, but from engaging in any effort *whatsoever* to collect the tax. The final sentence of the statute is an express *exception* to the Anti-Injunction Act. Its language is plain and the meaning is simple: When the IRS has violated the deficiency procedures, the "proper court" may enjoin

15. See also 28 USC §2201.
16. See Chapter Four.

the IRS from its efforts to collect the tax.[17]

Despite the clear condemnation of any assessment or collection efforts during the pendency of the 90-day grace period or the Tax Court action, IRS does *routinely* assess taxes in violation of the statute. It is common for the IRS to file tax liens while a case is pending in the Tax Court, or even to levy wages and bank accounts prior to a decision from the Tax Court. This is in defiance of the statute. With the passage of the Taxpayers' Bill of Rights Act, Code §6213(a) was amended. The amendment specifically handed the Tax Court the authority to enjoin the IRS from carrying out any action or proceeding to collect a tax when a timely petition was filed with the Court. However, an injunction against collection of the premature assessment is available through the Tax Court *only* if a timely petition is filed. In this regard, §6213(a) reads:

"* * *The Tax Court shall have no jurisdiction to enjoin any action or proceeding under this subjection unless a timely petition for a redetermination of the deficiency has been filed and then only in respect of the deficiency that is the subject of such petition."

The addition to the statute of the right to obtain a collection injunction from the Tax Court when the IRS is collecting pursuant to a premature assessment is a breath of fresh air. Too often the IRS ignores the restrictions on assessment contained in the law, banking upon the fact that most citizens may become bogged down in the mire of complicated court procedures, thus rendering relief from the premature assessment difficult or impossible. While relief was never impossible, the *new right* to request the Tax Court to enter the collection injunction lends much greater simplicity to the problem.

The Wrongful Levy. The *second exception* to the Anti-Injunction Act is found within Code §7426. That section of the tax law is referred to as the "Wrongful Levy Statute." The Wrongful Levy Statute *specifically and expressly* provides the district court with jurisdiction or authority to entertain lawsuits for injunctions when the IRS has levied upon or sold the property of any person, "other than the person against whom is assessed the tax out of which the levy arose."[18] In particular, the law reads:

"If a levy has been made on property or property has been sold pursuant to a levy, any person (other than the person against whom is assessed the tax out of which

such levy arose) who claims an interest in or lien on such property and that such property was wrongfully levied upon may bring a civil action against the United States in a district court of the United States. Such action may be brought without regard to whether such property has been surrendered to or sold by the Secretary." Code §7426(a)(1).

The premise of the Wrongful Levy statute is the well-settled proposition that *assessed taxes cannot be collected from any person other than the person who owes the tax.*[19] Whenever the IRS attempts, knowingly or otherwise, to levy or seize the property of a citizen against whom *no assessment* is made, in an effort to satisfy all or part of the liability of *another citizen,* the Wrongful Levy statute applies. It may be employed to provide the former with judicial relief from the improper acts of the tax collector. The statute reads:

"The district court shall have jurisdiction to grant only such of the following forms of relief as may be appropriate in the circumstances:
"(1) Injunction.—If a levy or sale would irreparably injure rights in property which the court determines to be superior to rights of the United States in such property, the court may grant an injunction to prohibit the enforcement of such levy or to prohibit such sale.
"(2) Recovery of Property.—If the court determines that such property has been wrongfully levied upon, the court may—

"(A) order the return of specific property if the United States is in possession of such property;
"(B) grant a judgment for the amount of money levied upon; or
"(C) if such property was sold, grant a judgment for an amount not exceeding the greater of—
"(i) the amount received by the United States from the sale of such property, or
"(ii) the fair market value of such property immediately before the levy.* * *" Code §7426(b)(1) and (2).

The Wrongful Levy provision of the Code has been a particularly useful tool in preventing IRS abuse. As we read, the court is expressly empowered to either enjoin the IRS from executing the levy, or it may order the IRS to return the proceeds of any property sold pursuant to the levy. The one and only important limitation to the Wrongful Levy statute is that the protections of the

17. *Mall v. Kelly,* 564 F.Supp. 371 (DC Wyo. 1983); *Stroman v. McCanless,* 391 F.Supp. 1344 (DC Tex. 1975); *Rodriguez v. United States,* 629 F.Supp. 333 (DC Ill. 1986).
18. See 26 USC §7426(a)(1).
19. See *Aquilino v. United States,* 363 U.S. 509 (1960).

statute *do not apply* to the person *against whom the assessment was made.* When the IRS is levying upon the property of a person against whom the assessment was made, other provisions of law, some of which we have already examined, must be employed to minimize the effects of such an act.

In this regard, the statute stipulates that:

"For purposes of an adjudication under this section, the assessment of tax upon which the interest or lien of the United States is based shall be conclusively presumed to be valid." Code §7426(c).

This language makes it plain that one proceeding under the Wrongful Levy statute may not attack the validity of the assessment made against another person. Rather, the basis of the court action must focus upon the propriety of the IRS' *efforts* to collect the assessment of another by levying upon your property. Thus, while the *assessment* will be considered valid and left undisturbed for purposes of this statute, the improper acts to collect the assessment from you can be prevented or remedied by the court.

A very common example of the manner in which this exemption operates applies in the case of a married couple where just one of the partners, say the husband, has a tax liability assessed against him alone. This occurs regularly when the husband files a *separate,* rather than a joint, income tax return. When a separate return is filed, the liability growing out of that return may be satisfied *only* from the property of the person who signed the return. In this example, only the husband's property could be seized to satisfy the debt.[20]

Despite this fact, the IRS very often attempts to satisfy such an assessment by levying upon the property of the wife. This is unlawful. The wife's *separate* property may not be sold by the IRS to satisfy a valid, individual assessment pending against her husband.[21] Even when the property is held *jointly* by the husband and wife, but the assessment is made separately against the husband, the IRS may not apply the wife's half-interest in the property against her husband's liability.[22]

The §7426 remedy is not limited to the husband-wife scenario I just reviewed. Another common example is when the IRS levies upon bank accounts belonging to children over which their father or mother has signature rights. The fact that the father may be acting as a custodian of the funds does not render him the owner of those funds. Under that circumstance, the children would be entitled under §7426 to either halt the seizure of the funds or to recover the funds if they were seized.

Section 7426 may be used as a tool to protect the non-taxpayer's interest in property which the IRS has levied upon. When the non-taxpayer commences the action under §7426, the Anti-Injunction Act does not apply to prevent the court from issuing an order halting the IRS from seizing or selling the property in question.

***The* Shapiro Doctrine.** *The third,* and perhaps most complex exception to the Anti-Injunction Act is not grounded in any statute passed by Congress. Rather, the exception is "equitable" in nature and finds its basis in court decisions. The term "equity" or "equitable" as used here refers to that which is just, fair, and right. *Black's Law Dictionary*[23] teaches:

"EQUITY. In its broadest and most general signification, this term denotes the spirit and the habit of fairness, justness, and right dealing which would regulate the intercourse of men with men—the rule of doing to all others as we desire them to do to us; or, as it is expressed by Justinian, 'to live honestly, to harm nobody, to render to every man his due'. (Citation) It is therefore the synonym of natural right or justice...It is grounded in the precepts of the conscience, not in any sanction of positive law.

"In a restricted sense, the word denotes equal and impartial justice as between two persons whose rights or claims are in conflict; justice that is, as ascertained by natural right or ethical insight, but independent of the formulated body of law." Revised Fourth Edition, page 634.

The "formulated body of law" relevant to this discussion is the general rule expressed within the Anti-Injunction Act. As we learned, the rule provides that the courts may not prevent the IRS from taking any action with respect to the assessment or collection of federal tax liabilities. Yet, the federal courts, exercising their "equity jurisdiction," have carved out of this granite an *exception* based upon the concepts of fairness, justness and righteousness.

The concept of relying upon the equity jurisdiction of the federal courts to enjoin IRS collection action grows out of three Supreme Court decisions on the subject. The case of *Miller v. Standard Nut Margarine Company,*[24] was the first to speak. Later came *Enochs v.*

---

20. In "community property" states such as Arizona, California and Wisconsin, state law automatically vests ownership of all property in both the husband *and* the wife, whether or not the property is held separately.

21. *United States v. Rogers,* 461 U.S. 677 (1983).

22. *Rogers,* supra. However, it should be noted that when the property is owned jointly, the IRS is permitted under certain circumstances to sell the property. It must, however, compensate the wife for her one-half interest in the property when this occurs.

23. West Publishing Company, St. Paul, Minnesota.

24. 248 U.S. 498 (1932).

Williams Packing Company,[25] followed by the latest Supreme Court statement on the question, *Commissioner v. Shapiro.*[26] This latest case was in essence, a capsulization of the earlier two. In my opinion, it settled, once and for all, the long disputed question of the *circumstances* under which a court may in fact impose an injunction upon the IRS.

Under the *Shapiro* doctrine, an injunction against the tax collector will be issued only when the applicant can demonstrate the existence of three factors, known as the elements of an injunction. The *first* element is, that *under no circumstances* can the government sustain its claim that taxes are due, based upon all of the facts available to it at the time of the suit. This allegation suggests that the tax assessment itself is *patently* invalid. While it may have been obtained in a fashion which comports with the procedures of the Code, if the facts do not justify the amount of the assessment, the first prong of the test is met. When the IRS is attempting to collect a tax, the amount of which is patently improper, the Supreme Court held this to be "an exaction in the guise of a tax."[27]

The *second* element is, the citizen must show that he will suffer *irreparable* harm if the IRS is permitted to collect the improper tax assessment. "Irreparable harm" is the kind of damage inflicted upon a person which cannot be remedied by money or money's worth compensation.

The *third* element necessary to invoking the *Shapiro* doctrine is, the citizen must demonstrate to the court that he has no *adequate* alternative means of preventing the damage likely to occur if collection were permitted to go forward. Stated another way, there are no administrative remedies which will permit him to rectify the problem before the harm is inflicted. In this regard, the IRS will suggest that payment of the tax and pursuing a claim for refund is an adequate remedy. You must, however, demonstrate that you are financially unable to pay the tax and have no means of acquiring sufficient funds to do so. Also, the government will suggest that the remedy of Tax Court was available to you if a notice of deficiency was mailed.[28] You must be prepared to set forth facts which demonstrate *sound reasoning* why the Tax Court remedy was inappropriate. One example would be where the IRS mailed the notice of deficiency to you, but for reasons other than negligence, you did not receive it within the 90-day deadline.

When these factors can be proven to exist to the satisfaction of the court, the "equity jurisdiction" of the court may be invoked to enjoin collection. Speaking of this power, the Supreme Court, in *Miller,* stated:

"* * *And this court. . .recognizes the rule that, in causes where the complainant shows that in addition to the illegality of an exaction in the guise of a tax there exists special and extraordinary circumstances sufficient to bring the case within some acknowledged head of equity jurisprudence, a suit may be maintained to enjoin the collector. (Citations)"

The latest Supreme Court analysis of the question appears in *Shapiro,* a 1976 decision. There, the Court elaborated upon and clarified the three standards just described. *Shapiro* explained that the first element, whether the Government could ultimately prevail, is determined on the basis of the information available to it at the time of the suit. Those facts upon which the government based its assessment must be disclosed to the citizen and the court in order that the determination of "probably success" can be made. All are agreed that where the tax assessment is so excessive, arbitrary, capricious, and without any foundation in fact, then it is a mere exaction in the guise of a tax and may be enjoined.

The burden to prove this rests squarely upon the citizen applying for the injunction. Based upon the information obtained from the IRS relative to the manner in which the assessment was made, you must demonstrate to the court that the assessment is wholly invalid in light of the facts of the case. This is purely a "numbers" test. In the absence of your ability to accomplish this task, you will not be successful in your bid for an injunction.

Let us now turn our attention to the second element, that being, if the IRS is permitted to carry out collection, you will suffer such injury as may be termed "irreparable." In this respect, *financial destruction* has been held to be sufficient irreparable harm to precipitate the granting of an injunction.[29] One federal court described it in this manner:

"When it is made to appear that the rights and property of the alleged taxpayer will be utterly destroyed if he is compelled to pay the tax that is not in fact his obligation and the pursuit of his remedy by suit for the recovery will not adequately restore to him that which he has lost, a court of equity may take jurisdiction to grant relief in advance of payment notwithstanding the

---

25. 370 U.S. 1 (1962).

26. 424 U.S. 614 (1976).

27. *Miller vs. Standard Nut Margarine Company,* supra.

28. Of course, if no notice of deficiency was mailed, the assessment may be enjoined on grounds other than the *Shapiro* doctrine.

29. *Midwest Haulers, Inc. v. Brady,* 128 F.2d 496 (6th Cir. 1942).

prohibition in Section (7421)." See *Midwest Haulers, Inc. v. Brady*, supra.

In another federal case of more recent vintage,[30] the IRS arbitrarily assessed a citizen the sum of $25,549.00 on the *mere suspicion* that she was engaged in the sale of illegal drugs and derived income from that source. She brought a suit to enjoin collection. In it she proved the erroneous nature of the assessment and the fact that prepayment of the alleged tax would destroy her financially. In holding that she was entitled to the injunction, a federal court stated:

"The proof made on the preliminary injunction established that the sole basis for the seizure of Mrs. Willits' property was the altogether fictitious assessment which (IRS) agent Zahurak implemented on the basis of Officer Ahearn's speculations. Furthermore, Mrs. Willits alleged, and the proof she adduced tended to show, that the seizure was sufficiently extensive to deny her all means of supporting herself and her children."

Even more recently, federal courts have held that when an IRS levy will deprive a citizen of the means by which to support his family, irreparable harm is said to exist.[31] The Ninth Circuit Court of Appeals observed:

"The record before us indicates that Jensen earned $1,087.38 per month and the IRS seized $664.76 of these earnings. After other deductions Jensen was left with $144.82 per month to support his family of five. If these facts are true, and if Jensen had no other income or assets at his disposal from which he might pay the claimed deficiencies, the levy on his wages caused more than monetary harm. It deprived Jensen of the ability to provide necessities of life for himself and family."[32]

Hence, when imminent financial ruin can be demonstrated from the facts of the case, that factor, taken together with the unjustified assessment, enables the court to enjoin the IRS even in the face of the Anti-Injunction statute.[33]

The third element to invoking the *Shapiro* doctrine is, that no adequate remedy is available as an alternative to the injunction. The government can be expected to excitedly argue that your "adequate remedy" under the law is to pay the tax, then file a claim for refund. You must demonstrate, with facts based upon the circumstances of the case, why this remedy is inadequate. When the amount of tax demanded by the IRS is sufficiently high so as to render payment out of the realm of possibility, that argument can be effectively used to prove lack of "an adequate remedy."[34] To prove this, a complete statement of your income and monthly expenses, as well as a statement of assets and liabilities should be submitted to the court as proof of your inability to pay, demonstrating that the remedy of claim for refund is inadequate under the circumstances.

When you have met this burden of proving the presence of each of these three elements, the Anti-Injunction Act does not apply and the court possesses the lawful authority to enjoin collection of the tax.

The Procedurally Incorrect Assessment. The *fourth* exemption to the Anti-Injunction Act grows out of a combination of case law and Congressionally enacted measures. This argument applies when the IRS has failed to follow the appropriate procedures when making an assessmet. Our previous discussion assumed that the IRS may have followed the correct procedures in obtaining its assessment. Here, however, the premise is that *it did not* follow the deficiency procedures, bypassing statutory protections within the Code.

A leading case in this area is *Bothke v. Fluor Engineers and Constructors.*[35] In that case, the court determined that a citizen has the right and authority to seek judicial intervention against the IRS when the assessment the government is attempting to collect has been obtained improperly in violation of the deficiency procedures.

The administrative provisions of the tax code are clear. There are only two legitimate ways in which the IRS may obtain an assessment against a citizen. *The first* is the most common. The citizen signs an income tax return on which he declares a liability, then files that return with the IRS. The IRS is then authorized to assess the tax and undertake collection if the tax is not paid with the return. The *second* arises out of the completion of an audit, or in the event no return is filed by the citizen. In these circumstances, the IRS may make a determination that taxes are due beyond what may have already been paid. According to the law,[36] no assessment of that additional tax may be made *unless* the

30. *Willits v. Richardson*, 497 F.2d 240 (5th Cir. 1974).

31. *Jensen v. IRS*, 835 F.2d 196 (9th Cir. 1987), citing *Lopez v. Heckler*, 713 F.2d 1432 (9th Cir. 1983).

32. *Jensen*, supra, 713 F.2d at 198; footnotes and citations omitted.

33. *Goldberg v. Kelly*, 397 U.S. 254,264 (1970); *Sniadach v. Family Finance Corp.*, 392 U.S. 337, 341-42 (1969) (temporary deprivation of wages may "drive a wage-earning family to the wall.")

34. *Lucia v. United States*, 447 F.2d 912 (5th Cir. en banc 1973); *Pizzarello v. United States*, 408 F.2d 579 (2nd Cir. 1969).

35. 713 F.2d 1405 (9th Cir. 1983).

36. Code §§6212 and 6213(a).

citizen is first mailed a notice of deficiency.

The notice of deficiency, as explained, provides the citizen with the option of paying the tax, or, within 90 days of receiving the notice, filing a petition with the Tax Court. If either of these two processes is not followed, any purported tax assessment made by the IRS is *invalid*.[37] The *Bothke* court correctly determined that when the IRS fails to follow its own administrative procedures in obtaining an assessment, the assessment is invalid. "Merely demanding payment," the court stated, "even repeatedly, does not cause liability...The Service may assess the tax only in certain circumstances and in conformity with proper procedures."[38] Under these conditions, the IRS may be enjoined from collecting the tax.[39]

Specific examples of courts enjoining the IRS from collecting taxes when procedures were violated are:

1. When it has failed to issue the notice of deficiency;[40]

2. When the assessment was made simultaneously with the notice of deficiency in violation of the 90-day grace period;[41]

3. When the assessment was made during the pendency of the case before the Tax Court, and prior to the Tax Court's decision on the matter;[42]

4. When the IRS made an assessment in violation of the terms of a waiver agreement signed by the citizen and the government;[43] and

5. When the IRS failed to issue a notice of deficiency to the citizen, and violated the terms of a conditional waiver.[44]

The language of Code §6213(a) plainly states that when the IRS is in violation of the deficiency procedures, an appropriate court may enjoin the collection of the tax. In order to prevail with respect to such a claim, you must prove that the IRS' assessment was made without regard to the deficiency procedures. The availability of your IMF will greatly assist you in this particular. As the IMF will reflect all administrative action taken in your case, you may effectively rely upon it to show that the assessment was made without regard to a notice of deficiency. The IMF will also reflect any other procedural failure which may be fatal to the assessment.

Applying for an Injunction

The matter of approving the application for an injunction is, as you might imagine, solely within the power of the court. The court's approval of your application for injunction is dependent upon several factors. The first is whether you have properly invoked the "equity jurisdiction" of the court. This question is answered by reference to your complaint. If you have set out allegations within the complaint which are sufficient to open the door of equity, the matter will be ripe for review by the court.

The second consideration bearing upon whether the court will grant your application is whether the facts of the case *justify* its approval. As the applicant, you will bear the burden of proving that the facts of the case do justify granting the application. Keep in mind, when applying for an injunction the courts are predisposed *against* such relief due to the mere presence of the Anti-Injunction Act. The exemptions we have studied apply in certain narrow factual situations. You must establish to the court's satisfaction that the facts render one or more of the exemptions we discussed applicable to the case.

The final consideration by the court in ruling on your application is the question of whether the law—the statutes and relevant case authorities—*authorize* the court to issue the injunction. It is a common practice for IRS lawyers, when under fire by a citizen in this regard, to rally behind the presumed protection of the Anti-Injunction Act. Uncreative lawyers seeking a quick and painless remedy to the problems posed by citizen attacks will *almost always* raise the Anti-Injunction Act as a defense to the claim. The general harangue offered by them is to suggest that the Act prevents *all* suits against the IRS, regardless of the circumstances. An example of the typical argument is discussed and *rejected* by the court in *Rodriguez v. United States*. See footnote 17.

Government lawyers do not like to admit that exceptions to the Act do indeed exist, and the courts are quick to side with them in these debates. Therefore, in order to prevail in battle with the IRS, you will have to understand the premise of the Anti-Injunction Act, as

---

37. There is *one* exception to this rule. Under very rare circumstances, the IRS may assess a tax without regard to the "deficiency procedures" if it determines that collection of the tax is "in jeopardy." Even then, however, the citizen must be afforded prompt notice and an opportunity for review. See 26 USC §7429.

38. See *Bothke*, 713 F.2d at 1414.

39. Accord, *Rodriguez v. United States*, supra, at note 17.

40. *Mall v. Kelly*, 564 F.Supp. 371 (DC Wyo. 1983).

41. *Bromberg v. Ingling*, 300 F.2d 859 (9th Cir. 1962).

42. *Dierks v. United States*, 215 F.Supp. 338 (DC NY 1963).

43. *Stroman v. McCanless*, 391 F.Supp. 1344 (DC Tex. 1975).

44. *Parsons Corp. v. United States*, 87-1 USTC Para. 9211 (DC Cal. 1986).

well as the legal premises which have established binding exceptions to the rule.

The following is a more detailed discussion of the mechanics of completing each of the three steps we have just identified as being essential to an effective application for an injunction against the IRS:

The Allegations of the Complaint. The first step is that "necessary allegations" must be set forth in your complaint. The complaint, you will recall, is your formal claim of wrongdoing against the IRS and a request from the court for specific relief. Within the paragraphs of the complaint, you must set forth facts which will open the door of equity, thus enabling the court to exercise its equity jurisdiction over the IRS.

Within the *Background Facts* portion of your complaint, you must set out the events which have led you to the threshold of judicial action. Specific examples of this are shown in the forthcoming chapters in this manual. However, you must be mindful of the need to demonstrate, in a factual, rather than an argumentative context, the manner in which the IRS has unlawfully obtained its assessment, or is proceeding unlawfully to collect an assessment. These allegations of fact are critical and great care should be taken to ensure that they are sufficient.

In addition to setting forth, in an historical context, the events which led to judicial action, you must include in your complaint a statement of the *three specific factual claims* which, under the *Shapiro* doctrine, authorize the court to grant an injunction against the IRS. You will recall that the three-pronged *Shapiro* test is:

1. That under no circumstances can the IRS justify its assessment, based upon the facts known to it at the time of the suit. This is known as the "probability of success on the merits" test. If there is any probability that the facts will justify what the IRS has done, it will not be enjoined by the court. Remember, this test is addressed to the *amount* of tax demanded. Within the complaint, you must state, in a factual context, that the IRS cannot prevail in the case, since the facts known to it at the time of the suit will not justify its assessment.

2. That the damage and injury which will be inflicted upon you by reason of the IRS' assessment will be "irreparable." Irreparable damage is the kind of injury which cannot be remedied by money or money's worth compensation. For example, if the IRS is permitted to seize your paycheck week after week, you will lose not only the amount of that paycheck, but also your home, your ability to provide for your family and your good name and reputation when you fail to pay others whom you owe. This is the kind of irreparable injury which will justify an injunction when the other elements are shown.

3. That you have no adequate remedy at law available as an alternative to the injunction. Whenever the law provides a remedy for you to pursue as an alternative to an injunction, the court will not issue the injunction. You must allege that no adequate remedy exists which will afford you the opportunity to correct the unjust assessment without suffering irreparable damage. Most importantly, you should address the question of why the remedies of payment and Tax Court are either unavailable or inadequate.

These three essential factual allegations must be set out in the complaint. They are usually contained in a separate section of the complaint, entitled *Equity*. Examples of this are shown in forthcoming chapters.

The Motion for Injunction. After you have drafted your complaint and have followed all the steps necessary to file it, (see Chapter Two) you may bring the issue of injunction before the court. Injunctions in effect during the pendency of a case are referred to as "preliminary injunctions." Their purpose is to preserve the status quo until such time as the court may pass upon the ultimate issues raised in the case.

Assuming the preliminary injunction is granted, if it is ultimately found that you are correct in your allegations and the court rules in your favor on the merits of the case, the preliminary injunction will be made "permanent." The tax assessment which formed the basis of your lawsuit will be uncollectable. As a matter of fact, the IRS will most likely abate the liability if you are succesful in your case.

Assuming that you are not successful in your bid to prove all of the factual allegations of your complaint, the preliminary injunction will be dissolved, and the IRS will be permitted to move forward with its collection action.

In the federal courts, *motions* are filed by persons seeking some immediate relief from the court. In this example, we are seeking relief in the form of a preliminary injunction issued against the IRS preventing collection of what we claim to be an unjust assessment. The motion must be filed in written form, with copies served upon the government's attorney, just as was the complaint. (See Chapter Two.) Included with the motion is a "notice" which establishes a time and place for a hearing. It is the responsibility of the person filing the motion to schedule a hearing. This is done by contacting the clerk's office. With the help of the clerk, you will have your motion placed on the calendar for hearing before the judge assigned to the case.

The courts are very particular about the advance notice which must be provided to any party who may wish to oppose a motion. Rule 6(d), FRCvP, provides that at least five days notice must be afforded when making a motion in the case. However, local rules of court may modify that rule, enlarging the time period. You should check with the clerk to determine the

Exhibit 8-1: Motion for Preliminary Injunction

UNITED STATES DISTRICT COURT
DISTRICT OF MINNESOTA
THIRD DIVISION

Mrs. Andrea Citizen,	)	
	)	
Plaintiff,	)	File No. _____
	)	
vs.	)	
	)	
The United States of	)	
America, and the Internal	)	
Revenue Service,	)	
	)	
Defendants.	)	

NOTICE OF MOTION AND MOTION FOR PRELIMINARY INJUNCTION

PLEASE TAKE NOTICE, that the above-named Plaintiff will move this Court at courtroom ____, Federal Courthouse, (address, City, State, Zip) at (time), on (date), or as soon thereafter as counsel can be heard, for said Court's order granting the following relief:

1. That the Court enjoin the Defendants, and any of their agents or employees from seizing or attempting to seize the property located at (Address, City, State, Zip), pending the outcome and determination of the above-entitled litigation.

2. For such other and further relief as the Court may deem just and equitable.

Said motion is based upon all of the files, records and proceedings herein, pursuant to the Federal Rules of Civil Procedure, upon the attached Memorandum of Law and Affidavit, and further, upon any oral argument which may be had at the hearing.

Dated:

_____
Mrs. Andrea Citizen
Address
City, State, Zip
Area Code and Phone Number

amount of advance notice required by local rules. When scheduling your hearing, this time requirement must be taken into consideration.

Exhibit 8-1 is an example of a written motion for preliminary injunction. Note the blank spaces in the "notice" portion of the document. These spaces are filled in when you obtain a date and time for hearing from the clerk. The motion, in specific terms, requests that the court grant a preliminary injunction.

Establishing the Facts You Allege. While it is critical to allege facts in the complaint sufficient to justify the court's granting an injunction, it is not sufficient to rest upon the allegations of the complaint when arguing your motion for preliminary injunction. The court will require that sworn testimony be placed before it, which testimony establishes the truthfulness of the allegations contained in the complaint. For purposes of the motion for preliminary injunction, this is accomplished by "affidavit."

An affidavit is a notarized statement which declares that it was signed under "on oath or affirmation." The effect of the notarized statement is the same as though a witness testified under oath. The affidavit is probably the most critical aspect of the preliminary injunction process. The reason is that the facts you allege in your complaint must now be "verified" through sworn testimony in an affidavit. Without a foundation of sworn testimony upon which to rest your claim that the facts justify the court's granting your motion for injunction, the court will not do so.

In drafting an affidavit, take care to avoid a common problem which is present in many affidavits. This common problem I speak of is to make "conclusory" statements in the affidavit, rather than true statements of fact. Let me illustrate. One of the facts which we must establish is that the citizen will suffer "irreparable harm" if the injunction is not granted. The tendency is for persons to make the simple claim, "The Plaintiff will suffer irreparable harm if the injunction is not granted."

Even though the Plaintiff might sign his name to this statement and have his signature notarized, that does not transform the bare bones statement into something which will be effective in the mind of the court. The statement we just read is a "conclusory statement." It merely states, as a conclusion, the point which is required to be proven with specific facts.

A more complete statement regarding irreparable harm is critical if you expect the court to rule in your favor. The proper procedure is to set out a statement of your assets and liabilities, and a statement of your monthly income and expenses. You should also set out the amounts demanded by the IRS and the manner in which it intends to collect; i.e., a wage levy leaving you $100 per month on which to live. From this picture *the court* is able to draw the conclusion that you will be financially destroyed if the IRS is permitted to proceed with collection. The affidavit in Exhibit 8-2 demonstrates the manner in which this is effected. Please review it carefully, *but note,* it is an *example only.* Your affidavit must be based upon *your facts.*

Establishing the Law Upon Which You Rely. The requirement to place before the court the law upon which you rely for the basis of your claims is critical. As I already stated, the IRS will take the tunnel vision view that the Anti-Injunction Act prevents the court from granting the relief you are seeking—period. We know, however, that important exceptions to the rule do apply. You will be required to establish that the law supports your claims.

This is accomplished by submitting a "memorandum of law." A memorandum of law is nothing more than a written statement of the points and authorities, including statutes and case law, which support your position. It is not necessary that a memorandum be particularly lengthy, but it is necessary that it address the points of law which support your position. Any statutes which support your legal stance should be referenced in the memorandum, as well as any case authority which applies.

Under the heading, *Exceptions to the Anti-Injunction Act,* I set out the major principles of law which act to override the Anti-Injunction Act. Building upon these principles, you should draft a memorandum containing arguments in support of your position which advance the legal posture of your case. In Exhibit 8-3, I have included an example of a brief memorandum which does just this.

Please note, that the memorandum and affidavit (Exhibits 8-2 and 8-3) are based upon the premise that the IRS is attempting to seize property which it is not entitled to seize; i.e., a Wrongful Levy case. It is important that the example not be viewed as the *only* way in which to argue in favor of an injunction against the IRS. I have provided four specific examples of when injunctive relief is available. However, Exhibits 8-2 and 8-3 incorporate *just one* of those examples. Be careful to adapt the examples to your particular facts and legal arguments.

The Court Hearing. After the motion and supporting documents are filed with the court and served upon the government's attorney, your case will be heard by a judge. Pursuant to the time and place which you established with the help of the clerk of court, you must appear at the courthouse prepared to argue your motion.

A hearing on the motion will be conducted in court, but without a jury. This is not a trial on the merits of your case. It is a preliminary hearing before the court for the purpose of adducing arguments from both

Exhibit 8-2: Affidavit

NOTE: The facts in this Affidavit are hypothetical and are based upon the premise of a wrongful levy action under Code §7426. The facts assume that the IRS is attempting to seize the separate property of a non-debtor spouse to satisfy her husband's tax debt. See *The Wrongful Levy* discussion in Chapter Eight.

UNITED STATES DISTRICT COURT
DISTRICT OF MINNESOTA
THIRD DIVISION

```
Mrs. Andrea Citizen,            )
                                )
            Plaintiff,          )      File No. _____
                                )
vs.                             )
                                )
The United States of            )
America, and the Internal       )
Revenue Service,                )
                                )
            Defendants.         )
          _____

STATE OF _____)
                     ) ss
COUNTY OF _____)
```

AFFIDAVIT OF ANDREA CITIZEN

I, ANDREA CITIZEN, being first duly sworn on oath, depose and state the following:

1. That I am the Plaintiff in the above-entitled action.

2. That my husband's name is William E. Citizen. The two of us were married on (date).

3. That at the time of our marriage, I was the sole owner of a parcel of real property located at (Address, City, State, Zip). The property is legally described as:

(Insert Legal Description of Property Subject to Seizure.)

4. I have owned the above property as my sole property since (date). A copy of the Warranty Deed transferring the same to me upon purchase is attached to this Affidavit as Exhibit 1.

AFFIDAVIT, PAGE 1

5. That at the time of my marriage to William E. Citizen, the property was not transferred into his name in any way.

6. I have no tax liability with the Internal Revenue Service.

7. On (date), the United States Tax Court entered a decision against William E. Citizen in the case of <u>Citizen v. Commissioner</u>, Docket No. _____. The court found a deficiency in the income taxes of William E. Citizen in the amount of $15,562.85. That amount was later assessed against William E. Citizen alone, not me. A copy of the Tax Court opinion is attached to this Affidavit and is marked Exhibit 2.

8. On (date), the Internal Revenue Service, Collection Division, and (Name) Revenue Officer, began sending notices to William E. Citizen at (Address, City, State, Zip), demanding that the tax liability assessed by the Tax Court be paid in full "immediately." A copy of one such notice is attached hereto as Exhibit 3.

9. On (date), the IRS Revenue Officer, placed a federal tax lien upon my separate real property described above. The lien is in the amount of $15,562.85, which is the amount of the assessment against my husband. A copy of the Notice of Filing Federal Tax Lien is attached hereto and marked Exhibit 4.

10. Later, the Revenue Officer made continuous phone calls to my home demanding that the assessed amount be paid forthwith, and threatening to seize my separate property if my husband's tax liability was not paid.

11. On (date), I filed an Administrative Demand with the District Director, Internal Revenue Service, in (City, State), demanding that the tax lien in question be removed, and further

demanding that the Revenue Officer be prevented from threatening to seize my house. A copy of the Administrative Demand is attached hereto and marked Exhibit 5.

12. On (date), the District Director denied the Administrative Demand referred to in the foregoing paragraph, which denial constitutes a final administrative determination. A copy of the denial is attached hereto as Exhibit 6.

13. On (date), the Revenue Officer mailed a "30 day Notice before Seizure" to my home. The notice indicates that if the amount of $15,562.85 is not paid within 30 days, the home will be seized by the Internal Revenue Service. A copy of the 30-day letter is attached hereto and marked Exhibit 7.

14. For all of the years that I have owned the house in question, I have made all of the mortgage payments and have paid all of the real estate taxes on said property.

15. My only source of money on which I survive is the wages I earn from (name of employer, City, State).

16. The wages I earn are used to pay my personal monthly living expenses which, at present, consist of:

a.	House P.I.T.I.	$645.00
b.	Utilities	$100.00
c.	Food	$150.00
d.	Travel to work	$ 80.00
e.	Credit card payments	$ 61.00
f.	Auto purchase payment	$150.00
g.	Insurance	$ 40.00
h.	Credit union payment	$400.00
	Total	$1,626.00

17. My current gross wages are $2,550.00 per month. Mandatory withholdings for state, federal and social security taxes

AFFIDAVIT, PAGE 3

leave me with net monthly income of $1,785.00.

18. The amount of money left to me after all necessary living expenses are paid is not sufficient to enable me to secure a loan to pay the tax demanded by the IRS.

19. At present, the house in question is worth approximately $55,000. The mortgage balance on the property is $49,000. Thus, I have just $6,000 equity in the house. Even if I could make payments on a loan for $6,000, that amount would be grossly insufficient to pay the tax demanded by the IRS.

20. A distressed sale of the house will net insufficient funds to pay the liability in full.

21. The only automobile I own is a 1986 Ford, with an approximate value of $3,000.00. I still owe $2,500 against the loan on that vehicle. Hence, there is very little equity in that asset. Therefore, I would not realize sufficient funds from the sale of that vehicle.

22. I have no stocks, bonds, savings accounts or other assets, either real or personal, which I could sell or mortgage to raise the money demanded by the IRS. Therefore, the remedy of paying the tax is inadequate as I simply do have the ability to do so.

23. Because the assessment in question here is recorded against my husband and not me, I was never served with a notice of deficiency in connection with the liability. Therefore, I was never able to utilize the remedy of petitioning the Tax Court relative to this liability. Because of the lack of a notice of deficiency, the remedy of Tax Court is unavailable to me.

24. If the IRS is allowed to carry out the acts threatened by

AFFIDAVIT, PAGE 4

them, I will suffer financial ruin from which I will never recover. I
will have lost my home, but the liability to the bank on account of
the loan will not have been paid. My current financial condition
makes it impossible to purchase a second home. This leaves me in the
position of having no means by which to provide a home for my minor
children, of which I have two.

This Affidavit is made in support of the motion for
Preliminary Injunction which is attached hereto.

Dated:

_____

Mrs. Andrea Citizen
Address
City, State, Zip
Area Code and Phone Number

Subscribed and sworn to before me
on (date).

_____

Notary Public

My Commission Expires: _____

Exhibit 8-3: Memorandum of Law

NOTE: The facts in this Memorandum are hypothetical and are based upon the premise of a wrongful levy action under Code §7426. The argument assumes that the IRS is attempting to seize the separate property of a non-debtor spouse to satisfy her husband's tax debt. See *The Wrongful Levy* discussion in Chapter Eight.

UNITED STATES DISTRICT COURT
DISTRICT OF MINNESOTA
THIRD DIVISION

Mrs. Andrea Citizen,   )
)
            Plaintiff,   )   File No. _____
)
vs.   )
)
The United States of   )
America, and the Internal   )
Revenue Service,   )
)
            Defendants.   )
_____

MEMORANDUM OF LAW

The Plaintiff makes this Memorandum of Law in support of her Motion for Preliminary Injunction. Plaintiff asserts to the Court that she is entitled to a preliminary injunction for reasons set out in this Memorandum.

LAW AND ARGUMENT

The government is likely to argue to the Court that the Anti-Injunction Act, 26 USC §7421, is an absolute bar to the relief sought in this case. However, as shown in the Affidavit of Plaintiff, she has no tax liability whatsoever with the IRS. It is also shown that the debt which the IRS is attempting to collect is the separate debt of Plaintiff's husband.

Since Plaintiff has no liability outstanding with the IRS, the Anti-Injunction Act, 26 USC §7421, does not apply to her. She may bring an action to enjoin the IRS notwithstanding §7421. This action is brought under 26 USC §7426, the Wrongful Levy statute. It provides in part:

> "(a)(1) If a levy has been made on property or property has been sold pursuant to a levy, any person (other than the person against whom is assessed the tax out of which such levy arose) who claims an interest in or lien on such property and that such property was wrongfully levied upon may bring a civil action against the United States in a district court of the United States. Such action may be brought without regard to whether such property has been surrendered to or sold by the Secretary.
>
> "(b)(1) If a levy or sale would irreparably injure rights in property which the court determines to be superior to rights of the United States in such property, the court may grant an injunction to prohibit the enforcement of such levy or to prohibit such sale."

Thus, §7426 gives this Court the express jurisdiction to hear this suit for injunction. The complaint states sufficient facts which entitle the Plaintiff to the relief she is seeking. The law is clear that the property of one person cannot be seized to satisfy the separate tax liability of another person. The government can only satisfy the liability from the property of the person who actually owes the tax. See Aquilino v. United States, 363 U.S. 509 (1960).

Here, the government is attempting to levy upon property in which the debtor, William E. Citizen, has no legal interest. See the Affidavit of Plaintiff. Under the circumstances, the Plaintiff is clearly entitled to a preliminary injunction preventing seizure of the property pending the outcome of this case. This will provide her an opportunity to prove to the satisfaction of the court that she owns an undivided interest in the property in question. Once her undivided interest is established, she would be entitled to a permanent injunction. See Morgan v. Moynahan, 86 F.Supp. 522 (D.C. Tx. 1949).

The Affidavit attached to this Memorandum clearly shows that the elements necessary for the imposition of an injunction against the IRS are met in this case. First of all, it is shown that the Plaintiff does not owe the tax in question. It is the separate liability of her husband. Therefore, the IRS cannot prevail on the merits of this case. It is settled that the IRS cannot use the property of one citizen to satisfy the liability of another. Secondly, the Plaintiff will suffer immediate and irreparable harm if the injunction sought is not granted. The Plaintiff has insufficient funds to provide a home for her family in the event this home is seized.

In addition, since it is not her tax liability which the IRS is collecting, irreparable harm is apparent if her property is seized to satisfy the debt. Lastly, the Plaintiff has no adequate remedy at law. She cannot afford to pay the tax as demonstrated in Affidavit. Because she is not the debtor, she received no notice of deficiency from the IRS, thus rendering a Tax Court determination an impossibility. For all of these reasons, it is clear that the Plaintiff has met her burden to prove that she is entitled to the injunction sought here.

CONCLUSIONS

WHEREFORE, the Plaintiff respectfully requests that this Court grant the relief sought in her motion.

Dated:

_____

Mrs. Andrea Citizen
Address
City, State, Zip
Area Code and Phone Number

parties on the merits of the motion. The government will, regardless of the facts, argue that the Anti-Injunction Act applies and that your case should be dismissed. You must argue the contrary, drawing from your affidavit and memorandum.

Perhaps the most critical aspect of the motion hearing will be the *facts* as they are adduced during the hearing. The government may or may not have dedicated any time to preparing affidavits. It may or may not attempt to correctly and completely demonstrate the facts of the case to the court. My guess, based upon past experience, is that it will not. The government's interests are usually best served when the specific facts are left vague and undefined. Therefore, you must take extra time in preparing your affidavit and memorandum to be sure that the facts are before the court in clear, understandable form. Extra time should be dedicated in your *oral* argument to review the *facts* in order that the court will better appreciate the nature of your claim.

You should also argue orally the main points of your legal position. It is not necessary or desirable that you "read" your memorandum to the judge. However, you must be sure that the main points of the argument are presented in clear, understandable form. Prepare careful notes before the hearing and do not be afraid to read from them.

When the hearing is complete, the court will probably not announce a decision "on the spot." Rather, it is customary for the court to take the matter "under advisement" and to issue a written opinion later. If you have persuaded the court that you are entitled to the preliminary injunction, it will so order in its written opinion. The preliminary injunction will be binding upon the parties for the duration of the proceeding, or until such time as the court may dissolve it.

Conclusion

The time it takes to prosecute a case in the federal system, even under expedited procedures, often greatly transcends the time in which it takes the IRS to issue and act upon a notice of Levy. Therefore, the preliminary injunction remedy available under certain circumstances is of great importance if one is to preserve his assets while his case is pending.

The Anti-Injunction Act may be the most important piece of legislation on the question of preventing IRS abuse. Its bold statement, in the absence of a persuasive argument to the contrary, will cause a court to reject your efforts to stop IRS abuse, almost summarily. But as we have learned, there are important exceptions to the Anti-Injunction rule which apply when the IRS has overstepped its bounds. In any effort to quell IRS abuse, these exceptions to the Act must be studied to the end that one or more may be applied to the facts of your case. When this effort is successful, the IRS can be stopped dead in its tracks while on its march into lawlessness.

CHAPTER

9

The Arbitrary Notice
How to Counterattack!

Already in this manual I spoke at length on the subject of the IRS' mathematical recomputation. In Chapter Five, *Recapturing Your Losses,* I discussed in detail the steps a person could take to recover what was confiscated through the use of the mathematical recomputation. This chapter will assume a slightly different posture than that presented in Chapter Five. Here, the arbitrary notice will be featured as more of a *challenge* than a frustrating, invincible weapon wielded by the IRS. Without a doubt, the arbitrary notice is one of the principal ways in which the IRS takes advantage of an unsuspecting citizen. This chapter will show you how to turn the tables on the IRS *whenever* it attempts to unlawfully collect taxes through the use of the arbitrary notice.

For any person who may yet believe that the arbitrary notice (a bogus mathematical recomputation) is either, (a) non-existent, or (b) not a problem, let me offer a bit of sobering evidence. In *How Anyone Can Negotiate With The IRS—And WIN!,* I reported that according to *1987* IRS statistics, just over 460,000 such notices were

mailed to taxpayers. It was also reported that the bills netted the IRS over $22 million in additional collections.[1] The *1988* notice was used on 564,767 occasions. *That is a 22 percent increase over the previous year![2]* The story continues! The same statistics reveal that the *average* tax collected through the use of these notices in 1988 was *$1,327![3]*

Now you tell me, is this a problem or not? Can you afford to pay a bill in excess of $1,300 merely because some apparent authority has *demanded* it? Would you pay a phone bill in excess of $1,300 if nobody at the phone company is willing or able to provide a reasonable explanation of why it is owed? I do not believe that any reasonable person would. The one and only reason the IRS is successful in collecting a dime in most cases is that it has the authority to confiscate the money if the individual is unwilling to part with it freely. This does not magically transform an otherwise wholly unlawful bill into a legitimate one; all it does is complete the cycle of lawlessness.

In Chapter One, in my discussion *Planning the*

---

1. See *How Anyone Can Negotiate With The IRS—And WIN!,* page 45.

2. *1988 IRS Highlights,* page 32, Table 7.

3. Ibid, at page 33. It is not known what percentage of such notices were valid versus those which were patently bogus. I can only speculate.

Attack, I stated that the sooner one can take the offensive with regard to IRS abuse, the sooner that abusive tactic can be ground to a halt. Nothing could be more true with respect to the arbitrary notice. Immediate, decisive, affirmative action directed at the heart of the enemy's attack will bring this aggressive act to a pronounced halt. The correct offensive response will place you in a position to demand the enemy's *unconditional surrender.*

The Peaceful Solution

Nobody with any degree of sense desires a war with the IRS. The proposition of battle with the tax collector can be most disheartening. Regardless of the outcome, the cost in terms of time and money is often high. Even with this manual in hand and the knowledge that you have the Ultimate Defense Weapons at your fingertips, the wise commander will exercise every opportunity to find a peaceful solution to the problem, thereby avoiding a confrontation. Be mindful of the teaching of Sun Tzu, to the effect that the best policy is to *influence* the trend of events such as to cause the enemy to submit willingly. Master Sun instructs:

> "Therefore one who is good at martial arts overcomes others' forces without battle, conquers others' cities without siege, destroys others' nations without taking a long time.* * *This means that attacking at the planning and attacking at the alliances, so as not to come to the point of actually doing battle. This is why classical martial arts say that the best of strategists does not fight. One who is good at laying siege does not lay siege with an army, but uses strategy to thwart the opponents, causing them to overcome themselves and destroy themselves, rather than taking them by a long and troublesome campaign."[4]

All we have learned thus far in this manual, and all that we will discuss in subsequent pages is calculated to achieve victory without the need of a battle. The exhaustion of administrative remedies is much more than a means to an end. The process is by itself a viable and legitimate manner in which to accomplish the goal of defeating the IRS on the question of the lawfulness of its acts. I am quick to confess that we cannot always rely upon the IRS to admit the lawlessness of its own acts while in the throws of administrative confrontation. However, with or without an admission of wrongdoing,

administrative remedies properly pursued often do provide relief from the unlawful attack. That alone, as far as we are concerned, is the purpose of engaging the enemy.

The Origin of the Mathematical Recomputation

The mathematical recomputation (referred to as an arbitrary notice when bogus) is used by IRS service centers to communicate the fact that one or more mathematical or clerical errors were discovered in a tax return and were corrected. The IRS is authorized by law to make corrections to a return attributable to math or clerical errors. Any increase in tax growing out of such a correction is not initially subject to the deficiency procedures established by Code §§6212 and 6213(a). Specifically, the law reads:

> "If the taxpayer is notified that, on account of a mathematical or clerical error appearing on the return, an amount of tax in excess of that shown on the return is due, and that an assessment of the tax has been or will be made on the basis of what would have been the correct amount of tax but for the mathematical or clerical error, such notice *shall not* be considered as a notice of deficiency for the purposes of subsection (a) (prohibiting assessment and collection until notice of the deficiency has been mailed), or of section 6212(c)(1) (restricting further deficiency letters) or of section 6512(a) (prohibiting credits or refunds after petition to the Tax Court), and the taxpayer *shall have no right* to file a petition with the Tax Court based on such notice, *nor shall* such assessment or collection be prohibited by the provisions of subsection (a) of this section (requiring a notice of deficiency prior to assessment and collection). *Each notice under this paragraph shall set forth the error alleged and an explanation thereof.*" Code §6213(b)(1); emphasis added.

Without a doubt, the IRS is given authority under the law to correct income tax returns which contain mathematical or clerical errors. However, this authority is limited. The IRS may correct a return under the above statutory authority only when:

1. An error in addition, subtraction, multiplication or division has occurred;

2. An incorrect use of any table provided by the IRS

---

4. Sun Tzu, *The Art of War,* translated by Thomas Cleary pages 72-73.

with respect to any tax form has occurred;

3. An entry on a return of an item which is inconsistent with another entry of the same or related item has occurred;

4. An omission of an item which is required to be shown on the return to substantiate any entry on the return has occurred; or

5. An entry on the return for a deduction or credit in an amount which exceeds the statutory limit for such item has occurred. This can include a specific monetary amount or a percentage, ratio or fraction.[5]

A typical example of an illegitimate mathematical recomputation notice is shown in Exhibit 9-1.

The IRS has patently abused its rights with regard to the mathematical recomputation in several respects. First of all, it has failed in a vast number of cases to "set forth the error alleged and an explanation thereof." Please see Exhibit 9-1. This failure has left many a citizen in the lurch when attempting to determine whether the amount demanded in the notice is in fact correct. Phone calls or other efforts to determine the reason for the additional assessment, or the grounds upon which the assessment is based, are often futile.

Furthermore, the IRS has completely *failed and refused* to provide any reasonable explanation of one's rights when he has received such a mathematical recomputation. The IRS is silent on the fact that *since 1976*, citizens have enjoyed the right to demand an abatement of any tax assessed through this means if he is not in agreement with the IRS' reasoning. Code §6213(b)(2)(A) holds:

> "Notwithstanding section 6404(b) (limiting one's ability to demand an abatement of income tax assessments) *a taxpayer may file* with the Secretary *within 60 days* after notice is sent under paragraph (1) a request for an abatement of any assessment specified in such notice, and upon receipt of such request, the Secretary *shall abate the assessment.* Any reassessment of the tax with respect to which an abatement is made under this subparagraph *shall be subject to the deficiency procedures prescribed by this subchapter.*" Code §6213(b)(2)(A); emphasis added.

Subsection (b)(2)(B) provides:

> "In the case of any assessment referred to in paragraph (1), notwithstanding paragraph (1), no levy or proceeding in court for the collection of such assessment shall be made, begun, or prosecuted during the period in which such assessment may be abated under this paragraph."

In these provisions of §6213(b) we find a clear formula for dealing with the mathematical recomputation, or arbitrary notice, before it becomes a problem. As we have seen from subparagraph (b)(2)(A), the IRS is required by law to abate or cancel the tax when the citizen demands an abatement, in writing, within 60 days of the date shown in the notice. When the demand for abatement is made in this fashion, the IRS is required to *cancel* the liability, no questions asked! At that point, if it is persuaded that the assessment was valid, it must mail a notice of deficiency before the tax may be reassessed. Of course, when that occurs, you have the option of petitioning the Tax Court within 90 days of the date shown in the notice of deficiency. This further restricts the IRS' power to assess the tax. See Chapter Four.

The Demand for Abatement

The crime associated with the mathematical recomputation is not so much that the IRS, in violation of the law, fails to explain the alleged error it has corrected. The real offense is that it *has not* and does not, any place in the notice, inform the citizen of his right to demand an abatement and the restrictions placed upon collection when he does demand abatement. This failure has led many a citizen to fail to draft a demand for abatement which comports with the requirements of the law. If any letter is written, it typically raises questions seeking an explanation of the *reason* for the assessment, rather than *demanding* an abatement.

When an insufficient letter of response is mailed to the IRS regarding the mathematical recomputation, the wont of the IRS is to answer with a noncommittal letter indicating that it has taken the matter under advisement. The letter has the tendency to lull the citizen to sleep, secure in the belief that the matter is "under control." Exhibit 9-2 is an example of the typical IRS response to a letter *questioning* the notice, rather than *demanding* an abatement of the liability.

Please read with care the language of the second paragraph in the letter in Exhibit 9-2. It states that "we are giving special attention" to your letter. It further states that you will receive a response "within 45 days to let you know the action we are taking." Now I ask you, do you suppose it is an accident that the IRS will consume 45 days in the review process before it is capable of definitely responding to your request? Of course not!

The "inquiry" process requires 45 days only because by the time that period has expired, so has your

---

5. These limitations are expressed in Code §6213(g)(2).

Exhibit 9-1
Arbitrary Notice

Department of the Treasury
Internal Revenue Service
AUSTIN, TX 73301

Date of this notice: JULY 4, 1988
Taxpayer Identifying Number
Form: 1040A   Tax Period: DEC. 31, 1983

For assistance you may call us at:
291-1422 MNPLS.-ST. PAUL
800-424-1040 OTHER MN

Or you may write to us at the address shown at the left. If you write, be sure to attach the bottom part of this notice.

STATEMENT OF CHANGE TO YOUR ACCOUNT

WE CHANGED YOUR TAX RETURN TO CORRECT YOUR ACCOUNT INFORMATION.

STATEMENT OF ACCOUNT

ACCOUNT BALANCE BEFORE THIS CHANGE   NONE

INCREASE IN TAX BECAUSE OF THIS CHANGE $7,620.00
CREDIT ADDED -- TAX WITHHELD   5,478.00CR
FILING LATE PENALTY ADDED -- SEE CODE 01 ON ENCLOSED NOTICE   535.50
ESTIMATED TAX PENALTY ADDED -- SEE CODE 02 ON ENCLOSED NOTICE   55.00
NEGLIGENCE PENALTY ADDED -- SEE CODE 06 ON ENCLOSED NOTICE   967.75
INTEREST CHARGED -- SEE ENCLOSED NOTICE - CODE 09   1,451.66

AMOUNT YOU NOW OWE $5,151.91

YOU MAY AVOID ADDITIONAL INTEREST AND PENALTIES IF YOU PAY THE AMOUNT YOU OWE BY JULY 14, 1988. PLEASE MAKE YOUR CHECK OR MONEY ORDER PAYABLE TO THE INTERNAL REVENUE SERVICE. WRITE YOUR SOCIAL SECURITY NUMBER ON YOUR PAYMENT AND RETURN IT WITH THE BOTTOM PART OF THIS NOTICE. AN ENVELOPE IS ENCLOSED FOR YOUR CONVENIENCE. THANK YOU FOR YOUR COOPERATION.

To make sure that IRS employees give courteous responses and correct information to taxpayers, a second IRS employee sometimes listens in on telephone calls.
Keep this part for your records.

Return this part to us with your check or inquiry
Your telephone number | Best time to call

Overdtv 6 Form 8488 (Rev. 11-87)

AMOUNT YOU OWE.................$5,151.91
LESS PAYMENTS NOT INCLUDED.
PAY ADJUSTED AMOUNT.

34,159   33,159   0

515447855 KB 0000 30 0 6312 670 0000515191

INTERNAL REVENUE SERVICE
AUSTIN, TX 73301

6825 01,02,06,09   18254-551-64034-8

22A

Exhibit 9-2
IRS Response

Department of the Treasury
Internal Revenue Service
OGDEN, UT 84201

In reply refer to: 29684838
NOV. 08, 1985 LTR 191C Y
01896

Social Security Number:
Tax Period Ended: Dec. 31, 1983

Dear Taxpayer:

We apologize for not replying sooner to your inquiry of Oct. 29,1985.

We are giving special attention to the inquiry about the tax account identified above. We will write you again within 45 days to let you know the action we are taking.

If you have questions about this letter, please write us at the address shown on this letter. If you write, please attach this letter to help identify your account. Also, please include your telephone number and the most convenient time for us to call, so we can contact you if we need additional information.

If you prefer, you may call the IRS telephone number listed in your local directory. An IRS employee there will be able to help you, but the office at the address shown on this letter is most familiar with your case.

Sincerely yours,

Chief, Collection Branch

Enclosure:
Copy of this letter

allotment of time under §6213(b)(2)(A). Remember, you have just *60* days to demand the abatement. When you have used the first 10 or 15 days to write a letter *questioning* the assessment and the IRS expends the remaining time giving your case "special attention," the result is that *you have missed the deadline,* enabling the IRS to collect the assessment!

Therefore, do not waste a day attempting to discover the reason for the assessment or the nature of the alleged error. Unless the IRS has clearly communicated the nature of the error in its original notice *and* you are satisfied that the notice is correct, immediately demand an abatement. If the error is legitimate, the IRS has alternatives available to it under the law. By demanding the abatement, you shift the onus to the IRS to properly follow up.

In Exhibit 9-3, I have provided an example of a letter demanding abatement under Code §6213(b)(2)(A). It has proven effective in the past. Please review it, and take notice that it does not ask questions; it merely demands the abatement under authority of law.

The procedure for executing the demand for abatement was recently explained to us by the IRS. Still, its explanation *is not* offered on the face of the mathematical recomputation notice. In IRS Publication 1, *Your Rights as a Taxpayer,* an explanation of rights mandated by the Taxpayers' Bill of Rights Act, the IRS states with respect to the mathematical recomputation notice, on page three:

"Whenever you owe tax, we will send you a bill. Be sure to check any bill you receive to make sure it is correct. You have the right to have your bill adjusted if it is incorrect, so you should let us know the amount of an incorrect bill right away.

"If we tell you that you owe tax because of a math or clerical error on yor return, you have the right to ask us to send you a formal notice (a 'notice of deficiency') so that you can dispute the tax, as discussed earlier. You do not have to pay the additional tax when you ask for it within 60 days of the time we tell you of the error."

This represents the IRS' best effort to describe the right of abatement, and it does not even *mention* the need to demand abatement as I outlined! If the IRS is able to intimate the right of abatement in its Publication 1, why is it apparently unable to do so on the face of the correction notice? The reason is probably that if one's rights were fully explained in the notice itself, *more people would exercise them.* As it is, I submit that the uninformed citizen will have great difficulty associating the *general* language of Publication 1 with the *specific* demand for payment as shown in Exhibit 9-1. Thus, the unwary will continue to be misled, and will continue to pay taxes which are not owed.

When to Demand an Abatement

The statute authorizes the citizen to demand abatement of the tax shown due on the notice anytime within "60 days after the notice is sent." The notice bears a date at the top. See Exhibit 9-1, upper right corner. Your letter demanding abatement should be *received* by the IRS within 60 days of that date. You should mail the letter to the IRS office which issued the notice, and your letter should be mailed via certified mail, return receipt requested.

The deeper question which we must address at this juncture is, under what *circumstances* should one demand abatement of the tax assessed pursuant to a mathematical recomputation? In order to properly address that issue, we must understand that there are two types of correction notices. The first type I speak of we already exposed. It is used by the IRS as a means of collecting taxes *which are not* lawfully due. Obviously, when one is in receipt of such a notice, he is well-advised to mail an abatement letter in a timely fashion.

The difficulty arises when, upon review of the correction notice, one is unable, due to insufficient data, to determine whether the notice is valid or not. Too often, as is the case with Exhibit 9-1, the notice merely states that "we changed your tax return" to correct a mistake. Without an explanation as to what the mistake was, it is impossible to determine whether the actions of the IRS are legitimate.

Faced with this problem, I believe that the mandatory course of action is to demand an abatement. I do not say this to suggest that the IRS' collection system should be improperly disrupted. On the contrary, if the tax is legitimately due and owing it should be paid in a timely manner. But when, through the failure of the IRS, it is impossible to know whether it is correct or not, the only reasonable reply is to demand an abatement. If you do, the burden is then on the IRS to issue a notice of deficiency if it feels the assessment is justified.

The notice of deficiency, as we examined in Chapter Four, contains an explanation of the amount due, with accompanying computations fully describing the manner in which it was determined. After reviewing those worksheets, one is fully capable of ascertaining whether the IRS is correct or not. If it is correct, I would encourage you to pay the tax. However, if it is incorrect, I would encourage you to assert your right to petition the Tax Court in order that the matter be corrected.

This course of conduct affords much versatility to the citizen. The full advantages of time and alternatives rest squarely with the citizen, not the IRS. The power of

Exhibit 9-3
Letter Demanding Abatement

William E. Citizen
Address
City, State, Zip

Date

Internal Revenue Service
Service Center
Address
City, State, Zip

RE: Your Notice of (date -- copy enclosed)
    Tax Year _____
    SSN: 000-00-0000

Dear Sir:

Reference is made to your letter of (date), which states that my return for (year) has been changed by you due to an error. I have enclosed a copy of your letter for review.

Please be advised that I disagree with your statement that I owe additional taxes. This is notice to you under the provisions of Code §6213(b)(2)(A) that you are to immediately abate the tax assessment reflected in your notice (copy attached). You will please note that I have made this demand for abatement within the 60-day period prescribed by law. Therefore, the IRS has no alternative but to abate the assessment.

If the Internal Revenue Service insists that this assessment is legitimate and proper under the circumstances, I demand that the IRS mail a notice of deficiency to me as required by §6213(b)(2)(A) in order that I may exercise my right to petition the Tax Court.

I will look forward to your notice that the tax demanded has been abated pursuant to law.

Thank you very much,

William E. Citizen

encl. Tax Due Notice of (date)

Exhibit 9-4
Valid Mathematical Recomputation Notice

870803

Department of the Treasury
Internal Revenue Service
ANDOVER, MA 05501

If you have any questions, refer to this information:

Date of This Notice: AUG. 3, 1987
Social Security Number:
Document Locator Number:
Form 1040   Tax Year Ended: DEC. 31, 1986

Call: 291-1422   MNPLS.-ST. PAUL
or   800-424-1040   OTHER MN

Write: Chief, Taxpayer Assistance Section
        Internal Revenue Service Center
        ANDOVER, MA 05501

If you write, be sure to attach the bottom part of this notice. Please include your telephone number and the best time for us to call in case we need more information.

Correction Notice — Amount Due IRS

As a result of an error we corrected on your tax return, you owe IRS $ _____ 84.25. If you believe this amount is not correct, please see the back of this notice. Make your check or money order payable to the Internal Revenue Service. Please write your social security number on your payment and mail it with the bottom part of this notice. An envelope is enclosed for your convenience.

Allow for enough mailing time to be sure that we receive your payment by   AUG. 13, 1987

Thank you for your cooperation.

Correction Explanation

AN ERROR WAS MADE IN THE INCOME SECTION OF YOUR RETURN WHEN THE AMOUNT OF YOUR CAPITAL GAIN (OR LOSS) WAS TRANSFERRED FROM SCHEDULE D.

Tax Statement

Total Tax on Return ...... $	3,701.00	
Corrected Balance of Tax on Return .... $		3,783.00
Tax Withheld	3,560.00-	
*Estimated Tax Payments..	.00	
Other Credits	.00	
Other Payments	141.00-	
Total Payments and Credits		3,701.00-
UNDERPAID TAX......		82.00
**Penalty		.00
**Interest		2.25
Amount You Owe ...... $		84.25
Subtract Payments We Haven't Included .... $		
Pay Adjusted Amount Due .... $		

* **Estimated Tax Filers —** Please check to see if you should file an amended declaration of estimated tax because your tax was refigured.
See Codes   09   on the back for an explanation of penalty and interest charges.

If you have any questions, you may call or write us — see the information in the upper right corner of this notice. To make sure that IRS employees give courteous responses and correct information to taxpayers, a second employee sometimes listens in on telephone calls.
Keep this part for your records.

FORM 4084 (REV 8-86)

the IRS to force payment under mysterious terms or the hardships imposed by a wage or bank account levy are avoided altogether. In my own mind, this justifies requiring the IRS to issue the notice of deficiency before payment is considered.

Let us now examine the second type of mathematical recomputation notice. In Exhibit 9-4, I have provided an example of a legitimate recomputation which *does explain* the error which is alleged to have been made. Please review Exhibit 9-4 carefully to see what I am talking about. When your letter does provide sufficient explanation as to the supposed error, it becomes a simple matter to review your copy of the tax return to determine whether the allegation is correct. If it is correct, pay the tax. If it is not, demand the abatement. What could be more simple?

Parenthetically, I would like to direct your attention to Exhibit 9-4, under the heading, *Correction Notice— Amount Due.* In the second sentence, the notice states,

"If you believe this amount is not correct, please see the back of this notice." One would believe, in light of this statement, that the "back of the notice" will contain specific instructions for demanding an abatement. I have carefully reviewed the "back of the notice" and find it astonishing that not *one word* is mentioned on the subject of "abatement." Do you believe this to be an accidental oversight?

When the IRS Ignores Your Demand

In case you may not already realize this, the IRS does not always do what it is required to do under the law. If it is disposed to ignore its legal requirements in regard to your letter demanding abatement, you will receive from the tax collector further bills and demands for payment.

Exhibit 9-5
Second Letter Demanding Abatement

William E. Citizen
Address
City, State, Zip

Date

Internal Revenue Service
Service Center
Address
City, State, Zip

RE: IRS Demand for Payment of (date -- copy enclosed)
     Tax Year
     SSN: 000-00-0000

Dear Sir:

This letter is in regard to your notice of (date) informing me that if the amount of $_____ is not paid to the IRS within 30 days of the date of that letter, enforced collection action will be taken. I have previously written the IRS concerning this matter, and it has yet to be resolved. Enclosed you will find a copy of my letter of (date). In that letter, I demanded an abatement of the tax assessment in question as is my right under Code §6213(b)(2)(A). Apparently, this has not been done.

I again call your attention to the fact that your original notice of (date) indicated that my return was altered due to an error found by the IRS. I pointed out in my letter of (date) that I did not agree with your decision to change the return. My demand for abatement under §6213(b)(2)(A) was timely and hence, the IRS is obligated by law to abate the tax. In IRS Publication 1, Your Rights as a Taxpayer, it is explained, at page 3, that if the IRS sends a bill with which I do not agree, I have the right to "ask us (the IRS) to send you a formal notice (a notice of deficiency) so that you can dispute the tax, as discussed earlier." I have demanded such a notice of deficiency, but the IRS has thus far refused to mail one, continuing to demand full payment.

I have not received a notice of deficiency for the year at issue, and I do not agree with the assessed liability. I have responded within the 60-day period as required by law, but the IRS will not honor my demand. This is a violation of law and in contradiction of its own published statements of my rights and its obligations.

Be advised that if the tax is not immediately abated, I will pursue all legal remedies available to me, including taking such legal action as is authorized under Code §6213(a). Unless you have any questions, I will expect notice that the liability in question has been fully abated. If you feel I owe the tax in question, you may issue a notice of deficiency as per your Publication 1.

Thank you very much,

William E. Citizen

encl. Second Tax Due Notice of (date)
       First Letter Demanding Abatement

Rather than sending you notification that the tax was abated, or issuing a 90-day letter, the enemy may march on, oblivious to the warnings which you have issued. This can eventually lead to a wage levy if the problem is left unattended.

If the IRS ignores your first demand, I recommend that a second letter be mailed, again demanding an abatement of the liability. The second letter should be more specific and particular regarding the language of the statute. It should also point out that if the IRS does not abate the liability as mandated under §6213(b), you will assert your rights under §6213(a). Code §6213(a), describing the deficiency procedures in general, provides that if any assessment is made in contravention of the deficiency procedures, the "proper court" has jurisdiction to enjoin the IRS from collecting the tax. Please see Exhibit 9-5 for an example of the second letter demanding abatement.

I believe that it is necessary to issue two demands to the IRS for these reasons. First, it is fundamentally necessary to always exhaust administrative remedies with the IRS before turning to the federal courts for any relief. True, the statute we have examined provides that just *one* letter demanding abatement must be sent to shift the burden to the IRS. However, by mailing two such letters, we give the IRS the benefit of the doubt, considering that perhaps the first letter simply did not land in the hands of the proper authority.

Secondly, by going the extra mile and mailing the second letter, you have clearly demonstrated a desire and a willingness to resolve the matter at the administrative level. The IRS' failure to heed *two* demands will bode much worse than a mere failure to act upon one such letter. Lastly, and perhaps most importantly, your desire *should be* to resolve the dispute without the need of litigation. As we pointed out in the opening remarks to this chapter, under the heading, *The Peaceful Solution,* the superior commander achieves victory without battle. Therefore, every effort should be made to win the fight without engaging the enemy.

If your warnings have been ignored a second time, that is the time for swift and decisive action. Having ignored two warnings which clearly state your intent to exercise your rights, no court, and certainly not the IRS, should be surprised or dismayed when that is exactly what you do. Even more importantly, if the IRS continues to ignore your demands for abatement, it will inevitably either file a lien or begin to levy your bank account and paycheck. Such an eventuality necessitates a resort to Ultimate Defense Weapon Number Six.

Ultimate Defense Weapon Number Six

The Court Action to Abate Unlawful Assessment

In Chapter Eight, I spent much time examining the legal authority in support of the proposition that tax assessments made in violation of statutory authority may be enjoined by an action in the proper court. Recently, the Ninth Circuit Court of Appeals in California addressed this very question. The Court of Appeals reviewed a decision of a district court from Nevada. In its opinion[6] addressing the legality of a wage levy made in violation of the deficiency procedures, the court held:

"In his complaint, Jensen alleged that the IRS failed to comply with the notice provisions of 26 USC §§6212(a) and 6213(a) before levying on his wages. Section 6213(a) expressly provides that a levy may be enjoined 'notwithstanding the provisions of 7421(a)' (the Anti-Injunction Act). The district court had jurisdiction to hear Jensen's suit."[7]

To derail the IRS' oncoming attack, you must file an action in the federal district court which serves your state. The action must allege that the IRS made an assessment which is in violation of the deficiency provisions of the Code. You must also allege that you have exhausted administrative remedies in search of a solution to the problem, and that the facts of the case justify invoking the court's equity jurisdiction.

You will recall from Chapter Eight that a three-pronged test must be met in this regard. *First,* you must show that, based upon the facts available to the IRS at the time the case is filed, it cannot prevail on the merits. A plain violation of the statutory provisions of the Code will go far in this respect. *Second,* you must show that failure to grant the injunction you are seeking will cause immediate, irreparable harm. In this regard, we discussed the necessity of submitting an affidavit which will demonstrate this fact to the court. An outline has been provided in Chapter Eight. See Exhibit 8-2. *Third,* you must show that you have no adequate remedy at law available as an alternative to the injunction. When the IRS failed and refused to honor a demand for abatement of a mathematical recomputation notice and in turn, failed to issue a notice of deficiency, you have no remedy other than to pay the tax in full. When financial

---

6. *Jensen v. IRS,* 835 F.2d 196 (9th Cir. 1987).

7. 835 F.2d at 198. See also *Perlowin v. Sassi,* 711 F.2d 910 (9th Cir. 1983); *Laing v. United States,* 423 U.S. 161 (1975).

conditions make this impossible, such an argument should prove persuasive.

In Exhibit 9-6, you will find an example of a complaint which incorporates the issues and allegations which we have just identified. As with all sample court documents in this manual, the form contains hypothetical facts and circumstnaces built around the concept of an unlawful tax assessment. This form will have to be adapted to your specific facts before it could be put to use in your case.

Filing the Complaint

After the complaint has been drafted, one must turn his attention to the motion for preliminary injunction. The documents seeking and supporting the request for preliminary injunction should be filed simultaneously with the complaint. (See Chapter Two.) This will ensure that the question of the injunction will be placed before the court for a determination at the earliest possible moment. Chapter Eight should be reviewed for the particular forms which must accompany a request for preliminary injunction. One must pay especially careful attention to the requirements of the affidavit. Bear in mind that in order for an injunction to be granted, you must prove that *immediate* and *irreparable* harm will occur if the injunction is not ordered.[8]

The Government's Response

In my experience of over a decade of dealing with the IRS, I have never seen a lawsuit for injunction that was not opposed by Justice Department attorneys on the singular ground that the Anti-Injunction Act prohibits suits of this nature. Despite the plain, unmistakable rule of law which requires the IRS to follow clearly established procedures in making the assessment; and despite the plain unmistakable language of §6213(a) to the effect that federal courts possess jurisdiction to enjoin collection when those procedures are ignored, the Justice Department continues to insist that cases such as these should be dismissed by the courts.

Therefore, in anticipation of this attack, you *must* be prepared to present to the court an accurate picture of the facts of your case and the rules of law which bring it beyond the sweep of the Anti-Injunction Act. This will be done at the time of your hearing on the application for preliminary injunction. The reason for the duality of the hearing is generally that the Government's response to your complaint takes the form of a motion to dismiss it. In its motion and supporting documents, the government's representative will submit the proposition that Code §7421, the Anti-Injunction Act, *knows no bounds;* that its proscription is universal and may not be ignored under any condition whatsoever.

This statement, as we have seen, is patently false. Why attorneys within the employ of the United States, sworn to uphold the law and the Constitution of the United States will continue to advance a position of law wholly unsupported by statute or case authority, I can only guess. I can assure you that the reason is not because these lawyers are ignorant. I will leave further reasoning to your own imagination.

My point is that *you must be prepared* to assert the correctness of your legal position, lest your case be dismissed by the court. Moreover, you cannot expect the court to do your thinking for you while you are under the gun. I stated earlier that advance preparation is mandatory and will spell the difference between *success or failure* in the courtroom. Nowhere is this concept more poignant than in a hearing on a motion to dismiss your case. At every turn, the IRS attorney will attept to confuse the facts and the issues in an effort to persuade the court to dismiss your case. You must stand firm, pointing sternly to your affidavit which must establish the facts, and to your memorandum of law which stated the legal authorities. If you prevail in this hearing, you are home free!

Having just read such a pointed admonition of the need to study and prepare before the hearing, you may be suggesting to yourself that it is impossible to gain victory in this regard. Of course, that is not true. One case involving this very procedure will illustrate my point. Dave was the unlucky recipient of an IRS abrirary notice. For two tax years, the IRS determined that Dave owed over $4,200. In response to the notices, he demanded that the tax be abated and further demanded that a notice of deficiency be mailed in order that he could enjoy his right to petition the Tax Court. However, Dave's demands were ignored. The IRS, in total disregard of the law and Dave's rights to a notice of deficiency, filed first a lien, then a levy against Dave's paycheck.

Dave's response was to bash the IRS in the teeth with Ultimate Defense Weapon Number Six. The complaint was filed in late October after the IRS successfully levied two of Dave's paychecks. A hearing on the preliminary injunction was set for just a few days later in order that

8. *Jensen v. IRS, supra.*

Exhibit 9-6: Complaint for Abatement of Unjust Assessment

```
                    UNITED STATES DISTRICT COURT
                        DISTRICT OF MINNESOTA
                            THIRD DIVISION

William E. Citizen,              )
                                 )
          Plaintiff,             )    Civil Case No. _____
                                 )
vs.                              )    JURY TRIAL DEMANDED
                                 )
The United States of America,    )
                                 )
          Defendant.             )
```

COMPLAINT FOR ABATEMENT OF UNJUST ASSESSMENT

NATURE OF THE ACTION

1. This is a civil action to enjoin the collection of taxes pursuant to an unlawful assessment under Code §6213(a).

JURISDICTION

2. The Jurisdiction of the court is invoked under the authority of 26 USC §§6212, and 6213(a), providing jurisdiction to enjoin collection when the deficiency procedures of the tax code have been violated.

3. This case involves the internal revenue laws of the United States and hence, raises a federal question.

VENUE

4. Venue within the above-named court is proper according to 28 USC §1402, in that the United States is a defendant in this case.

PARTIES

5. The Plaintiff, William E. Citizen, (address, city, state,

COMPLAINT FOR ABATEMENT, PAGE 1

zip) is properly named as the Plaintiff in this action, as it is he against whom the unjust assessment was made, and it is he against whom the IRS is unlawfully proceeding.

6. The Defendant, United States of America, through its agency the Internal Revenue Service, caused the unjust assessment to be made and is proceeding against the Plaintiff to collect the same.

BACKGROUND FACTS

7. The Plaintiff filed a timely US individual income tax return, Form 1040 for the year 1986, with the Internal Revenue Service on or before April 15th, 1987. The return was filed with the IRS Service Center at (city, state).

8. On (date) the Plaintiff received a notice from the IRS that an error was discovered in said return, and that the IRS corrected the error. A bill for additional tax in the amount of $_____ was mailed to the Plaintiff. Attached to this complaint as Exhibit A is a copy of said bill.

9. On (date), within 60 days of the date shown on Exhibit A, Plaintiff responded in writing to the IRS. Said response explained that Plaintiff did not agree with the tax demanded in Exhibit A, and further, the letter demanded a full abatement of the assessed liability. Said abatement was demanded under the authority of Code §6213(b)(2)(A). Attached to this complaint as Exhibit B is a copy of said letter.

10. On (date) the Plaintiff received from the IRS a second demand for payment of the same liability. The letter demanded that if the amount was not paid within 30 days, enforced collection action

COMPLAINT FOR ABATEMENT, PAGE 2

would be taken. Attached to this complaint as Exhibit C is a copy of said second demand for payment.

11. On (date), immediately after receiving the letter in Exhibit C, Plaintiff mailed a second letter demanding abatement. Said letter pointed out that the IRS' intended collection action was unlawful under Code §6213(a) and (b). Furthermore, Plaintiff demanded that a notice of deficiency be mailed to him under Code §6212, in order that he may enjoy his right to petition the Tax Court. Attached to this complaint and marked Exhibit D is a copy of Plaintiff's second letter demanding abatement.

12. On (date) the Internal Revenue Service placed a levy against the wages of the Plaintiff. The levy demanded payment of $_____, the amount assessed for the year in question. The wage levy purports to seize all of the funds of the Plaintiff, leaving him with just $85 per week on which to live.

13. Plaintiff's personal living expenses exceed $1,500 per month, which amount is required for the support and maintenance of Plaintiff, his wife and their 3 minor children.

14. The amount of $85 per week, which IRS proposes to leave Plaintiff is grossly insufficient in which to pay all living expenses necessary to maintain the health and welfare of the Plaintiff and his family.

15. The Plaintiff properly pursued and exhausted all available administrative remedies in connection with his demand for abatement. However, IRS has failed and refused to honor such demands, in violation of Plaintiff's statutory rights under §6212 and 6213(a).

COMPLAINT FOR ABATEMENT, PAGE 3

16. This lawsuit is grounded upon the statutory language of Code §6213(a), permitting a suit to enjoin collection when the IRS has failed or refused to follow the established deficiency procedures of the code. This suit is not precluded by the Anti-Injunction Act, Code §7421.

COUNT I

17. Plaintiff restates all of the allegations contained in paragraphs 1-16 as though fully set forth here in Count I.

18. The Defendant made an assessment of taxes against the Plaintiff for the year _____, which assessment was based upon an alleged mathematical or clerical error as described in Code §6213(b)(1).

19. Upon receipt of notice of such assessment and demand for payment, Plaintiff made a timely demand for abatement in accordance with his rights under Code §6213(b)(2)(A).

20. The Defendant failed and refused to abate the liability, despite the statutory obligation to do so.

21. The Plaintiff repeatedly demanded a notice of deficiency but the Defendant refused to mail a statutory notice of deficiency as required by Code §§6212, 6213(a) and 6213(b)(2)(A).

22. The Defendant continues to demand that Plaintiff pay such liability, and in fact, has commenced enforced collection action in violation of Code §§6212 and 6213(a).

23. The Defendant's actions of failing to abate the tax in question, and of undertaking enforced collection action, have caused immediate and irreparable harm to the Plaintiff, and is in violation

COMPLAINT FOR ABATEMENT, PAGE 4

of the deficiency procedures set out in the Internal Revenue Code.

24. Plaintiff is entitled to an injunction and to the recovery of damages as hereinafter set forth as a result of the Defendant's violation of law.

EQUITY

25. The unlawful wage levy presently in effect against the Plaintiff will deprive Plaintiff of the ability to provide the necessities of life for himself and his family.

26. Such unlawful deprivation will cause immediate and irreparable harm to the Plaintiff unless the Defendant is enjoined by this Court because the Plaintiff cannot survive on $85 per week.

27. The Plaintiff has no adequate remedy at law as an alternative to the injunction sought here, in that he was unlawfully deprived of his statutory right to a notice of deficiency which would permit him to contest the liability in the Tax Court. Furthermore, the Plaintiff is without the ability to pay the tax demanded by the Defendant, making a suit for refund impossible.

28. For these reasons, the equity jurisdiction of this court is properly invoked, entitling Plaintiff to the injunction sought here.

DAMAGES

29. The Plaintiff has been deprived of the use of his wages in the amount of $_____ necessary for the support of his family as a result of the unlawful actions of the Defendant.

30. The Plaintiff will continue to suffer the unjust deprivation of his wages until such time as the unlawfully assessed

COMPLAINT FOR ABATEMENT, PAGE 5

tax is paid in full, unless this court intervenes.

REQUEST FOR RELIEF

WHEREFORE, based upon all of the foregoing, Plaintiff demands judgment against the Defendant as follows:

1. That the court enter an order enjoining the Defendant, and any of its agents or employees, from collecting or attempting to collect the unjust assessment at issue here.

2. That the court order the Defendant to abate the liability in question herein, pursuant to Code $6213(b)(2)(A)$.

3. That the Defendant be ordered to refund all of the Plaintiff's wages which have been seized pursuant to the unlawful levy.

4. That the court order the Defendant to pay all of the Plaintiff's costs and disbursements incurred in connection with prosecuting this suit for abatement.

5. For such other relief as the court may deem just.

Dated:

_____   _____
William E. Citizen   Jane M. Citizen

Address
City, State, Zip
Area Code and Phone Number

COMPLAINT FOR ABATEMENT, PAGE 6

the matter could be brought to a head as quickly as possible. Dave worked feverishly the next two days, rereading his case authority and yellow-highlighting the statutory language he intended to present to the court.

Finally, the day of the hearing came and Dave marched into the court, weapons in hand, poised for battle. He had the facts on his side; the IRS failed to issue the mandatory notice of deficiency as required by law. He had the law on his side; the very statutes which the IRS ignored handed the court the authority to prevent collection. Most importantly, Dave had *resolved* within himself that since he elected to engage the enemy, he would make every shot count!

When his case was called for hearing on a crisp morning in early November, Dave bolted to the front of the courtroom and confidently began unfolding his argument for the court. Dave briefly recited the facts of the case for the benefit of the judge. Pointing to his affidavit, he discussed his letters demanding abatement, (copies of which were attached to his affidavit) and the IRS' failure to adhere to his warnings. Turning to the law, he discussed the general principles of the Anti-Injunction Act, explaining the reasons why the act did not apply in this case. As legal arguments rolled off his tongue, Dave kept the IRS' lawyer entirely on the defensive. His rapid-fire assault sent the enemy scurrying for cover in every direction.

When the barrage died down and the smoke cleared, Dave stood alone. Almost no effort whatsoever was made by the government's attorney to gainsay what Dave had submitted to the court. Then the judge himself spoke. His remark was, "Sometimes plaintiffs come into this court and they are absolutely right and the government is absolutely wrong. This may be just such a case."

With that, an order was issued preventing the IRS from taking any further collection steps until the matter could be resolved. Hence, Dave nullified the effects of the wage levy within just a few weeks of the time it came into existence. With the exception of Dave's first two paychecks, the IRS never got another dime. Several months later, after some further legal fencing, the IRS made the ultimate gesture of surrender. It officially released the levy it had placed against Dave's wages a few months earlier. Eventually, the liability was abated in its entirety.

The Use of Discovery

Assuming you are successful in your bid for a preliminary injunction, the court will cast aside the government's motion to dismiss the case. This indicates that the fight is on! Since the burden of proof on all issues rests squarely upon your shoulders, you will want to employ the discovery tools contained within the Federal Rules of Civil Procedure at the earliest possible opportunity. Through the vehicle of discovery, you will be able to force admissions and statements from the lips of IRS representatives and personnel who were responsible for the acts taken against you.

In particular, you will want to focus upon the letters that you wrote in an effort to halt the impending unlawful collection. You must also establish that the IRS ignored the letters and made the assessment without first mailing a notice of deficiency. Whenever you involve yourself in discovery, your cause is best served if you first carefully review your complaint, listing each of the separate allegations you must establish with clear evidence. Next, determine which of those allegations may best be proven with documents, statements or admissions from the government itself. These are the areas in which your discovery should focus. You have completed your discovery when you have, in hand, all evidence you need to prove the allegations of your complaint, *and* you are in possession of the specific evidence which the government intends to use in its defense. This prepares you for the stages of litigation which are to follow.

Settlement Discussions

In any civil lawsuit, the issue of settlement will always rise to the fore sooner or later. We have discussed the topic of settlement in general terms already, and I do not intend to say much more here other than, if the question of settlement is broached anywhere along the way, *listen!* Avoid the attitude of stubbornness or belligerence which suggests that because they are wrong, you will "take them to the cleaners."

I do not mean to suggest that all cases should be settled and that the IRS should never be "taken to the cleaners." Rather, I suggest only that intelligent decisions to pursue litigation or explore settlement can only be made with *an open mind.*

Summary Judgment

The most likely resolution to the dispute over an unjust tax assessment is the remedy of summary judgment. However, as I state over and over, summary judgment is valid as a means of disposing of a case only when all of the facts material to a resolution of the problem are no longer in dispute. When, through discovery, the facts are agreed upon by the parties, summary judgment is appropriate.

However, care should be taken so as not to deprive one's self of the right to a jury trial by submitting a premature motion for summary judgment. On the isolated questions of the appropriateness of an injunction or the legal adequacy of the assessment in question, the court will rule upon these matters without a jury trial. Such questions will be looked upon by the court as pure questions of law which are said to be outside the province of the jury to determine.

This is not true with regard to questions of fact. When facts remain in dispute, a jury rightfully should be called upon to resolve these issues.[9] In the context of this case, questions of fact may involve whether and under what circumstances the IRS mailed a notice of deficiency, or whether demands for abatement were mailed by the citizen or received by the IRS. Questions of fact might also involve the manner in which the IRS responded, or failed to respond, to any letters demanding abatement. In my own mind, a most intriguing question of fact is, who authorized the mailing of a correction notice known to be false, and who authorized the IRS to ignore the letters demanding abatement?

The Trial

We have discussed in general terms the procedure which is followed in a civil tax trial. No purpose is served by restating the same points here, other than to say that if your case seeks the recovery of damages from the government as a result of the unlawful acts of an IRS agent,[10] it is my opinion that you are entitled to and should be afforded a jury trial on the issue of the damages. Therefore, care should be taken to insist upon the right to a jury trial at the outset of your case.

Exhibit 9-7 is a flowchart depicting the process which is followed in a case of this nature.

Conclusion

For too long, the IRS enjoyed the luxury of being able to simply send a bill and get paid. Relying on intimidation, confusion and the fact that in most cases it is more expensive for the taxpayer to object than to pay, the IRS collects millions of dollars that are not lawfully due. Like the bully who feeds on fear and inaction against his petty torment, the IRS has developed a false bravado that will be dashed when they pick on someone who possesses this Ultimate Weapon against IRS abuse. When you receive a bill for taxes that you do not owe, make them pick on someone their own size!

Exhibit 9-7 Flowchart of Action for Abatement of Unjust Assessment

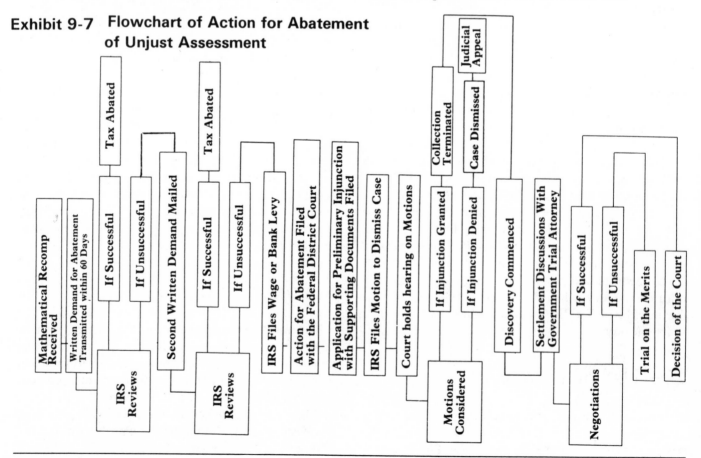

---

9. Seventh Amendment, U.S. Constitution; Rule 38, FRCvP.

10. See Chapter Twelve for details.

CHAPTER 10

Disarming the Tax Lien

Very early in the development of tax law in the United States, the Supreme Court recognized that "the power to tax involves the power to destroy."[1] If this statement were true when made, it must be more so today, given the nature of the federal tax lien and the manner in which the courts have fertilized and nurtured that power over many years.

This fact may best be illustrated by events which came to the fore in late 1984 and early 1985. Shirley and Tom lived in a small, rural community in eastern Pennsylvania. Though they were unmarried, they lived together since 1980 on Shirley's farm. Shirley was a horse breeder and Tom did the heavy labor for her on the farm.

In 1979, Tom's 1977 income tax return came under audit by the IRS. During the course of the examination, the IRS looked into subsequent returns as well. Eventually, the examination covered years 1978, 1979 and 1980. In February of 1982, the agent assigned to the examination came to the conclusion that Tom owed income taxes of just a bit over $247,000. At the same time, because Tom sold some property during the

course of the examination, the IRS obtained a jeopardy assessment against Tom. The jeopardy assessment is the only legally permissable manner of bypassing the deficiency procedures when making income tax assessments. As a result of the assessment, the IRS began to immediately collect the tax.

The IRS agents and revenue officers involved in the case contended that the jeopardy assessment was justified because Tom was selling property and allegedly depositing the proceeds into bank accounts owned by Shirley. As a result of the latter "observation" a lien was filed against Shirley's farm and the IRS executed levies upon her bank accounts, confiscating over $20,000. The liens prevented Shirley from obtaining the operating loans she needed to conduct her horse breeding operation. The levy on her account forced her to borrow money from personal friends upon which to live. She was unable to pay the mortgage on the farm and had no money of her own with which to buy food. She was humiliated by the IRS' acts which led to continuous threats by her creditors to foreclose upon her farm and machinery because of her inability to meet

---

1. Justice John Marshal in *M'Culloch v. Maryland*, 17 U.S. (4 Wheat.) 316 (1819).

mortgage obligations. Even an effort to sell the farm was squelched by the presence of the lien.

Knowing that the IRS' allegations against him were false, Tom executed an appeal of the jeopardy assessment to the Appeals Division. After some review, an appeals officer concluded that the assessment against Tom was "not reasonable" and ordered that it be abated in its entirety. He also ordered that the lien against the farm be released and that refunds be processed for money seized from Shirley. That decision was made on September 23, 1982. However, the revenue officer did not release the lien until November 30, over two months later. In the meantime, hindered by the lien, Shirley was unable to continue the day-to-day operations of the farm.

Later, the revenue officer was to explain that the delay was due to the lateness in his obtaining the abatement report. However, it was shown that he and the revenue agent responsible for the assessment were attempting to have the Appeals Officer's decision overturned. They were unsuccessful. In the meantime, however, Shirley continued to suffer the ravages of the lien. In addition, it was not until January of 1983 that the IRS returned to Shirley the funds they had seized from her bank account.

Years later, Tom testified before Congress in its hearings on the Taxpayers' Bill of Rights Act. His remarks were directed to a provision of the act which would afford citizens the right of administrative appeal of tax liens. Given the gross injustice imposed upon Tom's friend and companion Shirley, and the nightmare they both endured, Tom implored Congress to ratify that segment of the bill. Whether Tom's testimony was or was not the deciding factor in Congress' decision we do not know. We do know that with the passage of the Bill of Rights Act came a provision of law theretofore unknown in the tax code. That provision now allows the citizen the right to administratively appeal the filing of an erroneous lien, as well as the right to sue the IRS when damages attributable to an erroneous lien have been incurred by a citizen.

The Trouble with the Tax Lien

A federal tax lien is unlike any other lien known in law. A tax lien is considered a "general lien." It attaches to "all property and rights to property" owned by the person owing taxes to the government, whether that property is real or personal.[2] The principal contrasting factor with other liens under the law, is that the tax lien need not be addressed to a "specific" piece of property. As a general lien, it attaches to all property owned by the citizen at the time of its filing. Also, it attaches to all property acquired by him before the time of its expiration.[3]

The question of whether one "owns" property is determined by state law.[4] However, once it is determined that state law vests a present ownership interest in property, whether real or personal, federal law alone determines the extent to which the IRS may act to satisfy its lien *vis-a-vis* that property.[5]

Exhibit 10-1 is an example of a notice of Federal Tax Lien. It is mailed to the citizen by the IRS when the lien is filed with the county recorder for the county in which the citizen resides. It may also be filed in counties in which the citizen owns real property. The lien itself does not act to *deprive* a citizen of his property. Only a levy may actually seize property, transferring ownership from the citizen to the government. Like any other lien against property, the tax lien merely creates an "interest" in the property in favor of the United States to the extent specified within the lien. However, nothing but tenacious action by the citizen prevents the IRS from acting to seize property subject to a lien after it is filed.

Generally speaking, the IRS does not quickly act upon its liens after they are filed. For whatever reason, whether administrative, clerical, or in an effort to provide the citizen with an opportunity to pay the tax or make arrangements to do so, collection will often times (but not always) fall silent for a period of time subsequent to filing the lien. The other side of this coin, however, is that usually the lien is *the first step* taken by the IRS in enforced collection situations. The filing of a tax lien closely follows the expiration of the 30-day period for payment specified by law.[6] The government will take this step to protect its interests and prevent the citizen from divesting himself of all property prior to its undertaking enforced collection action.

Provided one is able to identify one or more disparities in connection with a federal tax lien, the aggrieved citizen must take immediate and decisive remedial action. The reasons are twofold. First, as we shall see later, efforts to "mitigate" any damages caused by an erroneous lien must be taken by the citizen if he

---

2. Code §6321.

3. *Glass City Bank of Jeanette v. United States,* 326 U.S. 265 (1945).

4. *Aquilino v. United States,* 363 U.S. 509 (1960).

5. *United States v. Rogers,* 103 S.Ct. 2132 (1983).

6. Code §6331.

Exhibit 10-1: Notice of Federal Tax Lien

Form 668(Y)	48	Department of the Treasury - Internal Revenue Service
(Rev. January 1989)		**Notice of Federal Tax Lien Under Internal Revenue Laws**

District	Serial Number	For Optional Use by Recording Office
ST PAUL, MN		

As provided by sections 6321, 6322, and 6323 of the Internal Revenue Code, notice is given that taxes (including interest and penalties) have been assessed against the following-named taxpayer. Demand for payment of this liability has been made, but it remains unpaid. Therefore, there is a lien in favor of the United States on all property and rights to property belonging to this taxpayer for the amount of these taxes, and additional penalties, interest, and costs that may accrue.

Name of Taxpayer

Residence

IMPORTANT RELEASE INFORMATION: With respect to each assessment listed below, unless notice of lien is refiled by the date given in column (e), this notice shall, on the day following such date, operate as a certificate of release as defined in IRC 6325(a).

Kind of Tax (a)	Tax Period Ended (b)	Identifying Number (c)	Date of Assessment (d)	Last Day for Refiling (e)	Unpaid Balance of Assessment (f)
1040	12/31/81		10/12/88	11/11/94	525.25
1040	12/31/82		10/12/88	11/11/94	2003.50
1040	12/31/83		10/12/88	11/11/94	830.94
1040	12/31/84		10/12/88	11/11/94	7638.69
1040	12/31/85		10/12/88	11/11/94	9110.47

Place of Filing

Total $ 20108.85

This notice was prepared and signed at _____ ST PAUL, MN _____, on this,

the _19th_ day of _May_, 19 _89_.

Signature

Title

(NOTE: Certificate of officer authorized by law to take acknowledgments is not essential to the validity of Notice of Federal Tax lien Rev. Rul. 71-466, 1971 - 2 C.B. 409)

Form 668(Y) (Rev. 1-89)

hopes to recover damages caused by the government. Second, and perhaps more importantly, the damages which can be inflicted as the result of a federal tax lien *are serious.* It should never be taken lightly, particularly when erroneous.

The Right to Appeal
The Federal Tax Lien

One of the largest and most prevalent complaints raised in hearings on the Bill of Rights Act was the fact that the IRS routinely files tax liens against citizens which are in error, causing much financial difficulty, *ala* Shirley. To compound the problem, the Code provided no remedy to the citizen faced with this most difficult situation. The Bill of Rights Act added Code section 6326, which now enables a citizen to *appeal* the filing of an erroneous lien.

When passed, I was critical of the new statute for its lack of specificity. It provided simply that the IRS was to issue regulations which establish the procedure under which "any person (may) appeal to the Secretary after the filing of a notice of a lien. . ."[7] Under subsection (b) of the new law, if it is determined that the lien is indeed erroneous, the IRS is required to "expeditiously (and, to the extent practicable, within 14 days after such determination) issue a certificate of release of such lien and shall include in such certificate a statement that such filing was erroneous."

While Congress did address the problem of erroneous and cumbersome tax liens, they left the matter entirely up to the IRS to determine how those erroneous filings would be handled. On May 5, 1989, the IRS issued regulations which took effect on July 7, 1989. The new regulations provide for the process of appealing erroneous liens.

Revenue Regulation 301.6326-1T establishes just *four* grounds upon which the filing of a tax lien may be appealed. In keeping with the Congressional Conference Committee recommendation, it states in the regulation that, "Such appeal may be used only for the purpose of correcting the erroneous filing of a notice of lien, not to challenge the underlying deficiency that led to the imposition of a lien." The four grounds expressed in the regulation for appealing the filing of a lien are:

1. The tax liability which gave rise to the lien, as well as all interest and penalties, was satisfied prior to filing the lien;

2. The tax liability which gave rise to the lien was assessed in violation of the deficiency procedures set out in §6213 of the Code;

3. The tax liability which gave rise to the lien was assessed in violation of Title 11 of the United States Code (the Bankruptcy Code); or

4. The statutory period for collection of the liability expired prior to the filing of the lien.[8]

When I originally read the provisions of the Bill of Rights which created this right of appeal, I had my doubts about whether the IRS would issue a regulation which would be useful in any way. I critized Congress for leaving the task of creating the procedure entirely to the discretion of the IRS. I must admit, however, after a careful review of the regultion, I am fairly pleased with what I see.

I do have one important reservation, and it is this: the law was enacted to permit the citizen to appeal the filing of an "erroneous" tax lien. I believe that a tax lien which is afoul of any of *nine* rules of law discussed later in this chapter is *erroneous* and should be subject to the remedy created by Code §6326. However, in its regulation, the IRS mentions just *four* reasons for appealing the filing of a tax lien. It is my opinion that such a regulation is overly *narrow,* a condition unique with regard to tax regulations. Historically, the IRS is guilty of drafting regulations which extend *beyond* Congressional intent in lawmaking. Here, it appears that the IRS has not gone far enough to provide citizen with the full and complete measure of protection which Congress intended. Whether or not I am correct in my reading of the regulation will be determined later by the courts.

Still, I am pleased with the provision which allows the appeal of a lien when the IRS has failed to follow its deficiency procedures. This is very important. We already discussed the "arbitrary notice" which the IRS mails to citizens creating bogus tax bills. The procedure under §6326 may go a long way toward remedying the injustice created by the arbitrary notice. It gives the citizen the power of administrative appeal when the IRS has not followed the proper procedures before assessing a tax liability. Under this new law, one can look forward to success if the IRS has not provided you the opportunity to contest the bill. Since this circumstance presents itself with monotonous regularity, I foresee that this new procedure will be most helpful when used correctly.

It should be noted, though, that in the case of the arbitrary notice, it is more common for the IRS to merely execute a wage or bank levy to collect the

---

7. New Code §6326.
8. Rev. Reg. 301.6326-1T-(b).

assessment. Under this condition, Code §6326 will be of no comfort. One will be forced to resort to Ultimate Defense Weapon Number Six. See Chapter Nine.

When to Appeal A Federal Tax Lien

From a regulatory point of view, the filing of a tax lien must be appealed by the citizen within one year of the time the citizen "becomes aware of the erroneously filed tax lien."[9] This is important because many people may tend to associate becoming aware of the erroneous lien solely with the date the lien was filed. Since the *IRS* has written the regulation prescribing the language of the time limit, it might be expected to argue that "becoming aware" of the erroneous lien is tied to the date it was filed. Clearly, however, this is not the intent of the regulation.

There are many ways one may "become aware" of an erroneous lien. In Shirley's case, the presence of the lien was apparent when Tom received notice in the mail that it was filed. Normally, notice of the lien is mailed to the citizen contemporaneously with its filing at the county recorder's office. Hence, your copy of the notice would arrive within days of it being filed. The date of receipt of your copy of the notice would begin the one year time limit for filing the appeal.

Just as often, the IRS does *not* mail a copy of the notice to the citizen when it is filed with the recorder's office. One explanation for this could be that it was not mailed to the citizen's last known address. When this occurs, you may not become aware of the erroneous lien until you make an effort to dispose of your property. Doug sold a parcel of real property on a contract for deed. Later, after the contract vendee defaulted on the property, Doug cancelled the contract and repossessed the property. He then sold it outright to a third party. When the third party attempted to refinance the property over one year after Doug sold it to him, and over two years after Doug repossessed it, the third party discovered that a lien was filed against the property.

The lien was for taxes owed by the original vendee on the contract for deed from whom Doug prepossessed the property. Unbelievable as it may seem, the property underwent not one, but two title searches before the lien appeared. As the notice of lien was mailed to the vendee, neither Doug nor the third party purchaser were aware that it was filed. The third party purchaser became aware of the presence of the lien some three years after it had been filed with the county recorder's office. The date they were notified by the bank that a lien was present was the date the one year time limit began for filing the appeal.

Another scenario involves Marilyn. She and her husband were separating and agreed to sell their home and equally divide the proceeds. Marilyn's husband had a long-standing dispute with the IRS which led to assessments and eventually, a lien for taxes. Marilyn had no tax liability with the IRS and the IRS recognized that fact. Despite this, just days before the sale of the home was to close and the purchasers were to take possession, the closing company phoned Marilyn and explained that a last minute title search revealed a second tax lien, this one in *her* name. As Marilyn was aware that a lien was in effect against her husband, she asked for clarification. After reviewing a copy of the actual document, Marilyn discovered that, yes, the lien did bear her name even though she never received notification from the IRS with respect to it. The date Marilyn received and verified the presence of her name on the lien is the date the one year time limit began for filing her appeal.[10]

These examples should not be permitted to limit one's application of the rule I am attempting to define. In actuality, the rule is quite simple. I have provided examples only to demonstrate that the date of filing the lien is not controlling in determining when the one-year period of limitations begins to run.

What Constitutes an "Erroneous Lien"

The right to appeal the filing of a federal tax lien is limited. The appeal may only be successful when the citizen can demonstrate that the lien is "erroneous." We have already briefly discussed the general rules in this regard, but I believe a more careful look is critical. In the first place, the regulation states:

> "Any person may appeal to the disrict director of the district in which a notice of federal tax lien was filed on the property or rights to property of such person for a release of lien alleging the error in the filing of notice of lien. Such appeal may be used only for the purpose of correcting the erroneous filing of a notice of lien, not to challenge the underlying deficiency that led to the imposition of a lien.[11]★ ★ ★"

---

9. Rev. Reg. §301.6326-1T(d)(3).

10. The reader will please note that each of these examples occurred prior to the enactment of the Taxpayers' Bill of Rights Act. Therefore, each problem was rectified using procedures other than the right to appeal a tax lien.

11. Rev. Reg. 301.6326-1T(a).

When it is found that the lien was filed in error, the IRS is required to "expeditiously, and, to the extent practicable, within 14 days after such determination, issue a certificate of release of lien."[12]

It is clear from both the language of the regulation and the Congressional Committee Report on the statute, Congress did not intend and the IRS will not allow one to litigate a deficiency determination through the vehicle of appealing the lien. Therefore, if one has lost a case in Tax Court or has otherwise failed to properly contest a deficiency determination, the remedy of appealing the tax lien will not offer any defense to collection.

At the same time, as I have already stated, the language of the regulation is, in my opinion, unjustifiably restrictive in defining the conditions under which a lien may be appealed. Based upon the federal statutes which regulate the administration of tax liens, I believe the list of potential "errors" is over *twice* as long as that given by the IRS in its regulation. There are the *nine* factors which I have distilled from the law, factors which determine whether or not a lien is "erroneous." Upon receipt of the notice of tax lien, one should review it to determine whether any defect is present. The nine factors are:

1. Is the lien for an amount *in excess* of that which was lawfully assessed, including interest and penalties?;[13]

2. Was the assessment in question made *outside* the statute of limitations?;[14]

Was the assessment made in *violation* of the deficiency procedures prescribed by the Code?;[15]

4. Did the IRS fail to send you adequate *notice* of the assessment and demand for its payment?;[16]

5. If a proper notice and demand was received, did the IRS provide the full *30-day period* required by law for payment?;[17]

6. Is *collection* of the tax barred by the statute of limitations?;[18]

7. Has the tax which is the subject of the lien already been *paid?;*

8. Is the lien filed in violation of the automatic stay provision of the Bankruptcy Code, applicable to a person in bankruptcy?;[19] and

9. Does the *property* mentioned in the lien constitute "property or rights to property" under the state law belonging to the person who owes the tax?[20]

While just four of these points were mentioned by the IRS as grounds for making an appeal, without a doubt, each has a bearing upon whether a lien is proper or "erroneous." When a lien is filed in violation of the notice and demand provisions of Code §6331, that lien is unlawful.[21] It must be considered "erroneous" under the regulation we are here discussing despite the fact the IRS ignored this reality in its regulation.

Most importantly, the language of the lien statute itself provides:

"If any person liable to pay any tax neglects or refuses to pay the same *after demand,* the amount. . .shall be a lien in favor of the United States upon all property and rights to property, whether real or personal, belonging to such person."[22] (Emphasis added.)

Thus we see the importance of the notice requirement to the question of a valid lien. The necessity to place a lawful demand for payment upon the citizen alleged to be delinquent is an integral part of the statute. In the absence of such a demand, the citizen would certainly have grounds to assert that the lien is erroneous. The written notice and demand for payment is described in Code §6331(d). That section stipulates that the notice required must be:

"(A) given in person,
"(B) left at the dwelling or usual place of business of such person, or
"(C) sent by certified or registered mail to such person's last known address, no less than 30 days before the day of the levy."

With the attention to notice and demand given by the Code, I believe that it is negligent for the IRS to have overlooked this aspect of determining whether a lien is "erroneous" under the law. The receipt of proper notice and an opportunity to be heard are fundamental elements of due process under the Fifth Amendment.

12. Ibid.
13. Code §6321.
14. Code §6501.
15. Code §§6212 and 6213.
16. Code §6331.
17. Ibid.
18. Code §6503.
19. 11 USC (the Bankruptcy Code) §362.
20. Code §6321.
21. *Kennebec Box Co. v. Richards Corp.,* 5 F.2d 951 (2nd Cir. 1925); *Coson v. United States,* 286 F.2d 453 (9th Cir. 1961); *Mrizek v. Long,* 59-2 U.S.T.C. Para. 9678 (DC Ill. 1959).
22. Code §6321.

Moreover, it is well-settled, as we have examined in Chapter Nine, that when the IRS ignores the statutory framework within which it must collect delinquent accounts, its actions are invalid. This principle must apply equally to the tax lien.

Given these factors, one must carefully review any tax lien which may be asserted by the IRS. Whenever it can be shown that the IRS has failed or erred in one of the nine areas identified above, steps should be taken in accordance with Code §6326 to appeal the lien.

How to Appeal a Tax Lien

As already explained, the administrative appeal of the lien must be carried out within one year of the date you "become aware" that the erroneous lien is in effect. The regulation we are examining specifies the procedures which must be followed and the form which must be employed when executing the right of appeal. At subparagraph (d) of the regulation, the IRS provides:

1. *Manner.* The appeal must be made *in writing* to the district director, marked to the attention of Chief, Special Procedures Function, of the district in which the notice of lien was filed. The office of Special Procedures is an adjunct to the Collection Division. SPF is responsible for the paperwork the Collection Division generates, including certificates of release of federal tax lien. Since SPF is responsible to release all liens, the appeal is made to that office.

2. *Form.* The appeal must include the following information and documents:

a. Your name, address, and social security number;

b. A copy of the notice of lien in question, if available; and

c. The grounds upon which the notice of lien is being appealed.

The grounds for appealing the lien are set forth above. There are just four of them recognized by the regulation, but we have explored a total of nine factors which must be considered when the validity of a tax lien is in question. Please note, however, that the regulation, in keeping with Congressional intent, is clear on the question of employing the process of administratively apealing a lien as a means to contest the deficiency determination. This is not permitted.

With respect to the requirement to include a copy of the lien, such is available from the county recorder with whom the lien was filed. As I pointed out above, the IRS will not provide a copy of the lien to the citizen at the time of filing in every case. However, anything filed with the county recorder's office becomes a matter of "public record" and is available for a small copying charge. The lien itself should always be obtained and included with the written appeal, if for no other reason, to avoid confusion.

In addition, when certain grounds are specified upon which it is asserted that the lien is erroneous, the IRS asks that supporting documents be supplied. For example, if the ground for appeal is that the liability was paid in full prior to filing the lien, proof of payment in full must be provided. Such proof includes a cancelled check in the full amount of the tax dated prior to the filing of the lien, an internal revenue cashier's check in the full amount dated in the same fashion, or any other manner of proof acceptable to the district director.[23]

If the ground for appeal is that the IRS failed to follow the deficiency procedures when making the assessment, the appeal must contain a statement as to exactly how the assessment was in violation of §6213 of the Code. Please see Chapters Four, Eight and Nine for further discussion of the deficiency procedures. The last proviso of the regulation is, if the ground for appeal is that the assessment was made in violation of Title 11 (the Bankruptcy Code) you must include in the appeal the identity of the Court and the district in which the bankruptcy petition was filed, with the docket number and the date the bankruptcy petition was filed.

Whenever grounds other than those set forth in the regulation are asserted in the appeal, you must take extra steps to ensure that you supplement your written appeal with documents supporting your position. Because we are asserting entitlement to relief under conditions not expressed in the regulation, but clearly affect the propriety of the lien, we must be prepared to bend over backwards to ensure that all of the elements of the appeal are adequately documented.

Just as an example, if you contend that the assessment of the liability was made after the statute of limitations expired, you may with to use your IMF as an attachment to the appeal. It will demonstrate both the date the return in question was filed and the date the assessment was recorded by the IRS. This kind of documentation will go a long way to verify the claims you advance in your written appeal. Anytime you can employ the use of the IRS' own internal documents or forms to establish the verity of your claims, your position is that much stronger.

Exhibit 10-2 is an example of the manner in which the written appeal of an erroneous lien may be structured. Please examine it carefully and note that the facts shown there are hypothetical. Also, for purposes of example, I

Exhibit 10-2: Administrative Appeal of Lien

IN THE INTERNAL REVENUE SERVICE
FOR THE INTERNAL REVENUE DISTRICT OF MINNESOTA

In re the matter of:)
)
William E. & Jane M. Citizen,   )
SSN: 000-00-0000   )
)
              Claimants.   )
)

**ADMINISTRATIVE APPEAL OF FILING OF FEDERAL TAX LIEN
AND APPLICATION FOR RELEASE OF FEDERAL TAX LIEN**

This is an Administrative Appeal of the filing of a Federal

Tax Lien and an Application for Release of Federal Tax Lien. It is

made pursuant to 26 USC §§6325 and 6326 and regulations thereunder.

This claim is made upon the following facts, arguments, and

disclosures:

1. <u>Taxpayer's identity</u> -- The claimants are William E. and

Jane M. Citizen, SSN: 000-00-0000, whose address is, (address, city,

state, zip).

(Note: these facts are hypothetical. You must use your own facts.)

2. <u>Tax Lien in Question</u> -- The Federal Tax Lien in question

was filed on (date) with the office of (recorder's office, city,

state). A true and accurate copy of the lien in question is attached

hereto and made a part of this appeal and application for release.

The Tax Lien in question covers the year _____ and is in the

amount of $_____. This appeal and application for release is

made in a timely manner.

3. <u>Grounds for Appeal and Release of Lien</u> -- The Lien for

taxes at issue here is based upon an assessment which was obtained in

violation of the deficiency procedures set out in §§6212 and 6213(a)

ADMINISTRATIVE APPEAL OF LIEN, PAGE 1

of the Code. In particular on (date) the claimants received from the IRS a letter informing them that a mathematical recomputation was performed in connection with their tax return for (year). By letter of (date) (copy attached), claimants informed the IRS that they were not in agreement with the recomputation and requested an abatement of the assessment pursuant to §6213(b)(2)(A). Further, they demanded that they be issued a notice of deficiency in connection with such liability if the IRS were to continue to insist that such amount was due and owing.

A notice of deficiency was never forthcoming. Rather, the next notification that claimants received from the IRS was a Notice of Filing Federal Tax Lien (copy attached). Section 6213(b) of the Code and its subparts makes it abundantly clear that the IRS must abate any assessment made pursuant to a mathematical recomputation if the citizen objects to that assessment within 60 days. Any reassessment of the liability is then subject to the deficiency procedures of §§6212 and 6213(a). In particular, those sections mandate that no assessment may be made unless the IRS first issues a notice of deficiency to the citizen. Once issued, no assessment may be made until after the expiration of 90 days, or if the citizen petitions the Tax Court within that 90-day period, no assessment may be made until after the Tax Court's decision has become final. See §6213(a).

Despite the plain language of the letter demanding that such rights be afforded to these claimants, the IRS failed and refused to abate the assessment in question and failed and refused to issue a 90-day letter to the claimants. This failure has acted to deprive the claimants of their right to Petition the Tax Court in respect to the alleged liability, in violation of the deficiency procedures established by the Code.

It is well-settled that any assessment which is obtained by the IRS in violation of the deficiency procedures is unlawful. Hence, it must follow that any lien recorded which purportedly secures to the benefit of the United States such an assessment must also be unlawful. For these reasons, the lien in question, a copy of which is attached hereto, must be released immediately.

4. Request for Relief -- By reason of the foregoing facts, the lien in question here is due to be released by the IRS in an expeditious manner, and in any event, within 14 days of approving this appeal and application for release.

5. Attestation -- Under penalty of perjury, the undersigned, William E. and Jane M. Citizen, hereby declare that the facts contained in this appeal and application, together with the accompanying documents, are true and correct to the best of their knowledge and belief.

Dated:

_____

William E. Citizen

_____

Jane M. Citizen

have addressed just *one* aspect of an erroneous lien. Keep in mind that we have discussed *nine* separate considerations which bear upon the correctness of a tax lien. If your grounds fall into one of the other eight, care must be taken to ensure that your appeal adequately addresses the relevant issues.

The regulation *makes it clear* that the above procedures "shall be the exclusive administrative remedy with respect to the erroneous filing of a notice of federal tax lien."[24] Therefore, if one were to overlook or somehow fail to exercise his right to appeal the lien within the one-year period, his administrative remedy is lost. It is also worthy of note that there is no limit in the regulation as to the number of times a lien may be appealed. I say this only to suggest that if, after your first appeal is denied, you find that you overlooked important issues which warrant consideration, a second appeal may be appropriate.

Applying For Release of the Lien

One final thought on the administrative process for disposing of a tax lien is appropriate to discuss. As we shall examine later, another new Bill of Rights provision establishes district court jurisdiction to sue the IRS for damages when it fails or refuses to release a tax lien under §6325 of the Code. I discussed in detail, in *How Anyone Can Negotiate With The IRS—And WIN!*, the manner in which one must make appliction for release of a lien under §6325.[25] I pointed out in that treatise that the IRS is under no obligation to release a lien *unless* a citizen makes an application for its release under Code §6325. That subtlety in the law explains why the IRS is guilty of failing to release liens on a wholesale level.

Under §6325, the lien is due to be released when the tax is paid in full or when the tax is uncollectable by reason of time. Also, the IRS may release the lien under such circumstances as will better facilitate full payment of the tax. These procedures are discussed at length in *How Anyone Can Negotiate,* Chapter Six, so I will not restate them here. In Chapter Six of that book, I have also provided a detailed formula on the manner in which the appliction for relief of the lien should be prepared. The application should be submitted to the office of Special Procedures serving the district where the lien is recorded.

What we have just learned is that there are *two* administrative procedures available when the IRS has a tax lien in effect. The first, available under Code §6326 is applicable when, for one of the reasons examined earlier, the lien is shown to be "erroneous." The *appeal* of the erroneous lien is the process by which one pursues that problem. The second procedure, available under Code §6325, is applicable when, for one of the reasons expressed in the statute,[26] the lien should be released. The *application* for release of the lien will address the latter situation.

In any event, it is my judgment that any application for release of the lien, or appeal of an erroneous lien, should make reference to *both* statutes governing the subject. Once more, those statutes are Code §§6325 (application for release) and 6326 (appeal of erroneous lien). The reason I encourage the reference to both statutes is simple. The new statute creating district court jurisdiction is somewhat ambiguous in its language. First of all, it provides that a suit for damages in connection with an improper lien may be filed when the IRS fails to release a lien under *Code §6325.* That statute, as already explained, provides for release of the lien only when *an application is submitted.* At the same time, the new law also states that unless *all administrative remedies available* under the Code are exhausted, no relief under the law will be afforded to the citizen.

Hence, a sort of duality in procedures is created. Each application for relief should also address the concept of an erroneous lien, and vice-versa. In this fashion, one will maximize the potential for success on the issue as well as preserving the widest possible range of rights and remedies available under the law. If this seems somewhat confusing, the doubts should melt after one has carefully reviewed Exhibit 10-2, Written Appeal of Tax Lien. Please examine it now.

When the Appeal is Denied

The IRS is required to issue a decision regarding the appeal as quickly as possible. If the decision is made to grant the appeal and discharge the lien, a certificate of release must be issued immediately. Consistent with the Congressional Committee Report on the statute, the regulation provides that the certificate of release of the lien "shall include a statement that the filing of the notice of lien was erroneous." The purpose of this clause, according to Congress, is to "facilitate repair of the taxpayer's credit and other financial records.[27]

When the written appeal is unpersuasive, the IRS can

---

24. Rev. Reg. §301.6326-1T(f).
25. See pages 207-223, *How Anyone Can Negotiate With The IRS—And WIN!*
26. See previous footnote.
27. Committee Report on P.L. 100-647.

be expected to unceremoniously deny the request with a letter to that effect. In that the appeal under §6326 is the "exclusive administrative remedy" available regarding tax liens, the issuance of a letter denying the appeal should be construed as a final administrative determination on the issue. Such a determination gives birth to Ultimate Defense Weapon Number Seven.

Ultimate Defense Weapon Number Seven
Court Proceeding to Recover Damages for Failure to Release a Lien

As an adjunct to the new section allowing for the appeal of an erroneous lien, the Taxpayers' Bill of Rights Act added Code section 7432. This new section acknowledges a citizen's right to sue the IRS for damages caused by its *failure to release a lien,* either "knowingly or by reason of negligence." The statute provides:

"(a) If any officer or employee of the Internal Revenue Service knowingly, or by reason of negligence, fails to release a lien under section 6325 on property of the taxpayer, such taxpayer may bring a civil action for damages against the United States in a district court of the United States.
"(b) In any action brought under subsecton (a), upon a finding of liability on the part of the defendant, the defendant shall be liable to the plaintiff in an amount equal to the sum of—
"(1) actual, direct economic damages sustained by the plaintiff which, but for the actions of the defendant, would not have been sustained, plus
"(2) the costs of the action."[28]

After reading the new Code section for yourself, you may now understand my reason for suggesting that all administrative actions you take regarding a tax lien should address *both* sections 6325 *and* 6326. As you can plainly see, Code §7432 addresses itself *only* to §6325 (*application* for release of lien). The wise citizen will therefore take steps to protect his interest and right to pursue the IRS in the courts by making reference to both the appropriate statutes.

In addition to Code §7432, another provision of law addresses itself to liens of the United States. Title 28, USC §2410 provides:

"(a) Under the conditions prescribed in this section and section 1444 of this title for the protection of the United States, the United States may be named a party in any civil action or suit in any district court, or in any State court having jurisdiction of the subject matter—
"(1) to quiet title to,
"(2) to foreclose a mortgage or other lien upon,
"(3) to partition,
"(4) to condemn, or
"(5) of interpleader or in the nature of interpleader with respect to,
"real or personal property on which the United States has or claims a mortgage or *other lien.*" (Emphasis added.)

Prior to the enactment of the new Code §7432, the above provision was a unique way in which to present to a district court the question of the propriety of a federal tax lien. Because of the broad language of 28 USC §2410 and its uncontested application to the matter of federal tax liens, I believe that such remains an important jurisdictional adjunct to Code §7432. Without question, it is settled that the district courts have the authority to resolve disputes over the propriety of federal tax liens under 28 USC §2410. This is important to appreciate because, as is always the case when the IRS is marched into court, we can expect the attorneys representing the government to suggest that the Anti-Injunction Act, Code §7421, is an all-inclusive bar to federal court jurisdiction where the IRS is concerned.

Limitations on the Proceeding

There are several important limitations on the right to commence a proceeding in court over an improper federal tax lien. These limitations are expressed in Code §7432(d). We shall address them in order.

First, under subsection (d)(1), *no relief* is available unless the citizen can demonstrate that all administrative remedies available under the Code were pursued and exhausted. This portion of the statute does not address itself to any particular provision of the Code. Therefore, I believe that its language must be liberally construed to mean that all possible administrative procedures relating to the disposition of a tax lien must be employed before a suit will be heard by the court. It is therefore important to submit *both* the appeal of the lien and the application for release of lien as described in detail above. See Exhibit 10-2.

---

28. New Code §7432(a) and (b).

Second, subsection (d)(2) provides that the "amount of damages awarded under (the law) *shall be reduced* by the amount of such damages which could have been reasonably mitigated by the plaintiff." This provision creates the responsibility for the citizen to take every reasonable step necessary to *prevent* or limit damages caused by the lien. The statute does not define what constitutes "reasonable steps" to mitigate damages. I can offer a few suggestions based upon common sense. First, it is common for tax liens to adversely affect one's credit rating and ability to secure funds from a bank pursuant to a loan. I therefore recommend that a person faced with an improper tax lien immediately notify the local credit reporting agency of the discrepancy so that the fact of your objection may be recorded in the credit report along with the lien itself. Next, I would notify the bank of the existence of the improper lien and provide the appropriate bank personnel with a copy of your written objections to the lien. These are just two examples. Other steps would include notification of any other appropriate persons or organizations that the IRS, through no fault of your own, has filed an improper lien against you. You should inform such parties that you have taken positive action to have the lien removed and, if necessary, provide copies of the relevant documents. Also, you should specifically advise such persons that you implore them not to alter their relationship with you or the manner in which they do business with you based upon the lien. Any other steps which would seem helpful under the circumstances should be taken.

The *third* limitation on the right to commence a proceeding regarding the improper lien is found under subsection (d)(3). This limitation is one of *time.* The statute provides that you have two years "after the date the right of action accrues" in which to bring the proceeding for damages in the district court. The Congressional Committee Report on the statute makes it plain that the right of action "does not accrue until a claimant has had a reasonable opportunity to discover all of the essential elements of a possible cause of action."[29] In this regard, you must have knowledge of the improper lien, you must have exhausted your administrative remedies without success, you must have incurred damages as a result of the lien, and you must have notified the IRS in accordace with the law as we shall examine presently. When these steps have been followed without success, the essential elements of a proceeding under §7432 become ripe and the two-year limitation period begins to run at that time.[30]

The *fourth* and final limitation on the right to commence a proceeding under §7432 is found in subsection (e) of the statute. That section provides that:

> "The Secretary shall by regulation prescribe reasonable procedures for a taxpayer to notify the Secretary of the failure to release a lien under section 6325 on property of the taxpayer."

As of this writing, the Secretary has not "prescribed reasonable procedures" for notifying the IRS when it has failed to release a lien for purposes of the proceeding under §7432. Because of the presence of the notice provision in the statute, it is fair to suggest that the notice is a mandatory aspect of the administrative procedures. It only stands to reason that the notice would be required, since it would provide the IRS with a final opportunity to correct the injustice created by the improper lien, thereby avoiding the need for litigation. At the same time, such a notice properly drafted and served upon the IRS prior to the suit would leave the IRS *defenseless* in the face of a §7432 proceeding. Since the IRS has failed thus far to issue the regulations establishing the content of the notice, I have some suggestions of my own. They are:

1. The notice should include your name, address and Social Security number;

2. You should state the tax year in question, the date of the lien in question and provide a copy of the document;

3. You should state than an application for release of lien under §6325 was submitted and either denied or ignored, or that an appeal under §6326 was submitted and either denied or ignored;

4. You should restate the grounds upon which you claim that the lien should be released, including copies of the original submission and all other appropriate documents in support of your position;

5. You should state that as a result of the presence of the improper lien you have incurred damages in spite of your efforts to mitigate them. You should specify the nature and extent of the damages you have suffered;

6. You should demand that the lien be released immediately and inform the IRS that in the event it fails to do so in a reasonable amount of time, you will commence a proceeding under §7432; and

7. You should state that the notice is intended to substantially comply with the provisions of §7432(e), regarding notice to the Secretary.

The notice should be mailed by certified or registered mail to the IRS district director in the district where the

---

29. Congressional Committee Report on P.L. 100-647.

30. *Rosales v. United States,* 824 F.2d 799 (9th Cir. 1987); *Zeidler v. United States,* 601 F.2d 527 (10th Cir. 1979).

Exhibit 10-3: Notice of Failure to Release Lien

IN THE INTERNAL REVENUE SERVICE

FOR THE INTERNAL REVENUE DISTRICT OF MINNESOTA

In re the matter of:

William E. & Jane M. Citizen,
SSN: 000-00-0000

        Claimants.

NOTICE OF FAILURE TO RELEASE LIEN PURSUANT TO CODE §7432(e)

PLEASE TAKE NOTICE, that this written notice is made in accordance with 26 USC §7432(e) and is meant to comply with all substantial elements thereof.

This notice is based upon and applicable to the following circumstances:

1. Taxpayer's identity -- The claimants are William E. and Jane M. Citizen, SSN: 000-00-0000, whose address is, (address, city, state, zip).

2. Tax Lien in Question -- The Federal Tax Lien in question was filed on (date) with the office of (recorder's office, city, state). A true and accurate copy of the lien in question is attached hereto and made a part of this notice. The Tax Lien in question covers the year _____ and is in the amount of $_____.

3. Appeal and Application for Release -- On (date) the claimants submitted to the office of the District Director, marked to the attention of the Chief, Special Procedures Function, IRS at (city, state, zip) a written Administrative Appeal and Application for Release of the said lien. A true copy of said Appeal and Application is attached to this notice and made a part hereof. Said Appeal and Application was substantially in compliance with all of the regulations applicable thereto, and set forth adequate grounds justifying the release of the lien at issue here.

4. Restatement of Grounds -- The Appeal and Application for release of the lien in question was based upon the fact that the IRS failed to adhere to the deficiency procedures of the Code. In particular, the assessment in question is in violation of Code §§6212 and 6213(a). Hence, the lien in question must also be invalid. A full and complete statement of the grounds justifying the Appeal and Application are set forth in the original submission. A copy is attached.

5. Damages -- The claimants have suffered damages as a result of the improper lien. Claimants have made every reasonable effort to mitigate those damages but have nevertheless sustained losses. The specific damages which claimants have suffered are: (set out a clear and concise statement of the nature and extent of all damages caused by the lien).

6. Demand for Release -- Claimants hereby demand that the IRS immediately release the subject lien without further delay. Claimants further hereby notify the IRS that if it fails or refuses to do so within 30 days of the date of this notice, legal action will be taken in accordance with Code §7432.

7. Attestation -- Under penalty of perjury, the undersigned, William E. and Jane M. Citizen, hereby declare that the facts contained in this notice, together with the accompanying documents, are true and correct to the best of their knowledge and belief.

Dated:

_____

William E. Citizen

_____

Jane M. Citizen

lien is filed. A copy of the notice should also be mailed to the Chief, Special Procedures Function of the Collection Division within the same district. Exhibit 10-3 is an example of the notice I have just described. Please bear in mind that no regulations have yet been issued regarding this notice. Therefore, the example shown in Exhibit 10-3 is based solely upon my judgment as to what such a notice *should* contain.[31]

Drafting the Complaint

A complaint under §7432 is a simple matter to draft. As with each complaint discussed in this manual, care must be taken to ensure that all of the essential elements of a violation under the law are stated in the complaint. Based upon our conversation thus far, it can be said that the essential allegations of a §7432 proceeding are:

1. That a lien for taxes is in effect against you, the plaintiff;

2. That you have made a proper application under the law to the appropriate officer or employee of the IRS for release of the lien;

3. That knowingly or by reason of negligence, such officer or employee failed and refused to release the lien;

4. That you have incurred damages which, but for the actions of the defendant IRS employee, you would have not incurred;

5. That you have made every reasonable effort to mitigate those damages to the fullest extent possible;

6. That you have exhausted all administrative remedies in connection with the lien, yet the IRS refuses to release it;

7. That you have served notice on the IRS regarding your intent to commence the proceeding; and

8. That your proceeding is brought in a timely manner.[32]

It is a good idea to include as attachments to the complaint copies of all relevent documents to which you refer in the text. For example, a copy of the application for release of the lien, or the appeal of the erroneous lien, and your notice to the IRS regarding your intent to commence a proceeding under §7432 are critical attachments. Also, when alleging that all administrative remedies were exhausted, you should state exactly what administrative steps were taken by you in an effort to resolve the conflict.

It is not uncommon for the IRS to file multiple liens, each covering separate tax years or types of taxes, such as income and employment tax liabilities. When the IRS has filed multiple improper liens, each lien should be made the subject of a *separate count* of your complaint. Exhibit 10-4 is an example of the manner one would structure a complaint for damages in connection with the IRS' failure or refusal to release a tax lien. As with each of the exhibits in this manual, the facts expressed in Exhibit 10-4 are hypothetical. You must substitute your actual facts when adapting this form to your personal use.

Prosecuting Your Case

The process by which one will prosecute his proceeding within the district court for damages resulting from an improper tax lien is not much different than that which we already discussed in previous chapters. One aspect of this case which is somewhat different from the others is that, in this case, you are proceeding against an *individual* IRS officer or employee, not necessarily the United States.[33] In a very real way, you put on the hat of the "prosecuting attorney" responsible for bringing to justice those within the IRS guilty of abusing your rights!

As with all cases in which you are the complainant, you will bear the burden to prove with evidence that the allegations of your complaint are true. To the extent that you must prove liens are in effect and the appropriate demands were made by you, this can be accomplished without much difficulty. However, one element of the case may prove a bit more cumbersome. The law provides that in order to obtain damages in connection with your suit, you must prove that the agent named as the defendant "knowingly or by reason of negligence" failed to release the lien.

As you might imagine, this will require that you inquire into the thought processes by which the particular agent governed his actions. In order to prove that he acted improperly in connection with your application, you must be prepared to question him, ideally in the context of discovery, regarding his acts or failures to act. You may also employ the IRS manual in this regard. As I explained in Chapter Three, the manual clearly delineates the procedures which IRS personnel must follow in given factual scenarios. If you are able to demonstrate that the defendant was aware of the procedures set out in the manual governing release of the lien, yet ignored its mandates, such will be helpful in proving your case.

Most importantly, however, is the idea that the facts and circumstances of the improper lien must be *known*

---

31. Through the medium of my newsletter, *Pilla Talks Taxes*, I will keep readers apprised of all developments in this area. PTT is available from WINNING Publications, $97 per year.

32. These elements are distilled from Code §7432.

33. It should be noted however, that any judgment you obtain against this person will be paid by the United States. See Code §7432(c).

Exhibit 10-4
Complaint For Damages Due to Unjust Lien

UNITED STATES DISTRICT COURT
DISTRICT OF MINNESOTA
THIRD DIVISION

William E. and Jane M. Citizen,)	
)	
Plaintiffs,)	Civil Case No. _____
)	
vs.)	JURY TRIAL DEMANDED
)	
Willard P. Mean, Internal Revenue)	
Officer, James R. Nasty, Chief,)	
Special Procedures Function, IRS,)	
)	
Defendants.)	

_____

COMPLAINT FOR DAMAGES DUE TO UNJUST FEDERAL TAX LIEN

NATURE OF THE ACTION

1.   This is a civil action for recovery of damages incurred as
a result of an unjust Federal Tax Lien imposed upon the Plaintiffs by
the Internal Revenue Service.

2.   Plaintiffs also seek an order from the court requiring the
Defendants to release the said lien.

JURISDICTION

3.   The Jurisdiction of the court is invoked under the
authority of 26 USC §§7432, and 28 USC §2410, relating to jurisdiction
of the district courts in suits for damages due to unjust tax liens.

4.   This cases involves the internal revenue laws of the
United States and hence, raises a federal question.

VENUE

5.   Venue within the above-named court is proper according to
28 USC §1391(e) and 1392, in that the Defendants are officers and

COMPLAINT FOR DAMAGES RE: LIEN, PAGE 1

employees of the United States.

PARTIES

6.   The Plaintiffs, William E. and Jane M. Citizen, (address, city, state, zip) are properly named as the Plaintiffs to this action, as the unjust lien in question is filed against them.

7.   The Defendant, Willard P. Mean, Revenue Officer (office address, city, state, zip) is named as a Defendant in this case as he is the employee of the Internal Revenue Service who caused the unjust tax lien to be filed against the Plaintiffs.

8.   James R. Nasty, Chief, Special Procedures Function, IRS, (office address, city, state, zip) is named as a Defendant in this case as he is the employee of the Internal Revenue Service who failed and refused to release the lien in question.

BACKGROUND FACTS

8.   On (date) the IRS mailed a notice to the Plaintiffs indicating that an assessment in the amount of $ _____ pursuant to a mathematical recomputation was made concerning their tax return for the year _____. A copy of said letter is attached as Exhibit A.

9.   On (date) the Plaintiffs submitted a timely demand for an abatement of such assessment and demanded a notice of deficiency. Such demand was made in accordance with 26 USC §6213(b). A copy of said demand is attached hereto as Exhibit B.

10.   The next word the Plaintiffs received from the IRS was a Notice of Tax Lien which was recorded with the office of the county recorder at (county, city, state). The lien is in the amount of $_____, the amount demanded by the IRS in its mathematical

COMPLAINT FOR DAMAGES RE: LIEN, PAGE 2

recomputation. A copy of said lien is attached hereto as Exhibit C. The said lien is signed by Defendant Willard P. Mean, Internal Revenue Officer.

11. On (date) the Plaintiffs submitted to the Defendant James R. Nasty, Chief, Special Procedures Function, IRS, at (city, state) an Administrative Appeal and Application for Release of said lien. Said Appeal and Application was made in accordance with 26 USC §§6325 and 6326. A copy of said Appeal and Application is attached as Exhibit D.

12. The said Appeal and Application was substantially in compliance with all IRS regulations governing such applications, and stated adequate grounds and facts entitling the Plaintiffs to release of the said lien.

13. Despite the Appeal and Application, the Defendants, and each of them, have knowingly or by reason of negligence, failed and refused to release the said lien.

14. On (date) the Plaintiffs submitted a written Notice to the District Director of the IRS, with a copy to Defendant James R. Nasty, pursuant to 26 USC §7432(e). A copy of the said notice is attached as Exhibit E. Said notice is substantially in compliance with the statute governing such notices.

15. Despite having received a copy of said notice, the Defendants have failed and refused, knowingly or by reason of negligence, to release the said lien.

16. The Plaintiffs have suffered damage and injury, which, but for the presence of the unjust lien, they would not have otherwise suffered. Said damages are hereinafter more fully explained.

17.   The Plaintiffs have exhausted all administrative remedies in connection with the herein lien, yet the Defendants continue to fail and refuse, knowingly or by reason of negligence, to release the said lien.

COUNT I

18.   Plaintiffs restate all of the allegations contained in paragraphs 1-17 as though fully set forth here in Count I.

19.   The Internal Revenue Service has caused a federal tax lien to be placed against the property and rights to property of the Plaintiffs.

20.   The said lien is improper because of the fact that it grows out of an assessment made in violation of the deficiency procedures established by §§6212 and 6213(a) and (b) of the Internal Revenue Code.

21.   Plaintiffs exercised all available administrative remedies under the Code in an effort to secure the release of said lien, but to no avail.

22.   The Defendants herein, and each of them, have knowingly or by reason of negligence, failed and refused to release the said lien despite the repeated applications of the Plaintiffs.

23.   Plaintiffs have suffered damages in the amount of $_____ which, but for the presence of the lien, they would not have otherwise sustained.

24.   Plaintiffs are entitled to recover the said damages in accordance with law.

DAMAGES

25. The Plaintiffs have suffered damages and injury of the following nature and in the following amounts: (list in subparagraphs the clear and concise nature of all damages sustained and amounts of losses caused by the lien.)

26. The Plaintiffs have   made every reasonable effort to mitigate said damages but have nevertheless suffered losses.

REQUEST FOR RELIEF

WHEREFORE, based upon all of the foregoing, Plaintiffs demand judgment against the Defendant as follows:

1. That the Defendants, and each of them, be ordered to compensate the Plaintiffs in the amount of $_____ for the damage and injury which they have suffered as a result of the improper lien.

2. That the Court order the Defendants to immediately release the said lien in accordance with 26 USC §§6325 and 6326.

3. That the Defendants be ordered to pay all of the Plaintiffs' costs and disbursements incurred in connection with prosecuting this proceeding to recover damages.

4. For such other relief as the court may deem just.

Dated:

_____   _____
William E. Citizen   Jane M. Citizen
                        Address
                  City, State, Zip
                Area Code and Phone Number

COMPLAINT FOR DAMAGES RE: LIEN, PAGE 5

to the agent at the time his acts or failures to act occurred. In this regard, you must establish his familiarity with your written demands, the facts upon which they were based and his cognizance of the law upon which they rely. Proof of these facts will be a potent way in which to "pin" responsibility on the agent in connection with the lien.

It is paramount to prove your damages with *specific evidence,* as well as the fact that you have taken every reasonable step to mitigate those damages. Care should be taken to review the allegations of your complaint to ensure that you have specific evidence for each allegation.

The Right of Trial by Jury

The question of whether the law authorizes the IRS to place a lien upon property and to maintain that lien is, I believe, a question of law. Under the present scheme of judicial interpretation, questions of law are resolved by a judge without a jury.

On the other hand, the question of whether a particular agent of the IRS knew or reasonably should have known that his actions were improper or illegal under the law is a question of fact. Questions of fact are properly tried to a jury. Moreover, the issue of whether

Exhibit 10-5
Flowchart of Proceeding to Recover Damages Due to Unjust Tax Lien

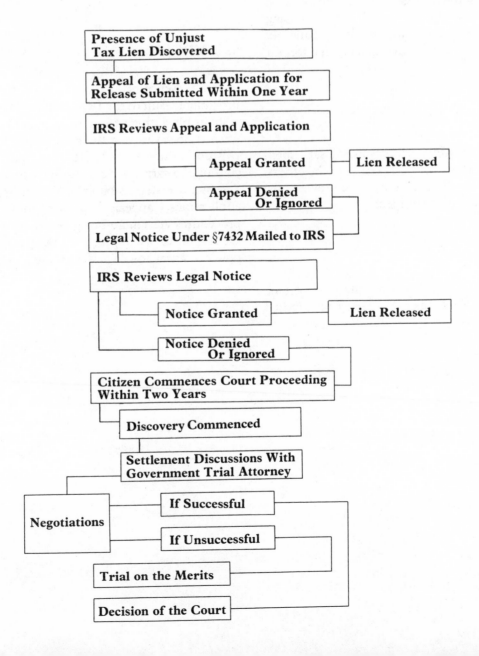

and to what extent you have suffered damages as a result of the lien, and whether you have properly attempted to mitigate those damages are purely questions of fact. Therefore, to the extent that your proceeding raises such questions of fact, you are entitled to a jury trial under the Seventh Amendment to the Constitution and Rule 38, FRCvP.

As we already know, however, it is common for government attorneys to employ the use of summary judgment (Rule 56 FRCvP) in an effort to dispose of cases against the United States. When such a motion is filed, one must be prepared to demonstrate that facts material to the issues involved in the case have yet to be resolved. When questions of fact remain unresolved, particularly those revolving around the question of agent's knowledge of the wrongfulness of his actions and the extent to which you have suffered damages as a result, summary judgment is a wholly inappropriate means by which to settle the case. Care should be taken to preserve the case for jury trial by submitting affidavits and other material authorized by Rule 56, FRCvP, in opposition to the government's motion for summary judgment.

Negotiating a Settlement

The principles already stated regarding settlement negotiations apply to this case as well as to the others. Please see Chapters Five and Six and review the remarks made there on this subject.

The Trial

If settlement cannot be reached, the case will be submitted for trial. Remember, you are legally saddled with the burden of proof on the issues in the complaint. Therefore, you must be prepared to go forward with evidence to prove your claims to the satisfaction of the court or jury. In this regard, all evidence you possess and have obtained through the discovery process, if relevant to the issues, should be presented.

In the trial, all evidence is submitted through the testimony of witnesses. You may testify on your own behalf or call witnesses whose testimony will be helpful to resolve the facts. After the evidence is submitted, the court or jury will determine the facts of the case and render judgment accordingly. A written instrument will be issued to the parties at the conclusion of the trial. The instrument will reflect the judgment and constitutes the final order in the case.

Exhibit 10-5 is a flowchart depicting the progression of a proceeding for damages relating to an unlawful federal tax lien.

Conclusion

The presence of §7432 in the tax Code is a direct, proximate result of the IRS' failure over the years to act responsibly with regard to releasing unjust tax liens. Be warned however, that the mere presence of the statute will do nothing to end IRS abuse on this front. *You* continue to carry the responsibility to see that the IRS does not overstep its bounds. You must file the correct applications, appeals and demands. When those procedures are ignored or given short shrift, you bear the responsibility to prosecute the wrongdoer! At least now you *know* how it may be accomplished effectively.

CHAPTER 11

How to Counter the Blundered Attack

"Don't drop your Guard!" With these words I cautioned the taxpaying public that the apparent coup of the Taxpayers' Bill of Rights Act *would not* spell the end of IRS abuse. "But why not?," curious and befuddled citizens would ask, questioning my skepticism. I remain guarded on the effects of the act for two reasons. First, the act did not, as its creators and advocates said it would, curtail the powers of the revenue officers such that his *ability* to abuse a citizen's right would fall in corresponding measure. My harshest criticism of the act was that the all-powerful revenue officers retains the vast majority of his nearly unlimited discretion. As anyone having the misfortune of dealing with a revenue officer can testify, those powers are awesome and exceedingly broad. Most of those powers, including the power to lien, levy, and seize assets, can be executed without the need of managerial approval.

Secondly, and perhaps most telling, is the fact that Congress—comprised of the same persons supposedly clamoring to the *aid* of the overburdened taxpayer—continues to hand the IRS *more* money and *more* manpower for the express purpose of collecting *more* taxes. In almost open defiance of the Bill of Rights Act, the Bush administration transmitted to Congress, on July 6th, 1989, its request for additional funding of the IRS, to the tune of *$58.5 million!* The date of July 6th is significant becuase it is just one week *after* many of the protections of the Bill of Rights Act went into effect!

The increased funding is even more ominous in light of recent Congressional rhetoric regarding taxpayers' rights. According to the Administration, the additional funding is for the express purpose of enabling "the IRS to increase tax collections by $150 million during the next (1990) fiscal year," and to "generate additional revenue of $500 million through *intensified tax code enforcement.* "[1] As I pointed out in my opening remarks to Chapter Eight, this *very attitude* is the *cause of IRS abuse!* Senators and Representatives lobbying for passage of the Bill of Rights Act cited chilling statistics in their hearings. They evidence the rise of the indis-

---

1. *Taxes on Parade,* July 12, 1989, CCH; (emphasis added).

criminate utilization by revenue officers of the infamous IRS lien, levy, and seizure in the early 1980's. Anyone believing that the seige is now over had better *wake up and take heed.* Congress and the Administration are *at it again!* Handing the IRS increased funds and "turning the dogs loose" will mean only one thing; innocent citizens *will be* caught in the net and unless they are prepared to take remedial steps, will become the next set of statistics quoted in the next wave of Congressional sentiment on the topic of IRS abuse.

No, America, we are not out of the woods yet. As a matter of fact, IRS' own records show that over the past three years, the number of revenue officers packing the weapons of lien, levy and seizure rose to 8,412[2] That is an increase of 14 percent over the number in existence in 1986.[3] Thus, America, the facts ring clear, the intent of Congress and the Administration seem plain. *You* will continue to feel the squeeze. You must stand ready and able to defend yourself when the IRS' collection machine begins to move in your direction. Given the fact of the IRS' continuing personnel and revenue increases, it is not a question of *whether* citizens will suffer from overly aggressive collection efforts. Rather, it is a question of *whom* will suffer and to what extent. In the final analysis, the choice is yours. You can prepare yourself now, while there is no impending threat to your liberty or property, or you can wait until you are hip deep in the quagmire of enforced collection. I am sure you will agree that now is the time to prepare!

The Wrongful Levy

One of the more common errors manifested by IRS aggressions on the tax collection front is the "Wrongful Levy." Chapter Eight discussed the wrongful levy in general terms, and only in the context of a preliminary injunction. Here we will address more fully the steps which are available to one injured by a wrongful levy. We have already defined the wrongful levy as one directed at the property of one person in an effort to satisfy the tax liability of another. It is settled law that an assessed liability may only be satisfied from the "property or rights to property" belonging to the person who owes the tax. When it can be shown that the property subject to the levy does not constitute the "property or rights to property" of the citizen in debt, the wrongful levy statute, Code §7426, may be utilized to *prevent* seizure, or to *recover* property if it has been seized.

A very important consideration when contemplating action under Code §7426 is the fact that an assessment made by the IRS is "conclusively presumed to be valid."[4] In nearly every other area of tax law, when a "presumption of correctness" is attached to the IRS' assessment or tax liability determination, that presumption is "rebuttable." This simply means the citizen has the right to present evidence to demonstrate that the IRS' determination is in fact incorrect. In the absence of such a showing, however, the IRS is not required to present evidence to *support* its assessment. Its assessment is "presumed" to be correct.

However, this rule of law does not apply to the wrongful levy statute. When contesting a levy under this statute, the citizen *may not* question the validity of the tax assessment. The presumption of correctness which attaches to the assessment will not be disturbed by the court. Therefore, the lesson this teaches is that the person against whom the tax is assessed will find no relief from an IRS levy within the embrace of Code §7426.[5] For purposes of Code §7426, a "taxpayer" is considered to be the person against whom the assessment is made. A "nontaxpayer" is a third party claiming an interest, in whole or in part, in property seized by the IRS in satisfaction of the "taxpayer's" debt.

"Taxpayers" will not obtain relief under the wrongful levy statute by reason of a simple theory. Under ordinary circumstances, citizens are afforded an opportunity to petition the Tax Court before a tax is assessed. When this alternative *is exercised,* the deficiency determined to exist by the Tax Court's decision may be assessed and collected.[6] Thereafter, the citizen is precluded from first paying the tax, then filing a claim for refund. He is also precluded from obtaining relief under the wrongful levy statute. If a "taxpayer" *has* not availed himself of the opportunity to contest the deficiency in *Tax Court,* his remedy lies in first paying the tax, then filing a claim for refund. In this manner, the courts maintain that all rights of the citizen to due process of law are protected.

On the other hand, an entirely different set of circumstances is presented when the property seized does not belong to the person who owes the tax, i.e., the "non-taxpayer." In the first place, since no notice of deficiency was sent to the "non-taxpayer," he will have no opportunity to petition the Tax Court. As we learned in Chapter Four, the notice of deficiency is one's ticket to the Tax Court. Without a notice of deficiency in hand, the Tax Court has no jurisdiction to resolve tax

---

2. *IRS Highlights, 1988,* Table 25, page 44.
3. *IRS Highlights, 1987,* Table 25.
4. Code §7426(c).
5. *Quinn v. United States,* 84-1 USTC Para. 9337 (DC La 1984).
6. The decision is, however, reviewable by the United States Court of Appeals.

disputes. Secondly, the remedy of paying the tax and filing a claim for refund is inadequte when collection is attempted from a person admittedly not in debt to the government. Surely you can appreciate that requiring a person to pay a tax, which the government concedes he does now owe, would be patently improper—never mind unconstitutional.

As a result of the great procedural and administrative handicaps presented when the IRS moves against the wrong property, §7426 fills the void. It allows the non-taxpayer to seek and obtain an injunction preventing the IRS from selling the seized property, and ordering the property be returned to the "non-taxpayer."

When to Begin A Wrongful Levy Action

The possible circumstances under which one may commence a wrongful levy action are limited only by the imaginations of the various revenue officers. I say this simply because the commencement of a wrongful levy action is dependent upon a wrongful *levy*. Thus, in order for any relief under §7426 to exist, the IRS must take action to levy the wrong property.[7]

The Statute of Limitations. Once the IRS has actually levied upon property belonging to a non-taxpayer, a suit under §7426 is limited by time in accordance with Code §6532(c)(1). Simply, the statute of limitations provides that a suit under Code §7426 must be commenced *within nine months* "of the date of the levy." After the expiration of that time, the courts are unforgiving and will dismiss such suits against the IRS.[8] There is *just one* condition under which this period of limitation is extended. When an administrative demand for return of property is made, the period of limitation is altered according to Code §6532(c)(2). That subsection reads:

> "If a request is made for a return of the property. . .the 9-month period prescribed in paragraph (1) shall be extended for a period of 12 months from the date of filing of such request or for a period of 6 months from the date of mailing by registered or certified mail by the Secretary to the person making such request a notice of disallowance of the part of the request to which the action relates, whichever is shorter."

Thus, when one exercises administrative remedies in search of a resolution to the problem created by the wrongful levy, one is afforded additional time in which to pursue the matter in the courts. Regardless of the grant of additional time, if the IRS refuses to approve the administrative request for return of the seized property, the suit in court must be filed timely in accordance with the terms of Code §6532(c)(2). Failure to do so will result in dismissal of the case.[9]

When considering the *circumstances* under which one should commence a suit to recover property wrongfully levied, one must be guided by this simple rule: when the IRS seizes property which does not belong solely to the taxpayer, any person claiming whole or partial ownership of the property has the right under Code §7426 to bring a suit against the IRS. Please allow me to provide a few common examples of when this occurs.

The Husband-Wife Relationship. Perhaps the most frequent wrongful levy involves the seizure of a wife's assets in satisfaction of her husband's separate tax liability (or vice versa). When the husband has a separate tax debt, only his separate property may be used to pay that debt. The wife's interest in property cannot be used in payment of her husband's debt. The husband may incur a separate liability for a number of reasons. First, he could have filed a separate, personal income tax return. When he alone signs the return, the wife will not and may not be held responsible for the assessment growing out of that return. As a matter of fact, even when the wife *did* sign the return, the "innocent spouse" statute (discussed later in this chapter) can provide relief to her such that she may not be held accountable for the unpaid tax liability.[10]

Secondly, the husband may be responsible for the debts of a business in which the wife played no active role or held no ownership interest. As an example, an assessment of the 100 percent penalty against the husband due to his failure to comply with the employment tax obligations of a corporation will not attach to his wife. Similarly, where the husband operated a small business as a sole proprietor, filed employment tax returns but did not pay the tax, the wife could not be held accountable for that liability.

Despite the separate assessment, the IRS often moves to seize the joint assets of the husband and wife, or worse, moves against the separate assets of the wife. When this occurs, the wife must commence a suit under Code §7426 to recover her property within nine months

---

7. *American Pacific Investment Corp. v. Nash,* 342 F.Supp. 797 (DC NJ 1972); *Standard Acceptance Co. v. United States,* 341 F.Supp. 41 (DC Ill. 1972).

8. *Ellis v. United States,* 87-2 USTC Para. 9418 (DC Wis. 1987); *Zimmerman v. United States,* 86-2 USTC Para. 9834 (DC Va. 1986).

9. *State of Vermont v. United States,* 75-1, USTC Para. 9175 (DC Vt. 1975).

10. Code §6013(e).

of the date of the levy (or 12 months from the time she submits a written demand for return of the seized property). The question of ownership is answered solely by reference to *state law.* Therefore, whenever one seeks to recover under Code §7426, he (or she) must be prepared to establish that state law vests ownership of the property, in whole in part, in the non-debtor spouse.[11]

Community Property Laws. Community property laws create an interesting, double-edged sword when it comes to applying the wrongful levy statute. As we established, the question of whether a person owns property or rights to property is answered solely by reference to state law. Many states observe community property rules when it comes to the marital relationship. Under the doctrine of community property, ownership of all property acquired by either partner automatically vests to *both* partners. Therefore, in a community property state, it does not matter that the family home, for example, is held solely in the name of the husband or wife. State law establishes that each spouse is legally recognized to own a present, vested, one-half interest in that property.

This rule of law may or may not operate to the advantage of the citizen, depending upon the circumstances. One *disadvantage* develops when the assessment is against the husband alone, but the wife holds the homestead solely in her name. The IRS would be entitled to move against the homestead on the premise that state law vests a present, one-half interest in that property in the husband, regardless of the fact that his name is not on the title. The IRS could attack the property to satisfy his debt.

On the other hand, the community property rules, creatively invoked, can act to *minimize* the reach of a federal tax levy. For example, let us continue to assume that the assessment is against the husband alone. Let us further assume that the husband is the only wage-earner in the family; the wife does not work outside the home. Let us further assume that the IRS has placed a wage levy against the husband's entire paycheck. We know that this is an all-too-common occurrence.

Interestingly, however, the wife, against whom no assessment is made, has a claim against the IRS under Code §7426. The claim is based upon the community property rules and is much the same as that advanced when the IRS moves against property held by the non-debtor spouse. Just as the home in the previous example is considered to be the property of the husband, the *paycheck* in the present example is considered to be the property of the wife! This fact gives the wife the right to commence a §7426 suit against the IRS in order to preserve her present, vested, one-half interest in her husband's paycheck.[12]

Thus, one must carefully examine the conditions surrounding any levy when living in a community property state. When the wife (or husband) can take steps to minimize the adverse effects of the levy, §7426 is the vehicle through which to proceed.

Property Held in Trust. Another area in which the IRS is aggressive regarding seizures involves property held in trust. A trust is created when the property of one person is transferred to the care of another (referred to as a trustee) for the benefit of the third party (referred to as a beneficiary). An example is when parents place funds in the care of a bank for the benefit of their minor children. Under a trust arrangemet, the trustee is responsible to oversee the assets in a responsible manner to ensure their availability to the beneficiaries at the time specified by the persons who created the trust.

When a trust is created in which the "grantors" (the persons creating the trust) divest themselves of all ownership interest and substantive control over the property, that property may not be seized to satisfy the separate debts of the grantors. However, the IRS commonly attacks such property under the theory that the trust was created and the property transferred to it solely as a "ruse" to avoid the payment of taxes. When such an allegation is made, the IRS contends that the "fraudulent conveyence" doctrine operates to cancel the transfer into the trust, making the property subject to levy.

When the IRS moves to seize the property of a trust, the trustees bear the responsibility of commencing a wrongful levy suit in the district court. The suit would undertake to prove that the property was not transferred in violation of the fraudulent conveyance doctrine. There are several elements which must be established before the court will determine whether a fraudulent conveyance occurred. These issues must be resolved in the context of the wrongful levy suit.[13]

Generally speaking, if the property was transferred *after* the liability for the tax accrued, the court will not look favorably upon a conveyance of property into trust. A tax is said to accrue at the time one becomes liable for the tax, not at the time the tax is assessed. For example,

---

11. *Broday v. United States,* F.2d 1097 (5th Cir. 1972).

12. *United States v. Mitchell,* 403 U.S. 190 (1971-Louisiana); *In re Ackerman,* 424 F.2d 1148 (9th Cir. 1970-Arizona); *United States v. Overman,* 424 F.2d 1142 (9th Cir. 1970-Washington); *Karaglanis v. United States,* 86-1 USTC Para. 9476 (DC Cal. 1986).

13. Chapter Four of *The Naked Truth,* pages 127-129, contains a more detailed discussion of the fraudulent conveyance.

the courts say that the liability for income tax *accrues* at the time the income is earned. Thus, if one earns income in 1988, the liability for tax accrues in 1988. Even though the tax may be assessed years later, any transfer of property occurring after 1988 will be looked upon with disfavor by the courts.

When it can be shown that the transfer of property was legitimate and not in violation of the fraudulent conveyance doctrine, a §7426 suit is the appropriate means to litigate the issue and preserve the property.

Non-Title Assets. The most difficult aspect of the §7426 suit is when the IRS has seized non-title assets. A non-title asset, unlike an automobile, home or other asset for which there exists a registered owner, is devoid of any tangible, extrinsic evidence establishing the rightful owner of the property. Therefore, the tendency of the IRS is to seize such property, such as cash, jewelry, furs, etc., under the *assumption* that it belongs to the taxpayer. It will then acquire the property through a kind of default if the rightful owner does not step forward to properly claim it. When one is ignorant of his rights or the proper procedure to follow, the property will be lost without a fight.

When making a claim to recover a non-title asset, there are two very important rules which one must observe in order to maximize his chances of success. First, he must be prepared to "trace" the property to himself as the owner. By this I mean that it is *insufficient* to merely claim ownership. When there is no title registration to establish ownership, the IRS and courts will require that the claimant provide sufficient historical background to justify his claim. Through the process of "pulling on the string," the claimant must demonstrate how he came into possession of the property, thereby verifying his claim of ownership.

Secondly, after "tracing" the history of the property, the claimant must be prepared to submit truthful, honest testimony to buttress his claim of ownership. Either through the testimony of himself or witnesses qualified to provide probative insight, the claimant must declare his ownership of the property. When these two steps are followed and there is no controverting evidence submitted by the IRS, the court will require the IRS to return the property.[14]

Whenever the IRS has wrongfully seized the non-title assets of one person on the assumption that they belong to the debtor-taxpayer, the citizen must take quick action to recover the property lest the IRS acquire it by default. The remedy of §7426 will provide the means to achieve this goal.

Establishing the Innocent Spouse Defense

Earlier I mentioned that when a joint tax return is signed by a husband and wife, both parties are equally liable for the tax shown on the return. Given this fact, the IRS may execute its levy against property belonging to either or both of the parties. There is one exception to this rule which bears discussion. The exception is the so-called "innocent spouse statute." The innocent spouse statute acts to *prevent* the IRS from collecting taxes from the spouse who is not responsible for the tax. When it can be shown that one spouse qualifies for innocent spouse treatment, the ravages of the levy can be avoided.

The protection of the innocent spouse statute is found in §6013(e) of the IRS Code. Under this provision, a spouse who signed a joint income tax return but had no knowledge the return was incorrect or incomplete cannot be held responsible for the additional taxes assessed in connection with that return. Specifically, the law provides that the innocent spouse "shall be relieved of liability for tax (including interest, penalties and other amounts)" if she (or he) can demonstrate that:

1. A joint tax return was made for the year in question;

2. On the return there is a substantial understatement of tax due to grossly erroneous items "of one spouse;"

3. The other spouse (innocent spouse) establishes that in signing the return "he or she did not know, and had no reason to know, that there was such substantial understatement;" and,

4. Taking into account all of the facts and circumstances, "it is inequitable to hold the other spouse (innocent spouse) liable for the deficiency in tax."[15]

Before I proceed to demonstrate exactly how this section of law was employed to relieve Cindy of almost $25,000 in taxes and penalties on account of her former husband's negligence, we must define some of the terms that are used in §6013(e). First of all, the term "substantial understatement" is defined as any understatement of tax liability which exceeds $500. The understatement is determined by subtracting the amount of tax *shown due on the return,* from the amount "required to be shown due on the return."[16] When the difference exceeds $500, we have a "substantial understatement" for purposes of the innocent spouse

---

14. *Marcus v. United States,* 73-2 USTC Para. 9516 (DC Fla. 1973); *Marotta v. United States,* 82-1 USTC Para 9115 (DC NY 1981).

15. Code §6013(e)(1).

16. Code §6631(b)(2)(A).

statute.[17]

Next, a "grossly erroneous item" means, either *any item* of gross income which is *omitted* from the return, or, any claim of deduction or credit for which there is no basis "in fact or law." When one spouse earned income in any amount and failed to report the income on the return, or has "dreamed up" deductions or credits, we have a "grossly erroneous item" for purposes of the innocent spouse statute.[18] Lastly, before the protections of this law will come to bear on the innocent spouse, the amount demanded by the IRS must exceed a certain percentage of the innocent spouse's gross income. If the innocent spouse's gross income for the most recent taxable year preceding the date of the notice of deficiency is $20,000 or less, the protections apply *only* if the additional tax demanded exceeds 10 percent of the innocent spouse's adjusted gross income. If the adjusted gross income is *more than* $20,000, the liability must exceed 25 percent of that amount before the law will apply.[19]

To illustrate this, let us look at the facts of a case in which this defense was successful. The IRS mailed a notice of deficiency to Cindy in April of 1988. In it, the IRS proposed an assessment of nearly $25,000 in taxes and penalties for the years 1984 and 1985. The tax was based upon unreported income and the disallowance of many deductions. To determine whether she could rely upon the protections of §6013(e), it was necessary to examine Cindy's 1987 income tax return. 1987 was the *most recent* taxable year preceding April 11, 1988, the date the notice of deficiency was mailed.

The amount of adjusted gross income shown on Cindy's 1987 income tax return was just $4,911. Since this is under $20,000, the 10 percent rule applied. The amount demanded by the IRS—about $25,000—was greatly in excess of 10 percent of Cindy's adjusted gross income. Ten percent of Cindy's adjusted gross income ($4,911) is just $491. Thus, she could rely on the statute's protections if the IRS were demanding anything in excess of $491. If Cindy's adjusted gross income were, say $23,000 (greater than $20,000), the amount demanded would have to be at least $5,751 (25%) in order for the statute to come into play. As stated, IRS wanted an additional *$25,000* in taxes and penalties. It is easy to see that Cindy was well within the statute's guidelines.

Next in line was the requirement to establish that

Cindy met each of the other requirements of the law necessary to be entitled to innocent spouse protection. She prepared and submitted to the Appeals Officer[20] an affidavit signed "under penalty of perjury." The affidavit set forth all of the applicable facts. She was careful to point out that during the periods in question, 1984 and 1985, she was a housewife/student earning no income. Tom, her husband, was the family's sole breadwinner. He worked as a real estate salesman and earned commissions.

Cindy pointed out that she had no control over the family's finances. By this, she would prove that she did not know or have reason to know that the tax returns for the years in question were incorrect. Cindy stated that Tom was responsible for paying the bills and he maintained a separate checking account. Cindy observed that Tom would give her only enough money to buy groceries and household necessities. It was important to truthfully point out that Tom did not shower expensive gifts of any kind on his wife, as this might indicate that Cindy had reason to know that Tom was earning more money than he declared on his tax returns.

The affidavit also declared that the returns were prepared by a reputable accountant within the community at Tom's behest. Cindy noted that she knew of this accountant's reputation and based on that, believed the returns were correct when filed. Finally, the affidavit noted that Cindy had no income and that she signed the returns *only* because it was her understanding that she was required to do so because she was married to Tom. Cindy persuasively stated later that if she had any clue that the returns were not correct and complete, she "never would have signed them."

The final element of proof addressed the "intangible" items which bear upon the issue of whether it was "inequitable" to hold Cindy responsible for the tax liability. Proof was provided that the couple was divorced as soon as September of 1986, just a few months after the 1985 tax return was filed. Also, it was shown that after being a housewife and mother for the 10 years of her marriage, Cindy was just beginning to get on her feet. She was about to complete her education and would then be able to provide for her son. Since Tom had refused to pay either the court-ordered child support or alimony, Cindy found even her day-to-day expenses difficult to meet.

---

17. Code §6013(e)(3).

18. Code §6013(e)(2).

19. Code §6013(e)(4)(A) and (B).

20. This particular case was resolved in the Appeals Division. The innocent spouse defense should be raised at the earliest possible opportunity. It must be set out either in the context of a Tax Court case (see Chapter Four), a suit for refund in the district court (Chapter Five), or at any other point in administrative negotiations with the IRS. Once established, §7426 becomes the vehicle through which the defense is enforced.

At the meeting with the Appeals Officer, the Affidavit was submitted and Cindy answered questions about the couple's financial affairs. Cindy truthfully and honestly described the conditions under which she existed during the periods in question. She openly explained how Tom kept full control of the money and never told her honestly how much he had earned from his job selling real estate. Shortly after the meeting, the Appeals Officer agreed that all essential elements of section 6013(e) were proved. The result was that the IRS could not attempt to hold Cindy responsible for any of the taxes demanded, despite the fact that she had signed two joint tax returns with her husband.

Innocent spouses must be aware of the right under §6013(e) to extinguish their liability for joint income tax returns when the fault is attributable solely to a recalcitrant partner. After one's right to protection under the innocent spouse statute is affirmed, Code §7426 provides the means whereby this right is *enforced* should the Collection Division become overly aggressive in collecting from the responsible spouse.[21]

Demanding Return of Wrongfully Seized Property

The administrative procedures prescribed for demanding a return of wrongfully seized property are short and sweet. Incredible as it may seem, these procedures are *not required* to be exhausted in order for a claim to arise under §7426. However, it is to the citizen's advantage to pursue these procedures prior to filing suit for two reasons. First, we already declared that it is desirable to win the war without engaging the enemy in battle. That is achieved by pursuing administrative remedies as completely as possible. Second, the period of limitations for bringing the suit under §7426 is *extended* when an administrative demand for return of the property is filed.[22]

Revenue Regulation §301.6343-1(b)(2) provides that the Demand for Return of Wrongfully Seized Property must take the following form:

1. It must be in writing and contain the name and address of the person submitting the request;

2. It must set forth a detailed description of the property seized;

3. It must set forth a description of the claimant's basis for an interest in the property levied upon; and

4. It must state the name and address of the citizen

against whom the tax was assessed, the internal revenue district in which it originated and the date of the lien or levy in question as shown on the notice of lien or levy. Ideally, a copy of the notice of lien or levy covering the subject property should be attached to the written administrative demand. The Demand should be mailed via certified mail to the Chief, Special Procedures Staff in the district where the levy was made. Exhibit 11-1 is an example of the written Demand just described.

The Application for Release of property must be made within the 9-month period set out in Code §6532. When this is done, the period of limitations for the suit *under* §7426 is extended. Once the demand is submitted, a waiting period is necessary to enable the IRS to act on the demand. If the demand is denied, the citizen has six months from the date of the denial in which to commence a suit under §7426. If no written response is received, the right to commence a suit dies *12 months* after the written demand is made. The right to file suit under §7426 is tied to the *shorter* of the two periods just mentioned.[23] Care should be taken to ensure that the written demand meets all of the requirements shown above. A demand which is inadequate will not extend the 9-month period of limitations as described in §6532(c).[24]

If the IRS either denies the written demand for return of the property or no action is taken on the demand, the right to sue for a return of the property exists under §7426.

Ultimate Defense Weapon Number Eight

Suit to Recover Property Wrongfully Levied

A lawsuit under Code §7426 may be commenced only against the United States. This vehicle is not the acceptable manner in which the unlawful actions of a particular agent are redressed. The complaint alleging the wrongful levy should be prepared, filed and served upon the United States in the fashion outlined in Chapter Two. As always, when drafting a complaint one must be aware of the elements of the statute under which he is alleging entitlement to relief. Those elements must be completely set forth in the complaint. The elements which must be delineated in a §7426 complaint are:

1. That the IRS has made a levy upon property, or property has been sold pursuant to a levy;

21. *Busse v. United States,* 78-1 USTC Para. 9294 (DC Ill. 1978).

22. Code §6532(c)(2).

23. Rev. Reg. §301.6532-3(b).

24. Ibid.

Exhibit 11-1: Administrative Demand for Return of Seized Property

```
                   IN THE INTERNAL REVENUE SERVICE
          FOR THE INTERNAL REVENUE DISTRICT OF MINNESOTA

In re the matter of:            )
                                )
Jane M. Citizen,                )
SSN:  000-00-0000               )
                                )
            Claimant.           )
                                )
          _____
```

ADMINISTRATIVE DEMAND FOR RETURN OF SEIZED PROPERTY

This is an Administrative Demand for the Return of Property Wrongfully Seized by the IRS. It is made pursuant to 26 USC §6343(b) and regulations thereunder.

This claim is made upon the following facts, arguments, and disclosures:

1. <u>Taxpayer's identity</u> -- The claimant is Jane M. Citizen, SSN: 000-00-0000, whose address is, (address, city, state, zip). **(Note: these facts are hypothetical. You must use your own facts.)**

2. <u>Property Under Levy</u> -- The property under levy which is the subject of this Demand is a parcel of real estate located at: (address, city, state). The legal description of the property is: (enter description of property from deed.) (If the property seized is not real estate, describe it in detail, whether it be an automobile, cash, a coin collection, etc.)

A copy of the notice of levy with respect to said property is attached hereto and marked Exhibit A.

3. <u>Claimant's Interest in the Property</u> -- The property in question was seized on account of the tax liability of William E. Citizen, the claimant's husband. The claimant has no outstanding

ADMINISTRATIVE DEMAND FOR RETURN OF PROPERTY, PAGE 1

liability with the IRS. Claimant is the sole owner of the property in question here as is evidenced by the deed of ownership, a copy of which is attached hereto and marked Exhibit B. (If the property is non-title property, describe how and when you acquired ownership of it and attach copies of purchase receipts if possible.) The delinquent taxpayer, Williem E. Citizen, owns no right, title or interest in the property in question. Under state law, the property is owned separately by the Claimant and therefore is due to be released to her under Code §6343(b).

 4. <u>Request for Relief</u> --   By reason of the foregoing facts, the property subject to the levy in question should immediately be released by the IRS.

 5. <u>Attestation</u> -- Under penalty of perjury, the undersigned Jane M. Citizen hereby declares that the facts contained in this demand for release, together with the accompanying documents, are true and correct to the best of her knowledge and belief.

 Dated:

_____

Jane M. Citizen

ADMINISTRATIVE DEMAND FOR RETURN OF PROPERTY, PAGE 2

2. That the property in question *did not belong* to the person against whom the tax was assessed, or that the person bringing the suit had a lien on the property superior to that of the United States, thus creating an interest in the property;

3. That the person bringing the suit *is not* the person against whom the tax was assessed; and

4. That levy or sale of the property would irreparably injure the rights of the claimant in the property.[25]

These elements should be framed in the complaint together with a full set of background facts setting forth the history of the case. Nothing about this complaint is substantially different from those we have already examined in this manual. An example of a complaint under §7426 is shown in Exhibit 11-2.

Applying for an Injunction

If the IRS has levied upon but not yet sold the property subject to the suit, you will want to immediately move the court for a preliminary injunction preventing its sale until the matter of ownership can be established. We have discussed at length the issues one must demonstrate when applying for an injunction. They are set out in Chapter Eight. To review briefly, the three elements are:

1. That the IRS has no probability of success on the merits. In regard to a §7426 suit, this test is addressed to the issue of the seizure, not the correctness of the assessment. Bear in mind that when proceeding under §7426, the assessment is conclusively presumed to be correct. Therefore, you must attack on another front, that being the question of ownership of the property.

2. That irreparable harm will result if the property is sold. When discussing irreparable harm in the previous chapters, I demonstrated that such harm occurs when the acts of the IRS will lead to financial destruction; the kind of harm which cannot be rectified by money or money's worth compensation. However, the test of irreparable harm is not quite so stringent in the context of the §7426 suit. The statute provides that an injunction should be issued when the applicant can demonstrate that "a levy or sale would irreparably injure the *rights in property* which the court determines to be superior to rights of the United States in such property..."[26] This test of irreparable harm goes only to the issue of property rights, not to the overall financial constraints visited as a result of a levy. Surely, however, if the levy is against one's homestead, the irreparable

harm may certainly rise to the level of outright financial destruction. But such a showing is not necessary to win the injunction under the statute. One must only show that in levying upon the property, your rights in and to the property would be extinguished and the IRS has made no effort to "make you whole" in that context.

3. The final element necessary to prevail in the motion for injunction is the question of the availability of an adequate remedy at law. When the law provides an alternative mode of relief other than injunction, the applicant is expected to exercise that remedy prior to seeking equity intervention by the courts. While it is not required under the language of the statute, it certainly could be argued that the right to make an administrative demand for return of the seized property[27] constitutes a "remedy at law." Because of the existence of the remedy, I encourage one to exercise it. However, when it is clear that the IRS intends to sell the property regardless of a pending administrative claim, no delay should occasion the application for injunction.

The matter of your application for an injunction will be placed before the court through your motion. You will recall from our discussion in Chapter Eight that there are two critical aspects of applications for injunction against the IRS. The first has been beat to death in this manual, but its importance justifies another refrain. The IRS can be expected to argue that the Anti-Injunction Act precludes the relief you are seeking. You ask, "How can such an argument be advanced in the face of a statute which clearly and expressly provides for such relief?" The answer lies nowhere in the law books. The only answer I can suggest is that the argument is indicative of the hearts of the commanders whose orders mobilize the IRS' armies. Perhaps it is that justice is simply not in them. Rare is the occasion where the government will state, "we made a mistake." Rather, every effort, legitimate or otherwise, is made to defend the unlawful acts, thus leaving the hapless citizen, who can least afford it, to bear the loss.

We have examined exceptions to the Anti-Injunction Act and the Wrongful Levy statute, Code §7426 *is one of them!* Make no mistake about it, when the terms of the statute are met, you are entitled to enjoin the seizure or sale of property wrongfully levied. Both §§7426 and 7421 itself so provide. Nevertheless, do not get caught flat-footed. Be prepared for the argument! You can expect it in a motion to dismiss your case.

The second critical aspect of injunction procedure is

---

25. These elements are distilled from Code §7426.

26. Code §7426(b)(1); emphasis added.

27. Code §6343. See the above heading, *Demanding Return of the Property.*

Exhibit 11-2: Complaint for Wrongful Levy

UNITED STATES DISTRICT COURT
DISTRICT OF MINNESOTA
THIRD DIVISION

Jane M. Citizen,	)
	)
Plaintiff,	) Civil Case No. _____
	)
vs.	) JURY TRIAL DEMANDED
	)
The United States of America,	)
	)
Defendants.	)

COMPLAINT FOR WRONGFUL LEVY BY IRS

NATURE OF THE ACTION

1. This is a civil action for an injunction preventing the IRS from selling property which it has wrongfully levied, and for return of the property to the Plaintiff.

JURISDICTION

2. The Jurisdiction of the court is invoked under the authority of 26 USC §§7426, and 28 USC §1346, relating to jurisdiction of the district courts in wrongful levy suits.

3. This case involves the internal revenue laws of the United States and hence, raises a federal question.

VENUE

4. Venue within the above-named court is proper according to 28 USC §1402 in that the United States of America is the Defendant.

PARTIES

5. The Plaintiff, Jane M. Citizen, (address, city, state, zip) is properly named as the Plaintiff to this action, as her property was unjustly levied upon by the IRS.

6. The Defendant, United States of America, through its

agency the Internal Revenue Service, has caused the wrongful levy to occur against the Plaintiff's property.

BACKGROUND FACTS

7. On (date) the IRS through its agents and officers caused the property of the Plaintiff to be levied upon. Attached hereto and marked Exhibit A is a true copy of the Notice of Levy attaching such property.

8. The property in question is located at, (Address, City, State) and is legally described as: (enter legal description from deed.) A copy of the deed of title is attached as Exhibit B. (If the property is non-title property, describe how and when you acquired ownership of it and attach copies of purchase receipts if possible.)

9. The levy in question purports to be made on account of the tax liability of William E. Citizen, the Plaintiff's husband. The Plaintiff has no outstanding tax liability with the IRS.

10. The delinquent taxpayer William E. Citizen has no ownership interest in the property in question. The property is the sole property of Plaintiff.

11. On (date) the Plaintiff submitted to (name), Chief, Special Procedures Function, IRS, at (city, state) an Administrative Demand for Release of the Property. Said Demand was made in accordance with 26 USC §§6343(b). A copy of said Demand is attached to this complaint as Exhibit C.

12. The said Demand was substantially in compliance with all IRS regulations governing such demands, and stated adequate grounds and facts entitling the Plaintiff to return of the property.

13. Despite the Demand, the Defendant, through its agency the IRS, has failed and refused to return the said property.

COMPLAINT FOR WRONGFUL LEVY, PAGE 2

14. The actions of the Defendant, throught its agency the IRS, will irreparably harm the property rights of the Plaintiff if not enjoined by this court.

15. The Plaintiff has exhausted all administrative remedies in connection with the herein levy, yet the Defendant continues to fail and refuse to return the said property.

COUNT I

16. Plaintiff restates all of the allegations contained in paragraphs 1-15 as though fully set forth here in Count I.

17. The Internal Revenue Service has caused a levy to be placed against the property of the Plaintiff.

18. The Plaintiff has no outstanding tax liability with the IRS.

19. The said levy purports to be in satisfaction of the outstanding liability of a third party, namely, Plaintiff's husband.

20. The Plaintiff's husband has no ownership interest in or to the property which the IRS has levied.

21. If the IRS is permitted to sell the property as it intends, the Plaintiff's property rights, which are superior to that of the United States, will be irreparably harmed.

22. Plaintiff is entitled to an injunction preventing the sale of said property, and to an order requiring the IRS to return the said property.

EQUITY

23. The United States cannot succeed on the merits of this case in that the Plaintiff can demonstrate that she alone is the owner of the property and that this fact was known to the government at the time of its levy.

COMPLAINT FOR WRONGFUL LEVY, PAGE 3

24. The Plaintiff's property rights in the said property will be irreparably harmed if the intended sale is permitted to proceed in that the IRS intends to apply all proceeds of the sale to her husband's tax liability.

25. The Plaintiff has no adequate remedy at law to prevent the impending irreparable harm in that she has exhausted all administrative remedies prior to bringing this suit.

DAMAGES

26. If the Defendant is permitted to go forward with the sale of the property as threatened, the Plaintiff will suffer monetary losses in the amount of $_____, in addition to the irreparable harm shown above.

REQUEST FOR RELIEF

WHEREFORE, based upon all of the foregoing, Plaintiff demands judgment against the Defendant as follows:

1. That the Defendant and its agency the Internal Revenue Service be enjoined from selling the property in question here.

2. That the Court order the Defendant to release the said property from levy and return it to the Plaintiff in accordance with 26 USC §6343(b). (If the property has already been sold, you should demand a monetary judgment from the court.)

3. That the Defendant be ordered to pay all of the Plaintiff's costs and disbursements incurred in connection with prosecuting this suit to recover wrongfully seized property.

4. For such other relief as the court may deem just.

Dated:
_____
Jane M. Citizen
Address
City, State, Zip
Area Code and Phone Number

COMPLAINT FOR WRONGFUL LEVY, PAGE 4

the need for a concise, descriptive affidavit. You will recall that the affidavit is the means by which you place before the court the facts upon which you rely as the basis for your motion. The facts are of paramount importance in regard to an injunction. You must be careful that your affidavit is complete. Also, do not fall into the trap of making "conclusory allegations" in your affidavit. Be sure that the facts shown there are set out in such a fashion as to allow the reader to independently come to the conclusions desired. Please see Chapter Eight for more details.

If the court grants your application for preliminary injunction, you may then proceed to aggressively prosecute your case.

Prosecuting the Wrongful Levy Case

We briefly discussed the burden of proof in a wrongful levy case. As with all cases in which you have alleged wrongdoing on the part of the IRS, you will bear the burden to prove that your allegations are true. On the wrongful levy front, courts have said that:

". . .the plaintiff (citizen) has the initial burden of coming forward with evidence to prove that he has title or some other ownership of the property and that the government had made a levy on that property because of a tax assessment against another taxpayer, and that after such showing. . .is made by the (citizen), the burden then shifts to the government to prove a nexus (between the delinquent taxpayer and the property seized).[28]

To explain further, once you have created a *prima facie* case of ownership of the property, it becomes the responsibility of the IRS to *justify* its acts by showing a "nexus," or connection, between the delinquent taxpayer and the property seized. When it cannot or has not shown such a connection sufficient to justify a finding of "ownership," the court is duty-bound to order a permanent injunction preventing the seizure of the property. In the event the property was already sold by the IRS at the time the §7426 suit is commenced, the citizen is entitled to a monetary judgment against the government.[29]

The Use of Discovery

I believe that discovery in the §7426 suit plays a crucial role. The reason is, in all other cases we have discussed, the burden is on you alone to prove each and every allegation of the complaint.[30] Never does it shift to the government. The §7426 case, however, is different. The burden of proof *does shift* to the government *after* you make the initial showing that you own the property in question. Thereafter, the government must prove a "nexus" between the delinquent taxpayer and the property seized.

If you are to be successful in the trial of the case, you *must learn* the government's theory of the case and obtain all the evidence it intends to offer to support that theory. In this case, the facts are critical. Only advance intelligence as to the government's witnesses, documentary exhibits and statements to be submitted as evidence will equip you to counter its case. You should never put yourself in the position of having to explain or refute the government's evidence *without* the opportunity of having reviewed it prior to trial. Only discovery affords the means to accomplish this necessary task.

Settlement Discussions

Nothing more can be said about settlement than has already been said in other chapters. My rule, as you are aware, is to keep an open mind.

Summary Judgment

The §7426 suit is perhaps the most "fact ridden" case we have discussed in this manual. By this I mean that the question of property ownership generally rises and falls upon a detailed series of facts. This is especially true when the dispute is over non-title assets such as cash, jewelry, coin collections, etc. When such is the case, summary judgment cannot rightfully be used as a means to dispose of the matter when questions of fact are yet to be decided.

When pivotal issues of fact remain in dispute, a jury rightfully should be called upon to resolve these issues.[31] In the context of this case, questions of fact

---

28. *Morris v. United States*, 87-1 USTC Para 9241 (11th Cir. 1987); *Marotta v. United States*, 82-1 Para. 9115 (DC NY 1981).

29. Code §7426(b)(2)(C).

30. The one and only exception to this is found in the FOIA Petition, Chapter Three.

31. Seventh Amendment, US Constitution; Rule 38, FRCvP; *Gordon v. United States*, 70-2 USTC Para. 9701 (DC 1972); *Fontana v. United States*, 528 F.Supp. 137 (DC 1982).

may involve the source of funds used to purchase the property in question. This question arises when one attempts to "trace" the property to himself as the rightful owner. Also, the circumstances under which the delinquent citizen was holding the property when it was seized bear on the issue of ownership.

The Trial

We have discussed in general terms the procedure followed in a civil tax trial. In this case, however, the government has a burden of proof after you have provided a foundation of evidence to buttress your claim of ownership to the property. This means that in the trial, the government will be required to bring forth specific evidence, through witnesses and documents, to support its theory of the case. You will have the right to interrogate those witnesses regarding their testimony and to offer such documents as you believe discredit or

contradict its position.

Exhibit 11-3 is a flowchart depicting the process which is followed in a case of this nature.

Conclusion

IRS Revenue Officers tend to be trigger happy when it comes to the seizure of property. The "shoot-first-ask-questions-later" attitudes leaves the property rights of many citizens trampled in its path. This is especially true where the husband-wife relationship is concerned. Innocent wives often become victims when the husband has a dispute with the IRS. It is common for the wife's property to come under attack when the IRS attempts to seize it to satisfy her husband's debt. In this event, and a broad range of other common abusive collection circumstances, the principles taught in this chapter will go a long way toward terminating the destruction of property rights at the hands of the IRS.

Exhibit 11-3

Flowchart of

Wrongful Levy Suit

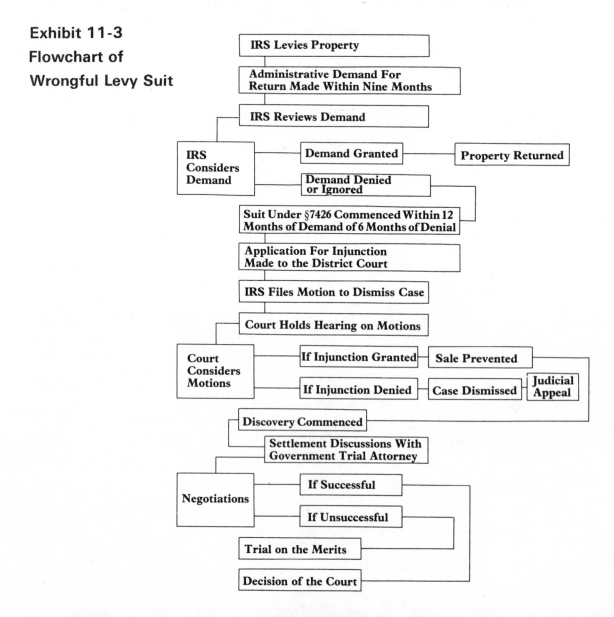

12
CHAPTER

How to Stop an IRS Rampage

In the early portion of this manual we studied the principles of law which set this nation apart from others in the world. The primary difference (finding its origin in the *Magna Charta*) is the concept that here, the *people* lawfully possess the power of government and merely delegate that power to their elected officials. Drawing from Jefferson's observations in the Declaration of Independence, I pointed out that when the designs of government run contrary to the interests of the people, the people possess the lawful authority to alter their government. This premise is present in our society in a number of ways, not the least of which is the First Amendment right to petition the government for redress of grievances. That First Amendment right is the foundational premise undergirding this manual.

At the heart of the right to petition for redress of grievances is the notion that government is *accountable* to the people for its actions. Government itself, and certainly the persons in government who act on behalf of the people, are not above the law. If they were, this country would be no different than the banana republics of South America which enjoy a military coup once a month, each giving birth to another self-important dictator who declares his own word to be law. The notion that the "King" is law personified and his acts sovereign was destroyed by Samual Rutherford in 1644, in his essay, *Lex Rex, or the Law and the Prince*.[1] Rutherford demonstrated that the concept of the "Divine right of Kings" and the "Sovereignty of the Crown" were contrary to the statement of rights in the Magna Charta and at odds with the general Biblical principles of accountability.[2]

Rutherford's declarations caused much stir in England. Eventually, they found themselves at the heart of the legal and social movement of Colonial America in the 1700's. It is beyond argument that the concept of the right of self-determination and the accountability of government were among the primary motivators of our forefathers in their act of casting off the chains of government which bound them to England.

---

1. Sprinkle Publications, Harrisburg, PA.

2. Rutherford was a Puritan minister.

Unfortunately, the ink was not yet dry on the Constitutional parchment when the concept of governmental sovereignty began to creep back into the thinking of our own early political leaders. It seems that, regardless of where on earth government is instituted, it becomes an end unto itself, greatly departing from its only legitimate purpose, the protection of its people. It seems that with the creation of government is born an entity which perceives that it is greater than the sum of its parts; an entity which, fueled by its own idea of synergism, has as its paramount goal, its own growth and propagation. Unfortunately, the United States government is not immune from the virus which infects each formal entity known as "government." The only difference is the extent to which the people permit the virus to spread and infect the entire body of government.

On January 8, 1798, the Eleventh Amendment to the United States Constitution was ratified with "vehement speed."[3] The Eleventh Amendment is recognized as the source of the "Sovereign Immunity Doctrine." It is interpreted to hold that no suit "in law or equity" may be maintained by any citizen against any State government or the Federal government in any court in the United States. The premise of the Eleventh Amendment is that the *government* is *"sovereign."* As such, it may not be sued by any person for any reason, lest it first *consent* to such suit. The doctrine of "sovereign immunity" ala the Eleventh Amendment is nothing more than the doctrine of the "divine right of Kings" disguised beneath a different cloak.

The Eleventh Amendment acts to *vitiate* the express language of the Constitution at Article III, sec. 2, para. 1. There, we learn that the judicial power of the United States *"shall extend to all cases,* in Law and Equity,"[4] including those involving a citizen and the government. Hence our founding fathers, in their wisdom, acknowledged the need to *hold government accountable* by permitting a citizen to demand such accountability through the vehicle of the courts. Yet the Eleventh Amendment declares *just the opposite,* holding that the "Judicial power of the United States *shall not be construed* to extend to any suit in law or equity," commenced by any citizen against the government.[5] Thus, the Eleventh Amendment is a dangerous departure from our Constitutional heritage. So much so, that Justice Felix Frankfurter described the concept of sovereign immunity as "an anachronistic survival of

monarchial privilege, and runs counter to democratic notions of the moral responsibility of the State."[6]

Despite the fact that it is alien to our accepted notions of government, the doctrine of sovereign immunity is routinely enforced in the courts of the United States. This fact has made it extremely difficult to pursue agents of the government, because early on, the courts determined that the same rules which govern suits against the United States also apply to suits against its officials.[7] Because of this rule, it was all but impossible to hold an individual IRS agent accountable for his unlawful acts. When efforts to do so were attempted, the agent would hide behind the shield of sovereign immunity, claiming that his actions were not subject to suit solely because of his status as an official of the United States.

In 1971, a crack in the sovereign immunity armor was achieved when a citizen successfully sued federal narcotics agents for violations of his Constitutional rights. In the case, the Supreme Court held that when agents of the federal government surpass the limitations of their authority, they no longer function as agents of the government, but rather, as individuals. Hence, they may be subject to suit.[8] *Bivens* created the so-called "Constitutional Tort," the right of action when one has suffered a violation of a Constitutional protection. However, subsequent decisions of the Supreme Court, in construing the concept of immunity and the *Bivens* claim, established a burden of proof which is so stringent, it is nearly impossible to prove that an agent acted outside the scope of official authority.[9]

This jurisdictional protectionism afforded the acts of federal agents, tax collectors in particular, created a sense of bravado which fueled the IRS' capacity to commit incredible acts. Many of these acts of lawlessness were the focal point of Congress' hearings on the Taxpayers' Bill of Rights Act. The result was the passage of new Code §7433. This new section of law permits citizens to sue to recover damages incurred as a result of violations of any Internal Revenue statute or regulation.

The Unlawful Acts of An IRS Collection Officer

The remedy found in Code §7433 is effective for actions which occur after November 10, 1988. The statute provides:

---

3. Justice Frankfurter dissenting in *Larson v. Domestic & Foreign Commerce Corp.,* 337 U.S. 682 (1949).

4. Emphasis added.

5. Eleventh Amendment; emphasis added.

6. Justice Frnakfurter dissenting in *Kennecott Copper Corp. v. State Tax Commission,* 327 U.S. 573 (1946).

7. *Tindal v. Wesley,* 167 U.S. 204 (1897).

8. *Bivens v. Six Unknown Named Agents of Federal Bureau of Narcotics,* 403 U.S. 388 (1971).

9. See, e.g., *Davis v. Scherer,* 468 U.S. 183 (1984).

"(a) If, in connection with any collection of Federal tax with respect to a taxpayer, any officer or employee of the Internal Revenue Service recklessly or intentionally disregards any provision of this title, or any regulation promulgated under this title, such taxpayer may bring a civil action for damages against the United States in a district court of the United States. Except as provided in section §7432 (see Chapter Ten), such civil action shall be the exclusive remedy for recovering damages resulting from such actions.

The problems previously existing in light of the doctrine of sovereign immunity and the corresponding immunity afforded federal agents acting in "the line of duty" are now behind us. This statute creates a clear remedy for recovering damages which is not subject to the traditional defenses offered by government lawyers when defending IRS employees accused of lawless acts. As a matter of fact, the last sentence of paragraph (a) of the statute makes it plain that other remedies which may have been possible prior to the passage of §7433 are now moot. The suit for damages under §7433, by its own language is the "exclusive remedy" for redressing the lawless acts of an individual IRS collection officer.[10]

When to Sue for Damages Caused by Unlawful Acts

The first consideration when determining whether to sue the United States for violations of law attributable to one or more of its tax collection agents, is whether the wrongful action constitutes a violaton of "any provision of this Title (Title 26, the Internal Revenue Code), or any regulation thereunder." When it can be shown that the IRS collection officer "recklessly or intentionally disregards" any statute or regulation within the scope of the tax law, he can be subjected to suit under §7433. Therefore, the primary issue to establish is that a right or remedy available to you under the code has been violated by the collection officer. If that can be demonstrated, the basis for a claim is in place.

An Important Limitation. You will notice that in the past few paragraphs I have used the words "collection officer" when discussing the relief available under §7433. These words are carefully chosen and reflect an important limitation of the right to sue under §7433. The statute provides that the violation must have occurred in connection with "any collection of Federal tax." This too is language which is very carefully chosen. The reason being, the Congressional

Conference Committee report on Code §7433 states:

". . .the provision is limited to reckless or intentional disregard in connection with the collection of tax. An action under this provision may not be based on alleged reckless or intentional disregard in connection with the *determination of tax.*" (Emphasis added.)

Consequently, the first point of concern is to acknowledge that the right to sue the IRS under §7433 does not exist when the alleged violation involves the *determination* of tax. This, of course, is the function of the Examination and Appeals Division. While it is inarguable that much abuse exists at the determination level (the Examination Division in particular) there is no right of recovery with regard to losses sustained there.

Therefore, it is clear that any suit alleging "reckless or intentional disregard" must grow out of the act of collecting the tax. The actions of a revenue officer, the Collection Division in general, including Special Procedures, or the Automated Collection Service (ACS) fall within the scope of this provision. Fortunately, the violations of law which are most costly to the citizen are those committed by persons engaged in the collection of taxes. The ability to recover damages incurred at that level should prove beneficial.

The Statute of Limitations. In subsection (d)(3) of new law, Congress has provided a statute of limitations. It reads:

"Notwithstanding any other provision of law, an action to enforce liability under this section may be brought without regard to the amount in controversy and may be brought only within 2 years after the date the right of action accrues."[11]

In order for the two-year period of limitations to begin, the citizen must be aware that a violation of his rights under the Code or regulations has occurred. Also, he must have incurred damages as well as exhausted all administrative remedies in connection with his claim. Only then, will the clock begin to tick on his claim.

Specific Circumstances Which May Constitute a Violation

As in each case where we discuss a specific remedy against IRS abuse, I attempt to paint a picture of when such remedy may be effectively employed. We will do

---

10. The only exception is the right to sue collection officers responsible for erroneous tax liens. See Chapter Ten, and Code §7432.

11. The right of action "accrues" after the citizen has had a reasonable opportunity to discover all the essential elements of a possible cause of action.

the same here with regard to the suit under §7433.

Unauthorized Disclosure of Information.
Section 6103 of the Code provides that your tax return in its related information "shall be confidential." The law enjoins any officer or employee of the IRS from disclosing information regarding your tax return or related matters to "any unauthorized person." In particular, the law defines "tax return" and "return information" as:

"The term 'return' means any tax or information return, declaration of estimated tax, or claim for refund required by law, or provide for or permitted under any provision of this title which is filed with the Secretary...

"The term 'return information' means a taxpayer's identity, the nature, source, or amount of his income, payments, receipts, deductions, exemptions, credits, liabilities, net worth, tax liability, tax withheld, deficiencies, overassessments, or tax payments, whether the taxpayer's return was, is being, or will be examined, or subject to other investigation or processing, or any other data, received by, recorded by, prepared by, or furnished to, or collected by the Secretary with respect to a return or with respect to the determination of the existence, or possible existence, of liability (or the amount thereof) of any person under this title for any tax, penalty, interest, fine, forfeiture, or other imposition, or offense, and any part of any written determination or any background file document relating to such written determination. . .which is not open to public inspection under section 6110,★ ★ ★"

As you can readily see, the proscription regarding disclosure is quite broad, and rightfully so. Given the vast amount of intimate information known to the IRS about you, it could easily cause irreparable harm if all or part of your tax affairs were leaked to others. When such a leak occurs, a violation cognizable under Code §7433 exists.

An example of this is the case of John. John was embroiled in a garden variety dispute with the IRS. When the case was sent into collection, an overly aggressive revenue officer violated the clear mandate of §6103. John's mother owned rental property which John managed on her behalf. Because John was responsible to run ads to rent apartments, interview applicants, collect rents and pay bills, the revenue officer was convinced that John actually owned the property but his mother was holding title merely as a ruse.

One day, the revenue officer arrived at the apartment building and announced to the tenants, one at a time, that the IRS would soon be seizing the property because

"John was delinquent in his taxes and refused to pay." He further explained that the IRS determined that he in fact owned the property and that due to the imminent seizure, they should vacate the premises. Obligingly, each tenant moved within days of the announcement. As it developed, the IRS never did attempt to seize the complex but the building stood empty for months. The act of disclosure was unlawful and certainly occasioned damages in connection with the collection of tax.

Unauthorized disclosures, althouth admittedly not to the extent of that shown here, occur all the time. The IRS is notorious for "dropping hints" regarding a person's problems in as much an effort to cause hardship as to collect tax. These disclosures are subject to redress under §7433.

Disregarding Notices and Demands. In the previous chapters of this manual, I delineated the procedures necessary in order to obtain an injunction against the collection of an unlawful tax assessment. I was careful to point out that those procedures would not allow a person to recover damages against a particular agent, but of course, §7433 does permit one to recover his damages. In the case of unlawful collection efforts brought on by the IRS' disregard of demands for abatement of mathematical recomputations or failure to mail a notice of deficiency as required by law, §7433 provides a means to recover damages suffered as a result.

Failure to Disclose Rights. In Chapter Seven I declared that one should, when in doubt, demand of IRS officials a statement of what your rights and remedies are in any situation. The IRS is under an affirmative duty to inform you of your rights when you make a specific request for them. This duty is reflected in Congress' passage of the Taxpayers' Bill of Rights Act, of which section one requires the IRS to prepare and distribute to "each taxpayer" a definitive statement, in simple, non-legal terms, as to what his rights are. That statement is IRS Publication 1, *Your Rights as a Taxpayer*. However, it is unavoidable that the document, all four pages of it, is grossly inadequate in describing all remedies available to a citizen and procedures necessary for invoking them. After all, the tax Code contains *thousands* of pages. This manual is well over *200 pages* in length and discusses *nine* remedies. How complete can a four-page statement possibly be?

This gives rise to the need, whenever in doubt, to demand that the IRS collection officer with whom you are dealing provide a clear and concise statement of procedures available to you under the circumstances, as well as the *specific* manner in which to avail yourself of those procedural protections. When you make a specific request for help and receive none, or worse, you receive incorrect informatoin, I believe that is a violation of your rights results and that you are entitled to recover the damages you suffer.[12]

The Bizarre and Unusual. There is no limit to the kind of unlawful conduct one can expect from IRS Collection Officers. I have been dealing with the IRS for over a decade. In that time, I have spoken with thousands of persons under the gun from every possible angle. The things that I have seen and heard would chill the most staunch IRS critic. I have come to the point where each new horror story, believed by the victim to be the "most incredible thing possible" is common place. Among those which top the list are the stories which cause even me to shake my head in disbelief.

My "favorite" occurred in a Detroit suburb in November of 1984. On that day, several collection officers of the IRS appeared at a day-care center to collect the back taxes allegedly owed by the center's owner and operator. The events which followed their arrival are nothing short of infuriating. Witnesses tell us through affidavits that agents of the IRS "hearded nearly 20 children" into a single room within the center. The room was then "sealed off" when the agents placed a large table in front of the door. They prevented the children from leaving the room.

Soon, the parents of the terrorized and crying children appeared at the center to claim their young. At a table in the lobby, IRS Collection Officers met each parent with a demand as he or she came through the door. The demand was that any debt owed to the day-care center be "paid now." The parents were not allowed to see or take their children home until they paid the bill! Imagine how you would feel if agents of the United States Government were holding your young son or daughter *hostage* for federal tax debts! *Ransom* was demanded in the form of immediate payment. The bizarre part of the story is that the parents did not owe the tax. The owner of the day-care center *allegedly* owed the tax. Yet the parents were required to pay in order to gain release of their children. I don't know about you, but to me, that's *going too far!*

Those agents should have been sued, sued, sued!; every one of them, and to the fullest extent of the law!! Without a doubt, §7433 provides a remedy to accomplish just that. We cannot tolerate this kind of lawlessness any further. As I stated in Chapter Seven, we must *wake up!* We must begin to call these agents to account for their unlawful acts. Each and every citizen subjected to lawlessness at the hands of the IRS must *not hesitate* to take lawful action. Only when the lawlessness of the IRS is attacked *at every turn* will we bring the monster under control. It requires courage and it requires knowledge. Most importantly, it requires a dedication to the principles of liberty and justice and a desire to pass those Constitutional attributes to posterity. If we do not take action to redress this kind of lawlessness, it will not take long for the notions of Constitutional liberty and justice to truly ring hollow, devoid of any substance. Act America, before it is too late. We have the tools!

A Double-Edged Sword

In Chapter Four, under the heading, *Exhausting Administrative Remedies,* I discussed Code §6673. That provision allows the Tax Court to award damages in favor of the United States against any person who commences a proceeding in the Tax Court solely for the purposes of delay, or in which he raises issues which are "frivolous or groundless." (See Chapter Four.) This section of law *also applies* to actions commenced under §7433. The law states:

> "Whenever it appears to the court that the taxpayer's position in proceedings before the court instituted or maintained by such taxpayer under section 7433 is frivolous or groundless, damages in an amount not in excess of *$10,000* shall be awarded *to the United States* by the court in the court's decision. Damages so awarded at the same time as the decision shall be paid upon notice and demand from the Secretary." Code §6673(b); emphasis added.

CAUTION: Do not take a lawsuit under §7433 *lightly.* Just as the violation of law by federal agents is a very serious matter, so is the institution of frivolous or groundless claims for purposes of harrassment. I demand that the IRS' lawless conduct not be returned in kind. This applies to actions under §7433. No action under that statute should be taken without adequate justification. In short, do not start a war if you do not intend to win the war! The costs are too great.

Exhausting Administrative Remedies

Section 7433(d)(1) reads:

> "A judgment for damages shall not be awarded under subsection (b) unless the court determines that the plaintiff has exhaused the administrative remedies available to such plaintiff within the Internal Revenue Service."

---

12. *Golden v. United States,* 86-2 USTC Para. 9626 (DC Mo. 1986); *Belton v. United States,* 82-2 USTC Para. 9455 (DC D of C 1982) and 83-1 USTC Para. 9181 (DC D of C 1983).

Administrative remedies are an integral part of every action against the IRS. We have gone to *great lengths* in this manual to ensure a complete treatment of the subject. When discussing the provisions relating to §7433, we must be somewhat general in our approach. Because the unlawful act of a revenue or other collection officer may be broad, we can say that *any* administrative remedy applicable to the situation should be employed prior to suit. For example, when the claim under §7433 involves an arbitrary notice, the citizen must have mailed his letter demanding abatement prior to commencing the suit.

In addition to the general statement just made, a more specific administrative remedy is available when the IRS is proceeding unlawfully to collect taxes. The remedy is found within new Code §7811. Under §7811, the "Ombudsman" has the authority to issue a "Taxpayer Assistance Order if, in the determination of the Ombudsman, the taxpayer is suffering or about to suffer a significant hardship as a result of the manner in which the internal revenue laws are being administered by the Secretary."[13]

The statute affords the Ombudsman (Problems Resolutions Officer) the power to do any of the following:

1. Require the IRS to release property which has been levied upon;

2. Compel the IRS to *cease* any action, or *refrain* from taking any action in connection with:

    a. the collection of taxes;

    b. any bankruptcy or receivership proceedings;

    c. any examination and investigation of possible tax liabilities, and enforcement of the tax code.[14]

Relief under §7811 is obtained by filing an application with the IRS. The IRS' sense of humor, to the extent that one exists, is seen in the regulations under §7811. For years, we have used the 9-1-1 phone number as a means of obtaining emergency police, fire and medical assistance. As a result of the concept of 9-1-1 *emergency* assistance, the IRS has cleverly dubbed its new *Application for Taxpayer Assistance Order (TAO)* Form *911*. An example of Form 911 and its instructions is reproduced in Exhibit 12-1. Please carefully review this form. Any relief under new Code §7811 will be contingent upon completing and filing that form.

In particular, please examine Line 11 of Form 911. There it provides, "Description of Hardship and Relief Requested." Thereafter, several blank spaces are provided for one to enter the particular problem he is having with the IRS and the manner he would like that

problem resolved. True to form, however, the IRS does not provide sufficient information to allow the uninformed taxpayer to make a legally correct, and hence effective, request for relief. For example, nowhere in the form or the accompanying instructions are we told the scope or limitations of the Taxpayer Assistance Order and authority of the Office of Ombudsman. That is why it is important to review the *statute* itself, §7811. It is the statute which governs the process by which all Form 911 applications will be heard. The statute sets *limitations*, and anyone wishing to avail himself of the possible benefits of the statute must know these limitations. Take a moment to review the scope of the statute as shown above.

While it is necessary in my judgment to employ the Form 911 before any action is taken under §7433, I view this statute with *guarded optimism*. The reason is found within the language of subsection (c) of §7811. It holds:

"Any Taxpayer Assistance Order issued by the Ombudsman under this section may be modified or rescinded only by the Ombudsman, *a district director, a service center director, a compliance center director, a regional director of appeals, or any superior of such person.*" (Emphasis added.)

Now correct me if I am wrong, but is not the purpose of the Ombudsman to *rectify* improper conduct on the part of the IRS? And is not the reason the Ombudsman has the authority to issue a TAO to *prevent* the IRS from taking or continuing its improper conduct? Why then is the IRS, the agency over which the Ombudsman is to have such authority, empowered to *rescind* the very orders which this Officer may issue?

In addition to this problem, the IRS has made it clear that it has wide discretion in determining whether or not a Form 911 Application will be granted. IRS News Release IR-89-11, issued January 27, 1989, provides some guidelines on this issue. In that bulletin, the IRS cautions that TAO's are *not* to be used to contest the "merits" of any *tax liability*. Rather, the "significant hardship" referred to in the statute addresses itself to "the administration of the law and not the law itself."

The term "significant hardship" is defined by regulation as:

". . .a serious privation caused or about to be caused to the taxpayer as the result of the particular manner in which the internal revenue laws are being administered by the Internal Revenue Service. The term means more

---

13. New Code §7811(a) created by the Taxpayers' Bill of Rights Act.
14. Code §7811(b).

Exhibit 12-1: Form 911 and Instructions

INSTRUCTIONS

FORM 911—APPLICATION FOR TAXPAYER ASSISTANCE ORDER
To Relieve Hardship

Purpose of Form.—You should use Form 911, Application for Taxpayer Assistance Order to Relieve Hardship, to apply for a review by the Taxpayer Ombudsman, or his designee, of actions being taken by the Internal Revenue Service. Such application may be made in cases where you are undergoing or about to undergo a significant hardship because of the manner in which the Internal Revenue laws are being administered. This application can not be used to contest the merits of any tax liability. If you disagree with the amount of tax assessed, please see Publication 1, Your Rights As A Taxpayer. While we are reviewing your application, we will take no further enforcement action. We will contact you after our review to advise you of our decision. The Internal Revenue Code requires us to suspend any statutory period of limitation until a decision is made on your request.

Where to File.—This application should be addressed to the Internal Revenue Service, Problem Resolution Office in the district where you live. Call the local Taxpayer Assistance number listed in your telephone directory or 1-800-424-1040 for the address of the Problem Resolution Office in your district. If you live overseas, and have other than an A.P.O. or F.P.O. address, mail your request to the Assistant Commissioner (International), Internal Revenue Service, Problem Resolution Office, P.O. Box 893, Washington, D.C. 20044. If you have an A.P.O. or F.P.O. address, you should send this application to the Internal Revenue Service, Problem Resolution Office where the return was filed.

CAUTION: Requests submitted to the incorrect office may result in delays. We will acknowledge your request within one week of receiving it. If you do not hear from us within 10 days (15 days for overseas addresses) of submitting your application, please contact the Problem Resolution Office in the IRS office to which you sent your application.

PART I. TAXPAYER INFORMATION

1. Name(s). Enter your name as it appeared on the tax return for each period you are requesting assistance. If your name has changed since the return was submitted, you should still enter the name as it appeared on your return. If you filed a joint return, enter both names.

2. SSN/EIN. Enter your social security number (SSN) or the employer identification number (EIN) of the business, corporation, trust, etc., for the name you showed in block 1. If you are married, and the request is for assistance on a problem involving a joint return, enter the social security number in block 2 for the first name listed in block 1.

3. Spouse's SSN. If the problem involves a joint return, enter the social security number for the second name listed in block 1.

4. Tax Form. Enter the tax form number of the tax form for which you filed for which you are requesting assistance. For example, if you are requesting assistance for a problem involving an individual income tax return, enter "1040." If your problem involves more than one tax form, include the information in block 10.

5. Tax Period Ended. If you are requesting assistance on an annually filed return, enter the calendar year or the ending date of the fiscal year for that return. If the problem concerns a return filed quarterly, enter the ending date of the quarter involved. If the problem involves more than one tax period, include the information in block 10.

6. and **7.** Self-explanatory.

8. Person To Contact. Enter the name of the person to contact about the problem. In the case of businesses, corporations, trusts, estates, etc., enter the name of a responsible official.

9. Telephone number. Enter the telephone number, including area code, of the person to contact.

10. Description of problem. Describe the action(s) being taken (or not being taken) by the Internal Revenue Service that are causing you hardship. If you know it, include the name of the person, office, telephone number, and/or address of the last contact you had with IRS. Please include a copy of the most recent correspondence, if any, you have had with IRS regarding this problem.

11. Description of hardship and relief requested. Describe the hardship which is being caused by the Internal Revenue Service's action (or lack of action) as outlined in Part I, block 10. Please tell us what kind of relief you are requesting.

12. Your Signature(s). To be valid this application must be signed by you in Part I, block 12, or by your authorized representative, acting in your behalf, in Part II, block 19. If your name has changed from the name that appears in Part I, block 1, sign using your current legal name. If the request is for assistance on a problem involving a joint return, both you and the spouse shown in block 3 must sign this form in order for the statutory period of limitations to be suspended. If one of the taxpayers is no longer living, the taxpayer's spouse or personal representative must sign the form and write "deceased" after the deceased taxpayer's name. If the taxpayer is your dependent child who can not sign the application because of age or other reasons, you may sign your child's name in the signature provided followed by the words "By (your signature), parent (or guardian) for minor child." If the application is being made for other than an individual taxpayer, a person having authority to sign the application should sign the application. Enter the date the application is signed.

Part II. REPRESENTATIVE INFORMATION

If you are the taxpayer and you wish to have a representative act in your behalf, your representative must have a power of attorney or tax information authorization on file for the tax year(s) and period(s) involved. Complete Part II, blocks 13 through 18. (See Form 2848, Power of Attorney and Declaration of Representative and instructions for more information.)

If you are an authorized representative and are submitting this request on behalf of the taxpayer identified in Part I, complete blocks 13 through 18. Sign and date this request in block 19 and attach a copy of Form 2848, or the power of attorney.

18. Centralized Authorization File (CAF) Number. Enter the representative's CAF number. The CAF number is the unique number that Internal Revenue Service assigns to a representative after a valid Form 2848 is filed with an IRS office.

Form 911	APPLICATION FOR TAXPAYER ASSISTANCE ORDER	OFFICIAL USE ONLY
(January 1989)	To Relieve Hardship	

NOTE: Filing this application will result in extending the statutory period of limitations (see instructions).

PART I. TAXPAYER INFORMATION

1. Name(s) (as shown on tax return)	2. SSN/EIN	3. Spouse's SSN
	4. Tax Form	5. Tax Period Ended

6. Current address (number and street, apt. no., rural route)

7. City, town or post office, state, and ZIP Code

8. Person to contact:	9. Telephone number: ( )	Best time to call:

10. Description of problem (If more space is needed, attach additional sheets.)

11. Description of hardship and relief requested (If more space is needed, attach additional sheets.)

12. Your Signature(s) (see instructions)	Date	Signature of Spouse (shown in block 1)	Date

PART II. REPRESENTATIVE INFORMATION (if applicable)

13. Name of Authorized Representative	14. Firm Name

15. Street address or P.O. Box	16. City, town or post office, state, and ZIP Code

17. Telephone: Best time to call: ( )	18. Centralized Authorization File (CAF) number

19. Signature	Date

PART III. INTERNAL REVENUE SERVICE USE ONLY

20. Initiating Employee Information—Name	T/P Request	Function	Telephone	Office	Date

IRS USE ONLY	APPROPRIATE	NOT APPROPRIATE	STATUTE SUSPENDED
	☐ No change (05)	☐ PRP case (02)	Number of days
	☐ Change (06)	☐ Referred to function (03)	PRO initials
	☐ TAO/complied (07)	☐ Denied (01)	Date
	☐ TAO/sustained (08)		
	☐ TAO/modified (09)		
	☐ TAO/rescinded (10)		
	☐ Reserved (11)		

Form 911 (1-89)　　Department of the Treasury—Internal Revenue Service

than an inconvenience to the taxpayer. Further, the term means more than financial hardship alone. Instead, even where financial hardship is involved, a finding of 'significant hardship' will depend on an examination of the action taken, or to be taken, by the Internal Revenue Service which produces or would produce the financial hardship. The action or proposed action must be such that it would offend the sense of fairness of taxpayers in general were they aware of all the surrounding facts and circumstances."[15]

Certainly, actions taken or proposed which are *unlawful* and in violation of the Code and regulations fall within the sweep of the above definition. The News Release mentioned earlier provides one example (just an example) of undue hardship. It reads:

"For example, a levy served on a taxpayer's checking account after the taxpayer had entered into a formal installment agreement with the IRS could result in a significant hardship. In general, IRS does not issue levies after taxpayers have entered into formal agreements. If the levy resulted in insufficient funds in the account to cover checks that had been written, the taxpayer's credit rating could be affected. In this case the taxpayer could request that the levy be released. *If the Problems Resolution Officer agreed,* the levy would be released." (Emphasis added.)

Another important aspect of the TAO and Form 911 is, according to §7811(d), the "running of any period of limitation with respect to any action described in subsection (a)," is *suspended.* (See footnotes 13 and 14.) What's worse, the period of limitation is suspended *beginning with the time the Application is submitted,* whether or not it is eventually granted! If the Application is granted, the suspension continues until the TAO is finally dissolved.[16] For this reason, great care must be taken in submitting a Form 911. If a Form 911 is submitted without first considering the implications of the applicable statute of limitation, it is possible for the unwitting citizen to *make matters worse* by handing the IRS *additional time* in which to rake him over the coals.

Nevertheless, the Form 911 created under Code §7811 is a viable administrative remedy which must be utilized before the commencement of a suit under §7433. The form is availble from the IRS and should be submitted to the Problems Resolution Officer within

the district where you reside. Processing of the Application for TAO will be handled through that office. You should submit the form as soon as possible upon discovering the lawless act in question. You should also make it clear that you intend, by submitting the Form 911, to comply with the requirement of §7433 to exhaust administrative remedies. The action should be taken *prior* to sustaining any damages as a result of the IRS' actions.

When the IRS fails to issue the TAO, or the TAO is overridden by later actions and you sustain damages due to the unlawful actions of a collection officer, Ultimate Defense Weapon Number Nine comes into play.

Ultimate Defense Weapon Number Nine
Suit For Damages Caused By Unlawful Collection Actions

At long last Congress has recognized what countless unfortunate citizens have known for years. The IRS often goes too far in the collection of taxes. The proximate result of those actions is that citizens suffer damages of a financial nature which in the past, were extremely difficult to recover. Now, Code §7433(b) provides:

"In any action brought under subsection (a), upon a finding of liability on the part of the defendant, the defendant shall be liable[17] to the plaintiff in an amount equal to the lesser of $100,000 or the sum of—

"(1) actual, direct economic damages sustined by the plaintiff as a proximate result of the reckless or intentional actions of the officer or employee, and

"(2) the costs of the action."

We have already discussed several limitations on the right to recover damages under this section, but one further limitation exists. In subsection (d)(2) we find the requirement that the plaintiff (citizen) "mitigate" or limit his damages. We have discussed at length in Chapter Ten the requirement to mitigate damages associated with an erroneous tax lien. The same principles apply here.[18] Whenever steps can be taken which will lead to the minimization of damages visited upon you as a result of the IRS' lawless conduct, such steps should be taken at the earliest possible moment. If efforts to mitigate damages are not taken, the amount

15. Rev. Reg. §301.7811-1T(a)(4)(ii).

16. Code §7811(d)(1) and (2).

17. When an IRS officer is found liable under this section, damages will be paid by the United States. Code §7433(c).

18. See Chapter Ten, under the heading, *Limitations on the Proceeding.*

you are entitled to recover "shall be reduced by the amount of such damages which could have reasonably been mitigated by the plaintiff."

Drafting the Complaint

The suit under §7433 must be commenced within two years after the right of action accrues. The right of action will accrue when the plaintiff has had an opportunity to discover the elements of a cause of action. When drafting your complaint, you must be careful to incorporate all essential elements of the violation. Under §7433, the essential elements of a cause of action are:

1. That an officer or employee of the IRS engaged in the *collection* of taxes recklessly or intentionally disregarded any statute or regulation under the Internal Revenue Code;

2. That you have incurred damages as a result of the reckless or intentional disregard of IRS statutes or regulations;

3. That you have exhausted all administrative remedies in connection with the lawless conduct; and

4. That you have made every reasonable effort to mitigate, or limit, the damages suffered as a result of the lawless conduct.

These elements, distilled from the language of §7433, must be set forth in your complaint in order for the document to sufficiently state a claim against the IRS employee in question. It is a good idea to include as attachments to your complaint copies of all relevent documents to which you refer in the text. An example of this would be your Form 911, Application For Taxpayer Assistance Order. As stated in Chapter Ten, when alleging that all administrative remedies were exhausted, you should state exactly what steps were taken in this regard.

Another observation in regard to §7433 is that this section will serve well as an *adjunct* to the other Defense Weapons we have discussed in Part IV of this manual. By this I mean that an allegation under §7433 could be made *in addition* to any of the other methods of eliminating IRS abuse. It is very common for civil complaints to charge *multiple* violations of law. One count of the complaint could allege that the IRS has wrongfully undertaken collection in violation of the deficiency procedures of the Code. A *second* count of the *same* complaint could set forth a claim that the particular collection officer recklessly and intentionally proceeded with collection in violation of the deficiency procedures. This tactic accomplishes two objectives. First, it halts the unlawful collection by stating a case in support of an injunction. Second, it states a claim against the officer or officers responsible, to the end that

your actual damages may be recovered.

Exhibit 12-2 is an example of the manner in which a complaint under §7433 would state a claim. Please note that the complaint shown there is identical in substance to that shown in Chapter Nine. (See Exhibit 9-6.) The only difference is that I have added a *second* count in Exhibit 12-2. The second count, in addition to the necessary background allegations, states a claim for entitlement to damages under §7433.

Applying for an Injunction

Despite the fact that the suit for damages is certainly authorized by §7433, you can expect the IRS' attorney to argue that the Anti-Injunction Act precludes any grant of injunctive relief. When you make an application for a preliminary injunction calculated to immediately end unlawful collection, you must set forth the facts which entitle you to the injunction. Chapter Eight has demonstrated the manner in which this is accomplished.

If your complaint seeks an injunction, the expected response offered by the government is a motion to dismiss, if not your entire complaint, then so much of it as seeks the injunction. You must stand ready to provide facts and legal argument to the court which will establish your entitlement to the relief sought when your request for injunction is set for hearing. Remember, the single most important aspect of this showing is the factual presentation made through your affidavit. This subject has been discussed in detail already. Therefore, I will rest upon those prior statements.

Prosecuting Your Case

Prosecution of the suit for damages under §7433 will very closely parallel the case against the erroneous tax lien. See Chapter Ten. Many of the elements are the same. For example, you must prove that damages were sustained as a direct result of the unlawful actions alleged and you must prove that you made every reasonable effort to mitigate those damages. In this case, however, your burden is to prove that the actions which are alleged to cause the damages were undertaken "recklessly or intentionally," in disregard of "any provision of (the IRS Code) or any regulation" thereunder.

As with all cases in which you are the complainant, you will bear the burden to prove with evidence that the allegations of your complaint are true, including the charge that the collection officer "recklessly or intentionally" violated the provisions of the Code or regulations. As in Chapter Ten, this will require that

Exhibit 12-2: Complaint For Damages Under Code §7433

UNITED STATES DISTRICT COURT
DISTRICT OF MINNESOTA
THIRD DIVISION

William E. Citizen,   )
)
                    Plaintiff,   )   Civil Case No. _____
)
vs.   )   JURY TRIAL DEMANDED
)
The United States of America,   )
)
                    Defendant.   )
_____

COMPLAINT FOR DAMAGES UNDER CODE §7433 AND INJUNCTION UNDER §6213(a)

NATURE OF THE ACTION

1. This is a civil action for damages under §7433 incurred as a result of the reckless or intentional violation of provisions of the IRS Code and Regulations.

2. This suit also seeks to enjoin the unlawful collection of taxes pursuant to Code §6213(a).

JURISDICTION

3. The Jurisdiction of this Court is invoked under the authority of Code §7433, permitting the recovery of damages as a result of the reckless or intentional violations of the Internal Revenue Code or regulations.

4. Jurisdiction is also asserted under the authority of 26 USC §§6212, and 6213(a), providing jurisdiction to enjoin collection when the deficiency procedures of the tax code are violated.

5. This case involves the internal revenue laws of the United States and hence, raises a federal question.

VENUE

6. Venue within the above-named court is proper according to

28 USC §1402, in that the United States is a defendant in this case.

PARTIES

7. The Plaintiff, William E. Citizen, (address, city, state, zip,) is properly named as the Plaintiff to this action, as it is he against whom the unlawful acts of collection were committed.

8. The Defendant, United States of America, through its agency the Internal Revenue Service, (office address, city, state, zip) caused the unjust assessment to be made and is proceeding against the Plaintiffs to collect the same.

BACKGROUND FACTS

9. The Plaintiff filed a timely US individual income tax return, Form 1040 for the year 1986, with the Internal Revenue Service on or before April 15th, 1987. The return was filed with the IRS Service Center at (city, state).

10. On (date) the Plaintiff received a notice from the IRS that an error was discovered in said return, and that the IRS corrected the error. A bill for additional tax in the amount of $_____ was mailed to Plaintiff. Attached to this complaint as Exhibit A is a copy of said bill.

11. On (date), within 60 days of the date shown on Exhibit A, Plaintiff responded in writing to the IRS. Said response explained that Plaintiff did not agree with the tax demanded in Exhibit A, and further demanded a full abatement of the assessed liability. Said abatement was demanded under the authority of Code §6213(b)(2)(A). Attached to this complaint as Exhibit B is a copy of said letter.

12. On (date) the Plaintiff received a second demand for payment of the same liability. The letter demanded that if the amount was not paid within 30 days, enforced collection action would be

COMPLAINT FOR DAMAGES, PAGE 2

taken. Attached to this complaint as Exhibit C is a copy of said second demand for payment.

13. On (date), immediately after receiving the letter in Exhibit C, Plaintiff drafted and mailed a second letter demanding abatement. Said letter pointed out that the IRS' intended collection action was unlawful under Code §6213(a) and (b). Furthermore, Plaintiff demanded that a notice of deficiency be mailed to him under Code §6212, in order that he may enjoy his right to petition the Tax Court. Attached to this complaint and marked Exhibit D is a copy of Plaintiff's second letter demanding abatement.

14. On (date) the Internal Revenue Service placed a levy against the wages of the Plaintiff. The levy demanded payment of $_____, the amount assessed for the year in question. The wage levy purports to seize all of the funds of the Plaintiff, leaving him with just $85 per week on which to live.

15. Plaintiff's personal living expenses exceed $1,500 per month, which amount is required for the support and maintenance of Plaintiff, his wife and their 3 minor children.

16. The amount of $85 per week, which IRS proposes to leave to Plaintiff upon which to live, is grossly insufficient to pay all Plaintiff's necessary living expenses.

17. After the wage levy was placed in effect, the Plaintiff pursued his remedy under Code §7811 by filing a Form 911 with the Problems Resolution Officer at (city, state). The Form 911 stated that the levy in question was unlawful and demanded the release thereof. The IRS failed to act upon (or denied) the Form 911 Application, permitting the levy to continue.

18. The Plaintiff properly pursued and exhausted all

COMPLAINT FOR DAMAGES, PAGE 3

available administrative remedies in connection with his demand for abatement. However, IRS failed and refused to honor such demands, in violation of Plaintiff's statutory rights under §§6212 and 6213(a).

19. The injunction sought in this lawsuit is grounded upon the statutory language of Code §6213(a), permitting a suit to enjoin collection when the IRS has failed or refused to follow the established deficiency procedures of the code. This suit is not precluded by the Anti-Injunction Act, Code §7421.

<u>COUNT I</u>

20. Plaintiff restates all of the allegations contained in paragraphs 1-19 as though fully set forth here in Count I.

21. The Defendant made an assessment of taxes against the Plaintiff for the year _____, which assessment is based upon an alleged mathematical or clerical error as described in Code §6213(b)(1).

22. Upon receipt of notice of such assessment and demand for payment, Plaintiff made a timely demand for abatement in accordance with his rights under Code §6213(b)(2)(A).

23. The Defendant has failed and refused to abate the liability, despite its statutory obligation to do so.

24. The Defendant has refused to mail a statutory notice of deficiency as required by Code §§6212, 6213(a) and 6213(b)(2)(A), despite demand for such a notice.

25. The Defendant continues to make demands upon the Plaintiff for payment of such liability, and in fact, has commenced enforced collection action in violation of Code §§6212 and 6213(a).

26. The Defendant's actions of failing to abate the tax in

question, of failing to issue a notice of deficiency, and of undertaking enforced collection action, have caused immediate and irreparable harm to the Plaintiff, and are in violation of federal law.

27.   Plaintiff is entitled to an injunction and to the recovery of damages as hereinafter set forth as a result of the Defendant's violation of law.

COUNT II

28.   Plaintiff restates all of the allegations contained in paragraphs 1-27 as though fully set forth here in Count II.

29.   The Defendant, through its agency the Internal Revenue Service, and (names), Collection Officers employed by the IRS, are actively involved in the collection of a tax unlawfully assessed against the Plaintiff.

30.   The assesssment and collection of the tax at issue here is in disregard of 26 USC §6212 and 6213, both of which are internal revenue statutes.

31.   The Defendant, through its agency the Internal Revenue Service, and (names), Collection Officers employed by the IRS, have recklessly or intentionally disregarded the language of 26 USC §§6212 and 6213, both of which are internal revenue statutes.

32.   The Plaintiff has suffered damages and injury as a result of the unlawful collection of tax at issue here, which damages and injury the Plaintiff has taken reasonable steps to mitigate.

33.   The Plaintiff has exhausted all administrative remedies available to him in connection with the unlawful assessment, but to no avail.

EQUITY

34.   The unlawful wage levy presently in effect against the Plaintiff will deprive Plaintiff of the ability to provide the necessities of life to himself and his family.

35.   Such unlawful deprivation will cause immediate and irreparable harm to the Plaintiff unless the Defendant is enjoined by this Court.

36.   The Plaintiff has no adequate remedy at law as an alternative to the injunction sought here, in that he has been unlawfully deprived of his statutory right to a notice of deficiency which would permit him to contest the liability in the Tax Court. Furthermore, the Plaintiff is without the ability to pay the tax demanded by the Defendant.

37.   For these reasons, the equity jurisdiction of this court is properly invoked and Plaintiff is entitled to the injunction sought here.

DAMAGES

38.   The Plaintiff has been deprived of the use of his wages in the amount of $_____ necessary for the support of his family as a result of the unlawful actions of the Defendant.

39.   The Plaintiff will continue to suffer the unjust deprivation of his wages until such time as the unlawfully assessed tax is paid in full, unless this court intervenes herein.

40.   The unjust actions of the Defendant have led to damages against the Plaintiff. Such damages can be summarized as: (list all specific damages caused by the unlawful actions, including dates and amounts).

41.   The Plaintiff has taken every reasonable step to mitigate

the damages mentioned above.

<u>REQUEST FOR RELIEF</u>

WHEREFORE, based upon all of the foregoing, Plaintiff demands judgment against the Defendant as follows:

1. That the court enter an order enjoining the Defendant, and any of its agents or employees, from collecting or attempting to collect the unjust assessment at issue herein.

2. That the court order the Defendant to completely abate the liability in question herein, pursuant to Code §6213(b)(2)(A).

3. That the Defendant be ordered to refund all of the Plaintiff's wages which have been seized pursuant to the unlawful levy.

4. That the Defendant be ordered to pay damages to the Plaintiff in the amount of $_____ which he has sustained as a result of the unlawful actions complained of here.

5. That the court order the Defendant to pay all of the Plaintiff's costs and disbursements incurred in connection with prosecuting this suit for damages.

6. For such other relief as the court may deem just.

Dated:

_____
William E. Citizen
Address
City, State, Zip
Area Code and Phone Number

you inquire into the thought processes (or lack thereof) by which the particular collection officer governed his actions. In this regard, the IRS Manual is replete with references to the Code and regulations. By establishing his familiarity with the particular manual sections governing the subject matter, you can demonstrate his knowledge of, and hence, disregard of, the statutes which protect you. Please note, however, that the test under the statute *is not* whether the collection officer violated a provision of the *manual*. A violation of the manual will not create liability for damages under the statute. The statute plainly declares that your proof must establish a violation of a *statute* or *regulation*.

It is also necessary to prove your damages with specific evidence, as well as the fact that you have taken every reasonable step to mitigate those damages. Care should be taken to review the allegations of your complaint to ensure that you have specific evidence of each allegation.

The Right of Trial by Jury

The character of a correctly phrased charge under §7433 appears to be entirely factual in nature. Unlike the question of a tax lien, which involves legal principles to be determined by a judge, §7433 involves purely *factual* determinations. Whether a collection officer ignored or disregarded, intentionally, or otherwise, a regulatory provision of the Code is a factual consideration. The law is not on trial, the acts of the collection officer are on trial. In addition, the issue of whether and to what extent you have suffered damages as a result of the unlawful acts alleged, and whether you have properly attempted to mitigate those damages, are purely questions of fact. I assert, therefore, that you are entitled to a jury trial under the Seventh Amendment to the Constitution and Rule 38, FRCvP, on these issues.

As we already know, however, it is common for government attorneys to employ the use of summary judgment (Rule 56, FRCvP) in an effort to dispose of cases against the United States. When such a motion is filed, one must be prepared to demonstrate that facts material to the issues involved in the case are yet to be resolved. When questions of fact remain unresolved, particularly those revolving around the question of the agent's knowledge of the wrongfulness of his actions and the extent to which you have suffered as a result, summary judgment is a wholly inappropriate means by which to settle the case. Care should be taken to preserve the case for jury trial by submitting affidavits and other material authorized under Rule 56 when opposing the government's motion for summary judgment.

Negotiating a Settlement

What has already been stated regarding settlement negotiations applies to this case. Please see Chapters Five and Six and review the remarks made there on this subject.

The Trial

If settlement cannot be reached, the case will be submitted for trial. As I stated, you are legally saddled with the burden of proof on the issues in the complaint. Therefore, you must be prepared to go forward with evidence to prove your claims to the satisfaction of the court or jury. In this regard, all evidence you possess and have obtained through the discovery process could, if relevant to the issues, be presented to the court.

In the trial, all evidence is submitted through the testimony of witnesses. You may testify on your own behalf or call such witnesses whose testimony will be helpful to resolve the facts. After the evidence is submitted, the court or jury will determine the facts of the case and render judgment accordingly. A written instrument will be issued to the parties at the conclusion of the trial. The instrument will reflect the judgment and constitutes the final order in the case.

Exhibit 12-3 is a flowchart depicting the progression of a suit for damages relating to the reckless or intentional violation of the tax code.

Conclusion

Ultimate Defense Weapon Number Nine is perhaps the *creme de la creme* of this manual. It represents a return, albeit gradual and limited, to the single most important rule of law upon which this nation was founded; the notion that government is accountable to the people for its actions. Ultimate Defense Weapon Number Nine, in the right hands, is a *powerful* and *useful* tool. It can emasculate the reckless, dangerously aggressive actions of callous collection officers. For the first time in contemporary history, we can force collection officers to look over their shoulders before considering a lawless act. I am speaking here of breaking the cycle of lawlessness in the purest sense. I am speaking of *forcing* revenue officers to observe your rights and respect their own limitations. I am speaking of evening the odds with the IRS once and for all!

Despite the attractiveness of the legal provision, it, like any other, is *useless* unless you are willing and able to aim and fire! The rhetoric holds that our's is a nation of law, not men. This precept is founded upon the doctrines which I discussed in the early pages of this chapter. Tax collection in the 20th Century, particularly in the past two dedaces, reflects a marked departure from that doctrine. Too often the IRS and federal courts adopt the view that the end justifies the means. As early as 1931, the Supreme Court declared that *exceptions* to the absolute protections of the Constitution should be afforded to the government while in the process of tax collection. Justice Brandeis, typically thought of as a champion of individual liberties, declared that when internal revenue is at stake:

> "Property rights must yield provisionally to governmental need."[19]

Under the flag of "governmental need" the IRS tramples the rights of citizens all the while the courts have debilitated the binding injunctions of the Constitution in cataclysmic proportion. It is most interesting that government has carved exceptions to individual rights out of the Constitution when the subject is the collection of taxes. Have we lost sight of the fact that this nation, and along with it the very Constitution of which I speak, were born out of a *dispute over taxation?* Washington himself declared in 1774:

> "I think the Parliament of Great Britian hath no more right to put their hands into my pocket, without my consent, than I have to put my hands into yours for money."

The importance of the protection of property rights *in the face of tax collection,* was espoused early on by, among others, John Dickinson, a colonial attorney and member of the Continental Congress. Dickinson was pre-eminent as a writer of pamphlets declaring the cause of the American colonies. Perhaps his most influential writings were compiled in a work entitled, *Letters of a farmer in Pennsylvania to the Inhabitants of the British Colonies.*[20] There he stated:

> "We cannot be happy without being free; we cannot be free without being *secure in our property;* we cannot be secure in our property if, without our consent, others may, as by right, *take it away."* (Emphasis added.)

The right of property, as expressed by Washington, Dickinson[21] and others, is of *paramount* concern. How has this most important point been lost on modern jurists? The answer lies, I believe, *in ignorance.* To protect and defend our rights, we must know and understand exactly what those rights are. We cannot expect that others will defend what we claim to be our own, even when the object under attack is our own political and economic freedom. The task is yours alone. Given the current state of our Constitution, I suggest you get busy!

Exhibit 12-3
Flowchart of Suit to Recover Damages

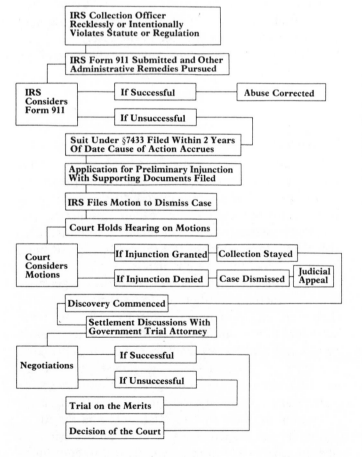

---

19. *Phillips v. Commissioner,* 283 U.S. 589 (1931).
20. Published in the *Pennsylvania Chronicle,* 1767-1768.

EPILOGUE

To extract maximum benefit from this manual, you should understand that there is a *secret* ingredient making this perhaps the most explosive expose' of IRS abuse prevention techniques ever written. What is this ingredient? It is the ability to conscript *IRS personnel* into your army! As we have seen, there are countless IRS officers, employees, agents, divisions and functions anxiously awaiting the opportunity to help you as a citizen. Well, maybe not "anxiously." When you know your rights as a taxpayer, the battle to defend those rights in the face of IRS abuse is half-won. The reason is that when, in the midst of battle with the IRS, you have the advantage of being capable to ask the *correct* questions of the *appropriate* IRS employees in order to obtain the *correct* answers. When you make *specific* requests for *specific* help and guidance, the IRS is under an affirmative duty to provide the needed assistance. This manual gives you the ability to, if nothing else, *push the right buttons.*

For example, as demonstrated in Chapter Twelve, when all else fails at the administrative level, simply "File 911." IRS Form 911, *Application for Taxpayer Assistance Order,* puts you in direct communication with the Problems Resolution Office. Within the PRO, we find reasonably well-informed IRS employees whose sole function is to aid in the resolution of citizens' compliance dilemmas. The Problems Resolution Officer best understands the inner workings of the IRS and the avenues to pursue in search of relief in a given case. With your *Taxpayers' Ultimate Defense Manual* in hand, you are able to talk intelligently with the PRO, comparing the advice offered to ensure its accuracy. In this fashion, you will obtain more information about taxpayers' rights than the vast majority of citizens in this country. The combination of your own knowledge of your rights and the PRO's knowledge of IRS functions, could likely prove to be the best defense package against IRS abuse ever introduced.

The information in this manual, as well as the author's other writings, are designed to provide the average citizen with the ammunition needed to fight the war against IRS abuse without the need of expensive legal talent. This is not to say, however, that legal representation is not desirable or necessary under certain circumstances. Should you find that you are unwilling or unable to fire an Ultimate Defense Weapon at the IRS, surely a competent, experienced attorney will. In your hands this manual will provide the information you need to effectiely and *intelligently* communicate with your tax attorney. In this manner, the possibility of success in your case is greatly enhanced.

Our earlier materials provide readers with important examples of how to fight back on your own against IRS abuse. For example, beginning with *The Naked Truth,* readers obtained their first exposure to the right to appeal an auditor's demand for payment of additional taxes. Later, in *How Anyone Can Negotiate With The IRS—And WIN!,* we demonstrated that the auditor *has no power* to assess and collect taxes, or to change your tax liability when *you* have determined that it is correct. The auditor's presumed power is emasculated simply by enlisting the services of an Appeals Officer.

These procedures are generally simple to understand and easy to execute. All it requires is that you spend a little time to learn how they function. In doing so, you effectively conscript IRS personnel into your army. Together with your own knowledge and the ability to use IRS personnel in your war effort, you possess the Ultimate Secret Formula for success against IRS abuse.

Appendix I

MAPS

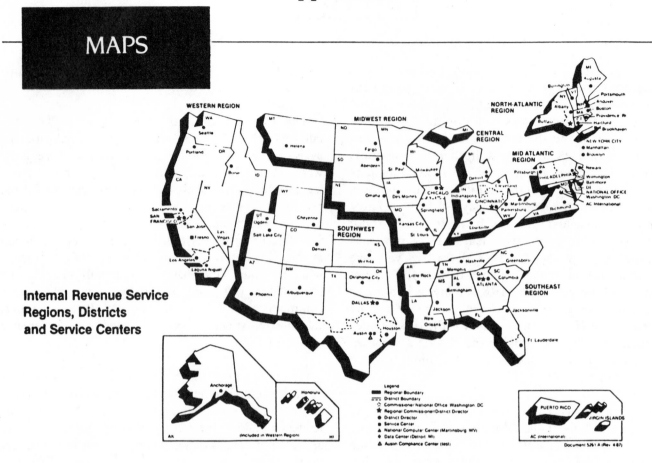

**Internal Revenue Service
Regions, Districts
and Service Centers**

**Chief Counsel
Regional and
District Offices**

✿ U.S. GOVERNMENT PRINTING OFFICE: 1989 231-926/00086

Appendix II

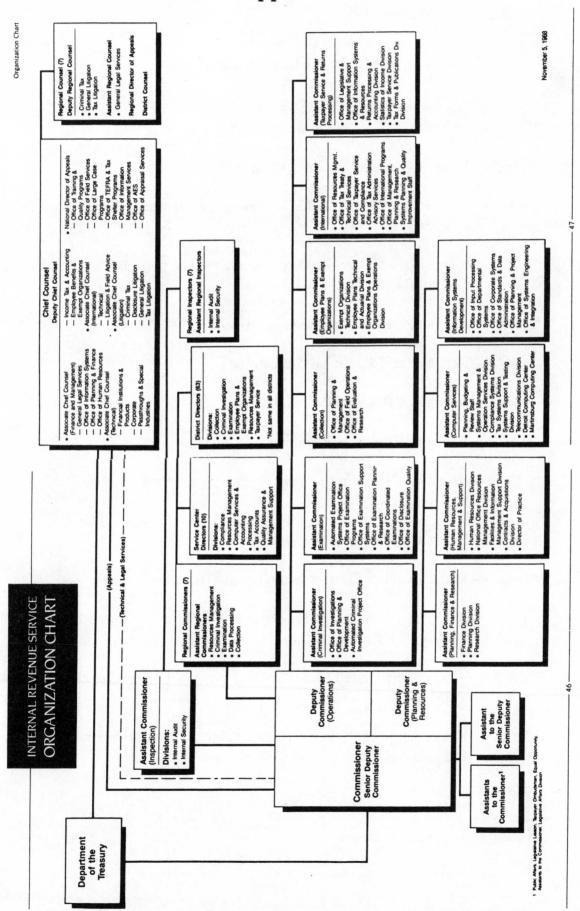

INTERNAL REVENUE SERVICE ORGANIZATION CHART

Department of the Treasury

Commissioner Senior Deputy Commissioner

Assistants to the Commissioner[1]

Assistant to the Senior Deputy Commissioner

Deputy Commissioner (Operations)

Deputy Commissioner (Planning & Resources)

— (Appeals) —
— (Technical & Legal Services) —

Assistant Commissioner (Inspection)

Divisions:
- Internal Audit
- Internal Security

Regional Commissioners (7)

Assistant Regional Commissioners
- Resources Management
- Criminal Investigation
- Examination
- Data Processing
- Collection

Service Center Directors (10)

Divisions:
- Compliance
- Resources Management
- Computer Services &
- Accounting
- Processing
- Tax Accounts
- Quality Assurance & Management Support

District Directors (63)

Divisions:
- Collection
- Criminal Investigation
- Examination
- Employee Plans & Exempt Organizations
- Resources Management
- Taxpayer Service

*Not same in all districts

Regional Inspectors (7)

Assistant Regional Inspection
- Internal Audit
- Internal Security

Chief Counsel Deputy Chief Counsel

Associate Chief Counsel (Finance and Management)
- General Legal Services
- Office of Information Systems
- Office of Planning & Finance
- Office of Human Resources

Associate Chief Counsel (Technical)
- Financial Institutions & Products
- Corporate
- Passthroughs & Special Industries

— Income Tax & Accounting
— Employee Benefits & Exempt Organizations

Associate Chief Counsel (International)
- Technical
- Litigation & Field Advice

Associate Chief Counsel (Litigation)
- General Tax
- Disclosure Litigation
- General Litigation
- Tax Litigation

National Director of Appeals
— Office of Training & Quality Programs
— Office of Field Services
— Office of Large Case Programs
— Office of TEFRA & Tax Shelter Programs
— Office of Information Management Services
— Office of AES
— Office of Appraisal Services

Regional Counsel (7) Deputy Regional Counsel
- Criminal Tax
- General Litigation
- Tax Litigation

Assistant Regional Counsel
- General Legal Services

Regional Director of Appeals

District Counsel

Assistant Commissioner (Criminal Investigation)
- Office of Investigations
- Office of Planning & Development
- Automated Criminal Investigation Project Office

Assistant Commissioner (Examination)
- Automated Examination Systems Project Office
- Office of Examination Programs
- Office of Examination Support Systems
- Office of Examination Planning & Research
- Office of Coordinated Examinations
- Office of Disclosure
- Office of Examination Quality

Assistant Commissioner (Collection)
- Office of Planning & Management
- Office of Field Operations
- Office of Evaluation & Research

Assistant Commissioner (Employee Plans & Exempt Organizations)
- Exempt Organizations Technical Division
- Employee Plans Technical and Actuarial Division
- Employee Plans & Exempt Organizations Operations Division

Assistant Commissioner (International)
- Office of Resources Mgmt.
- Office of Tax Treaty & Technical Services
- Office of Taxpayer Service and Compliance
- Office of Tax Administration Advisory Services
- Office of International Programs
- Office of Management, Planning & Research
- Systems Planning & Quality Improvement Staff

Assistant Commissioner (Planning, Finance & Research)
- Finance Division
- Planning Division
- Research Division

Assistant Commissioner (Human Resources Management & Support)
- Human Resources Division
- National Office Resources Management Division
- Facilities & Information Management Support Division
- Contracts & Acquisitions Division
- Director of Practice

Assistant Commissioner (Computer Services)
- Planning, Budgeting & Review Staff
- Systems Management & Operation Systems Division
- Compliance Systems Division
- Tax Systems Division
- Systems Support & Testing Division
- Telecommunications Division
- Detroit Computing Center
- Martinsburg Computing Center

Assistant Commissioner (Information Systems Development)
- Office of Input Processing
- Office of Departmental Systems
- Office of Corporate Systems
- Office of Standards & Data Administration
- Office of Planning & Project Management
- Office of Systems Engineering & Integration

Assistant Commissioner (Taxpayer Service & Returns Processing)
- Office of Legislative & Management Support
- Office of Information Systems & Resources
- Returns Processing & Accounting Division
- Statistics of Income Division
- Taxpayer Service Division
- Tax Forms & Publications Div. Division

[1] Public Affairs, Legislative Liaison, Taxpayer Ombudsman, Equal Opportunity, Assistants to the Commissioner, Legislative Affairs Division

November 5, 1988

46 — 47

Appendix III
Table of Abbreviations

"C.B." — Refers to Cumulative Bulletin.

"Cir." — Refers to the Circuit Court of Appeals, i.e., 8th Cir.

"Code" — Unless otherwise indicated, refers to the Internal Revenue Code of 1986, as amended.

"F.2d" — Refers to the Federal Reporter, Second Series, published by West Publishing Co., St. Paul, MN.

"IRM" — Refers to the Internal Revenue Manual.

"MT" — Refers to an IR Manual Transmittal.

"Rev. Proc." — Refers to a Revenue Procedure.

"Rev. Reg." — Refers to a Revenue Regulation.

"S.Ct." — Refers to *The Supreme Court Reporter,* published by West Publishing Co., St. Paul, MN.

"T.C." — Refers to a Tax Court Regular Decision.

"T.C. Memo" — Refers to a Tax Court Memorandum Decision.

"U.S." — Refers to the *United States Supreme Court Reports,* published by the U.S. Government Printing Office.

"U.S.C." — Refers to the United States Code, at the stated title and section, i.e., 26 USC §6334.

"U.S.T.C." — Refers to *United States Tax Cases,* published by Commerce Clearing House, Inc., Chicago, IL.

About the Author

Daniel J. Pilla has dedicated himself to the preservation of taxpayers' rights and their freedoms. As a Tax Litigation Consultant, he has recognized that there is a common ground on which both the citizen and tax collector can tread. He has also recognized that for the citizen to share this common ground, it will be necessary for him to assert his rights.

He will tell you, however, that before any rights can be asserted, one must have a working knowledge of those rights. Without this knowledge, history shows that the rights of the citizen will be trampled by those set to the task of tax collection. Without the assertion of these rights, there is no way to prevent abuse.

Just as Dan Pilla has dedicated himself to teaching Americans what these rights entail, he challenges each of us to learn and assert these rights whenever possible. He challenges each individual to protect the liberties afforded them by the Constitution. For only through the protection of individual liberties can we all work together to keep this country strong in the hands of God.

Other WINNING Publications
A Complete Package of Defense Materials

These materials, written by Daniel J. Pilla and published by WINNING Publications, comprise perhaps the most devastating package of IRS abuse defense materials known in America. With them you can know your rights and more importantly, you can know how to utilize them.

THE NAKED TRUTH

The first book to tell you of the IRS plan to audit each person every year. It exposes IRS Document 6941, dated May, 1984, which calls for the implementation of this plan over a ten year period. Upon release of our latest book, the *Taxpayers' Ultimate Defense Manual,* we are mid way through this period. It is shocking to learn why and how the IRS will accomplish this. Even more shocking are the realities around us that bear out the claims made in *The Naked Truth.*

.... $9.95 plus $2.50 P&H

HOW ANYONE CAN NEGOTIATE WITH THE IRS—AND WIN!

It has been said that, "If the taxpayers of this country ever discover that the IRS operates on 90 percent bluff, the entire system will collapse." This book provides you the ability to recognize and call IRS bluffs which could cost you taxes you do not owe. In it you also learn that the one IRS person that you fear the most, the tax auditor, is the one with the least power over you. Through this book, you will see exactly *How Anyone Can Negotiate With The IRS—And WIN!*

.... $12.95 plus $2.50 P&H

PILLA TALKS TAXES

This monthly newsletter is your link to current events in tax collection. Through it, Dan Pilla and those who subscribe have been able to put pressure on the IRS and Congress to the end that positive changes in tax administration have resulted. Years of IRS policy have been changed and an attitude of WINNING in tax disputes has begun to permeate the entire country. Serving as a means to provide up-to-the-minute tax collection news, you can't be without this valuable information that could save you hundreds, even thousands of tax dollars. America wins when *Pilla Talks Taxes.*

.... $97.00/year

A SPECIAL REPORT

On November 10, 1988, former President Ronald Reagan signed Public Law 100-647, enacting the *Technical and Miscellaneous Revenue Act of 1988.* The new law contained the much debated and long awaited *Taxpayers' Bill of Rights Act.* Touted as the most significant advance toward restoring citizens' rights, this bill was widely accepted and welcomed by taxpayers across the country. However, as discovered by Dan Pilla in his extensive analysis of the bill, danger lies in wait for the citizen who has been lulled into believing this law is his "saving grace." While certain aspects of this bill may be beneficial to some citizens, it will be very difficult for anyone to realize any benefit if its contents are not understood.

.... $29.95 plus $1.00 P&H

For any of the above materials, please send your check or money order in the amount indicated to:

WINNING Publications
506 Kenny Road
St. Paul, MN 55101
or call
612-774-0678